DREAMS THAT MONEY CAN BUY

Also by Jon Bradshaw

FAST COMPANY

THE CRUELEST GAME

DREAMS
THAT
MONEY CAN BUY

THE TRAGIC LIFE OF
LIBBY HOLMAN

BY JON BRADSHAW

WILLIAM MORROW AND COMPANY, INC. • NEW YORK

Library of Congress Catalog Card Number: 84-62077

ISBN: 0-688-01158-6

Printed in the United States of America

First Edition

1 2 3 4 5 6 7 8 9 10

FOR
CAROLYN
AND
SHANNON

CONTENTS

femme fatale: An irresistibly
attractive woman, especially one
who leads men into difficult,
dangerous or disastrous
situations. A siren.

—*Random House Dictionary of
the English Language*

MANHATTAN: SUMMER 1931

1

A T THE VERY SUMMIT OF HER SUDDEN AND SHORT-LIVED
fame, Libby Holman talked to a reporter from the New York
World. During the course of the interview, she attempted to de-
fine the limits of her life—her real life as she called it—its promises and possibilities. She had few doubts. But Libby was young
and still seduced by happy endings. She thought of herself as a
romantic optimist, believing the success she had achieved already
was merely a gorgeous harbinger of things to come.

"Here's my program," she said. "Five more years of the theater, but no more. I'll play big-time dramatic roles. Right now,
I'm coaching for *L'Aiglon* and I'm flirting with *Camille*. In five
years, I hope to have enough money saved up to give me a sure
income of fifteen thousand dollars a year. I'll go to France and
get a villa. Then I'll concentrate on the development of my
mind. I want to be rich inside.

"I want at least one great love. Maybe more, but no millionaires. I want a man who has achieved something in the arts.
He must be more than my match in physical vitality and artistic
achievements. You can say that I have not met a soul who
qualifies. But one thing is sure anyhow. I'll never be crying my
heart out over a guy that loves me and leaves me. After this
blues business, I'm positively immune to such silliness.

"I'll have a child. That's a necessary part of the experience.

11

I'll write stories, novels, poetry. There'll be a salon like Madame de Sévigné's. I want the sensitivity and understanding of Katherine Mansfield and the penetration of George Sand.

"While a girl is young and voluptuous, she can't help but be adored. Old age is the problem. I never want to envy youth. I never want to be dependent. At fifty, sixty and seventy, I want to have enough charm and fascination to draw the love of men, to make them forget lush young girls. I want to live to be a smart old witch who rules her kingdom with an iron scepter."

Libby had just turned twenty-seven and was making imaginary bequests to herself, creating a legacy for the worldly woman she intended to become. They were the dreams her money would buy. They were also prescient words—particularly the references to the millionaire and the child, and the desire to become a smart old witch. As it turned out, these were the cornerstones on which her tragic, madcap career would be built and prosper, before toppling into the ruin she had spent a lifetime attempting to avoid.

BOOK ONE:
THE MILLIONAIRE

2

THE SURNAME OF HOLMAN WAS AN AFTERTHOUGHT, LIBBY'S original name being Elizabeth Lloyd Holzman. She was born at home in Cincinnati, Ohio, on May 23, a warm and windless day in the leap year of 1904. Her parents, Alfred and Rachel Holzman, occupied a spacious house in the affluent suburb of Walnut Hills, and were of German-Jewish ancestry, the name *Holzman* meaning "one who cuts wood in a forest."

Cincinnati had a population of 325,000, more than half of whom were of German extraction. Many of these immigrants congregated in a tenement district north of the Miami and Erie Canal known as "Over-the-Rhine," where they had created a subculture of German bakeries and biergartens, rathskellers and music clubs. The narrow cobbled streets were glutted with trolley cars, horse-drawn fire engines and beer wagons, and the tidy, well-scrubbed shops and delicatessens emitted the pungent smells of schnapps and pretzels, bratwurst, sauerkraut and pumpernickel. Libby's birthplace was America's beer capital—Famous Golden Age Pale, Bohemian, Berliner Weiss, Old Honesty Lager—a boisterous town of traders, hagglers, brewers and barterers, built along the precipitous banks of the Ohio River.

Libby's father, a prosperous stockbroker of thirty-seven, maintained an office near Over-the-Rhine. A pragmatic man, Alfred would not have placed much credence in auguries or constellations, but on the day of Libby's birth, he considered himself decidedly ill-fated. That afternoon, he crossed Fountain Square and entered the sumptuous, brass-trimmed bar of the Sinton, Cincinnati's most fashionable hotel. Putting a ten-dollar bill on the mahogany bar, Holzman bought drinks for the house and confessed his disappointment. Alluding to Libby's elder sister, Marion, he claimed he had wanted a boy, not just another girl. Looking up from their lager and liverwurst, Holzman's cronies

15

teased him, claiming that anyone could beget a girl, but that it took a man to beget a boy. Holzman frowned and left the bar without a word.

Alfred Holzman was born in Cincinnati on August 20, 1867, the eldest of four sons, the others being Charles and the young twins, Ross and Wallace. At sixteen, Charles ran away from home, and although his family searched for him throughout Ohio and as far afield as St. Louis and Louisville, he was never seen again. At nineteen, Alfred graduated from the Cincinnati Law School. He called himself an attorney, but he would not become a member of the Ohio Bar for another twenty years.

On April 17, 1900, Alfred married Rachel Workum, a twenty-eight-year-old schoolteacher. Rachel was both pretty and intelligent and, while still in her teens, was said to have memorized the Psalms in Hebrew. Being a Workum, Rachel was considered an enviable catch, for the Workums were one of Cincinnati's first Jewish families. Levi J. Workum, for example, was the co-founder of one of America's largest distilleries, manufacturing such whiskeys as Lynchburg Rye and W. T. Snyder Sourmash. Rachel, however, was of an impoverished branch of the family.

A proud woman, Rachel liked to claim that her ancestors were of a noble line of Sephardic Jews that could be traced back to the noted sculptor, Sir Moses Ezekiel, and to Benjamin Disraeli, the 1st Earl of Beaconsfield and prime minister of Great Britain. These were spurious assertions, mere snobberies, but Rachel succeeded in persuading her children that they were not just anyone. Much later, whenever Libby was asked about her ancestry, she altered her mother's tale. She was of German-Huguenot descent, she said, with a trace of Scotch and Irish on the maternal side. Libby had never liked being Jewish, however impressive the lineage was meant to be.

Alfred and his younger brother, Ross, owned Holzman & Company, a firm of investment bankers trading in bonds and securities, with seats on the New York and Chicago stock exchanges and the Chicago Board of Trade. Alfred was the mainstay of the company, its founder and chief executive. A stern and taciturn man, he was also an amateur actor and athlete and was inordinately fond of the essays of Ralph Waldo Emerson, particularly "Self-Reliance," which he would later recite to Libby repeatedly.

Ross Holzman, the firm's dapper front man, was said to prize his silver tongue and seductive smile. He was extremely popular in Cincinnati. Like Alfred, he acted, but he also gambled and golfed and was elected treasurer of the Cincinnati Club, the city's most prestigious Jewish social organization. The Holzman brothers had a profitable partnership, and in 1904, when Libby was born, they seemed destined to achieve that most coveted of American dreams—becoming millionaires.

But less than a year later, rumors began to circulate through Cincinnati's financial community that Holzman & Company was in difficulties. The rumors were vehemently denied, but on May 25 a petition of bankruptcy was filed by Alfred Holzman, and subsequently, the company was adjudged bankrupt in the United States District Court. It was the largest failure in Cincinnati's financial history. Investors' losses were said to be nearly $1 million, although liabilities were ultimately assessed at $250,000. No immediate explanation was given for the bankruptcy, but it was attributed to reckless speculation on the cotton exchange.

At first, the Holzman brothers did not seem to realize the full extent of their losses. Toward the end of June, however, the despondent Alfred told his cronies in the Sinton Hotel bar that the handful of loose change in his jacket pocket was all he had left in the world. Ross was not so candid. He informed Alfred that he was going to Louisville to raise funds. A few days later, he disappeared.

That summer, officials of the Georgetown, Kentucky, Water, Gas, Electric and Power Company came to Cincinnati in search of $150,000 in bonds that, unknown to Alfred, Ross had borrowed from them. At the same time, the Cincinnati Club discovered that Ross had embezzled $7,000. At first, the club's Board of Governors hushed the matter up, but realizing the money would never be repaid, they decided to make it public. At a rowdy board meeting, the club's president cursed Ross Holzman, not only for embezzlement but for borrowing the money of friends and members in order to pay his gambling debts. Reluctantly, Alfred, too, denounced his brother.

Ross Holzman was never seen again. Rumor had it that he had bolted to France, to Mexico or Germany, but many of his friends believed he had fled to Honduras, a country he had often mentioned with inexplicable affection. Subsequent reports that he had met a violent death, that he had committed suicide, were never confirmed. His disappearance created a furor in Cincinnati and both Holzman brothers were publicly castigated, but Libby's father, knowing that he himself had done no wrong, chose to rise above the scandal. Like Ralph Waldo Emerson, Alfred Holzman would not brook "the yoke of men's opinions."

As a young girl, Libby viewed her uncle's disappearance in a somewhat more capricious light. She alluded to him as Uncle Honduras and gradually came to idolize his legend. By the time she was ten, he had taken on the mythic trappings of some knight-errant, a performer, if not of noble deeds, then at least of derring-do.

What Libby called his waywardness amused her and prompted, at last, a curious reverie. Lying awake in bed at night, she mused that Uncle Ross would return one day to Cincinnati, a wonderfully wealthy man. He would come steathily, by night. He would seek her out, confide his countless secrets and, before retreating to Honduras, would give her a million dollars. Libby spent long hours dreaming of how she would squander the windfall—the gowns, the baubles, the glittering prizes it would buy.

To be poor when one has been rich is unpardonable. But Alfred Holzman envisaged life as an absurd series of advances and reversals. He hardened himself to failure in the knowledge that it was inevitable and that it, too, would pass. He believed that one must bear and forbear, that one must forgive and seek forgiveness and that ultimately right would prevail. There was much of the stoic about him, influenced as he was by the prim and sober axioms of Emerson.

Rachel Holzman, on the other hand, was mortified. Being poor was an abomination. It had not been part of her plan and it seriously restricted her social aspirations for both herself and her children. But, like her husband, she was obstinate. She would make do, she would find a way, and she would not forget.

It was for them, "the doomed House of Holzman," as a local journal said, a dry and troubled time. Ross's perfidy preceded Alfred like a malodorous smog, but he found occasional employment as an attorney and general agent for two insurance companies. He was forced to sell his spacious house in Walnut Hills, and the family moved into the cramped apartment of Wallace Holzman, Alfred's younger brother and Ross's twin. Wallace would support Alfred's family for more than a year.

Despite his misfortunes, Alfred was considered an honorable man. As a matter of family pride, he and Wallace agreed to return every penny of the funds that Ross had misappropriated, a gesture that reduced both families to near penury for years. Although Libby remembered nothing of her father's wealth, she would never forget her mother's bitter jeremiads of what had been, what might have been. Growing up, she felt cheated, denied.

When Libby was four, the Holzmans moved into the dilapidated Cumberland Apartments at 808 Cleveland Avenue in the suburb of Avondale, renting a four-room flat for fifty dollars a month. A long narrow structure, bisected by a dark hallway running from the front door to the living room, it was what used to be known as a railroad flat. On one side of the hall was a dining room where Alfred Junior, who had been born in 1909, slept on a cot next to the dining-room table. Across the hall were Alfred and Rachel's bedroom and a smaller bedroom shared by Libby and Marion. There was one bathroom. At the front of the apartment was the living room, blocked off from the dining room by a large, ugly highboy. The Holzman children would spend more than fifteen years in these dingy quarters—Alfred Junior, known as Allie or Tinker Bell after the character in *Peter Pan*; Marion, called Mar or Dyli after her favorite expression, "Don't You Love It"; and Libby, whom everyone in the family called Baby.

To make ends meet, Rachel Holzman turned humble German thrift into what amounted to a sacrament. She was mightily mean. She made all her children's clothes, saving Marion's frocks and blouses, refashioning them for Libby and, when Libby had outgrown them, converting them into gentlemanly attire for young Allie. At picnics and church socials, she gathered all the scraps and leftovers, taking them home in order to make stocks and soups and stews. She maintained intimate ties with the wealthier Workums and managed, without too much loss of face, to obtain hand-me-downs for her children. Libby resented the clothes and, to begin with, refused to wear them. She also resented being sent to the bakery for day-old bread, which was sold at half price, informing the baker that her mother required the bread for stuffing.

Throughout Libby's childhood, the subject of money, its scarcity, its possibilities, was raised and aired repeatedly like a curse or an invocation. Money and position were Rachel's gods. She seemed to know, almost instinctively, that being poor required certain skills—an obstinate optimism, an unchallengeable cunning, an ability to seize each and every opportunity and, most important, to observe appearances until the malady was overcome—skills she imparted to her growing daughters.

Many years later, long after she had married a wealthy man and moved away, Marion would return occasionally to Cincinnati and drive with friends past the Cumberland Apartments, telling them that that was where her family had lived when they were "poories." Marion was consistently cheerful about her youth; but it was a period that Libby recalled with shame and loathing. She claimed her family had been so poor that she was forced to wear a showercap to bed at night to keep the cockroaches at bay. Nearly fifty years later, she and her friend Paul Bowles, the novelist and composer, visited Cincinnati. Bowles wanted to see the house in which Libby had spent her youth and Libby, almost angrily, refused to show him.

3

THE ORIGINAL REYNOLDS HOMESTEAD, KNOWN AS ROCK Spring Plantation, is situated near Critz, Virginia, a few miles north of the North Carolina border. The entire tract of 717 acres is dominated by No Business Mountain, a ridge running east and west in full view of the house. The first fifty acres of this property were purchased in 1814 by Abraham Reynolds, who settled there with his wife in a log cabin.

The log cabin no longer exists, but the brick house built by

Abraham's son, Hardin William remains. Originally containing two rooms, the house was enlarged to six rooms with a hall and an outside brick kitchen. The house was the birthplace of all sixteen of Hardin William Reynolds's children, all of whom were born in the same mahogany Empire bed. One of them, Richard Joshua, became the founder of the Reynolds Tobacco Company and the father of Smith Reynolds.

Born July 20, 1850, R. J. was too young to fight in the Civil War. At eighteen, he attended Emory and Henry College and then the Bryant and Stratton Business School in Baltimore, where, in his free hours, he sold his father's tobacco products to wholesale commission merchants. After graduation, he returned to Rock Spring Plantation, entering into partnership with his father. And there he might have remained, but the tall, bearded youth was restless and yearned to move farther south.

When R. J. was twenty-four, he sold his interest in Rock Spring and moved to Winston in North Carolina. Winston was a tiny town, but it was on a railroad and the center of a large area that produced the raw tobacco leaf that R. J. would one day process in enormous quantities. In 1874, the two adjoining hamlets of Winston and Salem were separate. Salem was the southern capital of the Moravian or United Brethren faith in America and the land had been legally deeded to Jesus Christ. Winston, a town of some three thousand people, was the trading center of the surrounding counties and for much of the remote mountain country.

R. J. began with a capital of $7,500. His dream was to make $100,000 and retire. In Winston, he purchased a lot on Depot Street and built his first tobacco factory in a small frame building. At the end of the first year, he was manufacturing 150,000 pounds of chewing tobacco. By 1887, his production had tripled and he was making chewing tobacco under eighty-six different brand names. In that year, his net worth was assessed at $262,932 and he never thought of retirement again.

R. J. Reynolds introduced the Camel cigarette in 1913. He designed the package and named it himself, choosing the word *camel* because it was simple and because he was partial to animals. Strictly speaking, the now famous emblem was a dromedary, a beast R. J. had first encountered at the Barnum and Bailey circus. As a result, countless Americans growing up in the first two thirds of the twentieth century believed that a camel was possessed of a single hump. But the Camel, known as the first truly American cigarette, would soon become the best-selling brand in the world. When asked by an admirer how his business would flourish when he was dead, "Old Dick," as his friends referred to him, replied: "I have written the book. Others need only read it when I am gone."

Reynolds did not marry until 1905 when, at fifty-four, he wed his distant cousin, Mary Katherine Smith. The year before, the Reynolds Tobacco Company had conducted a contest for the best letter advertising one of its products. Miss Smith won the thousand-dollar prize, and she and R. J. were married shortly thereafter. She was twenty-five, nearly thirty years younger than her husband. Within six years, they were to have four children— Richard Joshua, Jr., Mary Katherine, Nancy Susan, and finally, on November 5, 1911, Zachary Smith. Mrs. Reynolds always told them that R. J. had married her only in order to retrieve his thousand-dollar prize money.

A rural girl, Katherine Reynolds had never been partial to Winston-Salem and she persuaded her husband to move just beyond town to the countryside. When Smith was born, most of the land, about eleven hundred acres, had already been acquired, but the construction of the house took nearly four years and was not completed until the early winter of 1917.

Although Reynolda, as it was called, contained more than sixty rooms, Old Dick liked to call it the bungalow. The rambling white manor house with its green gabled roof occupied a knoll in the center of the vast estate. Southern similax and ivy grew over the wings, and, sloping away from the house, Japanese weeping cherry trees, magnolias and flowering shrubs had been planted periodically so that there would be continuous bloom.

The main drawing room, the largest room in the house, was, if rather stiff and formal, an architectural jewel. A huge white marble fireplace with inglenooks and love seats occupied the northern wall. Twin staircases wound above it to the gallery, which encircled the entire room. Hanging high above the gallery was a splendid crystal chandelier. The drawing room was decorated with tall Chinese floor vases, broad sofas and lounging chairs, English reading tables, Persian carpets and Flemish tapestries, an eighteenth-century grandfather clock, a four-manual Aeolian organ and a massive mahogany tobacco chest.

Dotted around the wide groomed lawns were an English formal garden, a life-size doll's house built for the Reynolds girls and rough log cabins for the boys. The estate contained numerous ancillary buildings—an Irish-potato house, a sweet-potato house, a blacksmith's shop and three large barns which sheltered the Percheron draft horses, the Tamworth swine, the prize herd of Jersey cows and bulls. Not far from the barns were the Reynolda Presbyterian Church, a general store, a private post office and, eventually, the Reynolda Day School.

Reynolda was intended to be self-sufficient. It boasted a power plant and cottages for its forty employees—the plumber, the electrician, the blacksmith, the gardeners and greenhouse keepers, the butler, the maids, the cooks and chauffeurs. Dairy, poultry and truck farms provided much of the residents' food. And so that the Reynolds children and their companions might keep themselves continually amused, there were tennis courts and bridle paths, a nine-hole golf course, an outdoor swimming pool fed by artesian wells, and a five-acre artificial lake, Lake Katherine, home to mallards and drakes and geese and swans. Reynolda was vast and self-contained, a miniature kingdom, its secrets concealed from the curious by walls and wrought-iron gates, by giant elms, thick shrubs and Southern pine.

The Reynolds family moved into Reynolda House three weeks before Christmas in 1917. Eight months later, R. J. Reynolds died. He was sixty-eight. At his death, the Reynolds Tobacco Company was producing more than twenty billion cigarettes a year, enabling R. J. to leave each of his four children twenty million dollars to be held in trust until their twenty-eighth birthdays. But Old Dick had been a wily man. His will also stipulated that, before coming into their inheritance, his children should be paid two dollars for every dollar they actually earned themselves.

Less than three years later, Katherine Reynolds married J. Edward Johnston, the headmaster of the Reynolda Day School. Although doctors had cautioned her not to have another child, in 1924 she produced a baby boy. The birth exhausted her and four days later she died of a heart attack. Her second son, Smith, only twelve, was shielded from her death. Coddled and pampered by bevies of nurses, governesses, and female relatives, Smith's world was, as it was meant to be, safe and elegant as a cocoon.

4

AT THE AGE OF FIVE, LIBBY WAS SENT TO THE AVONDALE Public School on Reading Road, a two-block walk from the Cumberland Apartments. A small school, with about thirty children in each class, it went from the first through the eighth grades. Libby was an exceptionally bright and precocious child; she skipped two grades in her first four years and triumphed as Puck in *A Midsummer Night's Dream*.

For as long as she could remember, Libby had been drawn to the stage, to singing and particularly to acting. The little olive-skinned, dark-haired girl was taken by her father when she was six to a performance of *Uncle Tom's Cabin*, and for weeks thereafter, remembering Eva's ascension into heaven, Libby longed to be a beautiful blonde and to look like an angel.

She had a peculiarly low and throaty voice. Concerning its origin, an improbable legend sprang up, which, whether true or not, Libby, at least, never denied: While she was undergoing a tonsillectomy, the surgeon's scalpel slipped, slightly perforating her palate, and her soprano voice was lost forever. Shortly afterward, one of Libby's teachers announced that she possessed the plangent voice of a bullfrog.

Both Libby's and Marion's theatrical ambitions were actively encouraged by their parents. Alfred and Rachel had performed frequently in plays and operettas presented by the Cincinnati Club, Rachel always being called upon whenever someone was needed for the part of an older woman. Rachel believed she understood the theater and felt that Marion was blessed with a genuine talent. In her view, Libby did imitations.

Superficially, Libby and Marion seemed the best of friends.

But Libby was morbidly jealous of her sister. Much later, she claimed her childhood had not been a happy one. Marion was older, Allie was younger, and Libby called herself "that terrible in-between." She was unable to conceal her awe of Marion. Marion was more beautiful, more talented, a mercurial girl with a quick bright personality. Libby thought of herself as an ugly duckling. And to make matters worse, her mother agreed.

During family dinners, Rachel would often belittle Libby, carping at her manners, her dress, criticizing her lack of what used to be known as deportment. She openly favored Marion. In consequence, Libby turned more and more to her father. Before the collapse of his company, Alfred had had a wide circle of friends, but he had now become something of a recluse. Although maintaining an office in downtown Cincinnati, he spent increasing periods at home, reading, writing, conducting research for other lawyers. Unlike Rachel, he was removed from all social ambition. And his very restraint, his dignity, captivated Libby, intensified her admiration. When he was away, she would creep into his closet, hiding there for hours, in order to be near his smells, his clothes.

For Libby, Rachel was little more than an ogre. When she was older, she often complained that her mother had castrated her father. "Kicked him in the nuts" was the bitter expression she favored. Libby felt her father had been a potent businessman, but a sheep at home. She thought of him as kind and giving and strong, while her mother had been merely grasping and avaricious. And yet it had been Rachel who had goaded her daughters, who had given them, despite their straitened circumstances, a real sense of superiority.

Alfred and Wallace Holzman had toiled for ten long years to repay the debts incurred by their brother Ross; and although they rarely alluded to that fact, they both suffered, as a result of it, from periodic bouts of depression.

Wallace invariably called his wife, Claire, each day at noon from his Cincinnati office, where he was employed as the superintendent of a wholesale liquor company. One April day in 1915, he failed to do so. Toward three o'clock, the apprehensive Claire, unable to reach her husband, telephoned Alfred. Alfred hurried over to his brother's office, only to discover that he had committed suicide by shooting himself through the head. He was forty years old.

In a note to his wife he had written: "Darling, I couldn't call you knowing this was to be. It is better thus, dearest one. Kiss the children. I am nearly dead and want it to end before the worst happens. Goodbye, Your own, Wallace."

Libby and Wallace had been particularly close and his death had a profound effect upon her. For years afterward, recalling it, Libby would suddenly burst into tears. Now, not quite eleven, she was terrified as her family was diminished one by one, and agonized, perhaps, that her father might be the next to abandon her. But one thing was certain: Of the four Holzman brothers, one was a bankrupt, two had simply disappeared, and now the fourth had put a bullet in his brain.

For once, Libby agreed with her mother. She too felt it was imperative to attend either Miss Kendrick's or Miss Dougherty's, the two fashionable private schools for young Cincinnati ladies. Three years before, Rachel had attempted to enroll Marion at Miss Dougherty's, but there had not been money enough. And now Libby too would have to settle for a less modish education. Thus, in September 1916, she entered Hughes High, Cincinnati's main public high school.

Hughes sat on a bluff in Clifton Heights. With its red brick battlements and castellated tower, it looked like some fraudulent fifteenth-century fortification. Libby would spend the next four years there. She was twelve and determined to excel, informing her father she intended to be singular, self-reliant.

America remained contentedly neutral during the first years of World War I. Indeed, in 1916, President Woodrow Wilson was reelected on a platform that included the slogan: "He kept us out of war." But the year before, the torpedoing of the British Cunard luxury liner S.S. *Lusitania* (killing 1,198 people, including 128 Americans) had kindled world opinion against Germany and, in the United States, against German-Americans. This anti-German prejudice was popularly expressed by Elsie Janis, the Broadway musical star, who wrote a poem that began: "Where are you, God?/I can't believe that you have seen/The things that they have done,/And yet upon this earth of Yours/There still exists the Hun."

In April 1917, when America finally entered the war, a wave of suspicion and fear swept over Cincinnati. The city's German-American residents, hitherto known as "Good Germans," now came to be regarded as an insidious threat to the American cause. Witch hunts ensued.

German language instruction was abolished in the public schools. German street and place names were summarily Americanized. Books of pro-German sentiment were removed from public library shelves, and many German newspapers ceased publication. Ernst Kuhnwald, the noted conductor of the Cincinnati Symphony Orchestra, was branded an alien and interned; and for a time, the playing of Wagner, Mozart and Beethoven was banned. Bratwurst was renamed victory sausage, sauerkraut was christened liberty cabbage, German shepherds became Alsatians, German toast was changed to French toast, and frankfurters were now more popularly known as hot-dogs. In Cincinnati, to have been German was tantamount to being a traitor and the city's German-American residents no longer boasted openly of their heritage.

Two months before the war ended, Alfred Holzman petitioned the Hamilton County Probate Court to anglicize his family name. His docket read: "Your petitioner states that he has from boyhood always been devoted to the English language and to the Anglo-Saxon institutions upon which he deems the United States of America to have chiefly relied for the social, cultural, ethical and commercial advancement of the said democratic federation of free states, that he accordingly deems the retention of the Germanic surname which now characterizes him as an ANACHRONISM and accordingly improper to the citizen of a country as above distinguished; and that accordingly he requests the honorable court to change his said surname of Holzman to Holman."

His petition was granted and his younger daughter, now fourteen, was henceforth known as Libby Holman. Secretly, Libby was ecstatic. She disliked being Jewish, even German-Jewish. The harsh Teutonic z was like a badge of shame to her. Holman was more euphonious and decidedly less offensive.

Libby spent her high-school years contributing to the war effort—participating in drives for Thrift Stamps, Liberty Loans and the Red Cross, and knitting mittens, scarves and sweaters for the doughboys overseas. Knitting was a popular American pastime during the war and Libby won a contest for being the fastest knitter in Cincinnati.

But she remained in the shadow of her sister, who had graduated from Hughes in 1918. Marion had studied drama and music and had been an exceptional student. Libby may have nurtured private envies, but she doggedly emulated Marion. She wrote pieces for the school magazine, *Old Hughes*, took a leading part in amateur theatricals, and made the honor roll in her first three years. Much later, she claimed that school had bored her, that she had learned more in six months from her father than she had learned in all her time at Hughes. "I studied Emerson and Wilde and Jung before I got the curse," she said.

At sixteen, Libby was five feet six inches and weighed one hundred twenty-four pounds. She had an ample, almost buxom figure and wore her unruly raven hair in a braid. Her weak chin embarrassed her as did her odd, abbreviated teeth, which would always seem too small for her mouth. Long afterward, a friend described them by saying: "Libby looked as though she'd been chewing on moccasins all her life." Her complexion was a dark and lustrous olive, causing her classmates to snicker among themselves, insinuating she had "Moorish blood." Libby had no Moorish blood, but there was something of the Gypsy about her. She had the Gypsys' reckless temperament, their uncheckable enthusiasms.

Libby's most arresting feature was her wide hazel eyes, but she was nearsighted, refused to wear glasses, and was compelled to walk right up to her classmates in order to see them. Her myopia disturbed her, but she compensated by joking about it, continually telling the tale of a young courting couple: They sat on a swing and the girl, in order to conceal her faulty vision, asked the boy if he could see a bright thumbtack in a distant tree—which she had placed there some time before. The boy could not see the tack and, haughtily, the girl offered to show him where it was. Approaching the tree, she tripped over a cow. Libby always implied that she was the heroine of the tale.

Since her parents did not own an automobile, Libby usually traveled to school by streetcar. Occasionally, however, her wealthy beaux gave her a lift and she was often seen hurtling through Cincinnati streets in Hudsons, Packards and Pierce-Arrows. Libby had numerous casual boyfriends, but three were particularly enamored of her. These youths thought her attractive—not as attractive as Marion, of course, but Libby was different; she was game and, more important, voluptuous. The youths assured each other that Libby, in the parlance of the day, was hot stuff.

During the early twenties, F. Scott Fitzgerald attempted to persuade his readers that the cities between Chicago and New York were one vast juvenile intrigue. But in Cincinnati, no one petted or necked with Libby. This did not initially dismay her suitors, who calculated that it was only a matter of time before she succumbed to their seductions. But Libby proved evasive and, while in high school, was not seriously involved with anyone.

Nonetheless, Libby's beaux escorted her to the movies and to plays at the Cox, the Grand and the Lyric theaters. She was driven to the zoo and to Crosley Field to watch the Reds perform. On weekends, she was taken to the Toadstool Inn, a popular nightspot for Cincinnati teenagers. The chairs and tables were designed to look like mushrooms and Libby and her friends sang "K-K-K-Katy" and "Melancholy Baby" and danced the fox trot, the toddle and the turkey trot to the hot jazz of Al Katz and His Kittens.

During her senior year at Hughes High, Libby wrote an anonymous gossip column for *Old Hughes* called "Remarks of a Rambler," in which she revealed her true identity in the final issue before graduation. The sole clue with which she had teased her readers was a bit of doggerel: "I am tall and slim. Am I a she or am I a him?" She wrote a short story entitled "What's a Girl Good for Anyway?" about two fourteen-year-old boys in love with the same girl. She also acted in the Quills, the women's drama group, and sang in the girls' glee club. Academically, she was ninth in a graduating class of two hundred sixty students— her proudest feat since Marion had graduated tenth in a somewhat smaller class.

Libby graduated from Hughes High School on June 11, 1920, less than a month after her sixteenth birthday. In all her class photographs, she wore the same black dress. One of Marion's hand-me-downs, it fell just below the calf, with wide white frills across the neckline. In each photograph, Libby stood in the front row and to the side, looking peeved and disappointed as though she had been persuaded to wear the wrong attire for the occasion.

Libby's precocity so impressed her peers that the class prophet wrote in her school yearbook: "Elizabeth is one of the most original girls in our class. Her contributions to 'Old Hughes' have made her famous. She is a talented actress too. We all expect to see Libby before the footlights some day. Indeed, she has already given us many manifestations of her art."

Libby was also nominated "the nerviest girl" in her class. " 'E' is for Libby, a girl of renown," as the yearbook observed. The yearbook contained one final reference to Libby, a wry limerick:

> There is a young lady named Lizzy
> Who is kept most exceedingly busy
> With the games and the shows
> The dances and beaux
> To think of it all makes me dizzy.

That autumn, Libby entered the University of Cincinnati where Marion had matriculated two years before. She would have preferred to attend an eastern university, but the Holmans were almost as impoverished as they had been when Libby entered high school and it had not been possible.

One of Libby's classmates at Hughes High and at the University of Cincinnati was Louis Kronenberger. The slim, bespectacled Kronenberger, later to become the drama critic for *Time* magazine and W. H. Auden's collaborator on anthologies of light verse, considered the university backward and unglamorous. For the most part, he was bored. He felt that a student "who applied himself could have acquired a good education of a kind," and that "except for the boredom, the university left no unpleasant memories. Except for the sterility, aroused no harsh judgments; in period terms, moreover, Middle Western colleges were something to make light of, not denounce; forget about rather than fume over."

But Libby was rarely bored and, concerning college life at least, held no grave opinions. She wanted to make her mark, to be conspicuous, and she began with her wardrobe. Arriving on campus, newly liberated from corsets and high shoes, Libby wore black lisle stockings, neatly rolled below the knee, pleated skirts, batiste blouses, black Oxfords and Shetland pullovers. But her most startling eccentricity, one that caused her classmates to turn and gawk as she passed by, was a man's gray slouch fedora, the brim of which was turned up and pinned in front and back, and worn at an appropriately rakish angle. Libby affected a kind of disheveled elegance as though her clothes had been thrown at her and had mysteriously fallen into all the right places.

At the beginning of her sophomore year, Libby had her black hair bobbed, an event that shocked both her colleagues and her professors. No other girl in Cincinnati had dared to adopt that infamous eastern fashion, and a faculty meeting was convened in order to attain the proper moral judgment. Eventually, they decided to let it pass, but they censured Libby for her distasteful lack of inhibition.

Libby had few inhibitions. She was one of the first girls on campus to smoke cigarettes (Camels were her favorite), and she flaunted mascara and bright red lipstick (her lips done up in the fashionable Cupid's bow). Once she attended a party given by one of her best friends only to be greeted at the front door by the friend's irate father, who demanded that Libby remove her makeup before entering his home. Only actresses and other fallen women, he implied, painted themselves in such a gaudy manner. Libby refused and was ordered to leave.

Libby much preferred the company of boys. Girls were catty and cavalier, tiresomely prim, and, in Libby's view, feigned bumptious poses of incorruptibility. Sensing, perhaps, these reservations, Libby's female classmates criticized her behind her back, calling her a vamp and sophisticated (meaning that she not only necked and petted, but probably went all the way). Even the boys considered Libby worldly, believing that she somehow knew more than they did, but precisely what that knowledge was, they were unable to express.

Libby was an audacious flirt, but her sexual explorations ended there. During her final year, having refused all invitations to the senior prom—the most important social event of the year—Libby chose to make a sensational entrance by turning up unexpectedly in a taxi. That evening, she danced with nearly all the boys, while, on the sidelines, the less popular girls reviled her. Shortly after midnight, the taxi returned and Libby went home as she had come, alone.

Best remembered in college for her roles in student plays, Libby appeared in the musical comedy *Fresh Paint* as the ingenue—described in the program as "an aesthetic flapper." For as long as she could remember, Libby had determined to become an actress; she liked singing (although she lacked a high range and her voice was considered more impassioned than good), but the drama, as she called it, consumed her. Her naturalness both mystified and impressed her more awkward colleagues. Libby jauntily explained that a respected director had told her that in order to make herself at ease on stage, she should first learn to walk naked and naturally in front of strangers. An improbable exercise, but Libby would later make a habit of it.

Both Libby and Marion performed at the small Art Theatre in downtown Cincinnati. Marion, a more accomplished actress, was given many of the starring roles, while Libby was given an occasional walk-on. In one of those amateur performances, Libby was cast as a nun. The director instructed her to sit silently at the back of the stage—as atmosphere. Piqued at Marion's more substantial role, Libby extracted a ball of wool from her habit and, during her sister's soliloquy, began to knit furiously. She knitted and knitted and knitted. The garment became longer and longer, and suddenly the audience broke into raucous laughter. Up front, the disconcerted Marion wondered what was wrong. Her soliloquy was tragic, not comic. Finally, she chose to ignore the outburst and finished her scene to puzzling applause. At the end of the act, the enraged director castigated Libby, but she was unmoved. She had not only stolen her sister's scene, she had also achieved a brief, but heady, celebrity.

Despite her impudent air of superiority, Libby was popular in college, particularly among the boys. But, again, she was not as popular as Marion had been. She lacked Marion's boundless charm, and she tended to snub those who bored her. Referring to a classmate, Libby told a friend: "He's a bore and he's also a boor. I trust you'll appreciate the difference."

Libby graduated from the University of Cincinnati on June 16, 1923, with a bachelor of arts degree. She majored in French, and by attending the University of Michigan for two summers, she finished in just three years. She was nineteen and was, up to that time, the youngest girl ever to have graduated from the university. One of her classmates described her as "smarter than an outhouse rat" and another claimed that it was because of Libby's tutoring that he managed to transfer to Yale. Libby tutored many of her friends, even writing their essays for them. Her French was fluent and she was often seen on campus reading Proust in the original.

During the graduation ceremony, Libby walked into the auditorium wearing her black mortarboard at an inelegant angle. Noticing it, a senior faculty member said: "Miss Holman, this is a *dignified* ceremony." Libby grinned. She passed the woman and, with one finger, pushed the cap upright and kept pushing it until it fell askew on the other side. The professor gasped but decided against further, and obviously pointless, reprimands.

That evening at a party at Castle Farm, the hostelry where the fashionable collegiate crowd drank and danced, Libby told her beau that although she had trifled with numerous ambitions, when she left Cincinnati, she intended to become a professional actress. The crowds, the applause, the encores and bows were all she had ever imagined. She intended, she said, to become a star, and to marry a millionaire. Of that, she was certain. Fame and luxury were alien to Libby, but they were never far from her mind.

5

SMITH REYNOLDS WAS A PETULANT AND MELANCHOLY BOY. He detested school. Educated at the Reynolda Day School, opened in 1919 by his mother on the family estate, he then attended R. J. Reynolds High School for several months, before transferring in 1925 to the Woodberry Forest School in Orange, Virginia.

Woodberry Forest was *the* school for boys of wealthy Winston families, but Smith was no happier here than he had been at home. At thirteen, he was a tall and slender youth with high cheekbones, a prominent aquiline nose, slanted eyes and fair hair. There was something enfeebled in his features, some inbred flaw, that gave his face the choked and sulky look of a spoiled boy denied some new extravagance. A typical Reynolds, he was nervous, high-strung, and suffered from sudden flurries of despair. Smith disliked being away from Winston; he disliked his studies, athletics, and the fact that his classmates had dubbed him "Camel." As the school year progressed, he took to spending more and more time in his room, brooding over imagined slights and injuries.

On at least two occasions before he was fifteen, Smith contemplated suicide. In one note to his friends and family, he wrote: "I will leave my car to Ab, if he finishes it. My money to Dick. My reputation to Virginia. My good looks to Mary (she needs it). P.S. You think I am tite, but I'm not. P.S. Hope you don't feel hurt about this will."

The second note, dated June 1927 and written on the back of a statement from Finchley Clothes & Haberdashery, stated: "My girl has turned me down. Give my love to Mary, Nancy, Dick, etc. Goodbye cruel world. Smith." Neither note was ever dispatched, but Smith saved them and, over the years, read them again and again, as some men read old billets-doux. They seemed to comfort Smith, reminding him, perhaps, that he had always suffered and been sensitive and that even when he was a youth, no one had understood him.

At fifteen, he left Woodberry Forest and did not return. It was the end of his formal education. His sole obsession was aviation. His heroes were Orville and Wilbur Wright and, of course, Charles Lindbergh. In late 1927, following his nonstop solo flight across the Atlantic, Lindbergh visited Winston-Salem in his plane, *The Spirit of St. Louis*, and Smith drove down to the local airfield to gawk at him.

Smith bought his first plane at fifteen for $6,500. He was a daredevil and was often seen executing outside loops and corkscrew falls in planes ill-equipped for stunts. He had already obtained his pilot's license and in 1929, at seventeen, became one of the youngest pilots in America. Smith loved to fly. He possessed a dislike for partitioned spaces and interrupted views, a hatred, in fact, for any obstacle that set a limit to his actions.

As befitted a rich man's son, he pursued his pleasures doggedly. Nothing was permitted to intervene. When the Depression began the following year, it would seem to him like some fantastic rumor, like one of those catastrophes that frequent the far side of the world—an earthquake or a tidal wave—which are horrible but ultimately unimportant, since no one he knew had been affected.

Smith would not come into the bulk of his inheritance until he was twenty-eight, but on his seventeenth birthday, his allowance increased from $5,000 to $50,000 a year. But the money was nothing, a means to an end. It was pleasure he required, the insatiable thrill of performing.

6

FOLLOWING GRADUATION, LIBBY HAD INTENDED TO GO TO New York immediately, but her father disapproved. In Alfred Holman's view, acting was a trivial pursuit, and he insisted that Libby remain in Cincinnati for another year, hoping, perhaps, that she would take up some sensible endeavor, an occupation more in keeping with those of her sober and industrious forebears. Libby reluctantly gave in. She was just nineteen; she would conquer Broadway when she was twenty.

Libby attended classes at the University of Cincinnati that year, concentrating on her French. She also sang and acted in college plays and went to all the openings at the downtown theaters. On at least two occasions, she was taken to the Roosevelt Theatre, listening, as she later said, "in a rapt daze," to Bessie Smith, whose first record, "Down Hearted Blues," had sold two million copies in 1923. Bessie Smith became Libby's newest passion, the only singer she had ever heard, she said, capable of singing "Glorias from the gutter."

During the Christmas holidays, Libby met a twenty-one-year-old Princeton senior named Howard Baer, who had come to

Cincinnati to visit a friend. The trim, dapper Baer encountered Libby for the first time in a performance of A. A. Milne's *Belinda*, and thought she was the most glorious girl he had ever seen.

The early twenties were Howard Baer's salad days. For him, it was a time when not only he "but the world itself was young. World War I had made the world safe for democracy," he recalled, "and President Harding's 'Normalcy' was the thing. Nice girls were still nice, but rebelliously now: they explored a little further than they had before and, in turn, permitted a certain amount of exploration." Baer was not pushy; he was no philanderer, but he was accustomed to being in command. Then he was introduced to Libby, and suddenly, everything changed. "Libby was bright and confident and sexy, although one never used that word in 1923. She was strong and dynamic and she burst like a new, more brilliant sun on my hitherto limited horizon." In short, Baer fell in love with her.

He knew that Libby was not conventionally beautiful and, despite her obsession with the stage, was probably not a competent actress. Concerning her voice, he was undecided. It was low and wonderfully husky, but music was not his métier. Libby's chief attractions were a superb figure, determination and an agile wit. She was simply different. Baer had always thought of himself as bourgeois, a man who would inevitably secure a position in a bank or brokerage, happily kowtowing to some as yet undefined middle-class morality. But Libby believed, she insisted in fact, that life should be lived to the hilt, and that made Howard Baer uncomfortable.

For nearly a fortnight, he and Libby went to the theater, to the movies, to Castle Farm, to dinner dances and cocktail parties. They held hands, they parked and hesitantly necked, and Baer soon realized that he was more in love with Libby than she would ever be with him. The realization frightened him.

Baer returned to Princeton and neither called nor wrote. It had been, he felt, the sensible decision. Many years later, he continued to believe that Libby had had some incandescent quality that would have burned him had he been foolish enough to pursue her. There had been in her a force, a vitality, that had seemed at the time unconquerable.

7

D URING THE SUMMER OF 1929, SMITH REYNOLDS MET ANNE Cannon, the nineteen-year-old daughter of Joseph F. Cannon, a multimillionaire towel manufacturer. In the industrial feudalism of the new South, the Cannons occupied a position in Kannapolis, North Carolina, analogous to that of the Reynolds family in Winston-Salem. American soldiers who smoked the Reynolds-manufactured Camel cigarettes during World War I were drying themselves with Cannon towels embroidered with such gaudy legends as "In God We Trust" and "To Hell with the Kaiser." By the late twenties, Cannon mills were producing 60 percent of all the towels in America.

Anne Cannon was a striking brunette, rich and unscrupulous. Her friends assumed she would marry her childhood sweetheart, F. Brandon Smith, the son of a wealthy hardware dealer, but Anne suddenly threw him over for Smith Reynolds. Smith and Anne had been courting for only a few weeks when Joe Cannon returned unexpectedly to his palatial Concord home to discover the young couple in an intimate embrace on the sofa in his living room. Outraged, he bundled the hapless teenagers into his Cadillac and ordered his chauffeur to take them down to York in South Carolina. During the forty-mile drive, Cannon brooded in the back seat, a loaded shotgun in his lap.

Throughout the Carolinas, York was known as a town where weddings were performed quickly and unquestioningly. When they reached the village shortly after midnight, Joe Cannon found a policeman and commanded him to procure a judge or a justice of the peace. Eventually, they awakened Probate Judge George F. Smith and, on November 16, 1929, Smith and Anne were summarily wed. When news of the marriage reached Winston-Salem, their friends alluded to it not as a shotgun but as a cannon wedding.

The next day, Smith and Anne drove to Winston-Salem in Smith's green Lincoln convertible. They decided not to reside at Reynolda House, moving instead to a ninth-floor apartment in the recently built Carolina Hotel Apartments on Fourth Street in downtown Winston.

A week later, a Christmas dance was held at the Robert E. Lee, Winston's finest hotel. The gala ball of the season, it was attended, as it always was, by the sons and daughters of Winston's wealthier families. Afterward, Smith, Anne, Smith's best friend, Ab Walker, and another friend, Jim Baggs, returned to the Carolina Apartments for drinks and dinner. Both Smith and Anne were drunk and, during dinner, they continued to drink, arguing volubly. Anne shouted loud profanities, some of which Jim Baggs claimed never to have heard a southern woman utter before. Smith slapped her repeatedly, and when she passed out, he put her to bed. Smith poured himself another drink and sulked at an open window. Then, taking the china dinner plates, he tossed them one by one into the street below, where they exploded like little bombs on the streetcar tracks.

The marriage lasted only a few months. Smith later claimed that he had never been in love with her and that the marriage had been more akin to a punishment. Although Anne was now pregnant, Smith left her in Winston and traveled north to New York. Exactly nine months and a week after their marriage, Anne gave birth to a daughter, Anne Cannon Reynolds II. Smith sent a congratulatory telegram.

In Manhattan, Smith cavorted with his sister Nancy and his brother, Dick, who had come to the city to relieve the tedium of rural life in North Carolina, to play, to spend and to ingratiate themselves with the fashionable theatrical set. The actress Louise Brooks encountered them occasionally at Connecticut weekends and Manhattan dinner parties. Smith was married, of course, but Miss Brooks believed that all three of them were casting about for potential mates, that they were simply up for grabs. But who would have them? In Louise Brook's view, the Reynoldses were a humdrum clan, little more than illiterate farmers.

8

I N JUNE 1924, LIBBY COMPLETED HER STUDIES AT THE University of Cincinnati and made preparations to leave for New York. She intended to enroll at the Columbia School of Journalism and, in her free time, to further her theatrical ambitions. Alfred Holman was, at last, resigned. He loved his daughter, wanted only the best for her, and he insisted that if, at the end of two years, she had not succeeded, she should follow his example and enter law school. As a going-away gift, one of Libby's beaux presented her with a carton of Camels. Her parents gave her $250 and Rachel expressed the hope that Libby would return to Cincinnati soon, marry a nice wealthy Jewish boy, as Marion had done, and raise a family.

Concerning the theater, Alfred Holman was never to change his mind. Even after Libby was well known, he continued to send her bulletins, solemnly stressing the poverty of fame. It was not, he cautioned, that he was a philistine, but, unlike the stage, the law was decent, dependable.

At Cincinnati's Union Station, Holman told his twenty-year-old daughter: "Libby, there are New York trains going both ways five times a day. Leave your college diploma behind and we'll frame it. It won't interest Florenz Ziegfeld, and neither, I fear, will you."

9

MANHATTAN IN THE TWENTIES WAS A BOLD AND BRASSY town, devoted to the pleasure of pleasing itself. New York's insularity was singular and profound and New Yorkers admired themselves tremendously. The city's signature was a careless grin, its catchpenny cynicism aptly expressed in the popular phrase "Oh, yeah?"

Prohibition—"The Great Foolishness," as the gossip columnist Lucius Beebe called it—had been in effect for more than four years. But from the beginning, the Volstead Act had been unpopular and practically unenforceable. The Anti-Saloon League of New York claimed that America had entered a new era of clean thinking and clean living, but few other New Yorkers were as naïve or sanctimonious. There were some thirty-two thousand speakeasies in the city and bootleg alcohol could be purchased almost anywhere—at soda fountains and shoeshine parlors, at fruit stands and barber shops, at laundries and delicatessens. Grocery stores sold gin disguised as cans of potatoes and whiskey masked as cans of beans. It seemed that almost everyone drank and to no apparent end.

But the Dry Decade was a glittering time—an era of hot jazz and flaming youth, of banjos, ivories and saxophones, of gilded skyscrapers and gaudy pleasure domes, of Channel swimmers, Atlantic fliers, Sultanic swatters, boardwalks and bathing beauties, Harlem slummers, flagpole sitters and marathon dancers, hip flasks and hootch, gold diggers and sugar daddies, cloche hats and raccoon coats, Mah Jongg, Model Ts and ticker-tape parades, rouged knees and bee-stung lips, lurid tabloids, intimate revues, glamorous torpedoes and bootleggers, blind pigs and speaks, the Charleston and cocaine, evangelists, flappers and Ziegfeld girls. Rhapsodies were blue, the beautiful were damned and, inevitably, gentlemen preferred blondes. Seriousness was unacceptable. Oh, Boy. Let's Do It. Ain't We Got Fun.

Smith Reynolds was besotted with Manhattan. He and his older brother coursed through the city on a rollicking spree, brash, extravagant young men, heirs to a fortune of $40 million. Nothing was beyond their means—the French restaurants and Harlem honkey-tonks, the grand hotels, the yachts, the planes, first nights at burlesques and musical comedies, the coveys of credulous showgirls. Dick was the leader in these escapades and Smith, who worshiped him, followed enthusiastically behind.

Dick was twenty-four. A large, tall and amiable youth, he was obsessed with sailing and flying. Unlike Smith, he had actually worked as a boy—packing cigarettes in one of his family's tobacco factories and, as an ordinary seaman, cleaning toilets and scrubbing decks aboard a freighter plying between New York and Hamburg. He attended North Carolina State College, where he played football, but decamped before the end of his freshman year.

When he was twenty, Dick formed the Ireland Amphibian Company, which owned Curtiss Field (later, Roosevelt Field) in Mineola, Long Island, and, from this connection, would subsequently become a major stockholder in Delta Airlines. But business rarely held him in thrall.

In 1927, having driven his Rolls-Royce into Long Island Sound, Dick disappeared with a blond chorine. There were rumors of murder and suicide, and a search ensued. Eleven days later, the police found young Reynolds eating chop suey in a St. Louis café and he explained his disappearance by saying: "I wanted to get away from Broadway and the nightclubs where only money talks."

Two years later, while driving recklessly through the English countryside, Dick struck and killed a cyclist. He was found guilty and served five months in Wormwood Scrubs. The prison's warden assured the press that, for all his money, Reynolds received no special treatment. "It don't make much difference who this chappie is," he said. "'E gets no more raisins in 'is duff than a Whitechapel leather snatcher."

Dick returned to Manhattan where he was joined by Smith. Dick's dark good looks, his charm and inexhaustible resources, gave him a certain cachet along the Great White Way. An enterprising playboy, he made the usual flamboyant gestures—giving a racehorse to a starlet for her birthday, financing part of a Broadway show.

Not yet twenty, Smith attempted to emulate Dick. He flew and sailed and drove his Rolls throughout the city. On one occasion, he fell in love with a chorus girl and informed the show's producers that she should be given a more substantial role. The producers barred him from the theater and Smith tried, unsuccessfully, to buy the show. Although Smith lacked his brother's flair, he seemed a romantic figure, an upstart perhaps, vainglorious, but the New York tabloids referred to him as the tobacco prince, and reported his comings and goings with tedious regularity.

10

THE FOUR CHIEF RESIDENCES FOR SINGLE WOMEN IN Manhattan were the YWCA, the Allerton House, the Three Arts Club and the Martha Washington Hotel. Even before Libby left Cincinnati, her mother had selected the Studio Club, a branch of the YWCA at 35 East Sixty-second Street, an establishment for young ladies engaged in the arts. Room and board cost twelve dollars a week. When Libby arrived in the late summer of 1924, her sole assets were an education, $250 in cash and, as a last resort, the train fare to Cincinnati, concealed in her new Boyishform bra.

"I had nothing practical to sell in New York," she said, "but a college education. And in New York, that's no asset unless you can type, run an elevator, sell notions or have a good enough memory for faces to be a hat check girl in a speakeasy.

"My mental torture was the thought of mother back home expecting terrible things to happen to me. And they were, but not the terrible things she imagined. Mother feared that I might be caught in the net of wily white slavers who lie in wait for girls with B.A. degrees and put chloroform in their coffee."

Libby resided at the Studio Club for nearly four months. Two girls shared each of the rooms or inhabited small dormitories containing six beds. The girls dubbed the dormitory the cuckoo room—a place where hijinks were permissible at any hour of the day or night. Libby lived in the cuckoo room. Late at night, she often sat up in her bed, playing the ukelele and singing songs to her roommates. Georgia Neese Clark, later to become Treasurer of the United States under President Harry Truman, shared the cuckoo room with her, as did Libby's new best friend, Mary Hoover, who would later marry the poet and novelist Conrad Aiken.

At first, Libby liked the Studio Club, the camaraderie of young girls gathered together in a strange and difficult city. Each morning, they scrutinized *Variety*. They trudged around to all the casting offices and cattle calls, drifting in and out of the two main centers of theatrical gossip and information—the Hotel Astor Drug Store on Broadway and the English Tea Room, situated in the basement of an old brownstone on West Forty-eighth Street. Searching for supplementary employment, they read the classified section of the New York *Times*, through which Libby finally found a job as a part-time model. But she was an ungainly mannequin and was astonished when she was hired, referring to herself as "Lizzie the hideous clothes machine."

Libby had also enrolled at Columbia University, selecting a course in short-story composition. She wrote nearly twenty stories that autumn and was unable to sell any of them. But Libby was determined to master the craft, and on numerous occasions, lacking subway fare, she walked across the park and trudged the fifty blocks up to Columbia and back again to Sixty-second Street.

Libby swiftly became disenchanted with the Studio Club. She was not permitted to smoke in the dormitory and was compelled to check in before ten-thirty each evening. She did not like rising early and, since breakfast was not served after nine, she often missed the morning meal. She detested the brilliant light in the club's downstairs parlor, where the girls were instructed to entertain their gentlemen callers, and she loathed washing her own laundry. "After making the rounds of all the theatrical offices, I used to come home so depressed that I'd lie in bed practically weeping," she said. "But, in spite of the rules, I continued to smoke and Mary Hoover did drawings of me in all my desolate poses."

That autumn, Libby met Jennings Perry, a fledgling journalist from Tennessee. Perry and a partner had recently purchased a newspaper in Rye, New York, called *The Courier*. Printed on a hand press, the weekly was published in an old curiosity shop in downtown Rye.

September 3 was Perry's twenty-fourth birthday, and late that afternoon, as he put the paper to bed, Libby walked into his office accompanied by an older man, a friend of her father's. The man had come to inquire about the possibilities of printing a book on Perry's press. Perry apologized and turned him down. He was too busy, he said; he was publishing a newspaper. But he was struck at once with Libby, her voluptuous figure and generous mouth, her deep throaty laugh, and the gold flecks he imagined he saw in her eyes. Ignoring her companion, the enamored youth invited Libby to dinner and, to his surprise, she accepted.

That evening, Libby suggested he come down to New York and have dinner with her at the Studio Club. Three nights later, Perry dined with some hundred and fifty girls in the club's main dining room. He was the only man. After dinner, he and Libby strolled into Central Park—in those days an unhazardous oasis where courting couples often walked in the evenings. In a drizzling rain, they stood under the eaves of the monkey house at the zoo smoking cigarettes. In a flat, midwestern accent, Libby spoke of her impoverished youth and how fond she was of her father. She was determined to become an actress, she said, and, should that fail, a successful singer.

Her dreams were ingenuous and touching, Perry felt, like those of some innocent campaigner who had yet to formulate a battle plan. For Libby, success was palpable and ever-present. She was both confident and convincing and, listening to her, Perry's secret doubts concerning his own ambitions were mysteriously washed away.

As Thanksgiving approached, Libby still had not been asked to read for a role. Only the week before, she had been forced to decide whether to use her return train fare to Cincinnati for travel or food. Being more hungry than homesick, she spent the

money on sardines and soup and imported tins of white as-
paragus.

One rainy morning, learning of yet another casting session,
she dutifully tramped crosstown to the Selwyn Theatre on West
Forty-second Street, where a sweaty stage manager listened to a
long line of girls reading for the role of a streetwalker in a play
entitled *The Fool*—candidates for a road company set to tour the
South and the Middle West.

Libby waited for three hours; she was thirty-eighth in line.
When it was time for the girl in front of her to read, the stage
manager announced that he was through for the day. He instructed the remaining girls to report to the theater in the morning. Libby was exasperated. As she left the theater, she heard the
stage manager asking for a cigarette. Proffering a Camel, Libby
explained that she had not been given an opportunity to read,
that it had not only been rude, it was an oversight.

The stage manager inhaled and looked Libby up and down.
Then, he smiled and said: "You look like you've got s.a. to burn,
kiddo. Okay, get up on the stage and take a try at it." Five minutes later, the role of the streetwalker with s.a. (sex appeal) was
Libby's. The job paid twenty-five dollars a week.

Based on the life of St. Francis of Assisi, *The Fool* had been a
hit on Broadway two years before. Its success had spawned seven
touring companies and Libby, billed as Elizabeth Holman, traveled through the provinces for four weeks in the role of "A
Woman of the Streets."

In early December, *The Fool* arrived in Memphis and Jennings Perry attended the one-night stand. The Rye *Courier* had
folded after only two months of publication and Perry was now a
reporter for the Memphis *Commercial-Appeal*. After Libby's performance, they walked into Tom Lee Park. They held hands and
Libby sang a popular song called "Jealousy," while Perry
hummed the harmony. And then, on a bench in the dark, they
kissed for the first time. It might have gone further, but, as
Perry knew, Libby was leaving for North Carolina at dawn. Even
so, that evening marked the beginning of what he would later
describe as a lengthy, though intermittent, love affair.

When the road show closed, Libby returned reluctantly to the
Studio Club, to the cuckoo room where she slept on the only
available bed, an old army cot. She hated it. And so, with her

friend Mary Hoover, who had wearied of the Studio Club herself, Libby moved into a small apartment on the top floor of a shabby brownstone at East Fifty-fourth Street and Madison Avenue. They paid a rent of fifteen dollars a month and bought their food from a neighborhood delicatessen, cooking it on a kerosene stove. Libby continued to make the tedious rounds between auditions and agents' offices. In the evenings, while Mary painted or sketched, Libby recited the grim litany of that day's reversals—it had snowed and there were holes in her only pair of pumps; an elderly agent had made a pass at her; an impertinent director had suggested she take up the violin. It wasn't fair, she said, it wasn't the way it was supposed to be.

Mary sympathized, but felt that Libby's appearance was her principal impediment. She was too tall; she was overweight with rosy chipmunk cheeks. She was nearsighted and refused to wear glasses. And then, there were her clothes, her ratty raccoon coat in particular, which Libby adored and refused to abandon. Her dreams were doomed to failure, Mary believed.

Casting directors may have objected to Libby's appearance, but it failed to discourage college boys. Libby had two or three different dates a week, almost always with Princeton undergraduates. During the twenties, some undefinable cachet was attached to Princeton, some inexplicable regard. Mary Hoover thought it very odd. It was well known, after all, that Harvard condescended to Yale, and Yale, in turn, looked down on Princeton. And yet, there existed among Princetonians an implied assumption of superiority. Libby was partial to Princeton men.

In early 1925, Libby's luck, her "potluck," as she called it, finally changed. She secured the part of a lady's maid in a play called *The Sapphire Ring*. One of her fellow actors was a suave and intelligent beauty named Helen Gahagan. She was only twenty-four and already, Libby noted, a Broadway star. When Libby informed her that she too would achieve stardom at a similar age, Miss Gahagan smiled (enigmatically, Libby felt) and said, "Of course you will, my dear." The play, a Viennese import, opened at the Selwyn Theatre on April 15, 1925, and closed that same week. For the next few days, Libby brooded at home with Mary Hoover, drawing obscene caricatures of drama critics and playing lamentations on her ukelele.

That spring, Mary painted a portrait of Libby in oil. She envisaged Libby as the consummate vamp, depicting her in a diaphanous veil which barely concealed her full, naked body. Libby's breasts were much in evidence. For reasons Mary never understood, the painting was ultimately displayed in the front window of the Steinway piano store on West Fifty-seventh Street. During the lunch hour and after work, curious crowds milled outside to gape at it. One afternoon, quite by accident, Libby walked by the window and gasped. She was very embarrassed and, thinking she might be recognized, turned and fled. At home, Mary asked Libby what she had thought of her portrait. Libby laughed and, paraphrasing the old Italian maxim, said: "See nipples and *die.*"

The Theatre Guild was considered the most prestigious avant-garde theater in Manhattan. That April, the junior members of the Guild were industriously rehearsing a new revue called *The Garrick Gaieties.* The young cast was comprised of serious talented professionals who had gained experience in stock companies and in other Guild productions as bit players, extras and understudies. They were all unknown or, as one of them said, "we knew every maid and butler on Broadway and only maids and butlers knew us."

The cast included Sterling Holloway, June Cochrane, Romney Brent, Betty Starbuck (described by Dorothy Parker as having "the prettiest little persecution complex you'll ever see"), Lee Strasberg, Sanford Meisner, and Harold Clurman, the only doctor of philosophy on the New York stage. The music and lyrics were to be written by two young graduates of Columbia named Richard Rodgers and Lorenz Hart.

The *Gaieties* cast was among the first rush of educated talent to enter the musical comedy theater. Some of its members had graduated from Columbia, Vassar, Yale, the Sorbonne. A contradictory mix, Strasberg, Clurman and Meisner read Proust and studied Stanislavsky, drawn together, as Clurman said, by their common dissatisfactions, their still unshaped ideals, while many of the others were passionately devoted to musical comedy, the Charleston, and college football games.

In 1925, Dick Rodgers was twenty-three and Larry Hart was thirty. At Columbia, they had produced several brilliant Varsity shows in succession. They had been on Broadway once before with *Poor Little Ritz Girl*, but five lean seasons had now elapsed. Hart was impoverished and losing hope. Rodgers was seriously considering joining the family baby's underwear business. When asked to write the musical numbers for *The Gaieties*, Rodgers was enthusiastic, but Hart was stubborn and balked. He was disenchanted with amateur shows and amateurs' salaries. Rodgers, however, talked him around, and the two friends would become the real impetus behind *The Garrick Gaieties*, behind what Edith Meiser, one of the show's young actresses, called the snowball that became an avalanche.

One cold April afternoon, Libby and a friend, actor Stanley Lindahl, met for lunch at Child's Restaurant on Fifth Avenue. Lindahl, an extra in the Theatre Guild's production of *Caesar and Cleopatra*, told Libby that auditions were currently being held for a new revue called *The Garrick Gaieties*. It was not thought that the show would come to much, he said, what with only four performances to be staged on two successive Sundays, but Lindahl persuaded Libby that a limited engagement was better than not working at all. Given the Guild's reputation, he added, all the important critics would attend opening night. Libby was almost destitute and had begun to trifle with notions of going home. Without finishing her lunch, she hurried down to the Garrick Theatre.

Auditions for the show were in their second day when Libby arrived. She knew no one and stood nervously on stage in a pink flannel suit. When the pianist began to play, Libby sang "Jealousy." Her voice, as it always would, swooped in and out of key. Philip Loeb, the director, felt she was "too Broadway," that her looks clashed with those of the other girls—girls he considered fresh and buoyant ingenues. Libby, he reckoned, was not a girl one brought home to mother.

But Libby was given another opportunity, auditioning for Richard Rodgers. He asked her in what key she sang. Libby shrugged. She didn't know but asked him to play. Rodgers began to play the piano and Libby urged him to play lower, lower, then lower. Rodgers was not impressed. At the last moment, however, the producers decided that Libby had beautiful legs and gave her a part in the chorus at thirty-five dollars a week.

One of the first numbers Rodgers and Hart wrote for the

show was entitled "Ladies of the Box Office," a sultry, naughty tune that members of the cast called "the aphrodisiac song." A spoof on the commercial theater, it satirized such stars as Jeanne Eagels, Mary Pickford and the Ziegfeld Girl. They had not yet selected anyone to portray the Ziegfeld Chorus Girl and, suddenly, because the producers found Libby uncommonly seductive, they gave her the song.

The four special performances of *The Garrick Gaieties* were scheduled for the afternoon and evening of May 17 and would be repeated the following Sunday. The show set out to burlesque its betters—Michael Arlen's novel *The Green Hat* ("The Green Derby"); Sydney Howard's hit play *They Knew What They Wanted* ("They Didn't Know What They Were Getting"). The sole political spoof was "Mr. and Mrs.," in which President and Mrs. Coolidge's idea of an enjoyable evening was seen to be listening silently to the radio and falling asleep by ten. "The Scopes Monkey Trial" was staged with a jury in monkey suits. In "The Three Musketeers," New York's police department and subway manners were twitted. Before an unadorned curtain, June Cochrane and Sterling Holloway sang Rodgers and Hart's "Manhattan," the hit song of the show. Then came a rapid succession of hilarious skits, sparkling parodies and freshly conceived songs and dances. The Sunday matinee audience gave the cast a standing ovation. Between acts, Larry Hart dashed backstage shouting that the show was going to run for a year, for a year or more.

The critics were effusive. Alexander Woollcott described the show as "fresh and spirited and engaging, bright with the brightness of something newly-minted." Robert Benchley said "these hitherto unknown youngsters have given us the most civilized show in town." And of Rodgers and Hart's songs, *Variety* observed: "They clicked like a colonel's heels at attention."

The Gaieties was the first of the small literate revues. Not since Gilbert and Sullivan had there been such brilliant lyrics on the Broadway stage. The demand for tickets was so great that six extra performances were given, even though an unprecedented heat wave had enveloped the city. In late May, the cast begged the Theatre Guild to put the show on a regular run and finally the Guild relented. On June 8, 1925, *The Garrick Gaieties* opened anew and eventually ran for 211 performances.

*   *   *

Before reopening, various sketches were dropped, a new song, "Sentimental Me," was added, and Libby, who had been given a solo number called "Black and White" (about miscegenation) was informed that she would no longer be singing it. She retained her "Aphrodisiac" song, but was relegated to the chorus. "Am I disgusted? Am I downhearted? Am I discouraged?" she told Mary Hoover. "Write your own ticket, but I'm *awfully* fed up." She contemplated quitting, but desperately needed the thirty-five dollars a week.

Richard Rodgers was the one who had recommended cutting Libby's number. He didn't think she could sing on key. She was either sharp or flat and there was something vulgar in her voice, what was known at the time as a "coon-shouter's voice," a contralto with a big vibrant sound. There were others, however, such as Harold Clurman, who believed that Libby sang with wonderful spunk and gusto.

Throwing his long arms around her, Clurman said that Libby was far better than most of the singers in the cast but that it would take time for others to understand. He counseled cunning, patience, resolution.

Following the show's critical acclaim, Libby became, if only by association, a minor celebrity. The cast were now the pets of New York society, both of the old guard and the nascent "café society." She was to be seen everywhere in New York, usually surrounded by a cadre of young Princetonians. Her favorite was Johnny Martin, a handsome youth from Philadelphia who had lost his left arm in a shooting accident. Martin had just graduated from Princeton where, despite his handicap, he had been an excellent athlete and an expert shot, and he would later hold the North American record for landing the largest game fish of the year. He had joined the staff of the recently launched *Time* magazine and would eventually become its managing editor.

Johnny Martin escorted Libby and her friends to parties that summer where Richard Rodgers played the piano and Larry Hart did Al Jolson imitations; Algonquin parties where Libby met Robert Benchley and Dorothy Parker; Sunday night parties at the Gershwins' home on East Seventy-second Street; British parties given by Bea Lillie and Gertrude Lawrence in the duplex apartment they shared on the West Side, where Libby listened to

Noel Coward playing his unpublished tunes; bohemian parties where Libby consumed bathtub gin; bathing parties at Long Island beach clubs where the *Gaieties* cast once masqueraded for charity as "the widows and orphans of celibate seamen;" society parties at secluded estates in Westport and Sands Point; weekend parties at Anne Boissevain's home in Jamaica Estates in Queens where Libby hobnobbed with cartoonist Peter Arno and met Edna St. Vincent Millay; plush parties and fancy-dress balls at Ezra Winter's vast studio on the very top of Grand Central Station.

And when the parties were over or not in full swing, Libby's group, wearing chiffon frocks with uneven hems, silk stockings with clocks, satin pumps with Baby Louis heels and bell-shaped cloche hats, met their young men beneath the clock at the Biltmore Hotel. They attended the Mayfair dances at the Ritz. They shimmied till dawn at the Club Chantee or went to the Embassy Club where Emil Coleman's orchestra played tunes from *The Gaieties* whenever one of the cast came in. After the theater, they met for drinks at Dinty Moore's or Barney Gallant's, or at the Casino-in-the-Park, where they listened to Eddie Duchin's piano.

Wearing little hats with veils, gloves and tailored suits, Libby and her friends gathered at the Lorraine Grill for tango dances or for tea dances at the Plaza. They ferried across the Hudson to Hoboken beer halls with H. L. Mencken and Ernest Boyd, shunning the Round Table at the Algonquin because Mencken thought it silly, and Libby had decided it "was little more than a cat fight really." On hot summer nights, they were taken to the Astor Roof for iced coffee and chicken à la king. They taxied up to Harlem to the Cotton Club where Josephine Baker cavorted in a skirt comprised of green bananas; or, at midnight, to the Inferno, a basement club, where the regulars, instead of taking the stairs, slid down a chute, at the bottom of which stood a large black man in a red devil's suit who caught them and carried them to their tables. At dawn, they taxied back again to Child's for hot cakes and coffee, their beaux lacing the cups with whatever remained in their engraved silver flasks.

"It was too perfect," Libby told the actress Erin O'Brien Moore. "When you're twenty-one, there's so much to do and so much time in which to do it. I did almost anything that popped in my head. It was *fantastically* exhausting. But, even then, I wanted more. I wanted more *everything* forever."

Libby had lived in Manhattan for nearly a year and could not now imagine living anywhere else. She was still not earning enough money, and she spent all of that and more, borrowing here and there for her extravagances. But Libby remained light-hearted. She had neither the time nor the inclination for cynical reflection, for sentimental melancholy. Many members of the *Gaieties* cast, in fact, resented Libby for what they called her wildness, her irrepressible self-assurance. But those qualities were precisely what attracted fellow actor Sterling Holloway to her, and during the run of the show, they became close friends.

A twenty-year-old carrot-topped Georgian, Holloway was the show's main attraction. He sang and danced and acted in almost every scene. Holloway adored Libby, loved her black, unruly hair, her ardor, her cheeky flair for self-dramatization. And Libby, in turn, adored him. She treated the tall, skinny, effeminate boy like a baby brother, and Holloway was pleased. They were inseparable and Theresa Helburn, the Theatre Guild's producer, begged Libby to stop hugging Holloway so much, insisting it would sap his strength, and they would have to close the show.

Because he had so many costume changes, Holloway never wore underwear onstage. In September, during a matinee, he suddenly came down with an attack of acute appendicitis. His fellow actors bore him from the stage and, in the wings, undressed him, since whoever would understudy him that evening would need his costume. Libby was the first to realize that Holloway wore only a jockstrap. "He can't go to the hospital dressed like that," she shouted. Reaching up under her skirt, Libby pulled off her pink lace bloomers and put them on her stricken friend. Several members of the cast were shocked, but Holloway laughed all the way to the hospital.

"Sentimental Me," Holloway's second-act number, contained the lyric, "I sit and sigh, she sighs and sits upon my knee." Each evening, before going onstage, some of the more mischievous members of the cast would whisper, "shit" in Holloway's ear, hoping he would heedlessly substitute "shit" for "sit" onstage. But the carefree Georgian was a professional and nearly five months went by without mishap.

One night, Libby whispered "shit" loudly and persuasively in Holloway's ear. He went onstage and began to sing his song, completing the first chorus successfully; but during the refrain, he suddenly sang: "I shit and sigh, she sighs and shits upon my knee." He sang it with suave assurance and with perfect diction, and, it was only when he had finished the line that he realized what he had sung. Richard Rodgers, conducting the orchestra, flipped his baton in the air and ducked into the orchestra pit. The audience became silent, then broke into howls of raucous laughter. The mortified Holloway completed the number and scuttled into the wings. He was greeted by a triumphant Libby, who embraced him, and said, "That's *doing* it, darling. You were *wonderful*."

On another occasion, Libby and Holloway hired a horse-drawn hansom outside the Plaza Hotel. Holloway had presented Libby with a dozen roses and, driving slowly down Fifth Avenue, she stood up in the open carriage, lofting the roses and blowing kisses to passing pedestrians. Startled, they turned to stare, and Libby shouted in her basso profundo, "I will do Carmen next season, and I will do it *even* better than I did this year."

Despite her bravado, and her sophisticated Princeton beaux, Libby was as sexually confused and puritanical as she had been at seventeen. She supported, in principle at least, the burgeoning sexual liberation movement of her time, but disapproved of women who slept around. She worried continually about contracting a disease or of becoming pregnant—superfluous concerns since she was still a virgin and was determined, for the moment, to remain one.

Libby was courted by many men, but she had no intention of letting them work their manly wiles upon her. Rather, she cultivated the company of weak and vulnerable youths, callow collegians or latent homosexuals, whom she could dominate. In the theatrical circles in which she moved, "gentlemen homosexuals," as they were known, were acceptable escorts. Their homosexuality was "overlooked." Moreover, Libby had strong maternal needs; she adored children and childlike men and was headstrong and parental in her dealings with them. Heterosexuals, on the other hand, men such as Johnny Martin and Harold Clurman, interpreted Libby's bravado as coquetry. Clurman felt that Libby signaled a sense of blood, as of something luscious, ripe, provocative. He thought of her as a budding vamp on the verge of shedding her provincial ways. And Clurman was right, but he could not have guessed the direction in which it would take her.

At summer's end, Libby and two other girls from *The Gaieties* moved into a furnished sublet on Lower Park Avenue. Eleanor Shaler was a featured dancer who hoped one day to star as a dancer-comedienne; Sally Bates, a talented young actress, aspired to the legitimate stage. The apartment, a single bedroom and living room, contained a piano and a small love seat. Because the bedroom had just two beds, the girls purchased a cot from Bloomingdale's, agreeing that the last one home each night would sleep on it. Eventually, the cot was monopolized by Libby.

The three girls played eight performances a week and, in their free time, took countless singing, acting and dancing lessons. They attended the movies, friends' performances at Sunday benefits and, occasionally, were driven to Long Island for abbreviated weekends. Sally Bates was the most reserved of the three. Libby and Eleanor Shaler were effusive and less discriminating. Eleanor admired Libby's vibrance and impulsiveness, but disliked the gossip and innuendo that flowered in her wake. Libby liked being talked about, liked being looked at; she wanted to be seen. Eleanor found it uncomfortable to be in Libby's company since she made her companions conspicuous too. Whenever Libby encountered a girlfriend in a public place, a theater lobby or a restaurant, she would call her name at the top of her voice, shrieking: "*Eleanor,*" or "*Sally,* my *favorite* person." And everyone in the room would turn and stare.

The girls shared the apartment for three months. Normally, Libby rose early, took a cold shower in the bathroom without closing the door and then traipsed around naked as though she inhabited a tropical isle. She displayed no sense of physical modesty and, among friends at least, felt more comfortable undressed.

Both roommates thought her terribly funny. In moments of high elation, she would cry, "Cut off my arm at the elbow and my body's just a shell," and Eleanor and Sally would laugh hysterically. She loved tiny objects that she could hold in the palm of her hand—little flowers, miniature teddy bears, anything small or broken. She possessed tremendous warmth, a genuine sweetness, and, as Eleanor said, "there was not a drop of bitch blood in her either."

Several of the girls in *The Gaieties* studied dance at Mary Read's studio on West Seventy-second Street. Miss Read choreographed the Tiller Girls, the first precision troupe of dancers in America, whom she had brought over from England. She also taught a ballet technique specifically designed for musical comedy. Because Libby wished to improve her limited talent for the dance, her friend Harriette Woodruff brought her to the studio one afternoon.

No sooner were they introduced than Libby was guided through a series of complicated steps. At the end of the lesson, Miss Read took Harriette Woodruff aside and, indicating Libby, said: "Don't ask me how or why, but that girl's going to come to a tragic end." Miss Woodruff laughed. "You don't know Libby," she said. "She's got real spunk." But Mary Read refused to look at Libby again and, claiming she lacked true balletic skills, asked her not to return.

11

SHEPHERD'S GIVEN NAME WAS ROBERT, BUT EVERYONE called him Slick. When he was in the seventh grade, his geography teacher had yanked his hair, claiming the boy had been impertinent. His classmates laughed and ribbed him about it after school. To ensure himself against further embarrassments, he promptly went to the barbershop and asked that all his fine brown hair be clipped and shaved. Thereafter, his classmates called him Slickhead, eventually abbreviating it to Slick.

Slick was born and raised in Winston-Salem. His family was not poor, neither were they well-to-do. As a child, he often played ball in the large, oak-studded yard of R. J. Reynolds's granite mansion at Fifth and Spring, in the days before the

Reynolds family moved out to Reynolda. Winston was a small town then. Everyone knew everyone else and Slick played with Dick and Smith Reynolds, with Bowman and Gordon Gray, and with other children whose parents had grown rich and prosperous from tobacco. Slick and the Reynolds boys were not close friends, but he considered them congenial companions.

After graduating from R. J. Reynolds High School, Slick obtained employment as a reporter for the Winston-Salem *Journal*, covering local sports, the courts and politics. In the course of his duties, he encountered Smith infrequently; but Smith would wave as he sped through town in his green Lincoln convertible, and occasionally they met for lunch at the Carolinian Coffee Shoppe. Because Slick had not seen Smith in more than a year, not since the moody youth had decamped for New York, he was surprised when Smith called one afternoon. Claiming to have an interesting proposition, Smith insisted they get together the following day.

They arranged to meet in Talman's Office Supply, a store in the lobby of the Nissen Building at the corner of Fourth and Cherry. Shaped in the form of a U, the eighteen-story building was then the tallest structure in North Carolina. Smith, dressed in slacks and an open sports shirt, was much as Slick remembered him, a little older, perhaps, somewhat more brash and confident. He talked excitedly about New York, claiming not to understand why Slick still lived in Winston.

Smith explained that he had recently purchased a new plane, a Savoia-Marchetti amphibian, and intended to make a solo flight around the world that summer. It would be, he felt, the supreme adventure, but it required publicity. To that end, Smith proposed that Slick ghostwrite his story, syndicating it through one of the national press agencies. He would give Slick his itinerary and, during the trip, would dispatch coded cables, verifying each day's journey, with colorful details of where he had been, what he had done, the difficulties he had surmounted. To give the story verve and authenticity, Smith suggested that Slick go to the library and research the towns and countries in which Smith intended to stop—Cairo, Constantinople, Burma, French Indo-China. Slick could write what he pleased. Smith asked only that his account be vivid, dashing, unforgettable.

In return, Slick would receive half of whatever he sold the

story for; but Smith wanted the proposed adventure kept secret. Only Slick, his brother, Dick, and his friend Ab Walker had been told about it. Slick agreed, and the two young men shook hands. Smith was returning to New York, but he would stay in touch. He did not expect to be back in Winston for donkey's years.

12

LIBBY HAD PLANNED HER OWN SEDUCTION CAREFULLY. IN-tending to make no innocent mistakes, she had selected the man, the method, the time and the place. She was twenty-two and could no longer tolerate the tiresome burden of her virginity.

During the spring of 1926, she had joined the midwestern road company of *The Greenwich Village Follies*. The show's large cast included Leonard Sillman, later to become known for producing the *New Faces* revues on Broadway; two ancient vaudevillians called McIntyre and Heath; Fred Allen, a rising young comedian with a bright, deadpan delivery; and a gaggle of tall chorines called The Sixteen American Rockets.

Sillman had become Libby's closest friend during the long tour. The diminutive actor and dancer envisaged himself as "a midget's dream of Clifton Webb." A weak and boastful homosexual, he was described by Libby as "not being able to bear the terrible weight of his own egomania." But she liked him in spite of that and Sillman, in turn, adored Libby.

He loved her looks—the slit hazel eyes, the bee-stung mouth, the bright japonica fingernails, and all her affectations—the tattered French beret, the corncob pipe, the shabby raccoon coat. Only her voice disturbed him. It was the seductive voice of a siren and, whenever Libby began to sing, Sillman claimed to put wax in his ears.

That spring, Sillman introduced Libby to a minor actor in the show named Robert Brandeis. Brandeis was a handsome youth of twenty-four and, because of his longish mane of palomino hair, was affectionately known as Horseface. He was passionately in love with Libby and, on more than one occasion, had made awkward advances, flustered retreats. Each night after the show, Sillman, Brandeis and Libby would gather in Sillman's hotel suite to eat and drink and discuss their mutual doubts and apprehensions.

Libby, though attracted to Brandeis, continued, brusquely, to reject his suit. Two weeks after the tour began, Brandeis was informed his part was being cut and was given a week's notice. During that time, Libby began to warm to the heartbroken youth. Sillman saw them holding hands and assumed that Libby had, at last, acceded to some of his less urgent blandishments. Sillman didn't know that Libby nurtured a more elaborate plan.

One night in Cleveland, following the show, Libby, Brandeis and Sillman withdrew to Sillman's suite and ordered dinner. At first, Libby seemed irritable, but she drank more wine than Sillman had ever seen her drink and, as the evening progressed, she became sure, unruffled, sensual. She toyed with Brandeis rather as a hungry lioness toys with fallen though still living prey. She ignored him, stroked him, abused him, pampered him, prodded him playfully. Brandeis was both confused and flattered. The more Libby drank, the more she seemed torn between devouring and being devoured. She almost purred.

After dinner, the young couple bid Sillman goodnight and adjourned to Libby's room. Sillman was impatient for morning to come and over breakfast Libby told him everything. She did not remember a great deal, in fact, but it had not been a distasteful exercise. It had been expedient, like having one's appendix removed, and she was much relieved. Brandeis was sweet, but she never allowed him to touch her again. Within the week, he was gone. Libby suffered no remorse. She had made, she felt, the sensible decision, her virginity having been dispatched with few of the usual complications.

In June, *The Greenwich Village Follies* closed for the summer, and Libby, who had contrived to save a little money, decided to travel to Europe. She had talked for months of going abroad. Everyone she knew had been to Europe or intended to go that summer; besides, she needed a rest. She had been in New York for nearly two years, working or searching for work without cessation. In early July, therefore, she sailed for Le Havre on the Cunard Line's *Franconia*. The return fare was $198 and she traveled in tourist class where most of the passengers were college students.

For the outward voyage, the Cunard Line had hired a jazz band called The Intercollegiate Aces—all of whom were Princeton graduates, former members of the Triangle Club. One of them, Avery Sherry, who played the saxophone and clarinet, had met Libby previously in New York. The band had been hired to play in the first-class lounge, but on their first night at sea, they trooped into tourist class and Sherry met Libby again.

That night, she pestered Sherry to let her sing with the band. Sherry refused, but on the second night, he relented and Libby was smuggled into first class where she spent all her subsequent evenings. Backed by The Intercollegiate Aces, she sang "If I Could Be with You One Hour Tonight," "Baby Face" and "When the Red Red Robin Comes Bob Bob Bobbin' Along." Employing her husky lower register, Libby sang the songs slowly and seductively, and although she was not much older than her audience, she gave an impression, Sherry felt, of worldliness.

Libby spent the summer in Paris. She loved the city, particularly at night. She lived inexpensively at the Hôtel Sainte-Anne near the Avenue de l'Opéra, went regularly to Bricktop's nightclub in Pigalle, saw Josephine Baker at the Folies Bergère, drank at the rowdy cafés in St.-Germain, and took long walks in the Tuileries. Much later, she described her time in Paris as the only real holiday she had ever had; she had remained alone, capricious, free.

Toward the end of her third week, Libby met Tommy Adler, an old friend from Cincinnati. Libby's tutoring had helped Adler gain entrance to Yale, where he was now in his final year. The youth had just arrived in Paris and Libby, adopting the role of the older, more experienced traveler, instructed him that the truly amusing *boîtes* in town were the Petite Chaumière, where boys dressed up as girls; a Russian cabaret in the Place Pigalle, and a gangster's dive called Le Rat Mort. Casually, she also mentioned Zelli's—every collegian's favorite hangout—implying that one should see it, for the sake of it, but that it was not as *drôle* as the other clubs.

Disregarding Libby's counsel, Adler's favorite nightery became Harry's New York Bar and he often took her there. The popular basement bar was located at 5 Rue Daunou on the Right Bank and was known, among its predominantly American clientele, as "Sank-Roo-Do-Noo." At cocktail time, a black piano player performed. One evening, Libby jumped up from her table and began to sing, the pianist swiftly adapting to her register and rhythms. When she finished, there was loud applause and a man claiming to be an executive of Brunswick Records stood up and told Libby that if she would come to see him when she returned to America, he would make her rich and famous. Libby shouted that she was going to be rich and famous anyway and then, in rapid French, ordered him to shut up and sit down. Libby's friends were much amused. They preferred her to be, as she liked to be, a madcap, the sort of girl who liked to think that a comic aside solved everything.

In late August, Libby sailed back to America, convinced that Paris had been the high point of her life, that it had changed her fundamentally and that, therefore, nothing would be the same again. She was blinded, as she had often been, by glimpses of some gorgeous, though indeterminate future. On the other hand, the two years her father had given her to succeed had now expired. No matter, she thought. She would persevere. Her dreams would not elude her for long.

In New York, Leonard Sillman met Libby at the pier. She seemed to him a little smug, a little more secretive than she had been. He was anxious to know if she had had a torrid romance that summer. He insisted she tell him everything. "Singers don't have romances," Libby said. "They inspire them."

Libby went out on the road again in a new version of *The Greenwich Village Follies* and, in late January of 1927, when the show closed, returned to Manhattan. She continued to live from hand to mouth. Unable to find work, she moved once more into the Studio Club. But Libby remained optimistic. She was ambitious; and the ambitious, like the fearful, look ahead.

She spent most of that winter in casting offices along Broadway—an avenue the gossip columnists were fond of calling "The Hardened Artery" or, simply, "Rue Regret." In the late twenties, newspaperman Mark Hellinger wrote that Broadway's "oversized signs blinked their come-ons so brightly that daylight, by comparison, seemed dim." Broadway was glutted with "cabarets and theaters and honky-tonks and dime-a-dance joints and checkered tablecloth speakeasies and chop suey restaurants and offices for fight managers, theatrical booking agents, Broadway lawyers, gangsters, private eyes, theatrical boarding houses on the side streets, lush apartments for kept women, beer drops and windfree corners for pathetic panhandlers. Minsky's burlesque, the Palace Theatre, Spinrad's barber shop, the El Fey, beautiful girls who had not yet felt the urge to go west. It was an expensive circus, nothing more, nothing less."

The most notorious and fashionable club on Broadway was the El Fey on West Forty-fifth Street—named after its backer, the gangster Larry Fay, whom the New York Police Department listed, after Legs Diamond and Waxey Gordon, as Public Enemy Number Three. A dapper figure, Fay operated New York's milk and taxicab rackets and eventually, on New Year's Eve of 1933, would be shot down in another of his clubs, The Napoleon. The El Fey was the most expensive club in town—bootleg champagne sold for thirty dollars a bottle and a pitcher of water cost two dollars. Despite her straitened circumstances, Libby went there frequently, taken by Johnny Martin and other wealthy Princetonians.

The El Fey was Larry Fay's in name only. It was run and operated by Texas Guinan, who had become the spirit of Prohibition in New York. The forty-three-year-old buxom blonde wore a gold police whistle around her neck to mock local police and federal agents. The critic Edmund Wilson described her as "this prodigious woman, with her pearls, her glittering bosom, her abundant beautifully bleached yellow coiffure, her formidable trap of shining white teeth, her broad bare back behind its grating of green velvet, the full-blown peony as big as a cabbage on her broad green thigh."

Nightly, the club was filled with Astors, Whitneys, Vanderbilts and Reynoldses, with such actors as Eddie Cantor, Harold Lloyd, and Gloria Swanson, with newspaper columnists Ed Sullivan and Walter Winchell and with gangsters such as Arnold Rothstein, Myron Lepke, Jack "Legs" Diamond and his younger brother, Eddie. The performers were equally well known. The fifteen-year-old Ruby Keeler performed her fast rhythm tap dances there. The featured dancer was George Raft, his specialty being a double-jointed Charleston. And a beautiful girl from Brooklyn named Rubye Stevens sang and danced in the chorus line, marking time until she moved to Hollywood where she would change her name to Barbara Stanwyck.

Entering the El Fey after midnight, Texas Guinan's invariable greeting to her customers was "Hello, Suckers." Her battle cry was "Curfew shall not ring tonight." She was famous for indoor fun after midnight and for such axioms as "Never give a sucker an even break," "Her brain is as good as new," "Give the little girl a big hand," and "It's having the same man around the house all the time that ruins matrimony."

Money was the magic word. Everyone Libby knew—that is, everyone she knew outside the theater—seemed to have unlimited resources. Polly Adler, Manhattan's most successful madam, believed that "in the Twenties, the only unforgivable sin was to be poor. People talked about ways of making it and ways of spending it, lived by standards and on a scale based on having plenty of it, grabbed for more with one hand and tossed it away with the other. Everybody had an angle, everybody was raking in the chips, there was no excuse not to have money."

One day at the English Tea Room, Libby told Leonard Sillman that when she married, it would not be for love, but for money. Putting aside her corncob pipe and emphasizing each of the syllables emphatically, she said: "I'm going to be *rich, rich, rich*." But, as she admitted, Libby did not yet know how such a thing might be accomplished.

Leonard Sillman believed in Libby's talent and did whatever he could to help her. That April, he was hired to perform in a new musical called *Merry-Go-Round*, and he persuaded the producer, Richard Herndon, to audition Libby. The audition was held in the basement of the Holy Cross Church on West Forty-seventh Street while morning mass was conducted above. Sillman was shocked when Libby arrived. She was late, wore her tattered beret, a shabby dress, and had apparently forgotten to apply her makeup. As Herndon waited, Libby stood up and sang a song entitled "Bim Bam Beedle Bum Bay."

Sillman soon realized that it was one of Libby's flat days; she was off by at least three tones. In desperation, he prattled loudly and inconsequentially to Herndon, telling him that Libby had a terrible cold, but that she was fabulous, a real find, better even than Helen Morgan. When Herndon signed Libby for the show, Sillman liked to believe that he had heard next to nothing of the song.

With lyrics by Morris Ryskin and Howard Dietz and music by Henry Souvaine and Jay Gorney, *Merry-Go-Round* opened in New York at the Klaw Theatre on May 31, 1927. Libby had been given two numbers—"What D'ya Say" and a torrid torch song called "Hogan's Alley." The next day, she received the best reviews of her brief career. Critics referred to her as "a witch," "a dark-eyed houri," and her voice was described as "the wail of a corned beef and cabbage Delilah." Another critic wrote:

> Dick Herndon's revue may hit you between the eyes or it may not, but either way, you can't miss the adorable Libby Holman, who chants Howard Dietz's song lyrics to the Souvaine-Gorney tunes so liltingly. The Holman houri is one of those angels worth waiting to see and hear. She's a portrait in high shading; Creolesque, annoyingly sweet to the eye. Poise in terms of exquisite style is hers; she's always the scene for without her the scene doesn't matter. Tie these virtues to a crooning vocal machine, plus a charm of delivery; there, my dears, you have a brief pastel of the Herndon lady.

That summer a black musical called *Africana* opened at Daly's Sixty-third Street Theatre. It, too, was a hit and the cast gave weekly midnight performances so that other working actors might see the show. Libby's new friend, the novelist Carl Van Vechten, whom she had met through Leonard Sillman, insisted that Libby see *Africana* since her voice reminded him of the show's star—a young black protégée of his called Ethel Waters. Miss Waters, already known for the singing of her "ungodly raw" honky-tonk songs, had long been Libby's idol and Libby put in a standing order for seats in the first row for every midnight performance of the run in order to hear Ethel Waters sing "I'm Coming Virginia," "Weary Feet" and "Shake That Thing."

Some critics had already made comparisons between the two singers, even down to their coloring—the most recent allusion to Libby's "Moorish blood." Convinced that Libby could pass for black, the producer of the all-black musical *Rang Tang* tried to persuade Richard Herndon to release her from *Merry-Go-Round* so that she could play the lead in his show. Herndon refused. Leonard Sillman thought it scandalous, but Libby was amused and always claimed she would have been perfect in the part.

During the late twenties, Manhattan whites were obsessed with black culture, an obsession popularized by Carl Van Vechten's 1926 novel, *Nigger Heaven.* By 1927, Harlem had never been so high-spirited, especially after dark. Whites congregated nightly in Harlem, becoming, in effect, tourists in their own city, "flocking," as Langston Hughes observed, "to the little cabarets and bars, where formerly only colored people laughed and sang, and where now the strangers were given the best ringside tables to sit and stare at the Negro customers—like amusing animals in a zoo."

Night after night, "the mink set" (a set into which Libby had thrown herself wholeheartedly) tooled up to Harlem in Stutz Bearcats, Cadillacs and Locomobiles in order to rub shoulders with the Niggerati, as they were known; to eat yardbird (fried chicken), strings (spaghetti), pig's feet and black-eyed peas, corn bread and chitterlings, spareribs with collard greens; to indulge in such delights as smoking reefers (marijuana) which, unlike alcohol, were not illegal; to listen to stride piano and jazz, variously described as hot, barbaric, junglelike; to dance the mess-around, the shimmy, the skate, the bo-hog and the buzzard; to drink whiskey and bathtub gin at their favorite blind pigs, cribs, and shock houses—at Basement Brownies, the Yeah Man, the Alhambra, Pod's and Jerry's, the Next, Small's Paradise, the Spider Web, or at Connie's Inn and the Cotton Club, both of which barred black customers, and where they could listen to such performers as Duke Ellington, Avon Long, Cab Calloway, Florence Mills and Lena Horne; to participate in slumming tours arranged by Monkey, a little black hunchback and one of Harlem's best-known characters; to attend live black-and-white sex shows in the back room of a clip joint owned by Sewing Machine Bertha—slumming in Harlem so that, as Polly Adler said, "the upper classes could have themselves a real lowdown time."

Libby spent the summer and early autumn of 1927 in *Merry-Go-Round*, which would run for 136 performances. She had never been so happy, so busy, so full of the possibilities of things.

She had now moved into a small apartment on Beekman Place. She worked on Broadway, went up to Harlem after the show, and weekended in Connecticut. She had become a close friend of the tall dark-haired lyricist Howard Dietz and his attractive Southern wife, Betty, whom Dietz described as "game for anything." She attended the theatrical and literary parties at the Dietzs' apartment on West Eighth Street; and because the parties were crowded and tended to last till dawn, the Dietzes usually moved all their furniture into the hall and lugged it back in the morning.

Libby had begun to drink excessively, explaining to a friend that it was because she had arthritis and alcohol helped to ease the pain. She had lost her once voluptuous figure, a result of crash diets during which she often subsisted on celery for weeks at a time. At twenty-three, Libby was an extravagant girl but curiously cold and controlled. All the young men she knew seemed to fall in love with her, but she continued to prefer the company of homosexuals. They were wittier, less intractable, and with them sex was not an issue, it was not even a point of view. Libby felt less inhibited in their company. Like most women who pretend to be uninterested in sex, Libby held outlandish sexual opinions. She once told Johnny Martin and Leonard Sillman she believed that the vagina and the penis ought to be located in the neck so that, when friends embraced, they could copulate at the same time. Johnny Martin was shocked, but Sillman thought it both shrewd and funny.

Merry-Go-Round closed in October and Libby was unemployed again; but she was making additional monies now. Toward the end of the run, the brash American she had railed against in Harry's Bar had called her, and Libby subsequently signed a contract with Brunswick Records. Her first release, the hit song from *Merry-Go-Round*, was "Hogan's Alley." The Brunswick brochure described Libby as a charming young lady who "Blues the Vamps and Vamps the Blues." The brochure contained a photograph of her in which Libby contrived to look both sensual and demure—a wench in virginal disguise.

In August 1928, Libby auditioned for the role of Lotta in Vincent Youmans and Oscar Hammerstein II's new musical *Rainbow*. The audition was brief and unrewarding and the producers rejected her: Her voice was too low and too peculiar.

The next month, Libby returned to the road in a one-hour tab show called *Texas Guinan's Padlocks*, playing the part of Texas Guinan. Tab shows were tabloid versions of Broadway plays, which played the vaudeville circuit, and *Padlocks* was a reference to the locks placed on Miss Guinan's numerous clubs when they were closed down by Prohibition agents. Libby despised the show, the dreary one-night stands in a succession of what she considered coarse, provincial towns.

While performing in Baltimore, Libby heard that the producers of *Rainbow* were recasting the role of Lotta, and she decided to audition again. The actress who had been hired to play the part continually fluffed an important line—one that read: "She dances with a broken heart and sings like a goddamn canary." The actress invariably said: "She sings with a broken heart and dances like a goddamn canary." The actress was fired. When Libby reapplied for the role, she was auditioned by Vincent Youmans and Oscar Hammerstein II.

Libby met the two men at their suite in the Bellvue-Stratford Hotel in Philadelphia. "Hum something," said Youmans when Libby arrived, and Libby began humming, making up the tune as she went along. Youmans experimented with a melody on the piano and told Libby to continue humming. Libby hummed and hummed, attempting to give Youmans an idea of her range and style. Hammerstein sat at a table scribbling on a pad. Some hours later, the two men completed a song called "I Want A Man," tailored specifically to Libby's vocal measurements. That afternoon she was hired, joining the cast of *Rainbow* just prior to its Baltimore tryout.

Set in 1849 during the California gold rush, *Rainbow* was the tale of a young scout at Fort Independence, Missouri, who kills an officer in self-defense, joins a wagon train heading west and eventually wins both a pardon and the colonel's daughter. With its realistic situations, lusty dialogue and intelligent use of music, *Rainbow* was in the grand tradition of Hammerstein's *Show Boat*, which had opened on Broadway the year before, and with which, unfortunately, it was all too often compared.

Rainbow opened at the Gallo Theatre in New York on November 21, 1928. On opening night, almost everything that might have gone wrong went wrong. The street was torn up in front of the theater and patrons were conducted to a side entrance on Eighth Avenue. Fanny the mule, who had a cameo, had been brought to the theater at seven but didn't go onstage until after nine. Just as the spotlight struck her, Fanny relieved herself copiously, and Louise Brown, the featured dancer, had to maneuver artfully around the fetid pile. The crosstown elevated trains rumbled past the rear of the theater, causing the backdrops to twitch and shake, and a critic wrote the following day that "one intermission was so long, the orchestra played everything but 'Dixie' to fill it up."

Most critics recognized *Rainbow*'s beauty and originality and believed it could be saved with cuts and revisions. But for all its strengths, *Rainbow* was flawed by unsympathetic characters, hackneyed humor and dialogue considered too raw for audiences in 1928. Despite strong performances from the principals, two minor performers stole the show—Charles Ruggles and Libby Holman.

"Miss Holman," the *Morning Telegram* said, "pouting, provocatively sulky, managed to run fleetly away with the honors of the premiere. She carried and sang a torch that made Liberty's enormous flambeau seem like a charred and whittled match stem." *The New Yorker* complained: "We regretted strenuously that Libby Holman of the velvet-contralto voice was on stage so little and had only one song to sing." But *Rainbow*, which Oscar Hammerstein II would call his gorgeous flop, closed after twenty-eight performances.

The week *Rainbow* opened, Whitney Bolton in his column, "Easy Stages," in the New York *Herald Tribune*, wrote a florid paean to Libby:

> The newest of the ladies who croon forlornly from husky, stirring throats is Miss Libby Holman. The possibility that some may be confused by the expression demands an explanation. The carrying of a torch means that a person is miserable because a still adored lover has deserted, leaving one desolate and brokenhearted.
>
> A stranger to major productions, Miss Holman burst upon me as a sensation. I rejoiced over what I thought was a discovery, but my rising chirrup was swiftly silenced by a contemptuous know-it-all who informed me icily that Miss Holman had been the pet of the disco record set for months. It seems she had made a series of torch-song records for phonograph

reproduction and that her thrilling plaints are bringing life to remote villages.

She becomes, therefore, one of the treasured sisterhood that has been my solace for countless weeks. The first of these to coo miseries in a provocative key was Miss Ruth Etting. I burned sacred oil there with undivided allegiance until Miss Helen Morgan began to hum the throaty "Can't Help Lovin' That Man of Mine." The third chauntress to join the purling group was Miss Helen Kane, whose torches were more vigorous and less dolsome than the Etting and Morgan flambeaux. Now, there is a fourth—come to titillate Broadway with enticing murmurs of dejection, sad, but ravishing whispers. Maybe an expert forger of jests can make up one about a torch-lit procession.

Within days of *Rainbow*'s closing, Libby obtained a role in Ned Wayburn's *Gambols*—a minor revue with little merit of any kind. The revue was largely concerned with choreography— Gypsy, Oriental and Indian dances—and at one point, two nearly naked gentlemen tossed a nearly naked lady back and forth in the air. The show opened at the Knickerbocker Theatre in New York on January 15, 1929. On opening night, there were several blackouts in the theater, which one critic thought amusing. The critics were not nearly so amused with the show itself.

Libby had little to do in *Gambols*, but introduced a splendid torch song called "There Ain't No Sweet Man Worth the Salt of My Tears." Again, her reviews were excellent. "Miss Holman is a ravishing brunette possessed of a remarkable blues voice," said one, and another referred to Libby as "a soft singer of lamentations." "In the dusk and sultry Libby Holman," wrote Percy Hammond in the *Herald Tribune*, "Mr. Wayburn has still another unusual asset, a lady who can act and sing anything from a naughty scene in a loose Longacre Square hotel to a Negro folksong, and still be a lady." But the show itself was dire and Ned Wayburn's *Gambols* closed after thirty-one performances.

Unemployed again, Libby turned to her friend Howard Dietz for assistance and advice. A wise-cracking Russian Jew from New York, the thirty-one-year-old Dietz had attended Columbia with Oscar Hammerstein and Larry Hart. While still an undergraduate, he created the Goldwyn Pictures (later MGM) trademark of a roaring lion with the accompanying slogan Ars Gratia Artis. In

1929, Dietz worked as a publicist for MGM and, when he wasn't praising the talents of Greta Garbo or Lionel Barrymore, he wrote, as Ernst Lubitsch said, "Broadway shows on MGM stationery." Dietz took his lyrics seriously, but not without a sense of humor. "I don't like lyricists who think," he said. "It gets in the way of their plagiarism."

Dietz liked Libby. He thought "there was no one in the theater more discussable." She seemed to him an outrageous woman, "who appeared in the nude in her dressing room and, therefore, had a lot of visitors." But he believed in her talent and would have a considerable influence on her career.

In early February, Dietz wangled a three-week singing engagement for Libby at a drab, dark honky-tonk called the Monsignor. He suggested that she be accompanied on the piano by a friend of his, a former lawyer and unemployed composer named Arthur Schwartz. Like Libby, Schwartz needed the work. The Monsignor was rather too far west on Forty-seventh Street, west of Ninth Avenue in fact, but it seemed a godsend to Libby and Schwartz.

The club was cramped and badly lit. There were only twenty tables and a tiny stage with an old piano that was not in tune. The brick walls were covered with tatty French posters, and an uneven shelf ran round the room, heaped with empty wine bottles. It looked like a neighborhood luncheonette (which it had been until recently) trumped up to appear Parisian.

They rehearsed thoroughly and, on opening night, gave what they believed to be a rousing performance. Libby sang several of her old numbers, "Hogan's Alley" and "Ain't No Sweet Man Worth the Salt of My Tears," and such currently popular tunes as "I'll Get By" and "She's Funny That Way." She sang them well, but the audience, most of whom appeared to be truckdrivers and their wives, all but ignored her.

Even so, Libby and Schwartz looked forward eagerly to the next evening's performance. But the club's manager, a small man in a big hat, paid them off and told them not to return. He was in business to do business, he said, and could not afford to support amateurs. Libby was livid. Extracting that evening's pay from her purse, she threw it in the small man's face. "You goddamned gorilla," she shouted. "Go out and buy yourself a stripper."

13

I N EARLY 1929, THE PRODUCERS TOM WEATHERLY AND WILliam A. Brady, Jr., joined forces to produce what they conceived as a new and modest revue. To be called *The Little Show*, it was the outgrowth of a series of Sunday evening divertissements that Weatherly had presented at New York's Selwyn Theatre.

His venture was backed by Dwight Deere Wiman, grandson of John Deere, the Illinois farming implements millionaire. Wiman drove around Manhattan in a wickerwork Rolls-Royce equipped with an elaborate bar—a conveyance Howard Dietz described as the most expensive car ever to appear in traffic. Known as the gentleman producer along Broadway, Wiman was also a close friend of Smith Reynolds and would travel, later in the year, to North Carolina to join the postwedding festivities of Smith and Anne Cannon.

For one hundred dollars a week and a half percent of the gross, Howard Dietz was hired to write the lyrics for the show. There were three principal roles. Dwight Wiman told Dietz that he had already signed Fred Allen and Clifton Webb, the dancer and interpretive vaudevillian. Dietz suggested they hire Arthur Schwartz to compose the music and, for the remaining principal role, he insisted they hire his young friend Libby Holman. Wiman acceded to both requests.

Dietz and Schwartz took up residence in the Warwick Hotel to write the score. "Working into the night," Dietz wrote, "the sound of the piano, however muted, endlessly repeating the same strain, penetrated the walls to an unwilling audience. We worked on borrowed time waiting for the manager to knock at the door. We became wandering minstrels, moving from room to room, hotel to hotel. The Warwick, the St. Moritz, the Essex House."

"They don't like what I'm playing," said Arthur sadly.

"That must be it," said Dietz. "They never complain about the lyrics."

Within weeks, they had composed nearly a dozen songs, including "Hammacher-Schlemmer, I Love You" and "I Guess I'll Have to Change My Plan," but *The Little Show* still lacked a memorable dramatic number.

"Moanin' Low," the song that, more than any other, would come to be identified with Libby, had its origins in Harlem. Clifton Webb, one of the most stylish dancers of his day, had long wanted to do a scene in which he could dance and play the part of a pimp—a sweetback, as the breed was known in Harlem—"a young man who allows a lady friend to keep him in change." Libby, Webb and Dietz worked on the idea together, attempting to devise a scene and an appropriate song for Libby's husky voice. For inspiration, they went up to Harlem—to slumming parties, to the black-and-tan cafés, to the Easter Parade on Lenox Avenue. But inspiration eluded them. One afternoon, Dietz heard the composer Ralph Rainger tinkering with a blues tune on the piano. It sounded just right and Dietz sat down and wrote the lyric to "Moanin' Low" in less than thirty minutes.

Ultimately, the staged scene of "Moanin' Low" would show Webb, the drunken sweetback, asleep in his gaudy suit, tan makeup and exaggerated sideburns. Libby, his high-yaller whore, creeps into their dingy Harlem bedroom and, while crooning her love for him, hides part of her earnings in her stocking. Webb wakes up, takes his money and performs a frenzied dance, utilizing the "snake-hip" movements he had learned from Buddy Bradley, the famous black dancing instructor. He then makes love to Libby, practically raping her, and discovers the concealed cash in her stocking. Outraged, Webb chokes her to death, he believes, and exits terror-stricken. Libby recovers, crawls to the door, beating futilely against it, while singing a throaty obbligato, a scatting improvised growl, that no white woman had ever attempted on Broadway before.

Libby and Webb rehearsed the number in secret for days before showing it to their producers. They even created their own scenery—a rumpled bed with a half-empty bottle of Gordon's gin beneath it. The producers thought it wonderful, but felt it should be toned down; it was too overtly sexual. Both Libby and Webb were adamant that what they called "the primitive implications" remain. In protest, Webb called in his friend Noel Coward, who, after seeing it, said that if "even a *soupçon* is changed," the producers would be "*quite, quite mad.*" Weatherly and Wiman relented.

When the revue opened in Atlantic City, Deitz and Schwartz came down from New York by train, but the train stalled, and they didn't arrive at the theater until after the final curtain. Dwight Wiman and Tom Weatherly greeted them in the lobby with hangdog expressions. Wiman was drunk; Weatherly was sober; both men were disconsolate. They advised Dietz and Schwartz to return to New York since the show would almost certainly close in a few days. It was a shambles. Even Clifton Webb, a veteran trouper, was full of dark predictions. But Dietz and Schwartz decided to stay for the next performance.

The following night, the revue played to a half-empty house. Despite this handicap, there was real enthusiasm for Libby, Webb and Allen, and the show seemed anything but a failure. "Hammacher-Schlemmer" and "Moanin' Low" were given loud rounds of applause and when Libby appeared onstage in a dark cerise strapless gown to sing "Can't We Be Friends?" the audience rose to its feet. The young composer Alec Wilder was in the theater that night. He watched as Libby stood in a slit in the curtain singing "Can't We Be Friends?" She sang very slowly and stood perfectly stationary. "A freak," Wilder later said, "but so dramatic. Such daring, the balls of it." It was one of the most theatrical moments he had ever seen.

From the very first tryouts, the audience responded to what they believed to be one of Libby's affectations. As she walked offstage, she always clutched the curtain as though she were afraid of falling. The audience didn't know that Libby was myopic and employed the curtain as a means of navigation.

The performance that evening was an unqualified success. "All I can say," said Weatherly, "is that what was a flop last night looks like a hit tonight."

"That's all you're allowed to say," said Arthur Schwartz.

The Little Show opened at the Music Box Theatre in New York on April 30, 1929. At the end of the second act, when Libby finished singing "Moanin' Low," the first-night audience was silent for a moment and then a great wave of applause swept through the theater. Libby was summoned for a dozen curtain calls. Eventually, she became so exhausted that Howard Dietz came out onstage and begged the audience to let her go.

The Little Show was an immediate success and would run for 321 performances. After years as a struggling bit player, a chorine, a minor singer in provincial tours, Libby was, at last, a star. Her reviews were remarkable. The New York *American* singled out "that dark crooning balladiste, Libby Holman, who comes into her contralto profundo own." *Variety* said that "Libby Holman sells the blues like a Gideon salesman to a hotel chain." Brooks Atkinson of the New York *Times* referred to "the dark purple menace of Libby Holman in the blues." Percy Hammond in the *Herald Tribune* wrote, "Miss Libby Holman is to be seen in her dusk beauty, moaning contralto dirges in a rain-barrel voice." And the *Mirror*'s critic wrote: "The theater had few to match her peculiarities of vocal enchantment; in addition, she possesses striking and colorful adjuncts: a bronzed complexion, luxury of figure, a fine grace and control. Of the youngsters in musical comedy or revue, she is one of a species so decidedly rare that one speaks her name with unmistakable sanctity. For this Holman girl is an artist."

Libby was Broadway's newest star. During the summer of 1929, Manhattan columnists alluded to her as a singer "of sullen sex hymns," "misery chanting," "the kid with the tropical voice" and, most frequently, "the Statue of Libby." Walter Winchell wrote: "She is the torch singer par excellence—the best of those female troubadours with voices of smoke and tears, who moan and keen love's labors lost to the rhythm and boom of the Roaring Twenties."

With the composure of one who has suddenly come into a long-awaited inheritance, Libby acquired the accouterments of stardom, its rewards and transient distinctions. "Moanin' Low" became one of the big hits of the year and music publishers were unable to print enough copies to satisfy the demand. She appeared frequently on record and on radio programs. She was invited and expected to sing at parties, private entertainments and jazz festivals. She sang at the Apollo Theatre in Harlem interpreting what the newspapers called Coon Songs. She was featured in the glossy magazines in Lux soap advertisements, the copy of which read: "The Queen of the Blues, they call her—the alluring Libby Holman. And who that has ever heard her husky voice moaning inconsolable woes would dispute the title?" Her popularity was such that the National Silk Manufacturers Association named a new spring shade in her honor—a pale pastel called Libby Holman blue.

She cropped up regularly in Walter Winchell's gossip column in the New York *Daily Mirror*—a column William Randolph Hearst claimed appealed "to the younger degeneration." Winchell and other gossip columnists likened Libby to the scent of rare, ripened fruit, to black orchids, or to the pulse in a savage throat. Libby talked endlessly and without restraint to the tabloid reporters, who, studiously and at considerable length, observed that she had abundant beauty and a sense of humor, which colored everything she said; that she possessed a mood of gentle mockery that prevented her from becoming melodramatic about her success; that she had embarked on a diet of crackers and milk; that the opera bored her since she had an aversion to trained voices in ensemble; that Paul Robeson was her favorite singer because his voice was earthy and elemental; and that she was partial to the works of Aldous Huxley, particularly *Point Counter Point*, published the year before, because it was, quite simply, the best British novel ever written. Her primary passion was the blues song, which, for Libby, symbolized the pain and hope of the entire colored race; and, finally, Libby cautioned her fans that marriage was not a state of absolute bliss and that she had not yet met a man capable of fascinating her for longer than it took to drink a dry martini.

She purchased what was claimed to be New York's first town car and took such new friends as the journalist John O'Hara for leisurely afternoon drives. The impecunious O'Hara, who would not write his first novel for another five years, had recently been fired from *Time* magazine for malingering by Libby's old boyfriend Johnny Martin. "The first real town car I ever rode in was owned by Libby Holman," O'Hara wrote, "who bought it with the money she made singing 'Moanin' Low.' It was a Model-A Ford, but it was a genuine town car, with the chauffeur outside in the rain. There was something about a town car, an extra touch of chic, that was not inherent to the limousine. Chauffeurs, getting rained on while Madam sat snug under a robe and flowers waved in the cut-glass vase, hated town cars."

Libby's newest and closest friend was Clifton Webb. The suave singer-dancer and Libby were seen together everywhere in Manhattan, at parties and openings, at benefits and country weekends. There were even rumors that Libby and Webb were about to become engaged or had been secretly married the week before. But Webb was another of Libby's "gentlemen homosexuals"; and always, in the background, like some vigilant mastiff, hovered the formidable presence of his mother, Mabelle.

Clifton Webb, born in Indianapolis in 1896, had been christened Webb Parmalee Hollenbeck. Mabelle often told the story that when Webb was two, while telling him a fairy tale, she was interrupted by a visitor. On her return, the little boy uttered his first word—"Proceed." Leaving her husband, a businessman, behind in Indiana, Mabelle moved with Webb to New York, enrolling him in dancing school and the Children's Theatre. When asked her husband's whereabouts, she always said: "We *never* speak of him. He didn't care for the *theatuh*."

At eighteen, Webb had a one-man show of his portraits and still lifes in New York. He had already performed in provincial grand opera and by 1925 was featured in musicals on Broadway. Often mistaken for an Englishman, he was a fastidious dandy and loved the company of women. The domineering Mabelle was not only Webb's mother but acted as his conscience, his banker, his agent and guardian angel. She negotiated his fees and billings. She criticized and pampered him, and they fought continuously. When she and Webb were on the road, she always employed a chauffeur and a maid so that, as Mabelle said, "We can live like human beings." Libby was devoted to Webb; she admired his charm and his mischievousness, and he knew everyone in the theater. Webb, in turn, was enamored with Libby and his mother resented it. She was polite to Libby, but eagle-eyed. Once, when Libby and Webb lost a small sum to a fellow actor in a poker game, Mabelle said, "Libby, you're just like Webb, a profligate." And, throwing her arms in the air in exasperation, she cried: "*Everything* goes out and *nothing* comes in. We'll all be in the poorhouse soon."

After the curtain fell on *The Little Show* each night, Libby rarely went home. Rather, and usually in the company of Webb, she spent several hours at one of the dozens of fashionable nightclubs in Manhattan. Never had contraband alcohol flowed so freely nor had it been consumed in such enormous quantities. Nightclub entertainment in New York was of a kind that would not be seen again for a generation.

The gossip columnist Louis Sobol called Manhattan's wealthy revelers "the mink and ermine crowd" and nightly they flocked to the Stork Club, "21," El Morocco and Sardi's. Libby favored Bea Lillie's comic routines at the Sutton Club, Clifton Webb moonlighting as a dancer at Ciro's, Helen Morgan singing at the House of Morgan, Fred and Adele Astaire performing intricate ballroom numbers at the Trocadero or Helen Kane singing "I Want to Be Bad" at the Casanova.

Perhaps the most fashionable speakeasy in Manhattan was Tony's on West Fifty-second Street, occasionally called "The Tony's" to differentiate it from all the other Tony's in town. It was Libby's favorite speakeasy and she spent three or four evenings a week there. Tony's was a popular hangout for the literary and theatrical crowd—for Robert Benchley, Howard Dietz, Peter Arno, John O'Hara, Dorothy Parker, Wolcott Gibbs, James Thurber and Heywood Broun. One night, on the piano in the back room, Vernon Duke composed "April in Paris," and Cole Porter occasionally played his current hits.

Tony Soma, the speakeasy's proprietor, was dark and distinguished looking. His regular patrons often introduced him as Admiral Balbo, the Italian Facist leader and intrepid aviator. He had an irritating habit of singing Verdi or Puccini arias while standing on his head, a feat he had mastered by studying yoga. And by serving inexpensive Italian food and highly suspicious alcohol, Tony felt he was performing a valuable service for the intelligentsia.

One evening, Libby was drinking champagne cocktails at Tony's with Clifton Webb. Across the room, actor Ronald Colman sat alone at a table near the wall telephone. Webb wagered Libby five dollars that she couldn't persuade Colman to ask her for a date. Libby promptly accepted, borrowed five cents, and walked across the room to the telephone. She pretended to ring a number and then conducted a breathy, and blatantly sexual, conversation—whispering just loud enough so that Colman could not fail to overhear. A few minutes after Libby returned to her table, the handsome actor walked over and introduced himself. "And what do you do?" Libby asked as Webb attempted to stifle his laughter. Colman smiled and asked her out the next evening. Libby was triumphant. Collecting the money from Webb, she turned to Colman and said: "Darling, don't torment yourself with luxuries you can't afford."

At twenty-five, Libby was in full bloom—"rotten-ripe," as Clifton Webb liked to say. She wasn't a conventional beauty; indeed, there were those who felt she wasn't beautiful at all. Her face was round, almost homely, with bountiful cheeks and a receding chin, surmounted by a bramble of black bushy hair. Her nose was flared and prominent, but her smile was swift and her pouty lips were openly seductive. It was an unusual face, dominated by narrow, naughty eyes, which, because of her nearsightedness, lent a real intensity to her features. Like many nearsighted women (particularly those who refuse to wear glasses), she had a soft come-hither look, and most men misinterpreted it, assuming Libby had accepted a proposition that they had not yet posed. A fellow actress surmised that Libby must have been used to lecherous looks from the time she was a very young girl.

Libby had an excellent figure and was inordinately fond of it. Actress Louise Brooks spent a weekend at *Tantallon*, Dwight Deere Wiman's house in Greenwich, Connecticut, where Libby was also a guest. Because the house was full, the two girls shared a bedroom. On Saturday morning, when the naked Libby left her bed to have a shower, Miss Brooks was amazed to see that she had a body like one of those exquisite bronze figurines that rise from Roman fountains. It was ripe and unashamed and Miss Brooks was full of admiration.

And yet, Libby's manner, her style, was infested with a kind of insistent vulgarity, most obviously reflected in her excessive use of expletives. Swearing, in fact, had become an integral part of her lexicon. In gracious surroundings, she liked to affect what used to be known as a piss-elegant pose and then drop some foul and unexpected epithet. Libby swore so often and with such apparent glee that Dorothy Parker, no stranger to vulgarity, once said to her: "Darling, you really ought to wear your drawers around your face."

That summer, Libby was escorted to parties and nightclubs by Richard Halliday, who would later marry Mary Martin; by Alan Campbell, who would later marry Dorothy Parker; and by Clifton Webb, whom Mabelle would never allow to marry anyone. And then, quite suddenly, Libby fell in love with a young Princeton graduate named Alan Jackson.

Jackson was born to a wealthy New York family which would later lose most of its fortune. A handsome youth of twenty-four, he was known, because of his prematurely gray hair, as "the Silver Fox." Employed as a writer for *Time* magazine, he seemed to spend more of his time drinking with writers than actually writing himself. But his friends considered him an excellent dancer and a convivial companion, and he liked to stroll from bar to bar with a large English sheepdog in tow.

On Saturday nights, when *The Little Show* closed, James Warburg and his wife, Kay Swift (who had written the music and lyrics to "Can't We Be Friends?"), dispatched their limousine to the stage door of the Music Box Theatre, and Libby and Jackson were ferried up to their North Greenwich home where the lovers spent numerous weekends that summer, occupying the Warburgs' guest cottage. Obsessed with Libby, Jackson felt she was the sexiest woman he had ever known, and he was much impressed with her celebrity. For Libby, it was the first serious love affair of her life, the first sexual relationship to last beyond a single dawn. Their affair would continue for nearly a year and would end as swiftly as it began.

Much later, Libby would say that Alan Jackson had been little more than a boy, a carefree companion, who sported and drank with the capricious enthusiasms of an undergraduate. And yet Libby sought out such men. They soothed her, amused her, they performed in her shadow like supplicant clowns. Then, in late 1929, Libby abruptly broke her pattern in a manner that suggested long years of submerged feeling and sexual frustration.

Toward the end of the run of *The Little Show*, Libby was introduced to Louisa d'Andelot Carpenter Jenny. First and foremost, Louisa was a Du Pont—the great-great-great-granddaughter of Pierre Samuel du Pont de Nemours, founder of the colossal Du

Pont empire. Louisa's mother, Margaretta du Pont, had married R.R.M. "Ruly" Carpenter, head of Du Pont's "development department" during the period of the company's most rapid expansion. Louisa was their eldest child.

A tall, beautiful, strawberry blonde of twenty-two, Louisa was passionate about the theater, about actors and actresses especially, and aspired to become a theatrical producer. But Louisa was, and would remain, a country girl. She loathed cities, shoes, elevators, traffic and hotels. She much preferred to hunt and fish, to drive tractors and bale hay. A superb shot, particularly with the twelve-gauge shotgun, she hunted fox, pheasant, quail and doves. She was the first woman master-of-hounds in America and would become one of the first licensed women pilots.

In July 1929, Louisa married John King Jenny. A graduate of the Kent School and Princeton, Jenny joined the Du Pont company in 1925 as a salesman and became associated with its foreign activities. He was endorsed by Louisa's domineering father, who considered him, in the parlance of the monied classes, "well-situated." Louisa had not wished to get married but did so in order to please her mother and to escape her father's house. The young couple were given a home at Montchanin, one of the many Du Pont estates on the outskirts of Wilmington.

Louisa tried to be an acceptable wife, but she despised the role. For as long as she could remember, she had considered men base and horrid. But she wanted desperately to become a mother, and within months of the marriage, became pregnant, only to miscarry. The loss seemed to reinforce her as yet unrealized preoccupation with women—a predilection Jenny never understood. He knew only that Louisa had been in one world when they were married and that, shortly thereafter, she entered another. Following her miscarriage, Louisa began to consort with women, though secretly. She and Jenny were not divorced until 1931, but Louisa had left her husband for Libby long before.

Libby was introduced to Louisa by Clifton Webb at an international horse show in Manhattan. The next night, Louisa waited for her outside the stage door of the Music Box Theatre in her chauffeur-driven limousine. She had already fallen in love with Libby and Libby, though hesitant, was attracted to her. The following weekend, Louisa invited Libby to sail aboard her father's yacht, *The Galaxy*, anchored at Port Washington on the north shore of Long Island. When Libby arrived at the dock, Louisa appeared on deck in white ducks and tennis shoes. She was, as she preferred to be, stripped to the waist. Her skin was milky white and contrasted distinctly with Libby's dark olive complexion. Libby was taken aback, but went aboard. Their affair began that afternoon.

Bisexuality was prevalent, even fashionable, in the theatrical world of the twenties and thirties. But prior to this, there had been little indication that Libby was partial to women. From time to time, the Manhattan tabloids had insinuated that Libby coveted the favors of such actresses as Jeanne Eagels and Josephine Baker, but these were low canards. For the first time, however, as Libby told her friends, she felt completely free and was not simply in love but in love with an equal. As for Louisa, she was not only rich and generous, but she would always be drawn to extroverted bisexual women and they, in turn, were attracted to Louisa because she treated them more kindly, with more understanding and love, than any man had done before her.

One of Libby's friends, actress Helen Lynd, called Louisa a "he-she." The first time she met her, she asked Libby and Clifton Webb: "Who *is* that person? She *walks* like a man, she *talks* like a man. God, she even *dresses* like a man," and Libby and Webb giggled uproariously. But others approved of their liaison. "If I can't have you," said Clifton Webb, "I'd rather you had the next best thing"—and Noel Coward sent Libby an obscene rendition of "She's Funny That Way."

Kay Swift, on the other hand, did not know anything about lesbianism and initially disapproved. After the affair began, she was invited down to Montchanin for a weekend. On the Saturday afternoon, while Libby was shopping in Wilmington, Louisa complained that Libby was working too hard, that she needed a rest. Louisa fretted all afternoon and Kay Swift began to see just how much Louisa loved Libby. She decided at once that Louisa was "a great dame" and never thought about lesbianism disapprovingly again.

By the end of 1929, Libby and Louisa were inseparable and Libby had taken to calling Louisa her "white lover." Libby introduced her to her favorite clubs, they drove up to Harlem, and Louisa sat through many of Libby's performances. But Louisa remained uncomfortable in the city. She preferred that Libby spend weekends at Montchanin or on her yacht; they often hunted together, or sailed around Long Island and up and down the inland waterways.

The Galaxy, a steel diesel yacht, was 137-feet long with six staterooms, and cruised at eleven knots. On one weekend trip down the inland waterway to Virginia, Libby invited Alan Campbell, Clifton Webb, Mabelle, and Webb's two male dressers, Ramona and Kimono. It was obvious to everyone on board that Libby and Louisa were in love and, since everyone but Mabelle was homosexual, they were unaffected. In any event, Libby had a way of making the most outrageous behavior seem perfectly natural. She had just concluded her affair with Alan Jackson and her friends teased her about him, urging Libby to tell them what it had really been like. Libby laughed and, winking at Louisa, replied: "He was like a square peg in a round hole."

Since early September, ominous rumors and outlandish reports had swirled through Wall Street; and on October 24, a day that would come to be known as Black Thursday, the vast jerry-built structure that was American finance and industry collapsed. The Roaring Twenties were over and nothing would ever be the same again. That Thursday, an unprecedented 16.4 million shares were traded and the Dow Jones Industrial Average plummeted 30.57 points. Liquidation of securities continued as speculators were forced to sell stock they had bought on margin, and $30 billion in capital just disappeared.

The Depression had begun, and once the initial shock was over, dark jokes began to circulate on Broadway—best exemplified by comedian Eddie Cantor, who brought down the house one night with his story of a hotel clerk's question to a registering guest: "Do you want a room for sleeping or for jumping?"

The Depression had no noticeable effect on Libby's career. Indeed, in many ways, it was her heyday. Toward the end of the run of *The Little Show*, she began an after-theater singing engagement at the Lido Club for which she was paid six hundred dollars a week. Louis Sobol, the gossip columnist, noted that the Lido "was a snobbish gathering place where you were barred admittance if the sheen of your tuxedo lapel lacked the proper gloss or if there was dust on the windowpanes of your lorgnette.

The couvert was gauged to pace along with the monthly upkeep of your Isotta-Fraschini and, while the ginger ale and soda and the booze were not the best, the tariff was something to make you gasp. Here, you sat around and pretended not to be bored because your neighbors were certain, for the most part, to be paid-up members of the Social Register."

Libby, accompanied by Ralph Rainger, sang such standards as "Moanin' Low," "Got a Man on My Mind," "I May Be Wrong," and "Nobody Breaks My Heart." She was originally hired for four weeks, but because the club was crowded with ruined stock-market victims, drinking industriously to forget their troubles, she was held over till the end of the year.

On January 16, 1930, *The Little Show* finally went dark. It was a famous closing night on Broadway and both the audience and the cast broke into tears as the players took their final bows. The Music Box Theatre was sold out and the rows were crowded with such luminaries as Beatrice Lillie, Marc Connolly, Franklin P. Adams, Alexander Woollcott, Howard Dietz, and Edna Ferber. During the intermission, Dietz had distributed bags of pennies to his friends in the audience, and as the cast took their final curtain calls, handfuls of coppers were flung onto the stage and the actors stooped to pick them up, smiling and bowing in mock gratitude.

In early February, the show went on the road, opening in Boston, where it was advertised as the overnight and all-year sensation of Broadway—the show New Yorkers had paid $1,125,000 to see. Again, Libby's reviews were excellent. Elliot Norton, Boston's premiere theater critic wrote:

I saw her sing "Can't We Be Friends?" standing in a spot next to the piano without moving a muscle. All the movement was in her eyes and the emotion she created. She held twelve hundred people there in the Wilbur Theatre without moving, without a gesture. It was tremendous. I later heard that it was because she was as blind as a bat. But what an effect. She wasn't beautiful; she was very sensual, not sensuous, like an animal.

Louisa Carpenter was in the audience that night. At the subsequent party, she told Libby that it was unquestionably the finest performance she had ever seen. Libby smiled and kissed

Louisa on the cheek. "Yes, it was, wasn't it," she said. "It was a little jewel. And I owe it all to you. You bring out the best in me. And you always will."

14

THE LITTLE SHOW MOVED ON TO BALTIMORE IN APRIL. FOR the first Saturday evening performance, Dwight Deere Wiman invited his young friend Smith Reynolds to attend. During the middle of the first act, Smith strode into the theater sporting riding boots and jodhpurs and slumped down in the first row. The show bored him, but when Libby began to sing "Moanin' Low," he was mesmerized. He had never heard such a sound before nor had he seen such a beguiling woman. Afterward, Wiman introduced them, and during the following weeks, Smith followed the tour with dogged determination, dispatching flowers and notes of extravagant praise to Libby's dressing room. The eighteen-year-old youth was wild for Libby's favor, but so were many other men, and she ignored him.

But Smith was a persistent suitor. Although still determined to make his round-the-world flight, he now postponed it. When Libby and Louisa went to Florida for the long Easter weekend, Smith followed them there. When the road tour of *The Little Show* ended in late June, Libby and Louisa sailed for Europe, and again, a week later, Smith tagged dutifully after.

In early July, Sammy Colt, a freshman at Brown University, and Ethel Barrymore's son, sailed for Europe also. Among his numerous letters of introduction was one to Tallulah Bankhead, then performing in London in *The Lady of the Camellias* at the Garrick Theatre. Colt called her the afternoon he arrived, suggesting he pay a visit the following morning at nine. "*Absolutely not*," said Tallulah, speaking in an accent once described as a mixture of British and Pickaninny. "I wouldn't let God, Himself, see me at nine in the morning and I hope He has the decency to let me die in the afternoon."

Colt was invited to Tallulah's Farm Street mews house for tea the next day, where he met Noel Coward, Clifton Webb, Mabelle, Louisa and Libby. Over tea, they all decided to go to Paris for the Bastille Day weekend. Coward considered Paris "the sexiest town on earth," the ideal city for a group such as theirs to find some amusing diversions. Only Tallulah declined. "*Sex?*" she shouted. "I'm bored with sex. What is it, after all? If you go down on a woman, you get a crick in your neck. If you go down on a man, you get lockjaw. And fucking just gives me *claustrophobia.*"

Leaving Tallulah behind, the irreverent pilgrims, old Mabelle included, spent nearly a week in Paris where they were joined by Mercedes de Acosta, the diminutive Spanish poet and playwright. Miss de Acosta was partial to elegant dinner jackets and claimed to have been Greta Garbo's lover. Tallulah, who didn't like her, described her as looking like "a mouse in a topcoat." One evening, everyone dressed up as apache dancers and caroused in Montmartre. On another occasion, they gathered at Chez Florence, Paris's most popular nightclub. As Libby entered, she was recognized by the predominantly American crowd, who shouted for her to take the stage and sing. Libby refused, but soon relented, singing for nearly thirty minutes and bringing the house down. The next day, Noel Coward returned to London and the rest of the group drifted down to the South of France.

Many years later, Mercedes de Acosta, in her memoirs *Here Lies the Heart*, wrote that before leaving Paris, she and Libby had visited a fortune-teller, an old White Russian woman, who, after telling Miss de Acosta's fortune, drew her aside, asking if she was fond of Libby. Miss de Acosta insisted she was extremely fond of Libby and the White Russian said: "I did not dare tell her, but she is in some way going to be mixed up in a violent death scene with a man she will marry."

This episode always amused Libby, and much later, whenever she referred to it, she would say: "Mercedes de Acosta once wrote a book called *Here Lies the Heart—and Lies and Lies and Lies.*"

*   *   *

Libby, Louisa, Clifton Webb and Mabelle motored down to Saint-Jean-de-Luz, where they rented a farmhouse outside the little Basque town. The next morning, Smith Reynolds drove up in a yellow Rolls-Royce, announcing he had come for breakfast. Libby never knew how he had managed to track her down.

Although flattered by Smith's attentions, Libby thought him an impertinent youth. And there were additional problems he either refused to acknowledge or to understand. Libby was intimately involved with Louisa and Smith, nearly eight years her junior, was a married man. But he was, for the moment, a harmless diversion and Libby treated him like an amiable buffoon.

Still, he was always there. When the little troupe drove across France to Juan-les-Pins, Smith followed. Clifton Webb began calling him Libby's mascot—"Smitty, the traveling bear." But nothing, not even derision, deterred him.

At summer's end, Libby and Webb were summoned to New York to begin rehearsals for a new Broadway show, *Three's a Crowd*, in which they would again co-star with Fred Allen. Howard Dietz and Arthur Schwartz had already been retained to write the score, and supporting members of the cast included Portland Hoffa (later Mrs. Fred Allen), the Russian ballerina Tamara Geva, and a vaudeville band called the California Collegians, whose tenor saxophone player was a struggling young actor named Fred MacMurray. When Libby left Europe, Smith drove to Munich in Germany to see his brother, Dick, but he had vowed to Libby that he would be in the first row of *Three's a Crowd* on opening night.

Max Gordon, the producer of *Three's a Crowd*, envisaged an intimate revue of the finest quality, a production that would delight the eye without being ostentatious, that would aspire to be witty, sophisticated, intelligent. Eventually, the show contained more than a score of scenes and songs. Fred Allen performed a sketch—a travesty on Admiral Byrd, then much in the news for his polar explorations; Groucho Marx wrote an amusing sketch called "The Event"; and social protest was included with "Yaller," a song that bemoaned the plight of the mulatto, unloved by the white world.

Libby was given two songs—"Give Me Something to Remember You By" and what would become her signature tune, the classic torch song "Body and Soul." In early September, the cast assembled for rehearsals, and when *Three's a Crowd* headed for the Erlanger Theatre in Philadelphia, an air of cheerful confidence pervaded the company.

"Body and Soul" was the single outside contribution to *Three's a Crowd*. The music was composed by a brash young Harvard graduate named Johnny Green, and three separate writers collaborated on the lyrics. From the beginning, there were difficulties. Libby disliked the lyrics and asked Howard Dietz to write a new version. Several new orchestrations were fashioned, none of which worked. The staging of the number was catastrophic. The director, Hassard Short, had created what seemed at first a brilliant device. The curtain rose on a dark stage, and Libby, sitting on a kind of inverted bowl encased in black velvet, was conveyed slowly front stage by pullies. Only a pin spot picked out her face so that, as Libby moved forward, her features seemed to grow larger and larger. Unfortunately, the pullies failed to function properly; they jerked and pitched and created so much din, the audience was unable to hear the song. On opening night in Philadelphia, the only two people who applauded the number were Johnny Green and his then wife, Carol.

On the second night, the pullies, which had cost one thousand dollars, were scrapped. Libby sang the song in front of the curtain, but still there was no applause. At the Wednesday matinee, Johnny Green decided to conduct the orchestra himself. The podium, however, was so high that he blocked Libby from the audience. Different effects were employed on different nights, and none of them worked. Libby was distraught. She threatened to quit. "Instead of calling it *Three's a Crowd*," she cried, "you can call it *Two's Company*."

A few days later, Howard Dietz encountered Ralph Rainger in New York's Pennsylvania Station. Rainger had composed "Moanin' Low" for Libby. Dietz explained the problems he was having with "Body and Soul," pleading with Rainger to accompany him to Philadelphia. Rainger was sympathetic but uninterested. The persistent Dietz maneuvered the composer down the platform and into the train, talking incessantly, and before Rainger could marshal his final arguments, the train pulled away.

In Philadelphia, Rainger reorchestrated the entire number. Instead of bringing the orchestra in on the verse of the song, which preceded the chorus, he used a simple piano arrangement and then brought the orchestra slowly into the refrain. By that trick alone, "Body and Soul" was rescued from being cut from the show.

The number was then restaged. Libby now began her entrance stage left with just a pin spot on her, her left hand clasped across her heart. She wore a long black dress with a plunging neckline and, against a black velvet curtain, moved onto the stage with slow, slinky steps as she sang. During rehearsals, the number succeeded, and the following night Libby stepped out onto the stage with new confidence. Before the last note had sounded, the audience stomped and shouted, demanding encores.

But additional difficulties ensued. A short time later, "Body and Soul" was banned by the National Broadcasting Company and by all Boston radio stations on the grounds of obscenity. Such a provocatively sexual word as *body* had not been employed in a song title before. Moreover, the New York censors objected to the line, "My life, a hell you're making." The word *hell* was taboo and the frustrated lyricists searched frantically through rhyming dictionaries for some suitable replacement—deciding reluctantly on the weaker but more acceptable "My life, a wreck you're making."

Three's a Crowd opened in New York at the Selwyn Theatre on October 15, 1930. The critics agreed that it was devoid of conventional routines and that it surpassed *The Little Show* in quality, style, humor and song.

"Here we have the same triumvirate as in *The Little Show*," wrote Robert Benchley, "if Miss Holman doesn't mind being called a vir for a moment." *Time* magazine said: "The show has for its principals the triple-threat team of last year's *Little Show*: nimble, spindle-shanked, emaciated Clifton Webb; droll, ready-voiced Fred Allen; mellifluous, primordial Libby Holman. So excellent is the work of these three performers that the framework of the show seems almost negligible."

In *Three's a Crowd*, Libby achieved celebrity all over again, "basking once more," as she said, "in the luminous, but not unbecoming, light of fame." She had been given, it is true, two glorious songs, but it was not her voice alone that lured patrons into the theater. Libby exuded carnality. When performing, she walked perfectly straight and upright, yet she seemed to sashay across the stage. The effect on the audience was twofold: Her sensuality struck them forcibly, at once, and then, afterward, in the memory, like a drunken dream.

Libby was not a good actress. But she used her affectations with considerable dramatic skill—the hand on the curtain, the seductive carriage, the careless dropping of a handkerchief— only then beginning to sing. And when Libby sang of lost love, of misbegotten affairs and broken dreams, she was wholly believable. Her songs sounded like confessions.

But Libby had no tortured tales to tell, at least none of her own making. *Her* dreams had been fulfilled. She was, as she had always wished to be, successful, favored, and she had fallen in love with a millionaire—albeit a woman. Her love affair with Louisa was the talk of Broadway. One member of the *Three's a Crowd* cast witnessed Libby giving Louisa a deep soul kiss at "21" and was so shocked she was unable to finish her meal. But Libby loved to shock; it amused her that others looked upon her as a notorious woman.

During the run of the show, the beautiful twenty-year-old, Russian dancer Tamara Geva became friends with Libby. Geva had attended the Kirov School of Ballet in Leningrad. In 1923, at the age of fifteen, she married George Balanchine. They left Russia in 1925. She then joined Sergei Diaghilev's Ballet Russe in Paris. Two and a half years later, she arrived in America with the Chauve Souris Company. *Three's a Crowd* was her second Broadway show.

Geva thought Libby a selfish woman, solely intent on fulfilling her own narcissistic ends. In Geva's view, Libby was overly given to sensationalism and had become involved with Louisa only to flout the rules, to perform some outrageous beau geste. Even so, Geva liked Libby—it was difficult not to—but she believed the torch singer was secretly unhappy. She sensed unhappiness seeping from her—palpable as sap.

15

AS HE HAD PROMISED, SMITH REYNOLDS TURNED UP IN THE first row at the Broadway premiere of *Three's a Crowd*. Afterward, as Libby and the rest of the cast celebrated their success at Sardi's, and later at Tony's, Smith continued to ply his blandishments; but they were more urgent now. He had fallen in love with her, he said, and demanded she end her relationship with Louisa. He insisted that just as soon as he obtained a divorce, Libby should marry him. On that point, he was adamant. Hitherto amused, Libby became curt, then angry, telling Smith that if he continued to act like a rapacious boy, she didn't wish to see him again. In a vain attempt to forget her, Smith flew to California, where he drank late and long and inconsolably. He telephoned Libby almost daily, begging her to change her mind. But Libby had never been seduced by whimpering.

Superficially, at least, Smith resembled the weak and vulnerable men Libby had cultivated in the past. He was young, just nineteen, and although not homosexual, he preferred the company of men, particularly that of his childhood chum, Ab Walker. But there the similarities ended. When Smith talked of flying, he became intense and passionate. He exhibited an air of recklessness that appealed to Libby, an urge to perform gallantly in some as yet unrevealed romantic circumstance that was kindred to her own.

On his return from California, Smith saw *Three's a Crowd* almost every night, sitting always in the same seat in the front row on the aisle. Afterward, he would join Libby at Tony's. Smith loathed Tony's. He loathed Libby's life-style altogether and, most of all, her theatrical friends, whom he found cold and cavalier. They, in turn, thought Smith insipid, inarticulate, an outsider, acknowledging him only when he bought them drinks. Smith felt excluded, and Libby's heart went out to him. She told Tallulah that Smith had "a kind of secret treasure buried deep inside of him," and Tallulah laughed, retorting that Smith's riches were only too transparent.

In June 1931, after 272 performances, *Three's a Crowd* closed and Libby leased a house in Sands Point on the north shore of Long Island. Sands Point was then a fashionable vacation spot where Herbert Bayard Swope, John Philip Sousa, Irving Berlin, Ed Wynn, Clifton Webb and Bea Lillie rented summer homes.

That summer, Tallulah Bankhead was making a picture for Paramount Pictures in Astoria and, seeking respite, spent frequent weekends at Libby's Sands Point home. On the occasion of her first visit, Libby's other guests included Howard and Betty Dietz and Louisa Carpenter. On Saturday evening, Tallulah asked Louisa to draw her a bath; Louisa was stunned. "I didn't mean to shock you," said Tallulah. "It's merely that I'm accustomed to ordering women about."

"Not *this* woman," said Louisa.

Tallulah was, as always, exasperating. At the end of the weekend, Howard Dietz observed: "A day away from Tallulah is like a month in the country."

Smith had rented a home of his own in Sands Point that summer—near the Port Washington airport where he kept his plane, the Savoia-Marchetti 80HP amphibian. In July, he was joined by his friend, the eighteen-year-old Ab Walker.

Libby continued to see Smith, but infrequently and usually when Louisa was in Delaware. They almost always quarreled. When Smith arrived unexpectedly at Libby's home one afternoon and found Louisa there, he rushed back to his car and drove, as his brother had done earlier that year, into Long Island Sound. On another occasion, Bea Lillie invited Libby and Louisa to a dinner party and neglected to invite Smith. Smith pleaded with Libby not to go or at least to take him with her, but she explained it was a hen party, that no men had been invited. When Libby had gone, Smith moped about the house, then leaped into his car, driving swiftly to the local airport.

Peter Bonetti, Smith's flying instructor from Winston-Salem, was at the airport when Smith careened onto the field, great tears rolling down his cheeks. Smith told Bonetti he was going to end it all, that Libby's friends were attempting to sabotage their romance. He intended, he said, to fly out to sea.

Without giving his motor more than a minute's warming up, Smith took off. As the small plane wobbled in the air, Bonetti thought that Smith would crash, but he managed to lift the nose and headed north and east toward the Atlantic. It was getting dark and Bonetti decided to wait for Smith. At three in the morning, he finally returned, admitting he had intended to fly until his gas was gone but, at the last minute, had changed his mind. Bonetti thought Smith a tortured, hypersensitive youth and wanted to console him. Being an employee, he said nothing at all.

That summer, Smith was preoccupied with kidnappers and, wherever he went, he carried a gun. Claiming to have received numerous threatening notes, he took such precautions as placing a dummy wrapped in sheets and newspapers in his bed at night, while he slept beneath it on the floor. Late one evening, Smith thought he heard two men whispering in the adjacent room. Frightened, he crept from his bedroom window and ran into town for the police. When they returned, the house was empty.

Smith's morbid fears included Libby and he insisted that, in order to protect herself, she should learn to shoot a gun. One afternoon, in Libby's living room, Smith gave her his .32 caliber automatic Mauser, which he swore was set on an empty chamber. Guns frightened Libby, but Smith stood behind her, pressing the Mauser into her hand, helping her squeeze the trigger. The gun went off, shattering a baseboard across the room. Libby screamed, accusing Smith of being an amateur, but he dismissed her angrily. "I've had guns since I was a baby," he said. "It must have gotten jammed."

Libby created feelings of confusion and impotency in Smith. He was not able to persuade her to take his intentions seriously; nor was he able to compete with her celebrity. Smith had only to look at any of the Manhattan tabloids to see her photograph, her Lux soap advertisements, to read her views on Tin Pan Alley or the Broadway theater. He was nothing in comparison, he felt— another rich boy from the provinces.

As the Depression deepened, Libby not only endured, she flourished. During the run of *Three's a Crowd*, she had earned $2,500 a week and had managed to save much of it. Addressing Libby as "Dear Libido," her banker informed Libby that her current account stood at $23,481.25. She drove around Manhattan in her expensive town car, had purchased a townhouse in the east Seventies, and was photographed in privileged places, often in the company of Rex, her Great Dane, whom, in pig Latin, she called X ray.

Walter Winchell observed that Libby's "deep moaning wowed the silk hat crowd and made a sucker out of the Depression." He claimed that Libby had caused Yale and Harvard men to miss classes, to flunk exams and to ignore the girls they had summoned for weekends. During a photographic session at the Yale Co-Op in New Haven, Libby was mobbed by hundreds of hysterical undergraduates, the "gin generation," as they were known, and her recording of "Body and Soul" had become their anthem.

"What I'm singing is always a very present thing," she told the *Daily Mirror*. "It's here, it's now, it's what's happening at the moment. That's what makes the songs so vital. When I sing, I never spare my vocal chords. My singing is like Flamenco. Sometimes, it's purposefully hideous. I try to convey anguish, anger, tragedy, passion. When you're expressing emotions like these, you cannot have a pure tone." Libby assured the reporter that the songs she sang were about people who have had difficult times in love but who don't surrender. "They just say, 'that's my plight and I'm going to take it in my stride.' That's what torch singing is all about."

Throughout 1931, Libby's idiosyncrasies, her petty likes and dislikes, were scrupulously documented by the Manhattan tabloids. She could make any story brilliant by merely telling it. It took her three minutes to fall asleep and twenty-five minutes to fully waken. Only two things bored her—failure and success. She considered her friend Noel Coward the outstanding figure in the contemporary theater. She would rather laugh than eat strawberry shortcake and she adored strawberries. She considered anything above Seventy-ninth Street suburban. She never allowed her own gramophone records in her home. When reading a magazine, she read the advertisements first, the fiction afterward. She believed that lyricists who rhymed *love* with *skies above* should be publicly flogged.

She smoked cigarettes only on Saturday nights, affecting a long cigarette holder fashioned of ivory; lighting her cigarette, she inhaled, exhaled, then, using a small pair of gold scissors, snipped the smoldering tip, replacing the lengthy butt in a solid-gold cigarette case. Her toenails were polished a deep rose red; she was inordinately proud of them, calling them her most precious jewels. She favored net stockings and always wore evening gowns in the evening. When dieting, she ate four times a day. She maintained eight photographs on her dressing-room wall—all of Garbo, her favorite actress.

Smith Reynolds had read all of this and more in the gossip columns, and it galled him. Libby was scheduled to leave on the road tour of *Three's a Crowd* in a few days' time. When Smith begged her not to go, Libby was outraged. She was a professional, she said, pointing out that Smith, instead of sulking, should do something meaningful with his life. Again, they argued. And then, tiring of Libby's taunts, Smith fell back on an old plan—envisaging an adventure so grand, so heroic, it would still all of Libby's hectoring.

16

ADVENTURE WAS IN VOGUE IN 1931. THE NEWSPAPERS WERE glutted with the exploits of Admiral Byrd, Wiley Post, Amelia Earhart, Charles Lindbergh, and Smith's personal hero, Richard Halliburton, the explorer and writer, who had already traced on foot Cortez's route in conquest of Mexico and Balboa's march across the Isthmus of Darien, and was even now circling the world in his own airplane. Smith was entranced with tales of their feats, their hardships, their resolution, and he intended to emulate them.

Having purchased his Savoia-Marchetti amphibian that spring, Smith had test-flown it frequently in Winston-Salem. In late July, he brought the plane north to the Savoia-Marchetti factory in Port Washington, continuing to test-fly it, but to no apparent end. Now, everything had changed, and Smith began to make final arrangements for a solo flight from London to Hong Kong.

The 80HP amphibian, a two-seater with dual controls, was propelled by a Kulner 125-horsepower radial motor, placed high above the fuselage, just under the top wing. Equipped with a complete short-wave radio, receiver and transmitter, the plane had a wing span of thirty-five feet, a hull of laminated wood encased in fabric, and a collapsible landing gear. The amphibian had a cruising speed of eighty miles an hour and a fuel capacity of a hundred and fifty gallons, giving it a range of approximately a thousand miles.

Libby, who had thought Smith's plan a youthful boast, was suddenly stirred by his adventure; and, imperceptibly, her feelings toward him began to change. She was still in love with Louisa, but they had quarreled and Louisa had sailed for Havana aboard *The Galaxy*. Left behind, Libby saw more of Smith than she would ordinarily have done. Dressed now in polished boots, in cavalry-twill jodhpurs and a fur-trimmed flying jacket, Smith no longer looked the sullen juvenile. His proposed trip had given him a new assurance, an accelerated sense of purpose. One afternoon Smith buzzed the beach near Libby's Sands Point home in his plane, strewing the sand with yellow roses. Libby and Tallulah were sunbathing and Tallulah remarked: "Something seems to have made a man of the boy. Darling, perhaps we've misjudged him."

On Wednesday afternoon, August 26, Smith bade Libby good-bye and flew to the Forty-seventh Street pier on the Hudson River, where the Cunard liner *Berengaria* was moored. Without previously advising the liner's authorities that his baggage would include a plane, Smith taxied through the choppy water to the side of the liner and ordered the captain to haul his plane aboard. After a brief altercation, the captain relented, and the plane was placed on the *Berengaria*'s aft deck where it was securely lashed and braced. As the liner headed down the Hudson, Smith calculated that before his journey ended, he would have traveled some 17,000 miles by air and nearly 12,000 miles by sea.

Five days later, he arrived in Southampton and then flew on to London, where, at his small Mayfair hotel, he contracted a virus and was confined to his bed for a fortnight. Lonely and missing Libby terribly, he wrote to her: "I have been sick. I don't know what's the matter, but I never felt more like dying in a long time."

Libby answered, urging him to come home. But toward the end of September, Smith flew to Paris, cabling Libby: "Why return now? Meet you later—but suicide is preferable. This is the last cable. Goodbye. Love, Smith."

That same day, Libby also received a letter from Smith: "Darling Angel. I would gladly come home if you were not going on with the show. I'll gladly give up this trip or anything I have to devote all my time to you, if you would do the same for me. If I get to the point where I simply cannot stand it without you for another minute, well, there's the old Mauser with a few cartridges in it. I guess I've had my inning. It's time another team went to bat."

Libby attributed Smith's despondency to loneliness and a romantic turn of mind. She thought his tragic expostulations silly and showed his letters to such friends as Tamara Geva, explaining that they consisted, in the main, of boyish bleats and whimpers. Still, Libby was moved by Smith's attentions, by his strident claims that only she could help him to realize his unfulfilled desires. Besides, Louisa had chosen to remain in Cuba for several more weeks and Libby was lonely now. As she moved from town to town on the provincial tour of *Three's a Crowd*, Smith no longer seemed like such an improbable proposition. She may have ridiculed his letters, but Libby told Clifton Webb that she was proud of her young aviator.

The summer before, Libby had introduced Smith to Eugenia Bankhead, whom everyone called Sister. Now thirty, Sister was considered more beautiful, more intelligent, wittier even, than her younger sister, Tallulah. In Paris, she often encountered Smith at the bar in Chez Florence, drinking heavily, but with good humor. Sister liked him, but sensed he was a doomed and driven youth. In consequence, she called him Myth, which appealed to him. One evening, he confided his love for Libby, asking Sister's advice. "Don't be ridiculous, darling," she said. "Loving Libby is like loving chocolate mousse. Soft to the touch and sweet to the eye. But the pleasure is fleeting. And all you'll get for your trouble is a bellyache."

Somewhat later, when Sister heard that Smith had proposed marriage to Libby, she laughed and said, "Good God, Smith asked *everyone* to marry him. He even asked *me* and he was already married. But then . . . so was I." (Sister would ultimately marry seven times—thrice to the same man—and in between conduct a complicated love affair with Louisa Carpenter.)

Sister commuted between Paris and her home in Mallorca that year. Not trusting the Spanish mails, her mother had shipped many of her silver heirlooms to Sister in Paris. Unable to carry them to Mallorca herself, Sister persuaded Smith to transport the silver in his plane, stopping in Mallorca on his way to Hong Kong. On the appointed day, Sister hired a motor launch and drove out into the harbor to await Smith's amphibian. To while away the afternoon, she took her husband, a wind-up Victrola, some new records, and two chilled bottles of Krug '29. The afternoon passed pleasantly, although Sister spent much of it fruitlessly scanning the skies. After she had finished the champagne and it began to grow dark, she ordered her husband to put into port. The next day, she received a cable from Smith saying: "Plane sank. Love, Myth."

Smith's plane had not sunk. He was, in fact, disconsolate, unable to fly. To complicate matters, he now suffered from a disease of the mastoid, which his French doctors assured him required immediate surgery. Smith decided to postpone his trip, return to America and undergo the operation there. At the beginning of October, therefore, he sailed from Southampton to New York aboard the American liner *Leviathan*.

As the Depression slipped further and further into what was to be its darkest period, *Three's a Crowd* was one of the few fortunate shows to have recovered its initial investment. Before the 1931 season was over, most actors would be begging for work, and bankers, trying to protect their theater mortgages, would begin producing shows themselves. Even the powerful Shubert brothers were in grim financial difficulties.

The road trip of *Three's a Crowd* was unsuccessful. In Newark, New Jersey, where the potential gross had been reckoned at $30,000 a week, the show grossed $9,200. When the pattern repeated itself in Philadelphia, Max Gordon, the producer, informed the cast that they would have to take drastic cuts in salary. Libby, who had been making $1,500 a week on the road, was suddenly reduced to $50. The show was her major source of income and she complained to Clifton Webb that it was no longer possible for her to live on a beginner's salary.

When Smith returned to America, Libby was commuting between New York and Newark. He entered Doctors Hospital, where successful surgery was performed. Following the operation, Libby visited him. Smith told her that in a few days he would be flying down to Winston-Salem to recuperate; he suggested that Libby join him there for the weekend and she agreed.

Libby had less than two days between shows. When she arrived in Winston, Smith took her up in his brother's plane, circling the thousand acres of Reynolda House so that Libby might appreciate the vast extent of his estate; and, as Smith had hoped, Libby claimed she had never seen a house as spacious or as beautiful. Reynolda was even more sumptuous than Louisa's home, Montchanin.

That Saturday night, in order to introduce Libby to his southern friends, Smith threw a party on the back lawn of Reynolda. Some twenty members of the younger gentry arrived, and as the evening progressed, Smith was pleased to see that his friends approved of his Yankee girl. When dinner was over and as it grew dark, Libby sat on a table on the back lawn, singing "Moanin' Low," "Body and Soul" and other torch songs the guests requested.

Afterward, Albert "Judge" Wharton, one of Smith's friends, shook Libby's hand, thanked her for singing, and said that she was one of the most beautiful women he had ever seen. Libby was flattered and kissed the youth on the cheek. And, indeed, she actually felt beautiful that night, although it was not an image of herself she was ever able to sustain. Libby's sense of herself ebbed and flowed, like her moods.

Libby was ebullient, and perhaps because of that (and putting Louisa out of her mind), she went to bed with Smith that evening. It was not an act she performed lightly, but her time at Reynolda had impressed her deeply, and she may have allowed Smith to make love to her out of affection and gratitude, as a kind of celebration. Smith, on the other hand, was transformed, and forever after, was obsessed with Libby.

*   *   *

That October, Anne Cannon Reynolds, now twenty-one, sued Smith for divorce. She insisted on haste and Smith consented to travel to Reno, Nevada. Anne charged incompatibility, complaining that Smith continually nagged and swore at her, that he assumed so domineering an attitude that she had become terribly, and perhaps terminally, distraught. Smith did not contest the divorce, and on November 23, Anne received her decree without appearing in court. Under the terms of the court-approved agreement, a $500,000 trust fund was to be created for Anne and an additional $500,000 trust fund for their daughter.

Smith was indifferent. The divorce had been an indispensable step in his pursuit of Libby—a satisfactory conclusion to an unsatisfactory affair. To Libby, he blithely explained that their chief bone of contention was that he had liked small parties and that Anne preferred large ones. As soon as the decree was approved, Smith flew to Washington, where Libby was appearing in *Three's a Crowd*.

Smith Reynolds had been wooing Libby for nearly a year, and now that he had obtained his divorce, he insisted she marry him immediately. He had telephoned from Reno daily, often threatening to shoot himself unless she acceded to his demands. But Libby was uncertain. Smith's tantrums continued to distress her, as did his dark threats of suicide. Libby's predominant concern, however, was that Smith was becoming violently possessive. He no longer liked to watch her perform. Only the week before in New Haven, hearing the thunderous applause for "Body and Soul," he had run from the theater, vanishing for several days. When he returned, in tears, he pleaded with Libby to leave the stage, to devote herself entirely to him. He couldn't bear to share her with anyone, he said, not even her fans.

Libby's doubts and hesitations only spurred Smith on. Wherever *Three's a Crowd* toured, Smith followed—to New Haven, to Washington and Baltimore, to Philadelphia and, finally, to Pittsburgh. Using all his charm and guile, Smith wheedled, he cajoled, he pointed out that America was in the midst of what would almost certainly be a lengthy depression, that theaters were closing, that she was currently earning fifty dollars a week, that if Libby was sensible, she would weather the encroaching storm at home with him in Carolina. Gradually, Libby was persuaded.

Traveling by train between Philadelphia and Pittsburgh, Libby told Tamara Geva that she had decided to marry her moody suitor. When Geva scoffed, Libby explained that there was more to Smith than met the eye, that he was "like an arid surface from which a geyser suddenly erupts." Geva failed to comprehend what Libby meant unless the geyser was intended to represent an unexpected eruption of oil. Geva found Smith morbid, unpleasant and unattractive. His money aside, there was nothing to recommend him.

Smith preferred to keep the marriage plans secret, and he instructed Libby to tell no one, not even her family. He intended to continue his flight from London to Hong Kong and wanted Libby to accompany him. But Libby was contracted to complete the tour, a contract that would hold her in thrall for another three and a half months. She begged Bob Milford, the company manager, to release her. "I'm going to lose this fella," she told him. "The world's going to crash around my head, you son of a bitch. Let me go." But Milford refused, explaining that if Libby quit she would throw a hundred people out of work, himself included, and that was unacceptable. Reluctantly, Libby agreed to remain with the show till the end of its run.

On November 16, just three days after Smith's final decree of divorce from Anne Cannon was approved, he and Libby were hastily married by a justice of the peace in Monroe, Michigan, an inconspicuous hamlet between Toledo and Detroit, where *Three's a Crowd* had come to play. Michigan was a state in which one could get married, if under twenty-one, without the consent of a guardian. By state law, Smith had been compelled to publish banns five days before the ceremony, which meant he had posted them before his final divorce decree came through.

Their marriage license was marked "do not publish"—an arrangement then permissible in Michigan. Libby gave her name as Elizabeth Holman, her occupation as "at home." Smith gave his name as Zachary Reynolds, his occupation as student. He gave his true age as twenty. Libby, however, concerned at the disparity in their ages, gave hers as twenty-five. She was, in fact, twenty-seven and, from that day on, would always be two years older than she claimed.

Fred Schoepfer, the justice of the peace, had not known who Smith Reynolds and Libby Holman were—describing them as an ordinary young couple, deeply in love. But when news of the marriage became public, Libby's friends were not so generous. Tamara Geva felt that Smith had simply wearied Libby with his insistent suit, that she had married more out of compassion than love, and Howard Dietz predicted dire results from what he called their irrational knot.

But Libby's chief critic was Louisa Carpenter. They had met infrequently since Louisa had sailed off for Havana three months before, and had argued lengthily about Libby's liaison with Smith. Libby was confused. She loved Louisa still; Louisa was dearer to her than anyone. But Libby felt there was no real future in their relationship, by which Louisa assumed she meant marriage and children—the lack of which would hardly impede *her* future. Louisa did not disapprove of marriage itself; she preferred her lovers to be heterosexual. But when she heard that Libby had married Smith, she was incensed. She believed Libby had been foolish, opportunistic, and that the marriage would come to a wretched end. On that point, Louisa was never to change her mind.

Libby and Smith spent their wedding night in a little hotel in Toledo, Ohio, and the next day she rejoined the company of *Three's a Crowd*. Smith left immediately for New York, where, on December 1, he sailed again for England. Reckoning to reach Hong Kong in about three months, he had arranged to meet Libby at the Repulse Bay Hotel on April 1, 1932.

These were giddy times for the young aviator and yet, in his logbook, entitled "The Log of Aeroplane NR-898W," Smith wrote the following sober entry on December 12: "Since my last flight in September, I have had to return to America due to illness. After recovery and much delay in America, I arrived in Plymouth Dec. 7 and proceeded to London. In London I have encountered much delay due to flying permits, and after the short test flight today, a fitting on the undercarriage gave way due to corrosion. The weather has been cold and foggy."

Throughout the sixty-page log, Libby is never mentioned. On

one occasion, Smith wrote: "I must be in Hong Kong by April 1, so I had to do anything to hurry things up." And later: "That night I could not sleep. I was so near to my destination. All at once thoughts came to me that had been squelched for months." Libby, presumably, had crossed his mind at last.

The 128-day journey carried Smith from England to Paris and on to Marseilles, Milan, Rome, Tunis, Tripoli and Cairo, where he spent a week looking at the pyramids and contracted a severe case of jaundice, which laid him up for a further three weeks. From Cairo, he flew to Gaza, to Baghdad, Karachi and Jodhpur, where he met the maharajah; then on to Agra, visiting the Taj Mahal by moonlight, to Calcutta, Rangoon, Bangkok, Hanoi, Haiphong and finally to Fort Bayard in French Indo-China, some two hundred seventy miles west of Hong Kong. Smith had been having continual mechanical difficulties with his amphibian and in Fort Bayard the engine broke down and he was forced to abandon the plane. Aboard a Standard Oil steamer, Smith pushed on to Hong Kong, arriving on April 9, eight days overdue.

While Smith flew across Europe and North Africa, *Three's a Crowd* limped from town to town, grossing fewer and fewer receipts. The show was finally forced to close in late February 1932.

Libby left immediately for Vancouver, whence she sailed to Hong Kong. The day she embarked, March 1, the newspapers reported the kidnapping of Charles Lindbergh's nineteen-month-old baby. Although Lindbergh would pay the kidnapper a $50,000 ransom, the child was not returned, and his dead body would not be discovered until May 12. The papers also reported that the Sino-Japanese war had begun, and that Hong Kong was crowded with foreign soldiers.

Libby arrived in Hong Kong on April 1, her landfall coinciding with an outbreak of influenza, and she was quarantined on the ship for twenty-four hours. The next day she disembarked, taking a taxi to the Repulse Bay, up through the hotel's lavish gardens filled with red flame-in-the-forest and on to its wisteria-covered entrance. But Smith had not checked in and the hotel manager had no news of him. After taking a bath, Libby walked through town. The streets were crowded with Chinese soldiers and refugees, with merchants and hagglers promoting their wares, with pushcarts and rickshaws. Less than a block from the hotel, she was accosted by a Chinese waif, whose customary occupation was to prey on tourists. Strangely, he took a liking to Libby and, instead of fleecing her, agreed in broken English to act as her guide and interpreter.

Escorted by her newfound friend, Libby spent several days sightseeing before receiving a cable from Smith in Fort Bayard, explaining his difficulties and assuring her that he would soon be in Hong Kong. Four days later, the waif scurried into the lobby of the Repulse Bay shouting that an American flier had fallen from the skies and that he would take Libby to him. Because of the war, and to be less conspicuous, Libby disguised herself as a Chinese peasant woman and sailed into Hong Kong harbor in a rented junk.

Out in the harbor, beyond the floating tenements of junks, of scows and tramp steamers, Libby saw a Standard Oil freighter approach: On the foredeck, in a white linen suit, stood Smith. From beneath her wide-brimmed Chinese hat, Libby shouted and waved. Smith finally nodded—the perfunctory nod of a celebrity acknowledging the praise of an enthusiastic fan; she was just another coolie to him. Libby ordered the junk to return to shore. At the dock, as Smith unloaded his luggage, Libby embraced him, but it was not until she removed her hat that he recognized her and kissed her passionately.

Suddenly, Smith pulled back, announcing, mysteriously, that civilians were not permitted to carry cameras or guns in Hong Kong. Libby was perplexed. Smith grinned, then extracted a camera from one jacket pocket, a pistol from the other. Libby urged him to hide them, but Smith continued to grin, brandishing his toys in the air. Libby had never seen him so sure, so self-possessed. His confidence excited her.

Smith had promised Libby a real honeymoon in Hong Kong. And for the next two weeks the young couple caroused and sported in the town. They gambled in Macao and toured Kowloon; they attended the races at Jardines and waltzed beneath the crystal chandeliers in the plush dining room of the Peninsula Hotel; they drank gimlets by moonlight on Victoria Peak and on one occasion, as Libby described it, they "opiated" in Pok Fulam. Libby would always speak effusively of her honeymoon; as told to future friends and lovers, it was a fine, foolhardy time, tinged with danger and the romantic trappings of the Orient.

From the beginning, however, the honeymoon was fraught with difficulties. Smith detested Hong Kong; he loathed the Chinese and what he called "the middle-class Englishman." "There is nothing worse," he wrote, "disgustingly middle-class." Ignoring Libby's protests, they returned to Fort Bayard, languishing in that bleak, colonial town for several days, until his amphibian was mended. They then flew back to Hong Kong where it rained torrentially for the remainder of their stay. Two days prior to sailing for America, they moved from the Repulse Bay Hotel and boarded the Canadian liner *Empress of Russia*. Smith had had his fill of foreigners and foreign food.

Despite his marriage, Smith was becoming even more possessive of Libby. On their first night aboard, he locked her into his stateroom, and spent the evening in Macao by himself. He continued to badger her into giving up the theater and, on one occasion, brandished his Mauser, threatening to shoot himself unless she agreed. Only later, and in galling circumstances, did Libby claim that her love for Smith was greater than her love for the theater. But it was difficult to believe her even then. Nonetheless, on the voyage home, she finally submitted—agreeing to abandon the theater for a year in order to devote herself to her exacting husband in Carolina.

With the amphibian aboard, Smith and Libby sailed from Hong Kong to Victoria in British Columbia, arriving on May 12. Libby flew immediately to New York and checked into the old Ambassador Hotel on Park Avenue. Smith remained behind, hoping to repair his still-damaged plane, but the costs were formidable and he finally left it there. Arriving at the Ambassador, he had some difficulty in locating Libby until he discovered that she had checked in under the name of Libby Holman.

A few days later, the New York tabloids learned of Libby and Smith's secret marriage nearly six months before. Libby confirmed the rumors to reporters. Several of her friends wished to give parties for the newlyweds, but Smith adamantly declined all celebrations, instructing Libby to tell everyone that they were leaving immediately for an unspecified destination on Long Island.

On June 5, Libby and Smith motored down the East Coast to North Carolina. They drove through the night and, early the next afternoon, entered the grounds of Reynolda House. From the main gates, Libby could see the private nine-hole golf course, the numerous barns and stables and greenhouses. And there, at last, on a wooded rise, was the large green-gabled, white-columned mansion, a bevy of servants scurrying about the lawn. A few minutes later, she and Smith pulled up beneath the porte-cochere. They were home.

17

WINSTON-SALEM'S SMART SET HASTENED TO WELCOME LIBBY. The younger Carolina gentry were much impressed with the vivacious singer and with her celebrity, believing that Smith had made an excellent catch. Their elders, however, did not share their enthusiasm. They were polite, of course (they were southerners after all), but behind their politesse smoldered considerable resentment. They liked to think of themselves as simple, as down-to-earth, as elegant country folk. They took their wealth and their Anglo-Saxon ancestry seriously and, among themselves, referred to Libby as "that damned Yankee Jewess," "that *actress*," "that fortune-hunter."

Smith ignored their ruderies. In Winston-Salem, Smith did as he pleased and answered to no one. During May and June, he threw lavish parties, dances and barbecues at Reynolda for his friends. He idolized Libby and bore her like a trophy for everyone to see. Describing the parties at Reynolda, a reporter wrote in the New York *Sunday News*: "Whirligig: Speed: Faster: Crazier: Champagne cocktails . . . Corn liquor straight . . . Pour it on . . . Step on the gas . . . Shoot the works . . . Speed: Gin, rye, bourbon, sex. Dizzy dames. Dizzy house parties. A thousand acre estate. Private golf course. Tennis courts. Swimming pool. Lake. Moonlight dips. Dances. Joyrides. Airplanes. Yachts. High-powered car. Speed. Chasing a new thrill today. Tiring of it to-morrow. Nowhere to go but places. Nothing to do but things. Speed with youth at the throttle, millions to spend . . . and bored stiff. Life's blah. The world's a phoney. The whirligig spins on."

After only a few weeks at Reynolda, Libby began to invite her New York theatrical friends down for long weekends, and the Tarheels were thrilled to meet and mingle with actors and actresses. At Reynolda, they were introduced to Spring By-ington, to Blanche Yurka and Clifton Webb. They met Louisa Carpenter, who had overcome her opposition to Libby's mar-riage but not her disapproval. And they met Libby's parents, who, on one occasion, drove down to Winston in matching Cord automobiles—Christmas presents from Smith and Libby.

At almost every party, Libby was urged to sing. Many of Smith's friends had previously purchased her records or had heard her torch songs on the radio. Using a local pianist, or Clifton Webb when he was there, Libby sang in the large lavish drawing room or at early evening picnics out by Lake Katherine, where, one night, the frogs croaked so conspicuously that Libby was forced to conclude her song.

Smith's friends believed that Smith and Libby were happy to-gether, but thought it a peculiar match. They liked Libby; she was witty and charming and, in some way, needed them, since she knew no one else in North Carolina. Among themselves, they speculated on the nature of Smith and Libby's sexual life, wondering whether they had bedded before their marriage— some of them thinking it unlikely, while others believed that, sexually, Libby had simply overcome her youthful groom. Nice girls, they knew, didn't do that sort of thing, but Libby was a sophisticate: She may have come from Cincinnati, but she had been around.

As for Smith, his friends rarely knew what to make of him. He was moody, he was wild, he stammered, he was sullen and noncommittal, and he gave a palpable impression of stupidity, although he wasn't stupid. A few of them thought him pathetic, having been raised without parents, brought up by servants and guardians, having been given too much money too soon, so that he had never learned to put first things first. And though he loved giving parties, Smith didn't like to drink. Alcohol, rather than elating him, tended to reinforce his somber disposition. In spite of his two marriages, many of his friends believed that he had never been particularly enthusiastic about women, that he was sexually confused, ambivalent. But this was pure conjecture. Smith was a loner. He never confided in anyone.

One Friday night toward the end of June, Jim Baggs, a Georgia boy who had moved to Winston five years before, attended a party at Reynolda, an event he described as "little more than a convention of homosexuals." That night he met Clifton Webb, Blanche Yurka, Louisa Carpenter and a man from California named Bobby Froelich. When Baggs was introduced to Froelich, Froelich threw his arms around him and hugged him. Baggs was surprised, but thought that that, perhaps, was how people in California shook hands. He couldn't be sure; he was just a country cracker boy. But Smith, he knew, disapproved. Smith told Baggs he had gotten himself in a fine mess what with all these "fairyish folk" around. That night, Smith stood at the edge of the party, a grim, hardened look on his pallid features.

The following week, Libby invited Clifton Webb, Bea Lillie and Peggy Fears down for a long weekend, telling them that Louisa Carpenter would also be there. They arrived early on Friday evening and, as they walked into the drawing room, were astonished to see it filled with a group of rowdy, intoxicated youths. Smith was crouched up on the gallery overlooking the drawing room, shooting crystal ornaments from the chandelier, while his friends urged him on with lusty cries of approbation. They decided to leave.

Louisa Carpenter had intended to remain at Reynolda through the Fourth of July weekend, but she too changed her mind. It was enough that she disapproved of Libby's marriage, that she thought Smith a sulky youth and knew, in turn, that Smith detested her. But now she had come to believe that he was dangerous. Libby pleaded with her to stay, clinging to her as she strode from the house. But Louisa would not be deterred, not even by Libby.

In the beginning, Libby loved being lady of the country manor. She regularly rehearsed with Charles Vardell, the dean of music at Salem College. She and Smith swam, played tennis or golf, and rode horseback together through the large estate. Smith offered to teach her how to fly. There was so much to do and so much time in which to trifle, but secretly, Libby longed for New York. She missed the theater, the speakeasies, the spirited banter of witty friends. Still, she had promised Smith to remain for a year in the South and so, as a compromise, she persuaded him to invite her friend Blanche Yurka for an indefinite stay.

Blanche Yurka (née Jurka), an actress of Czechoslovakian extraction, was well known for her Broadway roles in *The Wild Duck* and *Lysistrata*. She was by far the eldest of Libby's friends and would celebrate her thirty-ninth birthday at Reynolda. An imposing woman, she spoke in what used to be known in the theater as pear-shaped tones. She was tall with piercing blue eyes, and Libby, who longed to play serious, dramatic roles, was much impressed with what she envisaged as her majesty.

When Blanche arrived, she presented Libby with a Czechoslovakian drama called *Periphery*. It was a wonderful play, Blanche claimed, and Libby would be perfect as the female lead. During the long June afternoons that ensued, Libby and Blanche sat beneath the flowering magnolia trees, reading *Periphery* over and over again.

Libby knew what she wanted, but she never wanted anything for long. By the end of June, she had become petulant, depleted. North Carolina was unpardonably pacific, and it had not taken her long to learn that her listless husband had little interest in books, the theater or even travel. He exhibited, in fact, a marked desire to be alone.

Seeking respite, Libby attempted to persuade Smith that they should spend the coming winter in Manhattan, where they could both take courses at New York University. To that end, she talked him into importing a tutor to Reynolda—a young man named Raymond Kramer, who coached Smith in algebra, trigonometry, plane and solid geometry.

Smith suspected that Libby's talk of wintering in New York was little more than a ploy, and he was hostile to the plan. But then, he suspected everything. Only days before, three of his mother's friends had paid a call in order to introduce themselves to Libby. Libby served the ladies tea and one of them asked if she would sing for them. Thinking it polite, Libby agreed. Smith rose and left the room. Libby sang a song; the ladies thanked her and departed. Libby then looked for Smith, but he had vanished. She finally found him crouched beneath a lilac bush, crying and vomiting. When Libby asked what was wrong, Smith winced and said he couldn't bear it when Libby sang *his* songs to strangers.

Smith was awash with trepidation. He resisted the idea of moving to New York, and yet he would tell Libby, in a high stuttering voice, that he was keeping her from her friends and the theater, that he was unable to make her happy, that he could not live up to her expectations of him. In these moods, he took out his Mauser, placing it gently against his head.

The Mauser was Smith's sole keepsake, his talisman. He would often sit by himself in his bedroom, firing it out the window. The automatic had a hair trigger. Two years before, it had accidentally discharged, almost hitting his friend C. G. Hill. Libby urged him to get rid of the lethal weapon. But Smith insisted he was a rich man, that he required protection. Why couldn't Libby understand?

On Saturday, July 2, Walter Batchelor, Libby's agent and theatrical manager, journeyed down from New York to see Reynolda and to discuss *Periphery*, the Czech play, with Libby. The thirty-six-year-old Batchelor was a well-known manager, representing such stars as Rudy Vallee, Fred Allen, Clifton Webb and Helen Morgan.

That night after dinner, Libby, Blanche Yurka, Batchelor, Smith and his friend Ab Walker sat in the opulent drawing room drinking coffee. The Reynolds family Bible lay on a long oak refectory table. Smith's full name was written on the flyleaf with the accompanying notation: "born, Sunday morning, November 5, 1911 at ten minutes after five o'clock." With a coy smile on his face, Smith produced a pen and wrote just under his birth date: "And died of old age shortly thereafter."

"Oh, God, Smitty, don't do that," Libby screamed. "It isn't even funny to write something like that in such a serious place." Smith put his arm around Libby and, laughing, said: "You take everything so seriously, darling."

*   *   *

Albert Walker, whom everyone called Ab, was Smith's best friend. They had known each other since grammar school and were inseparable. Unlike Smith, the short, slender nineteen-year-old was a rough, gregarious youth. He had attended R. J. Reynolds High School, where he played on the football team, and, like Smith, had failed to graduate. The only child of a successful realtor, Ab worked for eighteen cents an hour as a doffer at the Chatham Mills in Elkin, some forty miles from Winston—the only job he could find.

Ab was a ladies' man and would, as one of his friends observed, screw a snake if you held its head. Despite an ulcerous stomach, he drank to excess. But he was the only person Smith completely trusted, and Ab exerted a calming effect on his erratic friend.

On Sunday, July 3, Libby, Blanche and Walter Batchelor spent the afternoon in the library reading *Periphery*. Libby's role was that of a prostitute who seduces a young married architect. Her paramour, however, surprises them in bed, becomes enraged and accidentally kills the architect. They decide to place the architect's body in the street in such a way that it would appear he had died accidentally. A drab and inconclusive drama, it had nonetheless become the vehicle in which Libby envisaged her return to Broadway.

As the three colleagues read the parts, Smith drifted in and out of the library. Libby, wearing a red-and-white one-piece bathing suit, was reclining on the sofa. It was hot and she was restless. Toward two o'clock, Smith sat down beside her. Libby changed position, laying her head on Smith's knee. Moments later, Smith dropped his hand down to Libby's bare thigh. Libby stiffened and, holding his hand, moved it away. "You shrank away from me," Smith whispered.

"Oh, *darling*," said Libby with slight exasperation.

The couple excused themselves and went up to their bedroom. "You shrank from me," said Smith again; and Libby explained that she had not shrunk from him, but had only moved his hand in order not to embarrass their guests. "Libby," said Smith, "if you didn't shrink from me, then I'm crazy. I see things that aren't true. I believe you if you tell me, but I think I should have my head examined."

"Don't be silly," said Libby, "you're imagining things."

"You have gotten where you are by yourself," shouted Smith. "You *can't* love me."

After dinner, Smith changed into a dark suit. Taking Libby aside, he said, "I have to go to town. I'm going to stay at the hotel tonight and go see a doctor in the morning and have my head examined." Libby asked him to stay or at least to allow her to accompany him, but Smith insisted on going alone. Libby went downstairs. She walked past Ab without looking at him and Ab could see that she was furious.

Smith trailed after her, a small overnight bag in his hand. Ab asked him where he was going and Smith shrugged and said: "How about carrying me into town?" Before leaving, they had a highball and, just before ten o'clock, drove the four miles into Winston in Ab's old Plymouth roadster.

Smith wanted to go to the Robert E. Lee Hotel. "Well, you can't go in and register," said Ab. "There's liable to be quite a bit of talk about it. Suppose you let me register." Smith nodded and Ab registered in his own name, taking a room on the ninth floor. Upstairs, Smith took a full quart of Scotch from his bag and poured large drinks for both of them.

The evening was spent discussing Libby. As he drank, Smith explained that if he and Libby went to New York that winter, he would be in school all day, Libby would be at the theater, and they would rarely see one another. He didn't really want Libby to abandon the stage, he said, but if she had asked him to relinquish flying, he would do so at once. He expected a similar consideration from her.

That evening, Smith hired Ab to be his personal secretary at a hundred and twenty-five dollars a week. Ab was expected to perform favors and odds and ends and to master the art of navigation in order to help Smith accomplish his old ambition—a flight around the world. Ab agreed to leave his job at Chatham Mills and to move into Smith's former bachelor quarters at Reynolda House.

In the morning, they left the hotel for Miller Field, where Smith had recently equipped a new plane for night flying. Intending to take it up the following night, he wanted to assure himself that it had been properly serviced. Afterward, they drove back to Reynolda. It was early, just after nine, and no one was awake. Smith rushed upstairs to awaken Libby. Taking her in his arms, he said, "Libby, dear, I'm so sorry. That's what I do, I make you unhappy by leaving you."

"What could I have done?" she said.

"That's the whole trouble," said Smith. "Nothing, nothing at all. I swore I would never leave you and in a moment I did and I'm worried, afraid that I will go on having these terrible weaknesses of mine. That is the one thing I want to do, to make you happy, and I'm failing in it."

Smith was disconsolate for the rest of the day, but that evening, remembering that his friend C. G. Hill would be celebrating his twenty-first birthday the following day, he decided to throw a party. The prospect of roistering with his friends elated Smith, almost as though his life had taken on some rich and unforeseen dimension.

Upstairs in her bedroom in the west wing, Blanche Yurka was unaware of the impending party and, in any event, disapproved of frivolous gatherings. Sitting down at her desk, she wrote a letter to an old friend, John Stein, a well-known theatrical manager and agent in New York: "Here I am in this God-forsaken place," she said. "Only the silence of the grave reigns. It's going to be a very dull holiday."

18

THE NEXT MORNING, LIBBY MADE ARRANGEMENTS FOR THE party, deciding to hold it by Lake Katherine some two hundred yards behind Reynolda House. The guests were from some of Winston's finest families, and at about six-thirty that evening, they coursed through the main front gates—in time for what the local newspapers would eventually call "a wild barbecue and corn whiskey bash."

The guest of honor was C. G. Hill, who, after Ab Walker, was Smith's closest friend. C. G. was a playboy, a skilled pilot, a bachelor, the richest catch in town (his father had married into the Cannon family), and his friends considered him a gadabout. His date that evening was the petite, dark-haired Virginia Dunklee. She was twenty-three, and her family owned Winston's largest laundry, the Zinzendorf.

Behind them came Babe Collier Vaught. The tall, twenty-eight-year-old brunette worked at Montaldo's, the smart department store in downtown Winston. The stylish Babe was a widow, her young husband, Billy Vaught, having burned to death the year before. Jim Shepherd, owner of a chic Winston art shop, came also. At the time, he was courting Babe Vaught and later married her. With him was a friend, Billy Shaw Howell, a former World War I pilot, who worked as a radio salesman in Charlotte. He had arrived in Winston the day before on a business trip and, though he did not know Smith, Shepherd asked him to come.

The two other guests were "Fat Charlie" Norfleet, the wealthy head of the trust department of the Wachovia Bank and Trust Company, and Lewis McGinnes, formerly Dick Reynolds's personal pilot, who now operated Winston's only airport. He had taught both Smith and C. G. Hill how to fly. The guest list was supplemented by Blanche Yurka and Ab Walker, making, with Libby and Smith, eleven guests in all. Smith had promised them an unforgettable evening.

That afternoon, Ab Walker and Jim Baggs had driven to Lewisville to collect the corn liquor from the bootlegger. North Carolina had been dry since 1908. Most of the bootlegging activity was centered in Wilkes County in the northern portion of the state, but Lewisville was closer and the two boys drove over in Ab's Plymouth roadster.

Employing the customary caution of his trade, the bootlegger told them he didn't make the stuff himself, but knew the man who knew the man who made it. It was excellent corn liquor, one hundred proof, and cost three dollars a gallon. The boys purchased a five-gallon wooden keg and returned to Reynolda about an hour before the party began.

Libby greeted her guests at the front door. With her deep tan and hazel eyes, she looked singularly attractive. She wore sandals and white flannel lounging pajamas with a red stripe, like a sash, around the waist. As the party began, she was vivacious and talkative, but an odd tension darkened her gaiety.

Only a few servants were on duty that evening, their labors supervised by John Carter, the black butler. Ab had already transported the corn liquor, the tub of home brew and a case of White Rock down to the boathouse. The guests gathered in the main house, where highballs were served, then adjourned to the lake. Libby and Babe Vaught spent most of the early evening talking and drinking together. They concocted an impromptu drinking contest, Babe claiming that she could hold as much liquor as any man, and they matched one another with divebombers, glasses of home brew into which they dropped shot glasses of corn liquor—the purpose being to drink the corn liquor before it fell to the bottom of the glass. Before the party was an hour old, it was obvious to everyone that both women were drunk.

Smith was not pleased. Plummer Walker, a black maid who had known Smith all his life, could tell just by looking at his face. The drinking contest had offended him, but he had done nothing to stop it. He himself was not drinking; he sipped at a glass of home brew, which he would nurse for the remainder of the evening.

Suddenly, Libby jumped up on the wooden crate of White Rock and shouted to Babe: "Let's do something. Let's sing." And then she stumbled, almost falling off, knocking over a bottle of soda water. Babe laughed uproariously. Disgusted, Smith walked over to Libby and whispered furiously; Libby grinned, exchanging winks with Babe. Smith retreated.

Around eight o'clock, Ab and Babe changed into bathing suits, although neither of them went swimming. At the boathouse, Ab encountered Libby. She threw her arms around him, kissed him on the cheek, and said, "Ab, Smith doesn't love me anymore." When Ab protested, Libby frowned and flounced away. Minutes later, as the sun was setting on the far side of the house, Libby and Smith returned to the boathouse and Libby said, "Ab did I kiss you this evening?" She seemed to imply that such an action was preposterous. Ab looked nervously at Smith and denied it. Smith said nothing and, taking Libby's arm, propelled her toward the main house.

A few minutes later, Smith returned alone. "Ab, I want you to get it straight that I'm not accusing you of anything," he said. "I saw the whole thing."

"But there wasn't anything," said Ab.

"I saw what happened," said Smith.

Before Ab could reply, Smith turned and walked away.

Just after nine o'clock, Libby disappeared. No one was to see her for the next three hours. None of the guests even remarked on her absence except for Ab, who questioned Smith about it. Smith told him that Libby was probably roaming around the grounds. When Ab suggested looking for her, Smith said that if Libby had not returned by the time the guests were gone, he would look for her himself.

The other guests straggled up to the house at about nine-thirty, where they drank and listened to music on the Victrola. Ab, who had been drinking heavily all evening, was now quite drunk. Even so, he offered to drive down to the lake and fetch Babe Vaught's shoes, which she had left there. On the way back, he looked everywhere for Libby but was unable to find her. He couldn't understand why Smith seemed so unconcerned.

At eleven o'clock, the guests began to leave. Sometime before, Babe Vaught and Jim Shepherd had slipped away for a drive. C. G. Hill and Virginia Dunklee left together. Billy Shaw Howell departed, taking "Fat Charlie" Norfleet with him. When Lewis McGinnes left, Smith took him aside and told him to make certain the landing lights were fixed since he intended to take his plane up the next evening. At 11:45, Blanche Yurka excused herself and went to bed. She was sleepy and it was more than an hour past her customary bedtime. A few minutes later, Babe Vaught and Jim Shepherd returned from their drive. Babe was now so drunk that Smith suggested she spend the night. Shepherd helped her to an upstairs bedroom where she would sleep soundly till the following morning. By midnight, only Smith, Ab and Jim Shepherd were awake in the house. Libby had still not appeared.

The three friends sat in the drawing room drinking and talking. At about 12:30 W. E. Fulcher, the night watchman, was lounging on the running board of his car at the rear of the house eating a sandwich. Suddenly Libby walked into the basement yard. She wore her red-and-white flannel pajamas and there was a grass stain on the right knee. She was walking curiously, Fulcher thought, taking one short step and then a long one, stepping this way and that, in much the way he walked when he had drunk too much. Fulcher's German shepherd, chained to the car bumper, barked. The shepherd leaped toward Libby, but was constrained by the chain. Rising up on his hind legs, he stood as tall as Libby. "The dog won't bite you," Fulcher said. Libby grinned and embraced the animal.

It was very dark and Fulcher offered to guide Libby back to the house with his flashlight. Just then, Ab Walker shouted and walked up to them. Smith shouted from the other side of the house, and Fulcher said he was coming around with the madam. When Smith appeared, Libby grinned at him. He said nothing and led her into the house.

Libby and Smith walked immediately upstairs, around the gallery, and then, unexpectedly, into Ab's bedroom. Ab, still wearing his bathing suit, began to lock up the house. While Smith and Ab had been outside, Jim Shepherd had gone upstairs to check on Babe. As Ab locked up, he came back down again. Suddenly, the two men heard loud voices. Libby and Smith were having a violent argument, and although they could hear their shouts and screams, they were unable to make much sense of them. Shepherd decided he would go home, and borrowed Ab's car. About fifteen minutes later, Libby and Smith came out into the hall and began walking to their bedroom in the east wing. But Smith then told Libby to go to bed and came downstairs to talk with Ab.

Ab was later to claim that there was nothing unusual in Smith's features nor in his manner, that, regardless of how he actually felt, he always looked the same. Smith sat down on the sofa and told Ab their round-the-world trip was canceled. "And you've just lost your job as my private secretary," he added.

"What do you mean?" said Ab.

"I'm going out and end it all tonight."

"Don't be mad," said Ab.

"You needn't bother locking all the doors," said Smith. "I'm coming back downstairs, but I'm going out and I won't be back."

Ab said nothing. Smith started up the stairs, then turned and tossed Ab his wallet. "You can have that," he said. Thinking it contained his weekly wages, Ab thanked him. Smith went up the stairs and down the hall to his bedroom. Because Ab's bathing suit had no pockets, he put the wallet behind a cushion on the

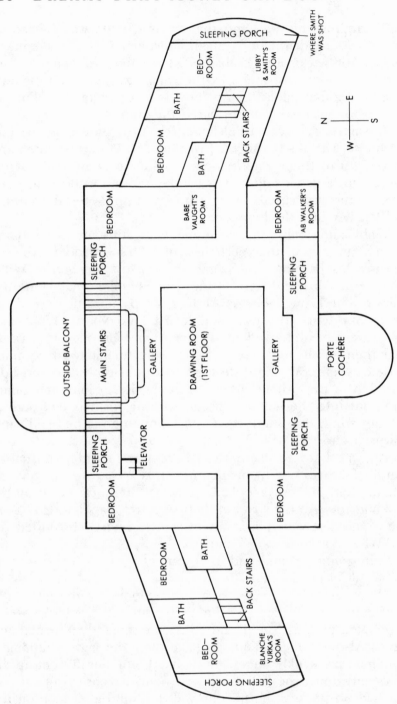

sofa. Not wishing to appear to be waiting for Smith, he pretended to clean up, to lock the outside doors, killing time until his friend returned.

Blanche Yurka had retired just before midnight. Less than an hour later, hearing what she believed to be male voices below in the kitchen and thinking she would join them for a glass of milk, she slipped on her black robe and descended the back stairs. But the kitchen was empty. Blanche walked into the drawing room where she found Ab. He told her the guests were gone and that he was closing up the house. Blanche returned to her bedroom.

At about 12:45, W. E. Fulcher heard what sounded like a gunshot, but was unable to discern from which part of the house it had come. He listened again, but heard nothing more—neither shouts nor screams. Since Smith had returned to Reynolda, Fulcher had grown accustomed to the sound of unexpected gunfire and thought no more of it.

Upstairs, in the west wing, Blanche Yurka heard what sounded like Libby's hysterical voice. But it was muted, indistinct. She rose from her bed, listening at the window, then walked down the hall and onto the gallery. Ab was still below in the drawing room. "I thought I heard somebody scream," she said. Ab shrugged. A few minutes before, Ab himself had heard what he thought was a muffled shot, but had dismissed it as improbable. He was still waiting for Smith to come down.

At that moment, Libby's voice sounded again, quite loudly this time, and Ab rushed up the stairs to the gallery. Both of them could now hear Libby crying, "*Ab! Ab! Ab!*" And then, wearing only a peach-colored negligee, Libby lurched toward them from the east wing, clutching the wall in order not to fall. Reaching Ab, she collapsed on a little settee, and when Ab leaned over her, she whispered, "Smith, Smith shot himself." Ab raced down the hall to the sleeping porch. Smith, still wearing his white ducks and a light-blue shirt, was lying on the bed. He was unconscious and blood seeped from a wound in his head to the floor below. Ab rushed down the back stairs and telephoned for an ambulance.

Blanche seemed to be in shock. She stood out on the gallery, doing nothing, not even attempting to assist Libby. When Ab returned to the sleeping porch, he lifted Smith up from the bed and dragged him, walking backward, down the hall and past the bedroom where Babe Vaught slumbered undisturbed.

At last, Blanche moved to help. Ab was carrying Smith by the shoulders, Smith's head lolling on Ab's shoulder, while Libby attempted to lift his feet. But the stronger, more sober Blanche pushed Libby aside and took hold of Smith's ankles. They carried his inert and surprisingly heavy body around the gallery, down the stairs, across the drawing room and out to the porte-cochere.

The ambulance had not arrived and they decided to drive to Baptist Hospital themselves. After Smith had been trundled into the back of Libby's dark green Cadillac, Blanche climbed in behind him. Ab drove. Libby sat next to him, her hands clenched to her face, sobbing hysterically. As they accelerated out the side entrance and into Reynolda Road, Blanche could see that Ab's face was smeared with Smith's blood.

19

N 1932, BAPTIST HOSPITAL HAD JUST UNDER A HUNDRED beds and, because of the Depression, a portion of the hospital had been closed down. Ab was driving fast. Turning into the hospital entrance, he crashed into the curb, riding up on it, and skidded to a stop outside. It was 1:10 A.M.

They were met at the emergency entrance by Miss Ethel Shore, the night supervisor. Ab jumped out of the car and shouted at her: "Goddamn it, *hurry up, hurry up.*" Libby got out of the car, began to stagger and, in order not to fall, clutched the front screen door. Smith's body was carried by Ab and an orderly into the hospital. The elevator rose slowly to the fifth floor, and when the doors opened, Ab was directed into the middle of the three operating rooms, where he laid his still-unconscious friend on a table. There was blood everywhere, from the emergency entrance up into the operating room. Miss Shore ordered it cleaned up.

The barefooted Libby had remained downstairs and the elevator returned to fetch her. Her negligee was not fastened and she wore nothing beneath it. When she arrived on the fifth floor, Miss Shore pulled a cot into an alcove near the operating room and sat Libby down. She was covered in blood, and Miss Shore washed it away.

Blanche Yurka wore a black robe over her negligee. She slipped off the robe and offered it to Libby. Miss Shore redressed Libby in it, fastening the front with a safety pin. Libby slumped back on the cot, crying softly and staring blankly before her. Blanche was escorted down to a private room on the third floor by one of the night nurses. While Miss Shore began calling doctors, Ab telephoned Smith's relatives, urging them to come to the hospital immediately.

In the operating room, Smith was being examined by two young interns—Dr. John Grizzard and Dr. Alexander Cox. Cox, a twenty-six-year-old graduate of the Medical College of Virginia in Richmond, had begun his internship at Baptist Hospital only five days before. He was the first doctor to examine Smith. He cleaned the wound, covering it with a four-by-four dressing. Smith was not restless nor did he seem to be in much pain. He did not have labored breathing but remained unconscious, and Dr. Cox concluded that it was only a matter of time before he would die.

Outside, through the open swinging doors between the operating room and the alcove, Dr. Cox could see Libby slouched on the cot talking to Nurse Shore. She was no longer hysterical. The interns had not been told who the victim was and were naturally curious. They searched his clothes for identification. Dr. Cox found only three pennies and a box of matches in the young millionaire's pockets.

One thing struck him as very curious. No one but the doctors were permitted in the operating room, yet Ab, despite admonitions from Nurse Shore, hovered around the body of his stricken friend. Dr. Cox felt he was waiting to see if Smith would talk, but Smith said nothing at all.

Just before two in the morning, Dr. Fred Hanes arrived at Baptist Hospital. A member of the Hanes hosiery family, he was the dean of the School of Medicine at Duke University. Dr. Hanes had been asleep at his home in Winston when Nurse

Shore summoned him to the hospital. Assisted by two other doctors, he examined Smith for nearly an hour. Using a strong light, he was able to see that there was a contusion on Smith's right temple, a swelling he would later describe as "large as a small orange," with a puncture wound of the skin in the center. There was another puncture just behind his left ear. Despite the loss of blood, Smith was not given a blood transfusion; and Hanes decided that his condition was too critical to risk an operation. Smith was moved to a bed in a private room.

Libby, accompanied by Ab, was taken to Room 311. Miss Ruby Jenkins, the third-floor head nurse, walked in behind them, and Ab told her to leave. "I want to talk to Mrs. Reynolds alone," he said.

"Can't you talk to her with me in here?"

"No," said Ab. "I would rather you go out."

Miss Jenkins turned and left. She had not quite closed the door when she heard Ab say: "Don't talk, don't say anything. Don't say *anything* to *anybody*."

Nurse Shore had instructed Miss Jenkins to watch Libby carefully. Already, she had noticed, Libby and Ab were smoking and although it was against the rules, she did nothing about it. She sat at her desk outside Room 311. About ten minutes later, she heard a noise inside. Without knocking, Miss Jenkins entered the room.

Libby had fallen out of bed and Ab seemed to have fallen too. He lay on his back on the floor and Libby was sprawled on top of him. They were trying to get to their feet. Miss Jenkins helped Libby back to bed and exchanged her negligee for a white hospital gown. As she was leaving, Libby said, "Oh, my baby, my baby," and Ab said, "What do you mean by that?" He turned to Miss Jenkins again and shouted, "Will you *please* go out of the room." She began to close the door, but not before Libby said, "Don't you know that I'm going to have a baby?"

At Reynolda House, meanwhile, the ambulance had arrived, its driver annoyed that he had been summoned on a false alarm. Fulcher, who had just completed his one o'clock round, apologized. He didn't know who had called the ambulance. Fulcher had heard a car pull away moments before and assumed Smith had gone to town, as he often did, for a late snack. When the ambulance left, Fulcher became concerned. He telephoned Stuart Warnken, Reynolda's manager, and the two men decided to search the house. All the doors, both front and back were open. They turned off some of the downstairs lights, then went upstairs to the east wing. On the sleeping porch, the overhead light was on, but Fulcher used his flashlight anyway. "*Good night*," he said. "Look at the blood on the bed."

"*You* look at it," said Warnken. "I don't want to see it."

Remembering the shot he had heard, Fulcher searched all around the bed. He saw the pool of blood on the floor, but there was no gun.

Downstairs in the drawing room, the men discovered two bottles—a fifth with a little gin in it and a quart bottle with about half an inch of whiskey. There was also a gallon jar of corn liquor, about half empty, and four or five glasses with varying amounts of corn liquor in them. Fulcher found Libby's red-and-white lounging pajamas lying on the sofa. Why were madam's pajamas in the drawing room and not up in her bedroom where they belonged? he wondered. What in the world had been going on?

At Baptist Hospital, Ab Walker had telephoned Edward Lasater, Smith's guardian, and J. T. Barnes, Smith's cousin by marriage, both of whom arrived at the hospital within the hour. At three A.M., Barnes motored out to Reynolda. Stuart Warnken escorted him up to the sleeping porch and the two men searched the room. Again, there was no trace of a gun. Barnes returned to the hospital.

At three-thirty, Ab took Ed Lasater aside, telling him, in confidence, that he wanted to go to Reynolda before the police searched his bedroom—a statement he would not remember making later. J. T. Barnes drove Ab to the house. En route, Ab explained he wanted to retrieve Smith's wallet and, because it was Prohibition, he felt he should remove the corn liquor and whiskey glasses before anyone discovered them. Ab expected to find his weekly wages in Smith's wallet, but when he extracted it from behind a cushion on the sofa, it contained nothing but a few business cards. Barnes then informed Warnken that Smith had been shot. And again, Barnes, Warnken and Clint Wharton, the superintendent of Reynolda Estates, trooped upstairs to the sleeping porch. Ab followed them, turning in to his bedroom to change out of his bloody bathing suit. Warnken didn't want to enter the sleeping porch again, but Barnes and Wharton went in and for the third successive time, the gun could not be found.

The three men returned to the drawing room, leaving Ab in his bedroom. Ab remained upstairs alone for about fifteen minutes. When he came down, Warnken thought he was terribly nervous. Warnken drove Ab and Barnes back to Baptist Hospital. As they cruised down Reynolda Road, Barnes said, to no one in particular, "I wonder where the gun is?"

"It's up on the sleeping porch," said Ab. He did not know that the sleeping porch had been searched three times previously. Warnken and Barnes exchanged taut looks and said nothing.

At 5:25 that Wednesday morning, July 6, 1932, Smith Reynolds died without regaining consciousness. Minutes later, his cousin Robert Critz reported his death to the authorities—the medical certificate stating that he had died a suicide from a pistol wound.

Toward six o'clock, Dr. Fred Hanes chauffeured Libby and Blanche Yurka back to Reynolda House. Libby was given a heavy sedative and put to bed. Stuart Warnken told Hanes that the gun had still not been found. Hanes, Warnken, Wharton, Lasater and Barnes went up to the sleeping porch. It was not fully daylight, but the overhead light was still on and, as they entered the room, Wharton said: "*Here* it is." The little .32 caliber Mauser automatic was lying on the blue-bordered carpet about three feet from the bed and just in front of the door. Dr. Hanes had almost stepped on the gun, and concerned that someone might kick it accidentally, causing it to discharge, he picked it up. "I can take the clip out of it," suggested Warnken. "Maybe you'd better for safety," said Lasater, and Dr. Hanes handed it over to him. But Warnken was unable to remove the clip, and he laid the Mauser down on the dresser.

Ab Walker had been driven from Baptist Hospital to his parents' home on Country Club Road, where he changed his clothes and went to bed. Unable to sleep, he walked downstairs and, after telling his parents that Smith had died from a bullet wound, asked them not to pester him with questions. "There is just one thing I want to ask you," his father said, "to get it off my mind. Do they suspect you in any way?"

"No, sir," said Ab.

In response to his mother's anxious entreaties, he admitted only that when he first entered the sleeping porch, he had found Libby leaning over Smith's unconscious body, a statement he would later contradict. He refused to say anything more and, borrowing his mother's car, left hurriedly for Reynolda House. Walking into the drawing room, he was greeted by Bob Critz. Critz asked him what had really happened the night before. Ab was reluctant to talk and began to cry. "Ab, I don't believe you're telling everything you know," said Critz. Ab rubbed his eyes. He looked blankly at Critz and said: "Well, there is something I'm going to take to my grave." But he would not elaborate.

Earlier, Babe Vaught had been wakened by J. T. Barnes and Ed Lasater. Informed that Smith was dead, she was cautioned not to say a word to anyone concerning the events of the night before. Later that morning, however, Babe told her friend Hannah Williams that she and Libby had drunk too much and that they had gone swimming in the outdoor pool. She admitted to passing out. She had not heard the shot, she said, but she vaguely recalled muffled voices and scuffling outside her bedroom door.

Shortly before seven, Sheriff Transou Scott arrived at Reynolda House. The thirty-four-year-old Scott, a former tax collector, had been sheriff of Forsyth County for two years. Bootleggers and domestic disputes were his specialties. This was his first encounter with death and, secretly, he was thrilled. He began by questioning Ab Walker. But Ab was sullen and uncommunicative.

Ab was heeding the advice he had given Libby—not to say anything to anyone. And it was not difficult to evade the sheriff's clumsy interrogations. Ab insisted there was no question in his mind but that Smith had committed suicide, that he had been expecting it for a week or more. Smith had not actually said he was going to kill himself, but he had "talked around in that direction." When Scott asked why, Ab shrugged and said: "Well, the truth of the matter is, Smith just thought too much of that woman."

The Reynolds family had agreed to make a united stand. Everyone was instructed to say nothing to outsiders, particularly the press. That afternoon, Ed Lasater stated that all the evidence pointed to the fact that Smith had committed suicide, adding that members of the family were satisfied with the verdict. Dr. W. N. Dalton, the Forsyth County coroner, signed a certificate of suicide—which meant that an inquest into the matter could be held only at the request of a Reynolds family member or at the instigation of Sheriff Transou Scott.

A single statement was released to the press and it concerned the Reynolds family's favorite subject—money. A relative, James Dunn, claimed that Libby would probably inherit nothing from the Reynolds estate. R. J. Reynolds's will had made no provision for the husbands and wives of his children, he said.

That afternoon, Smith's body was removed from Baptist Hospital and transported to the Vogler Funeral Home in downtown Winston. After being embalmed, it was carried home to Reynolda in a gray casket covered in mauve orchids and a sheaf of Easter lilies.

W. N. "Will" Reynolds, Smith's uncle and chairman of the board of the Reynolds Tobacco Company, arrived in Winston by train from Cleveland that afternoon. Aboard the same train were Libby's parents and her older sister, Marion. At the Winston-Salem train station, Alfred Holman told a reporter from the *Journal* that he was utterly baffled by Smith's suicide. In his view, Smith and Libby were one of the happiest couples he had ever known.

Libby had been placed in the care of Dr. Wingate Johnson, the Reynolds family physician. Only Blanche Yurka, who claimed to be nursing her, was permitted to visit. But the next day, despite the protests of Sheriff Scott, Ab Walker was allowed to see Libby and they spent more than an hour alone in her bedroom. Already the amateurishness that was to plague the investigation was evident. Sheriff Scott complained that he was being treated as little more than a security guard.

That evening, Blanche Yurka and C. G. Hill went horseback riding on the grounds of Reynolda. They discussed Smith's death at length, and Hill later reported to Sheriff Scott that Blanche had said that no one would ever reveal precisely what had happened that evening. Blanche heatedly denied Hill's report. "That boy has the most vivid imagination of anyone I've ever met," she said.

20

SLICK SHEPHERD'S DADDY HAD TAUGHT HIM THAT JOUR-nalism was history in a hurry, tall tales told by men with jaundiced eyes and hangovers. Slick, who had drunk too many highballs the night before, now remembered his father's words. It was a wretched time for a hangover. Only minutes before, United Press, his new employers, had called with the news that Smith Reynolds was dead. Slick promptly telephoned Sheriff Scott and arranged an interview.

Because Slick had been born and raised in Winston and knew everyone who had attended the tragic party, he would prove invaluable to United Press. He had already been informed that he would not be writing the story himself, his superiors deeming it too important an event for an inexperienced stringer. Instead, they were sending down a man from Washington, their chief crime reporter, Morris De Haven Tracey. Slick was instructed to provide him with contacts, with local color and interviews.

Slick strolled west on Fourth Street. It was already over seventy degrees, too hot for haste. He passed E. E. Hailey's Electric Shoe Shop and Shine Parlor, Gus Polite's Candy Kitchen, the Amuzu Theatre and the Alpha Cafe. In the distance he could see the twenty-story Reynolds Tobacco Company Building looming high over the town and the surrounding Piedmont plateau. From its parapets, one could look over Winston-Salem's three hospitals, its two newspapers, its one hundred and twenty-seven churches, the homes of its hundred millionaires, the R. J. Reynolds High School and the R. J. Reynolds Memorial Auditorium.

Turning down Cherry Street, Slick entered the Carolinian Coffee Shoppe where he had arranged to meet Sheriff Transou Scott.

Over a breakfast of ham and grits and eggs, Scott admitted to a genuine puzzlement. "In every suicide case, there is a reason," he said. "And I can find none here. But neither have I evidence of anything else."

"It doesn't make sense," said Slick. "Smith'd never try and kill himself. *Jesus*, he wasn't even twenty-one."

"Ain't never gonna be neither," said Scott. "This thing's gonna blow the lid off Winston."

Scott felt there was something wrong. There were just too many loose ends and inconsistencies. If Smith had been in such high spirits, as his guardian claimed, why had he committed suicide? And however you looked at it, it seemed unlikely that a man would shoot himself in the upper right temple, up next to the hair line; it was an awkward place to point a gun. The fatal bullet had still not been found and why had there been no blood between the sleeping porch and the car? Why had Libby's pajamas been found in the drawing room? Where had she been all evening? Why had it taken four searches to discover the gun? And, most interesting, what secret did Ab Walker intend to take to his grave? It still rankled Scott that although Ab had been permitted to visit Libby, she was, officially, too distraught to be interviewed by him.

Sheriff Scott was determined to solve the case. After leaving Slick, he scheduled a coroner's inquest to be held at Reynolda the following day. Six male jurors were promptly chosen. Guarded by a detail of policemen, they were driven to Reynolda and, in almost military fashion, were marched to the side of Smith's casket—wherein, as the Winston-Salem *Journal* reported, lay "the mortal remains of a boy who flew through a short span of life on the wings of adventure." The jurors were sworn in before the casket, since, by North Carolina law, they had to take their oath in the presence of the corpse.

Reynolda House was crowded with Smith's friends and relatives come to attend his funeral. Moments before the minister spoke, Libby, dressed in mourning, approached the casket. She stood between her parents, her face in her hands. The brief service was conducted by Dr. D. Clay Lilly, a soft-spoken Presbyterian minister. When he referred to Smith as a daring young aviator, Libby began to cry, her body shaking. Following the service, the funeral party drove to Salem Cemetery. Libby seemed on the verge of collapse. In the back seat of the limousine, she slouched against her father's shoulder, sobbing inconsolably.

Smith was buried next to his parents with some five hundred mourners gathered at the grave. The pallbearers included C. G. Hill and Ab Walker. As the graveside obsequies were concluded, Ab fainted and, supported by two friends, was pushed into a waiting limousine.

Libby was driven back to Reynolda House where the coroner's inquest was scheduled to begin. Coroner Dalton had cunningly contrived to bar the press from the hearing, a ploy that was, strictly speaking, against the law in North Carolina. Not until later in the afternoon did reporters win a favorable ruling from the state attorney-general's office in Raleigh—too late, however, to attend the first day's proceedings.

Within days of Smith Reynolds's death, some thirty reporters had flooded into Winston-Salem. They had traveled from New York, Cincinnati, Atlanta, Chicago and Washington, from Raleigh, Charlotte and Greensboro. Two New York *Evening Journal* reporters arrived on William Randolph Hearst's Sikorsky amphibian. Fulton Lewis, Jr., of Universal Services had come by private railway car. Grace Robinson, who had made her reputation reporting the abduction of Charles Lindbergh's baby, flew into town for the New York *Daily News*. According to Miss Robinson, Smith's death, whether murder or suicide, was more poignant, more dramatic, gorged with more dark and complicated mysteries than even the Lindbergh kidnapping. Slick Shepherd went even further. It was, he claimed, the most sensational story in America.

21

T HE CORONER'S INQUEST WAS HELD IN LIBBY AND SMITH'S spacious second-floor bedroom in the east wing of Reynolda House on Friday, July 8. The bedroom contained a double bed with small marble tables on either side. There was a settee beneath the window on the far side of the room, a fireplace at the foot of the bed, flanked by louvered doors leading to the screened sleeping porch where Smith had been shot. Painted in subdued patrician colors, the bedroom had not been altered since it was first decorated some fifteen years before.

By ten-thirty in the morning, the room was crowded and fold-up chairs had been erected to accommodate the participants. The six jurors were present, as were the court stenographer, the coroner, and Erle McMichael, the Forsyth County assistant solicitor. The first witness to be called and sworn in was Dr. Fred Hanes.

Dr. Hanes, who had conducted an autopsy on Smith, began by describing the bloody sheet that had covered his body when he arrived at Baptist Hospital, and the contusion, "as large as a small orange," but he was to devote most of his testimony to describing the bullet's path through Smith's brain, concluding that it had entered through the right temple and had proceeded diagonally across the brain cavity to about two inches behind the left ear. Concerning the distance from which the gun had been fired, Hanes said somewhat ambiguously: "I should think it would be reasonable to conclude from the fact that the skin was so slightly powder-burned that the muzzle of the pistol must have been resting almost, if not quite, on the skin itself, or close to it."

Dr. Hanes completed his statement by saying that he and two other doctors had examined Libby and Ab Walker at the hospital

Libby's favorite photograph of herself
taken at the height of her fame—with
her wild raven hair and Clara Bow lips,
wearing an embroidered silk Chinese
pajama suit.

Group photograph of Elizabeth Hart Workum and all her grandchildren, taken in Cincinnati in 1912. Libby, who was named after her, sits at the extreme left cuddling a bald doll in a christening dress. Her younger brother, Alfred, Jr., is the boy in the front row, far right. Libby's sister, Marion, stands at the back, second from the left.

Libby as she appeared in the University of Cincinnati production *Fresh Paint*, in which she was described as "an aesthetic flapper."

Libby at twenty-five.

FROM THE CINCINNATIAN

Libby as she appeared in Vincent Youmans and Oscar
Hammerstein's *Rainbow* in 1928. Libby sang the hit song "I
Want a Man," but the show was not a success.

The torrid bedroom scene from *The Little Show* in which Libby introduced "Moanin' Low" — Clifton Webb as the "sweetback" or pimp and Libby as his whore. Note the bottle of Gordon's gin beneath the bed.

A few of the members of *The Little Show* on the boardwalk in Atlantic City in 1929. Libby is second from left and Clifton Webb is on her left.

Clifton Webb, Libby, and Fred Allen in a dance routine from the 1930 hit Broadway revue *Three's a Crowd,* in which Libby introduced "Body and Soul."

The thirty-nine-year-old Howard Dietz was almost singlehandedly responsible for launching Libby's career. He composed the lyrics of "Moanin' Low" and wrote a clever version of "Body and Soul," which Libby preferred to the original.

Miss Tallulah Bankhead, Libby's longtime friend and enemy, whose voice was described as "a mixture of British and Pickaninny."

Zachary Smith Reynolds at sixteen: "The Tobacco Prince."

Louisa Carpenter posing at an equestrian event in Wilmington shortly after she and Libby met in 1929. Louisa was partial to this dashing pose.

The nineteen-year-old Ab Walker photographed by Slick Shepherd in the courtyard behind the jail where he was being held as a material witness in the Smith Reynolds case.

Heavily veiled and clad in black, Libby sits in the Wentworth, North Carolina, courtroom. Sitting beside her and holding her hand is her father, Alfred, while standing beyond him is Libby's lawyer, Benet Polikoff, making his plea for a reasonable bail.

Frank Spencer of the Winston-Salem *Journal* and R. H. "Slick" Shepherd who covered the Smith Reynolds tragedy for U.P.

The main drawing room of Reynolda House, Smith Reynolds's stately home on the outskirts of Winston-Salem. It was along the gallery above that Smith's unconscious body was carried en route to Baptist Hospital.

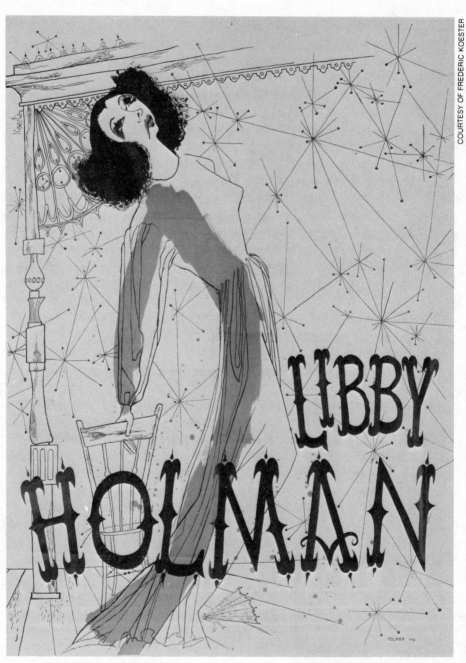

Libby's most dramatic portrait
fashioned by Fred Koester in Paris in
1950 for her one-woman show called
"Blues, Ballads, and Sin-Songs."

and held the opinion that both of them had been under the influence of alcohol—"to a rather marked degree."

Ab Walker was the next witness. Because he had just returned from Smith's funeral, he wore a black morning suit. His brown hair was closely cropped and parted in the middle. He looked older than nineteen, but his eyes were bright and childlike. As Ab took the stand, he appeared at ease; when Erle McMichael questioned him, however, he began to bite his fingernails, his responses were garbled and he repeated himself continually.

Ab denied that he had been drunk that night. He swore that he had had only a highball and a bottle of beer, that he had been "practically dead sober." He claimed not to have heard the pistol shot and said he had never seen the gun. He could not remember telling Ed Lasater that he had to get back to Reynolda House before the police searched his room—in the end, denying he had ever said such a thing. Nor could he recall, when answering J. T. Barnes's query as to where the gun was, that he had said it was upstairs on the sleeping porch.

When McMichael asked what secret he intended taking to his grave, Ab replied, "I don't know why I said that." McMichael interrogated him for nearly an hour, but Ab either evaded his questions or claimed he was unable to describe the events of that night with any real accuracy. "I remember these incidents," he said, "but don't remember the order they came in from here on hardly. I can't get them straight in my mind."

And then, oddly, before dismissing Ab, McMichael asked him a final question. "Did you know Mrs. Reynolds was a Jewess?" he said.

"No, sir."

"When did you find out?"

"I never knew she was a Jewess."

"Did you ever hear Smith express his opinion, or make any statement in regard to people of the Hebrew race?"

"No, sir."

"Did you know he had a very peculiar opinion about them?"

"No, sir."

"On Sunday night when he talked to you at the hotel, didn't he tell you he had just learned that Mrs. Reynolds was a Jewess?"

"No, sir."

* * *

The next witness was Blanche Yurka and a hush settled over the bedroom as she sat down. Erle McMichael questioned her and like Ab, Blanche dissembled also.

She claimed that Libby and Smith had had "the most beautiful companionship" she had ever seen, that she had seldom witnessed "two young people who seemed to have such a community of interests." To the best of her knowledge, Libby and Ab had been perfectly sober that evening. Libby, in fact, had been her usual self—"a very charming hostess." And it had been quite clear to her, Blanche volunteered, that Smith had committed suicide "on some utterly unexplainable impulse."

On only two points did Blanche's testimony differ from Ab's. Ab had insisted that when Blanche asked him if he hadn't heard screams, he had rushed up the stairs where he met Libby on the gallery. But Blanche stated that when she asked Ab if he had not heard screams, Ab had rushed upstairs to the gallery, where they both heard Libby calling Ab's name, and Ab had then raced down the hall to the sleeping porch. Blanche next saw Ab and Libby carrying Smith's body. But Ab had first gone to the sleeping porch. On that point, Blanche was positive. And Blanche had not seen Ab call for an ambulance; she had not even known one was called till later. Blanche was certain of that and said so over and over again. It seemed clear that if Ab had called for an ambulance, he had done so at another time. But if McMichael noticed these discrepancies, he failed to pursue them further.

The final witness to be called that afternoon was Libby. Because she was too distraught to leave her bed, the six members of the coroner's jury adjourned to her bedroom, bunching around the bed. Propped by a bank of white pillows, Libby wore a pale negligee. Her father sat beside her holding her hand. She was questioned by the Forsyth County solicitor, Carlisle Higgins, who had been too involved with a conspiracy case to appear at the hearing earlier.

The forty-four-year-old Higgins had been appointed solicitor two years before. A small and wiry man, he was reputed to be one of the best shots in North Carolina. Because of an accident while chopping wood, he had lost his right eye and now wore one made of glass. Higgins was inexperienced, but he got on with his business briskly.

"On last Tuesday, Tuesday of this week," he asked, "did you spend the entire day here?"

Libby began to speak, but her words were vague and incoherent. Her eyes were half closed, and if any of those present anticipated startling revelations, they were almost immediately disappointed.

"I spent the entire day here," Libby mumbled, "but I don't remember . . ."

"You don't remember Tuesday, the day of the party at all?"

"No."

"You don't remember anything you did?"

"No."

"Do you remember what you did on Monday previously?"

"Yes, that was the Fourth of July. I remember everything I did."

"You were feeling all right when you went to bed on Monday night?"

"Yes."

"You do not recall getting up, waking up Tuesday?"

"No, I don't remember any of that day. The last thing I remember is Monday night."

"So that you have no recollection at all of anything that happened after you went to bed Monday night until when?"

"The next thing I remember, and it is just a flash, is hearing my name called and looking up and seeing Smith with the revolver at his head, and then a shot, and after that I don't remember anything."

"Can you account in any way for the fact that you do not remember anything that took place on Tuesday?"

"No."

"You didn't take any medicine of any kind on Monday?"

"No, I don't think so. I never do."

"You didn't drink anything on Monday?"

"No."

"And the only recollection you have of Tuesday is a flash of your husband with the pistol?"

"That is the only clear thing."

"You and your husband had never had any differences?"

"We were terribly happy."

"You never had any differences at all? I mean by that, you never had any disputes?"

"No, no big ones at all."

"So far as you know, he was happy?"

"I *know* he was."

"Did you ever have prior to that, in your life, a day that was blank?"

"No, I never have, but I have never had a shock before."

"You don't remember the party?"

"No."

"Do you remember hearing a shot?"

"I remember the pistol to his head and the shot. I can't hear the shot now, but I remember, I don't know what it was. It was just, oh, I don't know. It was just like a crash."

"Do you remember anything after that?"

"No, I do not."

Higgins paused. "How old are you please, ma'am?"

"Twenty-six," said Libby, remembering her new age with remarkable facility. "Father said to tell you the feeling I had afterwards," she added. "It wasn't a mental picture or anything particularly clear after the flash . . . but I have this feeling that Smitty was in my arms and I felt this blood, but it is a haze, it is blurred."

It was nearly ten in the evening and Libby was too exhausted to continue. Therefore, Carlisle Higgins announced that the inquest would resume the next morning at nine. The first day's interrogations had proved inconclusive and, already, rumor and speculation ran rampant in the town. Sheriff Scott had found the shell of the bullet that had killed Smith, but the bullet itself had somehow disappeared. He hoped the resumption of questioning would help clarify the matter. But he was pessimistic.

That the inquest was not free from the suspicion that Smith had been murdered was indicated in a statement issued by Carlisle Higgins that evening. "We will determine tomorrow whether young Reynolds was right- or left-handed," he said. "If left-handed, then we will have a curious case, for he was shot in such a manner that, if he did it, he must have been right-handed." Higgins, in fact, suspected foul play. There had been entirely too much shuffling and dodging at the inquest for his satisfaction, too much "confounded poppycock."

The day's major surprise was saved till last. In an informal statement, Assistant Solicitor McMichael announced that Libby and Ab would be held as material witnesses, pending an investigation into the mysterious death of Smith Reynolds. The charge, however, did not imply suspicion of guilt, he said.

When notified of this, Libby became hysterical and was confined to her bedroom. Blanche Yurka was also ordered to remain at Reynolda House subject to call. Ab Walker was taken into custody and incarcerated in the county jail. At the insistence of Smith's two sisters, however, arrangements were made for him to spend the night in the more congenial surroundings of the Robert E. Lee Hotel.

Late that evening, Slick Shepherd managed to reach Alfred Holman by telephone at Reynolda House, but Holman was unexpansive. The detention of Libby had disturbed him deeply. "Are you a father?" Holman asked. When Slick admitted he was childless, Holman said: "Then I can't explain my feelings to you." He hung up.

Having won a ruling to attend the next day's inquest, the press corps assembled in a suite in the Robert E. Lee Hotel, affecting a gruff and edgy jubilance. Among them were staffers and stringers from AP, UP, Universal Services, the International News Service, the Cincinnati *Post*, the New York *Times*, the New York *Evening Journal*, the New York *Daily Mirror*, the New York *Daily News* and most of the major North Carolina papers. Concurring with the sentiments expressed in a Greensboro *News* editorial—"An unexplained corpse, whether of prince or pauper, is not a private matter"—they looked forward to the proceedings with the rapacity of hungry hounds who have been deprived of sustenance too long.

22

THE CORONER'S INQUEST WAS RECONVENED ON SATURDAY, July 9, in Smith and Libby's bedroom. Some twenty-five reporters were present, including Slick Shepherd who sat toward the back of the room with Morris De Haven Tracey. Both Western Union and Postal Telegraph had installed emergency telegraphic stations, and messenger boys were put at the newsmen's disposal.

From the beginning, Slick sensed that the two provincial prosecutors were incompetents. A crafty politician, Carlisle Higgins was an inept and unimaginative solicitor. Erle McMichael at least, was well intentioned, but a blunt and plodding man. When Ab Walker was recalled, Slick watched him spar with McMichael, slipping around his interrogations with surprising ease. Ab, Slick knew, was rough as pig iron and had never been able to get around anyone, yet he treated McMichael like a bantamweight.

In his testimony of the day before, Ab claimed that while Libby was sitting on a settee out on the gallery, he had found Smith on the bed and had raced downstairs to call an ambulance. Today, however, he altered his story, stating that when he had gone downstairs to make the call, he had left Libby on the sleeping porch with Smith's unconscious body. It was a crucial contradiction, but Erle McMichael failed to detect it. After an hour, Ab was dismissed for the second time.

An interminable parade of witnesses followed Ab to the stand. Stuart Warnken testified that he had searched the sleeping porch on two occasions and was unable to find a gun. He pointed out that Ab was the only person to have been left alone upstairs and that, during the ensuing search, the gun was lying in plain view on the floor.

Clint Wharton testified that he had made a meticulous examination of the house, discovering blood smears on the bathroom door of Smith and Libby's bedroom. Someone had attempted to wash them off with a bathroom towel.

Sheriff Transou Scott stated that he had found pieces of the fatal bullet on the sleeping porch. Given the placement of the cartridge and fragments of the bullet and what appeared to be the path of the bullet's exit through the sleeping-porch screen, Scott deduced that Smith must have been on Libby's side of the bed, either sitting or reclining when the gun was fired. And yet Libby claimed that Smith was standing, which, given the bullet's trajectory, seemed an impossibility.

J. T. Barnes claimed that Ab had not been surprised at Smith's suicide. Smith had intended to kill himself the night he and Ab stayed at the Robert E. Lee Hotel, but Ab had talked him out of it. According to Barnes, Ab felt that Smith wanted to kill himself because he loved Libby too deeply, that he had to watch her too carefully, that she worried him all the time.

Babe Vaught confessed, with some indignation, that she had been perfectly sober that evening, and that she had always intended to spend the night. She was a heavy sleeper and consequently had heard no disturbances—no scufflings beyond her door, no shot, no screams.

Deputy Sheriff H. A. Harris was then called to the stand. Having guarded Ab at the Robert E. Lee the night before, he testified that Ab had said, "I don't give a damn what they do to me, just so they take care of Mrs. Reynolds." Erle McMichael neglected to ask the deputy what Ab had meant by that.

An adjournment to Monday was now deemed necessary in order to investigate new evidence—the bloody fingerprints and smears found in the bathroom next to the sleeping porch. Once again, Libby and Ab were placed in custody. Libby was permitted to remain in her bedroom at Reynolda, a deputy sheriff outside her door, but Ab was transferred to the Forsyth County jail. The Reynolds family felt that Libby should have been jailed as well, but her delicate condition, it seemed, prevented that from happening. Libby, however, had recovered sufficiently to rail at the monstrous indignities she claimed to have suffered. The deputy sheriff, a genial southerner, took the brunt of Libby's Yankee invective, the likes of which he had never heard before.

*　　*　　*

By Monday morning, July 11, every person known to have been in the house at the time of the tragedy had been fingerprinted. R. G. Simpson, the fingerprint expert of the Winston-Salem Police Department, had developed photographs of the bloody prints on the bathroom door, but was unable to discern whether they had been made by a man or a woman. He was having similar problems with the fingerprints on Smith's Mauser; just too many people had handled it and the prints were smudged beyond recognition.

The coroner's inquest was resumed that afternoon in the ornate wood-paneled library of Reynolda House. Solicitor Carlisle Higgins conducted the questioning and, for the most part, covered familiar ground. His interrogations were long and tedious and, if the witnesses' facile answers were any indication, predictable. All the guests who had attended the barbecue were questioned and claimed that nothing untoward had happened, that no one had drunk excessively, that Libby and Smith had seemed perfectly content. They all concurred that Smith was not insane and had never suffered from moods or from any form of inferiority complex. In short, he had been a robust and gallant southern boy.

The most conspicuous prevarications were told by Slick's first cousin, Jim Shepherd. Shepherd explained that he and Babe Vaught had taken a ride shortly after dark, that Libby had not come with them, and that they had returned to the house before midnight. He was not asked why he had taken a two-hour drive in the midst of a party, where he had gone, or even why he had returned. Shepherd admitted being in the house from approximately 11:45 to 12:45, yet claimed not to have seen Libby return nor to have heard any portion of Smith and Libby's loud altercations in Ab's bedroom. It was a lame and faltering account, but Shepherd was never seriously challenged by Higgins and, after only twenty minutes on the stand, he was dismissed.

Slick had listened to his cousin's testimony with mounting astonishment. Only once had Shepherd seemed about to tell the truth. When asked precisely when he had left Reynolda, Shepherd said that he had been asked to spend the night, that Ab Walker had been quite insistent he remain, but he was expected at Charlie Norfleet's house and it was too late to call and cancel the plan. At that point, he was interrupted by Erle McMichael and thereafter became increasingly evasive.

The next day, Slick dropped by Shepherd's art shop on Fourth Street and, after discussing the case, Shepherd asked, "Do you believe I told the truth at the inquest?"

"Hell, no," said Slick. "You lied through your teeth and everyone knows it."

Jim Shepherd did not speak to Slick again for nearly thirty years.

During the late afternoon, in response to a signal from Coroner Dalton, Libby appeared wraithlike in the double doorway of the library, flanked by two nurses. She wore a sheer white negligee, sandals, no stockings, and her black unruly hair was partially tamed by a narrow white-silk ribbon. She could have walked directly to the witness chair. Instead, she moved slowly to the western end of the library where the afternoon sun shone through the windows, pausing briefly between the bright streaming light and the group of gaping reporters. "God, what an *actress,*" said Slick to Morris De Haven Tracey. "What a *figure,*" said Tracey. Only then did she walk to the witness chair.

Libby's eyes were swollen from weeping. Her deep tan was accentuated by the billowing white of her negligee. She cast a swift frightened glance at the strange faces of the jurors and reporters banked around her and began to sob in the low throaty voice that had brought her fame. Her mother and her sister, Marion, occupied seats at her side. Marion held Libby's hand, and Rachel fanned her forehead with a fashion magazine.

Alfred Holman, now acting as Libby's legal counsel, stepped forward and said to Carlisle Higgins: "You may ask my daughter any questions that would undertake to throw light on this mystery. I mean, I don't want you to consider Mrs. Reynolds at all." But Holman reserved the right to interrupt should he deem the questions objectionable. Throughout the next two and a half hours, Libby's testimony was broken by frequent bursts of sobbing—her mother pressing smelling salts upon her while Marion kneaded her hands.

"Mrs. Reynolds," said Carlisle Higgins, "it may be necessary for me to ask you some of the questions I asked you about on Saturday. I will try to avoid as many of them as possible."

Libby then recounted her first meeting with Smith, their courtship, and subsequent marriage. Higgins seemed particularly interested in her relationship with Ab Walker prior to her marriage, but Libby claimed that it had been purely casual. She spoke at length of Smith's obsession with guns and the number of times he had threatened suicide.

"Did you ever tell your people or his people anything about his conduct with a gun?" said Higgins.

"No, I wouldn't tell anybody," said Libby. "I was happy. I was terribly happy. It was only those moments. I knew it was a mood of Smith's and didn't want to go get sympathy from other people. We used to discuss those moods when he would come out of them and he would say, 'I know it. I make you unhappy. I can't help it.' I said, 'Those moments of unhappiness don't balance or even compare to the moments of happiness I have with you. I'm glad to be with you.' And he said, 'I have never seen you unhappy before we were married, never seen you crying.' And I said, 'I am only crying because you are unhappy.'"

"If it was a disease of the mind, as you seem to indicate," said Higgins, "how do you explain the fact that it manifests itself only in your presence and not in the presence of anyone else?"

"Because I knew Smith."

"Was he a jealous man?"

"He wasn't jealous of a soul because he always knew where I was."

"Now, last Tuesday, you do not remember anything that happened?"

"I have tried to reconstruct it, backward and forward, and I will swear I cannot remember one thing. And I would give anything in my life to remember."

"You don't remember being at the party at all?"

"I don't remember the party."

"Or anything that occurred?"

"That one memory is the only clear thing in my mind. And I have thought of it over and over and remembered what they told me I did and tried to picture it and the only picture I have in my mind is Smith standing over me. I don't even know where it happened, don't know where I was sleeping, but know wherever I was sleeping was where it happened, because I do remember the flash of Smith standing up with the gun at his head . . . first, my name being called, and then my waking out of the sleep and Smith with the gun at his head, and then that crash of the universe, just everything falling around me, and then feeling, I don't remember, a series of pictures, of him lying in my arms and the warm blood running over me and that is the only thing I have any recollection of."

"And then, you don't remember anything at all?"

"No, but I knew he was brooding on this before . . . and there was another thing that worried him terribly, that he told me . . ."

At this point, Libby lost all of her composure and began to sob, putting her fingers to her mouth, blubbering hysterically. Her mother dropped to her knees and placed her head in Libby's lap, attempting vainly to console her.

"It was on Monday night," she finally said, "after we had gone to bed, and it happened on Sunday too. That he tried to have physical contact with me and he couldn't and that worried him so much and I tried to comfort him and told him it was all right, that it didn't make any difference to me, and he said, 'No, I have read books and doctor's statistics say that women get irritable and can't do without that, and I want you to go out and have an affair with another man. Just don't tell me who it is.'" As Libby paused, the reporters jerked up their heads from their scribblings and waved frantically for the telegraph boys. Slick Shepherd couldn't believe his ears.

"And I said," continued Libby, "'I never would touch another man except you.' Then he said, 'I will have to do something to break up our marriage if you don't do that.' And I said, 'I couldn't ever in my life, no matter what happened to you, ever touch anyone else and I won't. That is a very little part of our love. The rest of our love is so big and great that it doesn't make any difference.'"

Libby paused and then said: "I just wanted to prove to him that I loved him, to save him from any danger he might inflict on himself . . . and that is true. *God*, that is true. He knows it."

During this long and operatic dirge, it could be seen that the jurors, at least, were not entirely unsympathetic, since two of them were now in tears. Libby seemed on the verge of collapse. She began to speak again, then broke into sobs and said, "Oh, such agony, oh, *God*."

"Buck up," said her father, stroking Libby's arm. "I can't bear it for you. I wish I could."

Libby then broke down completely and Carlisle Higgins dismissed her. Supported by her mother and father, she stumbled across the library. A hush fell over the room. No one spoke or moved. Only Slick Shepherd, who thought that Libby had given a remarkable performance, grabbed his notes and dashed outside to the telephone.

Coroner Dalton announced that the testimony was closed. The six jurors and the two prosecutors conferred and agreed to recess. It was six-thirty. They decided to reconvene at the courthouse, and the jurors retired to deliberate their verdict.

_____ **23** _____

MORE THAN TWO HUNDRED PEOPLE GATHERED OUTSIDE THE Forsyth County Courthouse to await the verdict that evening. Still under guard, Libby remained at Reynolda, but Alfred Holman mingled with the courthouse crowd. He anticipated a swift acquittal and wanted to be the first to bring his daughter the joyous news.

Toward midnight, after deliberating for more than five hours, the jurors finally reached a decision—concluding that Smith Reynolds had met his death "from a bullet wound inflicted by a party or parties unknown." The vagueness of the verdict left the fatal shooting open to official investigation; but it had legally excluded Smith Reynolds from being the unknown person, and automatically freed Libby and Ab Walker as material witnesses.

"The coroner's jury," said Carlisle Higgins, "composed of honorable men, have heard all the testimony and considered it carefully. They are not satisfied and, according to their verdict, do not know how Smith Reynolds met his death.

"At this time," he continued, "we have no additional information. We have presented to the jury all the evidence we had and unless something additional is discovered, I know of no reason why the solicitor's office will make any further move in this case. However, the grand jury, acting on their own initiative, have the right to make an investigation and submit a presentment of it if they feel in their judgment such an action is proper."

The next day, the grand jury decided to take no action. Legally, this left the case temporarily closed, but the way remained open for any subsequent grand jury to investigate the mystery. The next grand jury in Forsyth County, however, was not scheduled to convene until July 25—some two weeks hence.

Sheriff Transou Scott may not have been an imaginative sleuth, but he was obstinate. "So far as I and my office are concerned," he said, "this investigation is not closed. No case is closed so long as it remains an unsolved mystery."

There were just too many puzzlements for his satisfaction. The fatal bullet had still not been found. Why had Ab Walker told Ed Lasater that he had to get back to Reynolda House before the police searched his room? Why had he called for an ambulance and then, without waiting for it to arrive, driven Smith to the hospital? In the ten-minute interval between the time he said he had called the ambulance and when he reached the hospital, Ab had gone upstairs, carried Smith's cumbersome body back down and driven four miles to Baptist Hospital. Scott himself had made the drive at forty miles an hour and it had taken him seven minutes. It seemed to Scott that Ab had not had time to do all he claimed to have done.

Scott also knew that someone had removed the gun and smeared the fingerprints, before returning the gun to the sleeping porch. Someone had tried to wash the blood from the bathroom door. And why had there been no blood between the sleeping porch and the car? Had Smith, in fact, been carried that way? Again and again, Scott wondered where Libby had gone for nearly three hours during the party. He did not believe she suffered from some profound, if temporary, form of amnesia. It had still not been ascertained whether Smith was right- or left-handed. His tutor said that Smith had written with his right hand, but Smith's shooting friends assured authorities that he had always shot a gun with his left hand. One of them, George Orr, remembered this vividly, because Smith had been the only southpaw shot he had ever seen. These and numerous other puzzles continued to perplex the hapless sheriff. But he believed he would unravel them eventually. He needed only time and a little assistance from his laggardly superiors.

In Manhattan, the finer points of the case were not debated. It was, quite simply, a scandal. The tabloids were glutted with lurid tales of Libby and Smith Reynolds, a few of them implying that Libby, or someone, had murdered him. One of the chief offenders was Bernarr MacFadden's *Evening Graphic*, which rival newspapermen called the Porno-Graphic. The *Graphic* was published on faded pink paper, and its headlines, normally concerned with sex orgies and love-nest raids, were bigger and blacker than those of any other New York tabloid. MacFadden believed that "sex was the sirloin steak of true living," and his paper painstakingly reflected that philosophy.

Libby's theatrical friends supported her. Clifton Webb was outraged. "To call Libby a murderer," he said, "is as ridiculous as calling Lucretia Borgia a loving wife." Howard Dietz assured the *Daily News* that Libby was nearsighted and could not distinguish objects two feet away. "I don't think she could hit herself," he added. Tallulah Bankhead dismissed the rumors that Libby had shot Smith as "balderdash." Privately, however, she told her sister, Eugenia: "Darling, *of course* she did it. It was the only way to get Blanche Yurka out of the house."

Nothing more prejudiced Libby's case than the twenty-seven-part series that appeared in the New York *Daily Mirror*. The *Mirror* accused Libby of being haughty and tactless, of wearing mannish attire, of being a heavy drinker and attending mad midnight revels, of being a sensuous sex pirate, a red hot mama, an iceberg of disdain.

The series began: "Libby Holman's life story is one of poignant drama—of bittersweet. Of the shabby genteel, she fought her way, tooth and nail, to the pinnacle of Broadway with success as the most famous torch singer. . . . She isn't a genius, this Libby Holman. Indeed not. She's just a rather plump little Jewish widow, sophisticated, a rival for Clara Bow in sex appeal, yet retaining an air of charming girlishness; an actress of great enthusiasm, but not much talent. . . . Lucky professionally; in private life a child of tragedy and toy of fate. Intelligent, well-educated, cultured, yet strangely apathetic to that very culture and given to sympathizing with the Negro race, the mimicry of which brought her to the threshhold of fame and fortune. A queer creature of mixed emotions, the stark primitive emotions of a jungle girl, ranging from fulsome love to bitter hate, from kindness to cruelty. . . . Feted by the rich, applauded by the lowly, she hated men, yet she was capable of passionate love: As a little Cinderella out of the Middle West, she captivated Prince Charming, but their fairy tale of romance was blighted by murder—or was it suicide? All the facts will be laid before you. It is a thriller. Don't miss it."

Yellow journalism had not yet come to Winston-Salem, but extravagant theories as to how Smith actually died abounded. Most of the press corps believed there had been a coverup at the inquest, that those who attended the party had lied intentionally or by omission. Slick Shepherd was convinced of that, but what, he wondered, had they lied about? In Winston, particularly among the monied classes, it was customary for everyone to rally round when adversity affected one of their own. And so Virginia Dunklee, who admitted nothing at the inquest, subsequently told one of her friends that Libby and Smith had had a violent argument that night and that Libby had threatened to leave.

Other, more byzantine, suppositions circulated through Winston: Coroner Dalton claimed that he had received reports of a marital rift between Libby and Smith, instigated by the fact that Smith had only recently learned that Libby was of Jewish blood. This revelation, Dalton implied, would have had a profound effect on the proud southern boy. . . . Smith had been shot somewhere else in the house and then carried to his bedroom. Only then had Libby and Ab realized the seriousness of his wound and rushed him to Baptist Hospital. . . . Smith, bored with his marriage, had cabled his brother, Dick, then sailing off the western coast of Africa, that he wished to join him immediately. . . . The argument flared when Smith surprised Libby in a compromising position with Ab in Ab's bedroom. . . . Smith and Ab were homosexuals. When Smith saw Libby kissing Ab, he killed himself, not because he was jealous of Libby, but because he was jealous of Ab. . . . Smith was violently jealous of Libby's relationship with Louisa Carpenter. Libby refused to relinquish Louisa and it was this that precipitated Smith's death.

The evidence presented at the inquest troubled one other person also. Dr. Alexander Cox had been the first physician to examine Smith on his arrival at Baptist Hospital. And yet he was never interviewed by the press, he was not questioned by the police, nor was he asked to testify. In direct contradiction to the evidence presented by Dr. Fred Hanes, Dr. Cox insisted that Smith had not been wrapped in a bloody sheet on the operating table; in fact, there had been very little blood. There had not been a contusion the size of a small orange on his right temple and there had been no powder burns. Nor, he claimed, was the entrance wound on the right side of Smith's head. On the contrary, the wound ran like a tunnel straight through his head from left to right. Moreover, it was not the wound of a suicide—"unless Smith was taking target practice at a distance of more than eighteen inches from his head."

But few of these theories and contradictions reached the ears of the prosecutors; nor would they have heeded them. As far as Carlisle Higgins and Erle McMichael were concerned, the Smith Reynolds case was closed.

Libby was now at liberty to leave Winston-Salem. Her father intended to transport her to a peaceful place where she might recuperate. He would not reveal their destination. To all and sundry, Alfred Holman insisted his daughter was innocent and that the death of his son-in-law was an obvious case of suicide. He deplored the invidious suspicions created by the coroner's inquest.

On July 12, six days after Smith had died, Libby, accompanied by her father, her mother and her sister, vacated Reynolda House. Driven by Joe, the Reynolds' burly black chauffeur, they went first to Salem Cemetery, where Libby placed a bouquet of lilies on her husband's grave. Then the Holman family was driven to the Winston-Salem railway station in order to catch the 3:25 train bound north for Cincinnati.

More than a hundred people had gathered to witness Libby's departure. Braving a battery of photographers and some twenty reporters, Libby walked across the train platform. She was dressed entirely in black and wore a fur neckpiece, which she used to shield her face from the cameras. Supported by her mother and father, Libby shook convulsively, moaning, "This is terrible. This is terrible."

Libby had felt stultified in North Carolina—marooned too long in alien surroundings. She despised the Reynolds family, knowing also that they despised her because she was Jewish and because they believed she had married Smith for his money. For the rest of her life, Libby referred to Winston-Salem as "the hick town that tried to lynch me." She told her father she would never return.

Libby boarded the Norfolk and Western train and moments later it pulled away from the station. Libby looked forward to going home. Behind her, there remained an unsolved death and the inevitable backlash of local rancor and indignation.

24

THE NORFOLK AND WESTERN TRAIN SQUEAKED AND HISSED to a stop at the little hamlet of Clare, Ohio, a few miles south of Cincinnati. A white-coated porter promptly brushed the dust from the exterior handles of the Pullman door, placed his stool on the platform and waited.

During the overnight journey, Libby had remained in her private compartment and was not seen by the three reporters who had boarded the train in Winston. She and Marion spent most of the trip playing cards. Only Alfred Holman talked to the reporters and, in his desire to protect Libby, seemed both irascible and apologetic. He explained that Libby was not interested in rumors and suspicions. Her real concern was that the world should understand she had felt a great and genuine love for young Reynolds and that it should not be sullied.

In Clare, the rest of Libby's family rushed onto the platform to greet her—her younger brother, Alfred, her brother-in-law, Myron Kahn, and his young son. Libby stepped down to the platform, shielding her face from three photographers. Her father escorted her into a waiting limousine. The Holman clan was driven to Marion's home in Wyoming, a pretty tree-studded town, then some twelve miles north of Cincinnati.

As the car pulled away, an inquisitive scribe crept into Libby's train compartment and found in her crumpled bed an English novel entitled *Sleeveless Errand*, purporting to be a tale of sophisticated modern youth, of incessant rounds of dissipation, with a tragic climax: The beautiful heroine, "her passionate idealism bruised by the harsh realities of life," drives herself over a cliff. Inside the book, the reporter found a newspaper cutting—stating that Broadway, "which looks on life as merely a play," would be only too happy to welcome Libby Holman home.

Libby had been expected to remain at Marion's home for at least a fortnight, but on July 14, the day after she arrived, Louisa Carpenter's black Cadillac pulled up behind the little house; Libby slipped in and the two friends drove away. There was an encampment of photographers, reporters and a Movietone News crew at the front of the house. Discovering that Libby had bolted, they banged on the front door until it was opened by Libby's brother, Alfred. Alfred explained that Libby had been taken to a friend's cabin in the country. He discounted suggestions that Smith had been murdered. "The manner in which my sister's husband died is obvious," he said. "Libby's account of his suicide is the only true version." The youth seemed to believe that Libby actually had a version.

On July 18, Dick Reynolds secretly returned to Winston-Salem and concealed himself in the apartment of his lawyer, Stratton Coyner. For the past month, he had been sailing in his yacht off the western coast of Africa. Two days later, a laundry-supply salesman telephoned Slick Shepherd to tell him he had just been to the Zinzendorf laundry, where one of the salesgirls, noticing Dick's initials on his dirty shirts, had informed him that Reynolds was back in town. His address was on the laundry receipt.

Slick drove over to Stratton Coyner's apartment and banged on the door. Dick Reynolds finally let him in. The two old friends discussed Smith's death and Reynolds admitted he knew very little about it. "As of now, I am unable to form an opinion as to the cause of death," he said. "Naturally, I will insist on the sternest punishment for the miscreant if I find my brother was the victim of a foul deed. But I do not believe that Smith in-

tentionally took his own life." On that point, Dick Reynolds was
never to change his mind.

Because of Reynolds's instigation, a grand jury was finally
summoned in Winston-Salem for the purposes of investigating
Smith's death. Sheriff Scott was jubilant. For more than two
weeks, he had insisted that Smith's death was an unsolved
murder. His colleagues ignored him, but Scott had pressed
obstinately ahead—a tack that earned him the sobriquet "the
lone wolf."

"I am ready for the grand jury," he announced. "I have
positive evidence that Smith Reynolds did not kill himself, and
other evidence that was not available to the coroner's jury."
Then he added, cryptically: "There was a Broadway background
to the crime."

Sheriff Scott was now informed that Libby had disappeared.
He promptly cabled police departments in the Midwest and up
and down the eastern coast requesting her immediate apprehen-
sion. On July 26, Scott's investigations elicited an impassioned
outburst from Alfred Holman.

"Mrs. Smith Reynolds has not disappeared," Holman stated
in an open telegram. "She is available anytime the cause of justice demands, and her shattered mind and nerves permit. The
plain physical facts surrounding the death of Mr. Reynolds have
incontrovertibly established his self-destruction—sought now to
be overcome by zealous functionaries; such zeal must be attributed to self-seeking motives, ignoring every canon of decency
and right and humanism and justice. But, so was Jesus Christ
crucified and Jeanne d'Arc burned."

Libby, the irate attorney pointed out, had gone into seclusion
"from the morbidly curious, so that she may recover her sanity
and health, conceivably overcome by the grief over the loss of
her loved one and by the horrors to which she has been sub-
jected in an inquisition equaled only by those in the Middle
Ages."

Alfred Holman's florid exhortation did little more than anger
southern sensibilities, and in Winston-Salem there was a predictable wave of animosity. Coroner Dalton said that it was not the
policy of his office to persecute witnesses and that Libby had
been shown the utmost courtesy and consideration. Sheriff Scott

claimed he had done nothing more or less than his bounden duty—rather less, in fact, since he had failed to interview her. The Winston-Salem *Journal* concluded a long and passionate editorial by observing: "The truth is, the telegram of Mr. Holman's did not help the public satisfy its own mind with regard to the mysterious case. The father of Mrs. Reynolds protests too much. His unexpected outburst not only arouses resentment here, but suspicion."

On July 25, Judge Amos Stack charged the Forsyth County grand jury to investigate the Reynolds case without fear or favor. "It is hard for a solicitor to convict the rich," Judge Stack declaimed from the bench. "'Big Ikes' beat the law all too frequently and the law gives them every advantage. Those who do not fear the law know it is feebly enforced, that crime is not revealed, that they can leave the state. If you know of any offense that has been committed in this county, it is your duty to bring forth a presentment."

Two days after the grand jury convened, it was still not possible to ascertain what action it intended to take. During a brief recess, members of the jury shrugged and looked away when asked if the Smith Reynolds case had been discussed. Dozens of reporters and photographers skulked outside the closed door of the grand-jury room. Slick Shepherd sat there for nearly a week reading cheap thrillers and biding his time. He dogged the jury members everywhere—to coffee breaks at O'Hanlon's Drug Store, to lunch at the Alpha Cafe, to drinks and dinner at the Piccadilly Grill—for fear they would reach a verdict in his absence. Among his colleagues, the betting was five to one that Libby and Ab would be charged with murder, but not in the first degree.

On August 4, at 3:55 in the afternoon, the jurors filed into the Forsyth County courtroom and presented their bills to Judge Stack. As reporters, photographers and curious townsfolk milled impatiently in the rear of the room, the judge adjusted his bifocals and read the indictment.

"The Grand Jury do present," Judge Stack said solemnly, "that Albert Walker and Libby Holman Reynolds did unlawfully, willingly, feloniously, and premeditatedly of malicious aforethought, kill and murder one Z. Smith Reynolds."

By North Carolina law, this wording permitted a verdict of murder in the first degree, punishable by death in the electric chair. As reporters scurried to their telephones, the judge ruled that Libby and Ab would be detained without bail and warrants were issued for their arrest. Sheriff Scott admitted he did not know where Libby was, but that Ab would be arrested immediately.

That evening, Scott telephoned the police in Hamilton County, Ohio, requesting the prompt arrest of Libby. When Sheriff Joseph Shaefer arrived at the Holman home, Alfred Holman refused to disclose his daughter's whereabouts. "My daughter is in seclusion in the country," he said, "in bed under the care of a doctor and a nurse." He would surrender her at the proper time, adding "I will not give out any information on a frame-up."

25

KNOWING THAT LIBBY AND LOUISA CARPENTER WERE CLOSE friends, Sheriff Scott dispatched a request for Libby's arrest to Newcastle County authorities in Wilmington, Delaware. Once apprehended, Libby would be placed in the Forsyth County jail, he said. She would receive no favors. The jail contained a special section for women prisoners and if the singer was ill, as she claimed to be, she would be incarcerated in the hospital ward. Despite being sought by the police of North Carolina, Ohio and Delaware, however, Libby could not be found.

On August 5, Alfred Holman left Cincinnati for Winston, where, hoping to spare Libby the ignominy of confinement while awaiting trial, he intended to seek bond. After registering at the Robert E. Lee Hotel, the sixty-four-year-old lawyer led a group of newspapermen and town idlers to the limestone Forsyth County Courthouse. He walked up to the second-floor courtroom and asked for Solicitor Carlisle Higgins. "I want to

see if bail can't be arranged for my daughter," he said. "I understand that it can be done in extraordinary cases and I can convince anyone, I believe, that this case is extraordinary, because of
the delicate condition of my girl." Higgins curtly informed him
that his office had no intention of making a deal. "I will introduce you to the court," he said, "and that is all I intend to do."

Alfred Holman knew now that he had strayed into enemy
territory and decided to arm himself with local ammunition.
That evening, he retained as counsel William Graves, widely regarded as the finest criminal lawyer in North Carolina. He also
retained Benet Polikoff, Erle McMichael's law partner. Polikoff,
a burly man possessing great dignity and charm, was to become a
major influence on Libby's life and one of her closest friends.

From Aiken, South Carolina, Polikoff had moved his law
practice to Winston five years before, and was one of only two
Jewish lawyers in town. His given name was Benjamin, which he
had changed to Benet during college. He had also changed his
birth date from April to May because, in his experience, it had
always rained in April. Polikoff liked to say that it never rained
on his birthday again.

Polikoff and Graves contended that Alfred Holman was not
attempting to defy North Carolina law by shielding Libby. Given
her frail condition, he was doing all he could to make it more
comfortable for her and the merits of that argument should be
taken into consideration. The Forsyth County prosecutors ignored it.

While Libby remained at liberty, Ab Walker languished in the
red-brick county jail. Sheriff Scott claimed he had not been favored in any way, except to have his meals sent in from the Robert E. Lee. Given the quality of the hotel's cuisine, it was not
considered an extravagant concession. Reporters were not permitted to see him. Ab would not be able to tell them any more
than he had already done, his lawyer said.

Ab made one exception. Having known Slick Shepherd for so
many years, he consented to be interviewed and photographed
by Slick in the tiny courtyard behind the jail. Ab, dressed in a
dark suit and tie, was pleased to see Slick and accepted his offer
of a pack of Lucky Strikes. He agreed to tell Slick everything he
knew but, from the outset, gave an impression of muddled igno-
rance. "Some of the things I don't remember," said Ab. "I can't
get the sequence right."

"How was Smith shot?" said Slick.

"Can't rightly say," said Ab. "I wasn't up there."

Ab assured Slick that he had had nothing to do with Smith's death. He smiled when he was photographed and expressed what seemed a genuine desire to have the matter cleared up as quickly as possible. Slick told Ab he thought he was lying and, again, Ab smiled.

The next day, Ab's lawyers argued that the state did not have sufficient evidence to support a charge of first-degree murder, and after much deliberation, the court concurred. Walker was allowed a bond of $25,000, which his father paid, and he was set free. But Carlisle Higgins made it perfectly clear that the action had no bearing on the case against Libby, since, as Higgins said, "She is not in court."

Immediately afterward, Alfred Holman announced that Libby would surrender not later than Tuesday or Wednesday of the following week. He did not say where she was or how she intended to travel to Winston-Salem. Sheriff Scott thought Holman rather too high-handed for his liking, and admitted his frustration. Despite his far-flung investigations, Libby seemed to have disappeared. "I have no right notion where the lady is," he said. "She could be in an igloo in Africa for all I know."

That afternoon, while crossing Winston's courthouse square, Slick Shepherd encountered the tall, slender, bespectacled Alfred Holman. Holman sported a pale slouch fedora, which he doffed as Slick walked by. He seemed unusually affable and the two men exchanged humdrum pleasantries, sauntering up Fourth Street to St. Paul's Episcopal Church and into Cherry Street, walking toward the Robert E. Lee. It was a hot, muggy afternoon and Slick suggested they drop into Bobbitt's Drug Store for a Dr. Pepper.

Unexpectedly, Holman chuckled and said, "Aren't you a newspaperman?" When Slick admitted as much, Holman grinned and said, "Young man, you haven't asked me a single question about my daughter or the Reynolds case."

"Well, I reckon you've been asked every question on God's green earth," Slick said, "and if you had something important to say, you'd say so."

Slick never understood why Alfred Holman had singled him out that afternoon and was astonished at the nature of his confession. Taking the young reporter by the arm, Holman steered him to a nearby booth. "God's truth," said Holman, holding up his hand. "It was confirmed about an hour ago. My daughter is an expectant mother. She's two months pregnant." Slick almost dropped his Dr. Pepper.

"You're *sure*?" he asked.

Holman nodded. "You can do what you want with this," he said, "but I'm going to be hard to find."

"So am I," said Slick, "just as soon as I phone this in."

The wily Holman had divulged this news for his own and Libby's good. He knew the North Carolina courts had previously ruled (purely hypothetically) that if Libby had been pregnant, her child would be heir to half of Smith's estate. The courts were explicit on that point—stating that a child conceived during the existence of the marriage relationship, and born after the death of the father, inherited the same as if the father were alive. That child was presumed to be legitimate and the burden of proof would be upon anyone claiming to the contrary.

Holman confirmed Slick's exclusive story that evening to reporters: "I came to Winston-Salem today," he said, "in the hope that I might be able to arrange bond for my daughter's appearance here at such a time as the court might direct and thereby spare my daughter the discomfort of an arduous journey in her present condition. She is still suffering from shock and is an expectant mother. She will not require that the State of North Carolina request her extradition. She will voluntarily surrender to North Carolina and submit to the jurisdiction of the court in the full confidence that she will receive a fair and impartial trial."

The statement was cunningly veiled, extravagantly detached. Even so, Holman knew that it would shock the Reynolds family—loath, as they were, to part with any portion of Smith's estate—and that they would not surrender without a long and complicated legal battle. But Holman relished a struggle. He would enjoy bringing the Reynolds family to heel.

26

THE DU PONTS WERE UNQUESTIONABLY THE RICHEST INDUS-
trial family in America. In 1932, the family had been in the
country for one hundred and thirty-three years, and as they
accrued their wealth, they built vast family estates. Nemours,
outside Wilmington, was constructed of white marble with sev-
enty-seven rooms and three hundred landscaped acres, enclosed
by a nine-foot wall which Alfred du Pont, its builder, claimed
was necessary to repel intruders—"mainly in the name du Pont."
Nemours was surpassed only by Winterthur in New Castle
County, Delaware, an imposing castle of more than a hundred
rooms.

These were only two of more than twenty Du Pont properties
and it was to one of these estates, Montchanin, just outside
Wilmington, that Louisa Carpenter had brought Libby in July;
but even Montchanin had become too conspicuous for a woman
on the run, and it was subsequently decided to move Libby to a
more secluded hideaway.

Louisa Carpenter assigned Bill Broadwater to conceal Libby
from the police and the press. Broadwater, the chief engineer on
Louisa's father's yacht, *The Galaxy*, was part Cherokee and had
worked for the Carpenters since 1924. Born and raised on the
Elk River in the tiny fishing village of Port Herman, Broadwater
knew every creek and cranny in the northern Chesapeake.

He decided to take Libby to Benton Farm, a 346-acre property hidden in the brushy thickets along the Bohemia River in
northern Delaware. A hard slag road snaked down to the farm,
but it was remote, the nearest hamlet more than four miles distant. The sole house on the estate was Benton Lodge, which sat
on a ridge overlooking the Bohemia River. Built of white cedar
logs, it was ninety-six feet long, with huge stone fireplaces at either end of the living room. The Carpenters called it "the cabin."

But even this retreat was not considered safe enough and Libby was shuttled across Chesapeake Bay to Oakington in Maryland to the sprawling estate of Leonard Richards, Jr., a vice-president of the Atlas Powder Company (a Du Pont subsidiary) and a family friend of the Carpenters.

Because of police and reporters in the surrounding area, Libby was advised to vacate Oakington by day, and so, early each morning, Bill Broadwater picked her up in his boat, ferrying her back across the bay to Benton Lodge. During the three weeks of her concealment, while the combined forces of Ohio, North Carolina, Delaware and Maryland searched fruitlessly for her, Libby enjoyed herself, and Louisa Carpenter, flushed with the prospects of a genuine manhunt, thought it little more than a spirited, conspiratorial game.

Occasionally, Libby received visitors. Her mother and father came to Benton Lodge and there were official visits from Benet Polikoff. On one of Polikoff's trips, Louisa invited him to lunch. She then picked up her shotgun and went out on the deck overlooking the marshy Bohemia River. Polikoff heard two shots, and minutes later Louisa returned with a brace of mallards in her hand.

Libby spent most of her time with Bill Broadwater. Broadwater's speedboat, the *Oh, My*, a twenty-eight-foot Sea Lion, could cruise at forty-two knots. During late July and early August, Libby and Broadwater fished and sailed, picnicked and sunbathed on Pool's Island and at Hone's Point, secluded spots where no visitor ever came, or plied the backwaters of Chesapeake Bay.

On August 5, Benet Polikoff informed Libby that Ab Walker had been freed on bail and it was probable, he said, that a similar freedom awaited her. To that end, he had arranged a bond hearing for Libby two days hence in the little town of Wentworth, North Carolina. Libby, however, would have to devise a scheme of reaching Wentworth without being arrested en route. Libby and Louisa made immediate plans—envisaging the trip as an extremely dangerous military mission, but one not beyond their capabilities. The rest of the day, therefore, was devoted to the reading of maps, to tactics and strategy.

Shortly before midnight, they slipped out of Benton Lodge and down to the Bohemia River where the *Oh, My* was moored.

Despite the August heat, Louisa wore a mink coat, in the pockets of which she had placed $25,000 in cash to cover Libby's bond. They sped across the river. On the opposite bank, Louisa had parked her black Cadillac and the two friends headed south, driving through the night. In the morning, concealing the car in a remote Virginia wood near Bachelors Hall, they took turns sleeping.

Toward dusk on August 7, they rode triumphantly into the tobacco manufacturing town of Reidsville, North Carolina, eight miles from Wentworth. Checking into the Belvedere Hotel, they were greeted by Libby's father and younger brother, who congratulated the girls on what everyone agreed had been a splendid and successful escapade. With a flourish, Alfred Holman signed the hotel register—"Arthur Knapp and Guests"—and following a celebratory supper, they retired to their respective rooms.

27

THE NEXT DAY, ALFRED HOLMAN ANNOUNCED THAT LIBBY would surrender to Forsyth County police in Wentworth that afternoon. Wentworth had been selected for the bond hearing because Amos Stack, the circuit judge of the 11th District, resided there for the month of August. Wentworth had no railroad, no telegraph facilities and only one telephone line. A rowdy little farming community of less than eighty people, there were often more townsfolk in the jail than on the streets on Saturday nights.

At two-thirty, Libby left the Belvedere Hotel for Wentworth. Louisa elected to remain behind. Libby wore widow's weeds—a black felt turban, over which she had draped a long black mourning veil; a tight-fitting black crepe gown with satin trimming; black kid gloves and black satin pumps. The outfit was so opaque that it was almost impossible to distinguish the person within. As Libby climbed into her limousine, four or five of the town sports wagered trifling sums as to whether she would obtain bail.

She arrived at the Wentworth postmaster's residence on the main road just before three o'clock. While dozens of cameras clicked, she was helped from the car by her physician and a police officer, and went inside. After a brief interval, Benet Polikoff emerged from the house and announced that the warrant had been served. Officially, Libby was now under arrest.

A festive crowd of nearly five hundred people gathered outside the red-brick courthouse across the road. It was the most exciting event that had ever happened in Wentworth. Knowing that for miles around the country folk would come, the ladies of the district church had constructed a makeshift soft-drinks stand, above which a banner waved with the misspelled announcement: "Churc Benefit." Straw-hatted farmers were offering up to five dollars for seats inside the courthouse. Seventeen-year-old Dalton McMichael hawked copies of the local paper and would make a profit of ten dollars that hot afternoon. Other enterprising youths sold ice cream, grape juice and watermelons from the back of an old wagon; and Joe Rakestraw's general store did a booming trade in Brunswick stew.

Shortly after three, Libby walked to the courthouse, which sat on a grassy knoll some fifty yards across the road. Her lawyers, a physician and two constables bunched around, attempting to shield her from the unruly crowd. Photographers ducked and darted in her path, and near the courthouse steps, a Movietone News van began to film. As Libby approached, Slick Shepherd moved toward her, but was pushed aside by a burly farmer who wanted, he said, a closer look at "the Yankee hussy." But Libby's black veil concealed her features. As she ascended the courthouse steps, her head bowed, giggling farmers' wives screamed, "*There* she is, *there* she is," and Jack Simmons, a local high-school English teacher, shouted: "What an actress!"

Libby entered the courtroom and Judge Amos Stack rose gallantly. He seemed unable to keep his eyes off Libby's legs. Libby was seated within the bar—her father on her left, her physician, Dr. Cummings, on her right. She sat with her head resting on her right hand, her elbow on the arm of the chair; and aware, perhaps, of Judge Stack's reputation for lechery, she crossed her legs repeatedly.

The wood-paneled courtroom was overcrowded. Even the balcony was full. Again and again, Judge Stack called for silence. Finally, Carlisle Higgins rose to make his opening statement. "The solicitor of the state," he said, in his rapid mountain twang, "is of the opinion that the state is not in possession of sufficient evidence to support a premeditated charge." That being the case, Higgins said he would offer no objection to a reasonable bond. Libby turned to look at her father, surprised the bond had been granted so easily. But Higgins added: "I want it understood that I may reverse this stand and accuse the defendant of murder in the first degree when she is brought to trial."

Benet Polikoff then rose and, although he had Louisa's $25,000 in hand, he pleaded for a small bond of $10,000. The estate of Libby's father, he said, could not be valued at more than that. As for Libby, she had nothing except her potential earning capacity. Polikoff denied that Libby had run away from the murder indictment; she had given herself up voluntarily and had never intended to do otherwise.

"For there is no escape even if she desired to get away," he said. "Where could Libby Holman go without being recognized? She could not take six steps in the streets of New York or San Francisco without at least a dozen people following her." Polikoff paused. "Your Honor," he said, "a shot was fired and the body of the man she loved fell across her. When that shot was fired, Libby Holman was carrying in her body the child of that husband whom she loved. She wants to be tried as soon as her delicate condition will permit."

Listening to Polikoff's unexpected emotional outburst, Libby sat quietly. Occasionally, she raised a white handkerchief beneath her veil to her eyes. The following day, a local reporter described her as "a slim young Madonna of Sorrow in the dark role of widowhood." Judge Stack then asked if the amount of the bond fixed for Ab Walker, $25,000, was satisfactory, and, reluctantly, Polikoff agreed.

Libby rose and, leaning heavily on her father and her brother, walked haltingly to the Judge's bench. Judge Stack gave her his chair. Amid flaring flashbulbs, Libby signed the bond, swearing solemnly that she would return to North Carolina for trial.

A few minutes later, Libby left the courtroom, a free woman. As she descended the courthouse steps, a great cry rose from the assembled crowd. A black Cadillac sedan drew up and Libby and her relatives got in. The car moved slowly through the throng, many of whom screamed abuse and shook their fists in the air. An ancient farmer in a large straw hat complained: "Does seem to me we should have saw her face."

Slick Shepherd jumped into his Plymouth and drove hurriedly to Reidsville, overtaking Libby's Cadillac sedan on the way. Given her impenetrable disguise, Morris Tracey had instructed Slick to ascertain whether the woman behind the veil was really Libby Holman. Slick waited in front of the Belvedere Hotel, obstructing Libby's path. When she arrived, fully expecting to be slapped, Slick reached forward and lifted the veil. "Are you satisfied?" asked Libby. Slick grinned and moved aside, asking if she would agree to be interviewed. Alfred Holman refused. When Slick repeated his request, Holman retorted: *"Res ipsa loquitur."* Then, noting the look of incomprehension on Slick's face, he smiled and said: "Events speak for themselves."

That evening, Libby, her father, her brother and Louisa Carpenter dined in Louisa's suite on the second floor of the hotel. Alfred Holman had told reporters that Libby would remain in Reidsville for a day or two. But shortly after two in the morning, Libby and Louisa left the hotel. Louisa wore a dark suit and tie, her blond hair lifted up beneath a dark felt homburg. Gone now were Libby's widow's weeds. In their stead, she wore a natty white sports outfit, a white beret and gold-rimmed spectacles. The night clerk, who saw them leave, claimed Libby had skipped across the lobby, that she had seemed like a carefree college girl.

The next day's newspapers described Libby's companion as a mysterious blond youth, a wealthy admirer, heir to one of Ohio's great fortunes, who had sought to marry Libby before she yielded to the suit of Smith Reynolds. Now, attentive as ever, he had placed his fortune at Libby's disposal. The New York *Daily News* predicted that if this report was true, an epic battle between northern and southern millions would ensue. It was believed that the Reynolds family intended to aid the state with needed funds; and now Libby had her champion. How Libby and Louisa must have laughed as they drove north toward Montchanin. For once, all the reports had been accurate, except that Libby's wealthy admirer was a twenty-five-year-old woman.

Libby's immediate concern was the protection of her unborn child. "Libby wants a trial before the baby is born," said Benet Polikoff. "She wants vindication as soon as possible." But a trial date had still not been set. And Polikoff announced that he would resist any move to try Libby in Forsyth County since local prejudice would not permit the selection of an impartial jury.

On August 23, eleven weeks to the day after Smith had been buried, his embalmed corpse was secretly exhumed for the purposes of an autopsy. The court order had been signed by Carlisle Higgins in order to determine "the course of the bullet which caused his death, and which of the two wounds was the one of entrance and which was the wound of exit of the bullet, and also to determine whether the gun shot wound was fired with the muzzle of the pistol in contact with or very near the head, or whether same was fired with the weapon at some distance therefrom, and also the course and angle of the bullet through the brain, and the undersigned being advised that such post mortem will disclose these facts which are material as bearing upon the guilt or the innocence of the persons accused."

The autopsy was performed by W. N. Dalton, the county coroner; a Dr. T. C. Redfern; and Drs. Fred Hanes, Wingate Johnson and Arthur Valk—all three of whom had conducted a postmortem on Smith the night he died. Although prominent in their own fields, none of them was a pathologist or medical examiner. It was an astonishing procedure, since it implied that they had not examined Smith's body before, or that they were belatedly searching for evidence overlooked in their initial examination. Moreover, it supported Dr. Alex Cox's contention that Dr. Hanes's testimony at the inquest had been vague, equivocal or incorrect.

All persons connected with the autopsy were sworn to secrecy and not until September 1 did Carlisle Higgins admit that it had taken place, claiming that the findings fully confirmed Dr. Hanes's previous testimony. Higgins announced that the bullet that had killed Smith was fired "at *close range*, entering the right temple and, after coursing through the brain, emerged from the head behind the left ear."

At the time, the autopsy report was not questioned; but one fact was overwhelmingly clear, and rather than confirming Dr.

Hanes's previous testimony, it blatantly contradicted it. "Close range" did not mean that the barrel of the gun had been placed in contact with Smith's head, and it might reasonably have been interpreted as meaning any distance between three inches and three feet from the head. Again, this supported Dr. Cox's belief that Smith's wound had not been that of a suicide.

Three weeks passed. On September 24, Libby made her first, and what would prove to be her only, public statement concerning the death of Smith. She gave an exclusive interview to her old friend Ward Morehouse, a columnist for the New York *Sun*. Libby invited Morehouse down to Montchanin, where, in the company of Louisa Carpenter, she spoke to him of her trials and tribulations. Her account, calculated to curry public sympathy, was mawkish, effusive and, on the whole, improbable. As Libby talked, she knitted tiny pink garments for her unborn child.

"It's knowing that I'm going to give birth to the child of the man I loved that affords me my only gleam of happiness," she said, "that gives me any desire to live at all. The fact that within four months I will have a child, *his* child, makes me strong enough to fight for a complete and absolute vindication.

"I didn't shoot Smith Reynolds. God in heaven knows that. The Reynolds family know it in their hearts. I loved Smith as I never loved anyone before or will ever love again. The fullest and richest hours of my life were spent with that dear boy. I loved him tenderly and dearly and completely and to him I meant everything, everything. He was utterly dependent on me. When I realized that he was gone . . . I didn't want to live. My life was over. . . . And now I want to go through with the rial. I want no strings left, no doubts left in people's minds as to my innocence. I don't want only acquittal. I want a complete apology.

"I've got to be cheerful," she said, "for it's the only way. But it's the waiting that's hard. If the trial were tonight, right now, it would be easier. I'd just stand up and tell the truth. If they didn't believe me, they'd just have to go ahead and hang me.

"If I'd been in the state of North Carolina the day of that indictment, they'd have jammed me into a patrol car. The whole thing's been a terrible prostitution of justice, and the one man who could defend me, Smith Reynolds, is gone. . . . My baby will be named Smith, of course, boy or girl. That's to be the name."

Libby didn't know where she would live when the child was born. "Not Cincinnati," she said, "not the South. Maybe in France. I feel like a woman without a country. But tell Broadway I'm not weakening. Tell them it's my fight and I'm game. I can take it."

28

THE TRIAL OF LIBBY AND AB WALKER WAS FINALLY SCHEDuled for November 21, 1932. Despite her jaunty air of optimism, Libby dreaded the ordeal, knowing that in North Carolina at least, her guilt was a foregone conclusion.

Then, on October 18, a bizarre letter, written by Will Reynolds, Smith's legal guardian and chairman of the Executive Committee of the Reynolds Tobacco Company, arrived in the offices of Solicitor Carlisle Higgins. In polite, executive prose, the letter urged Higgins to abandon the case.

Dear Mr. Higgins,
    Ever since the death of my nephew, Smith Reynolds, I have been very interested in and have given very careful attention to everything I could learn about that tragic occurrence. Knowing Smith as I did and realizing the many fine traits of character he had, I am convinced that his attitude toward life was such that he would not have intentionally shot himself. Nothing I have been able to learn about the case has been sufficient to change my opinion.
    But it is true in my mind and in that of Smith's brother and sisters that the evidence fails to prove conclusively that Smith was murdered. I realize that the matter of handling these indictments rests officially in your hands as the representative of the State and that no individual has or ought to have anything to do with the question of whether these cases are prosecuted or dropped.

But there has been a great deal of curiosity and speculation as to what the attitude of Smith's family is toward these cases. With that fact in mind, I am taking the liberty of writing this letter to disclose that attitude and to say to you that if, in the discharge of your official duties, you deem it right and fair and in the public interest that the case be dropped, then the action will evoke no open criticism from me or other members of Smith's family.

In fact, under the circumstances, we would be quite happy if it should be your decision to drop the case. Distressed as we are over Smith's unfortunate death, none of us could find any pleasure in a prosecution not fully justified by the circumstances of his death. I am taking the liberty of sending a copy of this letter to Judge Stack for his information.

With personal regards,
W. N. Reynolds

There was considerable speculation in Winston as to why the Reynolds family now believed that the prosecution of Libby and Ab was not in their best interests. Despite Will Reynolds's conciliatory tone, the letter sounded like an ultimatum. Carlisle Higgins said that he would give it careful consideration but claimed not to know what action he would eventually pursue.

Both Libby's and Ab's lawyers thought the letter even-tempered and fairminded, the only possible conclusion Reynolds could have drawn after examining the evidence. But when Benet Polikoff read it to Libby, she was outraged. "I want this accusation against me cleared permanently, not temporarily," she shouted. "I am entitled to complete exoneration. I don't want that. I won't stand for it. It isn't justice. I am innocent and they know it." She demanded trial by jury. "That's exactly what I want," she said, "and nothing less will do."

Dick Reynolds agreed with his uncle's decision but added: "I have stated that I did not believe that my brother committed suicide and I'm still of the same opinion. His death might have been accidental. I believe that a lengthy trial with the evidence now available would accomplish nothing toward clearing up the mystery and would only result in undue hardship for the accused and heartaches for all concerned. The whole truth of what happened that night at Reynolda House will probably never be known."

THE MILLIONAIRE · 171

Three weeks later, on November 12, Carlisle Higgins announced he was now thoroughly satisfied that there was not sufficient evidence "to justify the state in going to trial."

"It therefore becomes my duty to determine what course the state shall pursue," he said, "and like any other question of human judgment, there might be an error of judgment. In determining the course I should pursue, I have decided that if I make a mistake it will be the one that leaves the way open for its correction hereafter. If the defendants are not guilty, the least the state can do now is to stop the prosecution. If they are guilty, then the door should not be closed to prosecution should sufficient evidence to justify it be available at any time hereafter." Thus, Higgins issued a nolle prosequi with leave—which meant that the case was temporarily closed but could be reopened at any time.

Two days later, the state of North Carolina formally dropped murder charges against Libby and Ab Walker. Judge Amos Stack directed that a nolle prosequi be entered in the record on the petition of Solicitor Higgins. "It is the duty of the solicitor," he said, "to protect the innocent as well as to prosecute the guilty and it is my custom to abide by the solicitor's wishes in such cases, since I do not investigate the evidence. Mr. Clerk," said the judge, "let the defendants be discharged and their bonds released."

In 1932, the Reynolds family wielded enormous influence in North Carolina. What they wanted, they tended to get. As head of the Reynolds clan, Will Reynolds did not want the trial to take place. Even before writing to Carlisle Higgins, Reynolds had taken the solicitor aside and told him he was satisfied there was not enough evidence to warrant a trial, and Higgins was persuaded. Young and inexperienced, Higgins was also an ambitious man (he eventually became a justice in the state supreme court), and it would have been politically unwise to have disagreed with Will Reynolds.

At the time, many people believed that a deal had been struck between the Reynolds and the Du Pont families, that in order to avert a trial, large sums had exchanged hands. But that seemed pointless and improbable. Besides, it was not Will Reynolds's way.

Will Reynolds was a profoundly conservative man, ultimately

concerned with the Reynolds family image, and anxious that it should not be sullied. He disliked publicity. He loathed scandal. And nothing now would bring Smith back. Will Reynolds did not believe that Smith had committed suicide. Much later, he confided to a friend that no Reynolds had *ever* committed suicide. Rather, he believed there had been a tragic accident, and based on numerous conversations with Ab Walker, he didn't want the unsavory details surrounding that accident made public. There had been too much squalid talk of suicide, shooting, drinking and impotence already. It would not do. It was bad for the family and, more important, it was bad for business.

There was also the delicate problem of Libby's pregnancy. Will Reynolds may have disapproved of Libby; he certainly disapproved of the widespread rumors in Winston that her unborn child was not Smith's at all but Ab Walker's. Following his conversations with Ab, however, he seemed convinced that the child was Smith's; and, if that was true, it had now become a Reynolds matter. For all these reasons, a public inquisition was unthinkable.

Libby had been proved neither innocent nor guilty and, contrary to her earlier demands, now seemed content with the state's decision. She would make no plans until after the child was born, expressing a wish that she be left alone, to live in privacy. "This writes *finis* to this chapter in the life of Mrs. Reynolds," said Benet Polikoff.

29

I T WAS A NEAT AND CONVENIENT SUMMATION. BUT BENET Polikoff could not have been more wrong. The death of Smith Reynolds would haunt Libby for the rest of her days. Like some mysterious, untreatable disease, it would infect her life and her career, and almost everyone who came to know her—friends, acquaintances, new husbands, lovers—were more than passingly curious to know what had actually happened on that summer night in 1932; and invariably, Libby tailored her tale to suit her audience.

The history of that night will always remain obscure, ambiguous, since everyone in a position to explain the facts intentionally lied about them. Over the years, however, whenever Libby spun her whimsical deceptions, she usually told more than she meant to, and almost as much as she knew.

To begin with, there was the public and the private Libby. The two masks rarely coincided and Libby herself often seemed unaware of the contradiction. Publicly, she spoke, as she felt compelled to do, of her rapturous love for Smith. But she harbored other, truer feelings. As time passed, Libby told trusted intimates that she had never loved Smith, that she had liked him considerably at first, had been flattered by his wealth, his insistent court, and that, finally, she had been seduced by what she called his boyish blandishments. Years later, Libby would tell a friend: "It's a tragedy that a woman has to undergo so much before she realizes that half the affection she feels for a man is maternal." Concerning her marriage, Libby would always believe that it had been folly for both of them, though for Libby at least, it had not been fatal.

The marriage elicited and emphasized all their mutual apprehensions. Smith feared Libby would return to the stage, that he would somehow be abandoned. He feared her witty homosexual friends, and may have believed that Libby's warmest, her most genuine affections, were being diverted by Louisa Carpenter. Finally, he feared his own personal inadequacies. His impotency, however erratic, weighed heavily on his already morbid mind, and two days before he died, he insisted that Libby conduct an affair with another man.

Libby, in turn, feared Smith's obsession with guns, his accelerating threats of suicide. She was older, stronger, more dominant than Smith and must have seen herself as little more than the elder statesman of their convoluted intrigue. And, finally, the country gentry bored her. After only five weeks in North Carolina, Libby had become increasingly morose—a sophisticate, compelled to participate, even to enjoy, the rural rough-and-tumble of teenaged boys. Such then, was the emotional background of their brief marriage as that innocent Fourth of July weekend began.

*   *   *

Libby testified that Smith had tried, unsuccessfully, to make love to her on at least two occasions in the week preceding his death; and there were probably other instances. As a result of this, they had argued violently. During the course of the party, they remained moodily apart. No one remembered them speaking at all. The first visible sign of conflict occurred when Smith berated Libby for cavorting indelicately with Babe Vaught. But even before then, it must have been obvious to the other guests that Smith and Libby were scrapping.

Shortly thereafter, Libby drunkenly flirted with Ab Walker, kissing him, though Ab was to deny this later. Smith then walked Libby back to the house and she disappeared. Libby was gone for nearly three hours. It is most unlikely that she passed out or simply wandered about the dark wooded grounds. She had some purpose, some destination, however slight or frivolous. All the other guests were accounted for that night, except for Jim Shepherd and Babe Vaught, who disappeared for about the same period of time. They later claimed to have gone for a ride in Babe's car, and Libby probably accompanied them. About midnight, they returned, depositing Libby outside. All the guests had now gone home and Shepherd took Babe, who was drunk, upstairs to bed.

At 12:20, Libby was discovered by Fulcher, the night watchman, walking drunkenly up the road and into the rear yard. She was then escorted into the house by Smith and Ab. Jim Shepherd awaited them. There seems no plausible reason why Shepherd should have denied seeing Libby, as he did at the inquest, but the next morning, Libby's red-and-white flannel lounging pajamas were found on the sofa in the drawing room. Following a custom she had adopted long before, Libby must have disrobed in front of the three men. She was drunk. She may have been taunting Smith or teasing Ab or simply showing off. Whatever her reasons, Libby stepped out of her pajamas and Smith angrily propelled her upstairs.

Jim Shepherd, a self-professed southern gentleman, would have considered it an indecent, embarrassing act and, rather than admit to having witnessed it, claimed he was not even there. While Smith and Libby were upstairs, Ab and Shepherd walked into the kitchen and, minutes later, Shepherd left, taking Ab's car.

At this point, Blanche Yurka, who had been wakened by their voices below in the kitchen, came downstairs and asked Ab where everyone had gone. Ab told her they had gone home. Blanche returned to her bedroom in the west wing, where, again, she fell asleep.

Ab now heard Libby and Smith upstairs in his bedroom arguing loudly, an event he would later confide to Virginia Dunklee. Libby had doffed the rest of her clothes and Smith was enraged—his jealousies and frustrations, Libby's drinking, her flirtation with Ab, her disappearance, undressing in front of his friends—how could he not have been? But Libby had just begun. It was at this point that she must have told Smith that she had missed her last period, nearly two weeks before, that she was almost certainly pregnant. It would have been the final blow. Given Smith's history of impotence, he must have wondered who the real father was. They continued to argue and Smith, now berserk, either summoned Ab from below or Ab came up independently. He had certainly not spent his time locking up the house, as he maintained, since Fulcher subsequently found all the downstairs doors open.

Now, at nearly 12:45, Libby, Smith and Ab moved down the hall to the sleeping porch. Their argument continued. Smith was incensed and inconsolable. Having put on her peach-colored negligee, Libby lay down on the bed. Smith then extracted his automatic Mauser from the marble side table and, lurching round to Libby's side of the bed, sat down, and threatened to kill himself. Libby was drunk. She may have lost her temper. Perhaps she goaded Smith, urging him to finish it at last. Perhaps she grabbed for the little gun. More probably, Ab did, wrenching it from Smith's hand; but Smith fought desperately, and the Mauser, which had a hair trigger, discharged, striking Smith in the head.

It didn't seem to be a serious wound. Ab fetched a towel from the bathroom and attempted to stem the flow of blood; but already a small bloody pool had begun to form on the floor at the side of the bed. Smith was unconscious. Libby became hysterical and Ab decided to go downstairs and call Baptist Hospital. But first, he haphazardly washed up the blood in the bathroom and, before leaving the sleeping porch, took the Mauser and hid it in his bedroom down the hall.

Downstairs, having called for an ambulance, Ab had another, and what seemed at the time more sensible, idea. He telephoned Dr. Douglas Craig, his family doctor. Ab told Craig there had been an accident, that he had to see him right away. Ab must have reasoned that if he could get Smith to a private doctor he might be treated discreetly. He seemed to think that Smith's reputation was in greater danger than his life.

Ab put down the telephone and walked into the drawing room. He had drunk excessively that evening, but the shock of Smith's accident had sobered him somewhat. At that moment, Blanche Yurka appeared above on the gallery. The shot, which had sounded some five minutes earlier, must have wakened her, but she claimed not to have heard it. She thought she had heard voices and wanted to know if Ab had heard them too. Ab said he had heard nothing. He started up the stairs, and then they both heard Libby screaming from the sleeping porch: "*Ab! Ab! Ab!*" Ab rushed down the hall.

Libby was on the bed cradling Smith's body when Ab returned. They carried him down the hall. Blanche pushed Libby aside and she and Ab bore the stricken Smith downstairs, his head pressed so tightly to the side of Ab's neck that whatever blood oozed from his wound was absorbed by Ab's bathing suit and did not splatter on the floor.

They drove rapidly to Dr. Douglas Craig's home at First and Stratford. As they pulled up, Dr. Craig came down the lawn to the car. He took one look at the wound and urged Ab to rush Smith to Baptist Hospital, where, just over four hours later, he died.

Only later did Ab realize that had he not wasted those precious twenty minutes, Smith might have lived; but it was too late now, which is why Ab, as he had cautioned Libby to do, said nothing, deciding instead to adopt the guise of the innocent and tragic bystander. That is why Ab told no one but Virginia Dunklee that Smith and Libby had had a violent argument, why he told no one but C. G. Hill of his furtive visit to Dr. Craig's, why he denied hearing the gunshot, denied he had ever seen the gun. But almost certainly, the gun had gone off in Ab's hand and he had concealed it, which is why he told Ed Lasater that he had to return to Reynolda House before the police searched his bedroom; he had to erase his fingerprints from the gun and replace it on the sleeping porch before it was missed.

Just prior to the coroner's inquest, Ab and Libby spent more than an hour alone in Libby's bedroom attempting to coordinate their stories. It was fortunate that Blanche Yurka had appeared on the gallery while Ab was downstairs calling Baptist Hospital. Blanche was a sober and reliable witness and she had sworn that Ab had not been anywhere near the sleeping porch during those crucial minutes. Libby's providential lapse of memory supported this version admirably. There was no one to contradict him now. It was a secret, Ab believed, that he would carry to his grave.

Libby, too, remembered more than she admitted . . . but not much more. For Libby, a surfeit of alcohol would always lead to at least a partial loss of memory. Many years later, following another night of prodigious intoxication, Libby begged her drinking companions: "Now, tell me what we did last night. I can't remember anything. And don't spare me. I want it blow by blow, word for word. Start at the beginning."

The morning Smith died at Baptist Hospital, Libby had returned to Reynolda House, having redonned the peach-colored negligee clotted and stained with her husband's blood. The Reynolds family physician told reporters that Libby was prostrate with grief, that she had been given a heavy sedative and would not be able to talk with them, or with anyone, not even the county sheriff.

But upstairs alone in her bedroom, Libby was wide awake. She had already telephoned her parents in Cincinnati. She had called her friends Howard Dietz and Clifton Webb in New York, and Louisa Carpenter in Delaware. She told Louisa that the Reynolds family were being horrible to her, almost as though they suspected that she had had something to do with Smith's demise. But unfortunately Libby could not remember anything. "I was so drunk last night," she said, "I don't know whether I shot him or not."

It is one thing to have known what happened and lied; the deeper tragedy is not to have known at all. To the end of her days, Libby wondered whether or not she had shot Smith Reynolds. It would have been unlike her—she was not inclined to violence—but her husband had died violently, and she remembered only the sound of her name, a crash, the warm blood, and a terrible, tantalizing apparition.

For Libby, Smith Reynolds's death had been a point of no

return—beyond which lay a future she would not otherwise have had. It had altered everything. But she didn't know that then. Nearly a lifetime would pass before Libby, looking back, was able to isolate that tragic moment and confide in a friend: *"There,* it was *there,* the detour began."

30

ON DECEMBER 13, LIBBY RENTED A WINTER HOME ON fashionable Owl's Nest Road in Christiana Hundred, Delaware. She was joined by her mother, who intended to remain at her side until the baby was born. Despite the wind and the heavy snow, Libby was often seen on the streets of nearby Wilmington in the company of Louisa Carpenter—Christmas shopping, taking tea in the lobby of the DuPont-Biltmore Hotel or attending theatrical performances at the Wilmington Playhouse. She made no attempt to disguise herself and the town grew accustomed to her frequent outings. The Reynolds scandal, as it was known, seemed, at last, behind her, although Associated Press and United Press regarded it—with the Lindbergh kidnapping, Franklin Roosevelt's presidential victory, the Olympic Games in Los Angeles, and the imprisonment of Al Capone—as one of the biggest American news stories of 1932.

The next month, Louisa Carpenter drove Libby to Pennsylvania Hospital in Philadelphia for a routine examination. Libby seemed unusually tense, and Louisa admitted that Libby not only was pregnant but was suffering from a nervous breakdown.

Her child was not expected until early February, but eight hours later, on January 9, 1933, Libby gave birth prematurely to a three-and-a-half-pound boy. The tiny infant was placed in a glass and metal incubator under the springs of which carbon lamps maintained a continuous temperature of ninety-eight degrees. Hovering just outside the delivery room were two Reynolds family lawyers—come to assure themselves that the child was, in fact, Smith Reynolds's. They seemed doubtful.

In Winston-Salem, there were many who shared this opinion, believing as they did that the child was Ab Walker's. Following his release from jail, Ab had been hired as a pump attendant at a Shell service station near Reynolda House. When news of the birth of Libby's son was announced, a gleeful group of his close friends drove up to the station and, in keeping with an old Tar-heel custom of burning a new father's hat, set Ab's brown fedora afire.

Contrary to an earlier court ruling, the Reynolds lawyers now contended that the birth of Libby's child did not improve her claim to Smith's estate: The terms of the will stipulated that only children living at the time of his death might inherit. Libby's lawyers contested this. Should it prove necessary, they stated, their fight would be taken to the Supreme Court.

Three days after his birth, Libby named her child Christopher Smith Reynolds. Because it was too dangerous to move him from his incubator and because Libby was too ill to leave her room, she had still not seen him. But the hospital corridor was crowded with Libby's friends—so many of them, in fact, that Libby described it as "a royal birth round which danced a jubilant peasantry."

On March 29, she granted an interview to thirteen reporters in the hospital solarium, insisting, however, that a list of questions be submitted in advance and that her answers would be read from a prepared statement. During the interview, Louisa Carpenter stood at her side.

"My only request," she said, "is that now we be allowed a private life surrounded by the peace and quiet which every baby needs and deserves." Although the infant weighed only seven pounds, Libby called him her "beautiful giant. The first sight of him," she said, "was a moment of ecstasy unlike any other moment in my life. He's the most perfect and adorable thing I have ever seen.

"If, when the baby becomes older," she continued, "his tastes turn toward the field of aviation, one of my fondest dreams will be realized. His father was an ambitious airman, idealistic and romantic and he loved adventure." Libby hoped her son would come to understand "the importance of work in life, the satisfaction of aspiring to an objective and the joy of concentrated effort toward a desired goal."

During the spring and summer of 1933, the Smith Reynolds estate became incredibly entangled. The Reynolds family was loath to give Libby anything. Joseph Cannon now contended that his daughter, Anne, had never been divorced from Smith Reynolds—despite her subsequent marriage to F. Brandon Smith. Cannon claimed that when Anne filed for divorce in Reno, she had been under the influence of morphine. He felt she was entitled to *all* of Smith's estate. As for Libby: She was an interloper.

The battle for Smith's inheritance dragged on; and it was not until March 13, 1935, that it was settled. The decree provided that Ab Walker would inherit $50,000; Anne Cannon Reynolds II would obtain $9.7 million; a similar sum would be given to Smith's brothers and sisters, provided it was used for charitable purposes; finally, Libby would receive $750,000 for herself and, after the deduction of taxes, her child would inherit $6.25 million.

Libby was overjoyed. It had taken more than two years of claims and counterclaims to settle her differences with the Reynolds family. But long before, the New York tabloids, with their tiresome bent for hyperbole, had taken to calling Libby's child the richest baby in America.

BOOK TWO:
THE CHILD

31

O N DECEMBER 5, 1933—AFTER THIRTEEN YEARS, TEN
months, eighteen days, eighteen hours and fifty-five minutes—Prohibition was finally repealed. That night, Libby invited Louisa Carpenter to her Manhattan duplex to celebrate. She
believed that the end of Prohibition signaled a new beginning, not
only for America but for the prospects of her eleven-month-old-
son. There was a good time coming. After dinner, Libby and
Louisa drank vintage champagne, and tiptoeing into Christopher's nursery, they raised their glasses to his boundless future.

Earlier that year, Libby and Louisa had rented a ten-acre estate called Rim Rock in the fashionable resort of Watch Hill in
Rhode Island. The twenty-five-room cream-and-white mansion
was perched on a grassy hill overlooking Long Island Sound,
and the two friends remained there in virtual seclusion until
after Labor Day. Libby had had her fill of captious headlines, of
tawdry scoops by vulgar scribes who claimed to be her friends.
And so she rested and read, and shepherded the fragile health
of her tiny child. Clifton Webb and Mabelle, Winsor French, Bea
Lillie, Franchot Tone and Howard Dietz were regular visitors.
Libby drove to Narragansett and to Newport in her new white
Cord convertible, played golf at the Misquamicut Club, and
raced to Fishers Island in a five-thousand-dollar speedboat that
she and Louisa had bought that summer. The boat, called *Three's
a Crowd*, was a whimsical allusion to their new life together.

The Boston train dropped off specially prepared milk for
Christopher each morning, and Libby dispatched her car to West-
erly Station in Watch Hill to fetch it. His milk was made of soy
protein with added vitamins and could be served only at seventy-
two degrees. Christopher, or Topper, as Libby had begun to call
him, was as pampered as a little prince. During the first nine

months of his life, Libby had received numerous anonymous letters assuring her that unless certain sums of money were remitted, Topper would be kidnapped or killed. In response, Libby hired six bodyguards to patrol Rim Rock by day and night. Woodie, the head guard, took to strolling about the wooded grounds in a bathing suit and a flannel dressing gown, beneath which he concealed a gun. No one was permitted to enter Rim Rock unless a written invitation on Libby's blue stationery was produced.

During the long hot afternoons, Maggie, the governess, usually took Topper out on the lawn, where he lay in a wicker pram in the shade of a red-and-yellow striped umbrella. Occasionally, Libby placed her dark glasses over Topper's eyes and, as he attempted to jerk them off, Libby or Louisa would shoot home movies. The two women, both of whom were deeply tanned, sported matching bobs, their hair cut short and swept to the side. Burlesquing and miming for the camera, they resembled adolescent country boys.

They returned to Montchanin in Delaware after Labor Day, rarely leaving the large estate. That winter, they flew to Palm Beach for a holiday, accompanied by their friends Margaret Perry, the eldest daughter of Antoinette Perry (after whom the Tony Awards were named), and Winsor French, the New York columnist. When French, a well-known homosexual, and Margaret Perry were married the following year, Libby quipped to Louisa: "instead of throwing the bouquet to the bridesmaids, Margaret should have tossed Winsor to the ushers."

In late September, Libby and Louisa traveled to New York for the opening of Irving Berlin's *As Thousands Cheer* starring Clifton Webb and Ethel Waters and introducing such songs as "Heat Wave" and "Easter Parade." Although Libby declined all interviews during the intermission, the next day's papers were filled with reports that she wished to return to Broadway. Libby was indignant. As she told Winsor French: "My torch singing was a fluke, you know. I haven't a trained voice and I never liked standing in front of a curtain singing songs of unrequited love. I think you can say that I have graduated from Tin Pan Alley."

Libby's instincts led her now toward the bucolic, toward the tranquil progression of time spent idling in the countryside. She needed nourishment, and preferred the relative solitude of Montchanin, the company of Louisa. Their relationship had ripened into what was known in the nineteenth century as a "Boston marriage"; that is, they were romantic friends—women who loved and trusted and depended on one another, but whose intimacy was not necessarily sexual. Libby felt all these qualities for Louisa, but she did not think of herself as a lesbian. Nor did she believe herself to be sick or sinful and, in any event, would have despised that narrow sexual stereotype. Rather, she considered herself emancipated.

For Libby, sex was an act of the imagination. Dedicated to the exploration of sexual possibilities, to the irresistible dream of conquest, she was, as she would always be, the aggressor. It was the pursuit of love that challenged her, that drew her on. Once her sexual ambitions had been achieved, however, she would become restless and bored. But Louisa had potent lures. Libby loved her; she was also seduced by her wealth and generosity. In addition, Louisa gave what Libby would ultimately demand from all her lovers—an adoration that was unwavering, unquestioning.

In the literary and theatrical circles frequented by Libby and Louisa, homosexuality (or bisexuality as it was often called) was fitting, even fashionable. The two women were accepted as a perfectly normal couple—outrageous in themselves, perhaps, but their liaison was commonplace. There were to be sure, the usual snickers and denigrations, particularly among Louisa's women friends, who also vied for her attentions. These women—playwrights, novelists, lyricists and rich young socialites—were invited regularly to Montchanin. Louisa called them her "Sapphic circle."

Whenever Libby and Louisa were out of earshot, the women would prate and gossip, their conspiratorial calumnies often directed toward Louisa's lavishness or Libby's lack of sexual ardor. "Louisa could buy Delaware, but she thinks it's overpriced" or "Libby may sing hot, but, trust me, that's where it ends" were typical remarks. Libby would have been amused. Louisa, she knew, was hers for as long as she desired. Their sexual affair had probably ended, but they were still emotionally entwined— Libby, the talented, unpredictable child; Louisa, the maternal, affectionate protector. Thus, a Boston marriage of sorts; and, to complete the complicated circle, they possessed a son.

*   *   *

By the time Topper was eighteen months old, Libby and Louisa treated him as the heir apparent in their romantic diarchy. Nothing was too good, too difficult, too extravagant for the little boy. But the women felt he should have a companion. With no natural means of procreation immediately at hand, Louisa decided to adopt a girl, a nice girl, someone of Topper's age, so that he would not grow up sisterless and unattached.

Libby and Louisa went shopping. Several days later, while looking at children in a Philadelphia orphanage, Louisa was smitten with a laughing little blond girl. She began to speak to her, but the nun interrupted, explaining that Louisa couldn't possibly prefer that one, she was much too difficult. "Then that's the one for me," said Louisa defiantly. The child was three years old. That very afternoon arrangements were made to adopt the girl and, given her disposition, Louisa elected to call her Sunny. Libby became Sunny's godmother, Clifton Webb her godfather.

On Sunny's arrival at Montchanin, Libby placed two Welsh terriors in her lap and the little girl, who had never seen a dog before, was terrified. But she was impressed at once with her new home. Montchanin was like some magical kingdom—complete with mansions, stables, barns and greenhouses, a vast roller-skating rink and a cockfighting pit where the Du Ponts gathered on Thursday afternoons to wager on their ferocious birds. The two-hundred-acre estate was ruled by Margaretta du Pont, Louisa's mother, and the Du Pont clan assembled at her home for an elaborate lunch each Sunday. Margaretta never openly discussed Louisa's relationship with Libby. That would have been beneath her, and impolite; in any event, she was the sort of woman who gave every indication of being unaware that homosexuality existed.

Sunny and Topper came to know better. They lived like outcasts, they imagined, surrounded by lesbians and homosexual "uncles" and "godfathers"—Libby and Louisa's weekend visitors. They became the targets of taunts by other children, particularly the other Du Pont children, who demanded to know if Louisa was really their father, and, if so, just how the procreative act had been performed. From the time she was eight, Sunny made a point of wearing her hair long, longer than Louisa's could ever have been. But nothing prevented the merciless mockery. The Du Pont children contended that Topper was fatherless, a bastard, and that Sunny had been found and carried into Montchanin like a stray cat. But Sunny remained aloof and proud, believing that she had been wanted, that, unlike other children, *she* had been chosen.

There were advantages, of course. Both children were overly indulged by their wealthy mothers. Topper was presented with bicycles, with shiny wagons and elaborate games. Sunny was given a splendid wardrobe, fashionable dolls and, when she was five, a palomino pony called Girlie. Seven brindle Great Danes roamed through the house—both pets and guardians—and whenever Topper and Sunny strayed too far, Greta, the largest of the dogs (whom Libby had named after Garbo), would drag them back by the seat of their pants.

When Sunny was eight and Topper was six, Libby and Louisa decided to take them to New York. Previously, they had traveled only in Louisa's plane; this time, they were going by rail. While the train sat in the Wilmington station for what seemed to the children an abnormally long time, they both shouted, almost in unison, "When does this thing take off?"

Surrounded more by detectives than by either family or friends, Topper and Sunny often felt like prisoners. Out there, beyond the gilded gates of Montchanin, was an unknown and perhaps unknowable world. It was frightening. Lying in their beds at night, the two children discussed their futures endlessly, concluding, finally, that since Topper was Libby's natural child, nothing untoward would happen to him. But Sunny's childhood was riven with the fear that one day she would be cast outside Montchanin's great front gate and it would never be opened to her again.

32

LIBBY MAY HAVE FORSAKEN TIN PAN ALLEY, BUT SHE CONtinued to nurture an old dream—to perform on Broadway in a noble role, to excel in "the drama," as she had called it in college. "I've always wanted to be a dramatic actress," she told a reporter. "I want to cover the whole range, play old women and gay women. I want to break your heart one minute and make you laugh your head off the next."

Libby had been taking acting lessons from Jasper Deeter at the Hedgerow Theater in Moylan, Pennsylvania, and in June of 1934, she made her dramatic debut in a comedy entitled *Spring in Autumn*. The comedy had been performed in Philadelphia the year before and was adapted so that its star, Blanche Yurka, could bring down the second act curtain by singing a Puccini aria while standing on her head—thus combining, as a local reviewer observed, "the best features of drama, the opera and the circus." The reviewer added: "The circus atmosphere pursued the play to Hedgerow, where it served as a vehicle to re-introduce to the stage, under a deep blanket of mystery, Libby Holman, singer of revue fame and the much publicized widow of Smith Reynolds."

Although Libby did not stand on her head, she briefly "lifted her voice in song—not a torch song—but a snatch from *Madame Butterfly*, a song soon quelled in the interests of the plot." It was, the reviewer concluded, an inauspicious dramatic debut.

But Libby was undeterred. That summer, she journeyed to Maine to perform with the Ogunquit Players at a salary of twenty-five dollars a week. "I'm not going to appear in a play in New York until I feel I'm completely ready for it," she said. "New York is going to be very critical of my first play. There are so many people who resent me trying to step out of the niche they put me in. They want me to stay put. They labeled me as a torch singer and they don't want me to do anything else. Well, let me tell you, the status is not quo.

"I have something to work for," she continued, "and I have a whole lot to learn. You see, I really don't know a thing about this acting business yet. Some day, I'd like to play Juliet and sing at a nightclub after the performance. Why not combine Juliet with jazz?

"I'm vain enough to think I'm a pretty good actress, and I'm going to be a much better one. I know as well as anyone that I'll have a job convincing the public I can act. So I've got to be better than good in order to convince them." Libby discounted rumors that she had been asked to go to Hollywood. "I was given several scripts to look over," she said, "and they all seemed cheap and sordid and mechanical. I prefer the Broadway stage."

Despite such optimistic pronouncements, Libby had more than her share of difficulties in Maine—none of them having anything to do with her dramatic abilities. Now, more than two years after Smith Reynolds's death, Libby's "scandal" remained a lurid subject of conversation. Behind her back, she was often referred to as "that woman." Before going to Maine, she asked her lawyer, Benet Polikoff, to find a suitable summer home in the vicinity of Ogunquit. Polikoff located a house almost immediately, but when it was discovered that the lessee was Libby Holman, the offer was withdrawn. In the end, Libby was forced to rent a house in Kennebunkport, some twenty-five miles from the theater.

At the Ogunquit Playhouse, where plays were staged for a single week, Libby's first role was in Maxwell Anderson's *The Gypsy*—a bizarre choice, the tale of a woman who drives her lover into killing himself. On opening night, during the second act, as Libby came onstage, the audience began to laugh. During the final act, they stamped their feet, hissed, hooted, and hurled spitballs and paper airplanes. Libby ignored them. But during the encores, she was booed again, and obscene cries of "whore" and "murderess" were shouted.

Libby also played roles in *The Farmer's Wife* with Mitzi Green and in *The Silver Box* with Ethel Barrymore. Although the audiences were not as hostile as they had been during *The Gypsy* they displayed a cool and tacit condemnation. Eventually, instead of asking the stage manager if the theater was full, Libby inquired: "How many enemies do I have in the house tonight?"

Because Louisa Carpenter had chosen to remain in Montchanin, Libby, for the most part, was alone in Ogunquit. That summer, she conducted a fleeting affair with a handsome young actor whom she called Square-eyes, or that, at least, is what she claimed. None of the young men with whom she now consorted ever met him, and they concluded that either Square-eyes lived in another town or Libby called him that in order to disguise his identity. These men, all of them actors, all of them lank and epicine youths, were dazzled with Libby. One of them, George Lloyd, a twenty-one-year-old, looked so much like Smith Reynolds that Libby almost fainted when they first met. On that occasion, Lloyd asked Libby if she was nearsighted. "Flatterer," she said, "I'm blind. But I like what I hear." Libby and Lloyd became immediate friends and their relationship would last until the early fifties.

Libby described George Lloyd as looking like a corrupt choirboy. Lloyd would become a well-known performer of pantomimes and character sketches in Manhattan supper clubs during the late thirties and forties. An adroit lyricist, he wrote a song that began: "I'm the guy that Libby Holman burned the torches for/that Morgan turned pianos into porches for." He wrote a poignant lamentation for Libby about a seller of daffodils who develops a narcissus complex. From the very beginning, he recognized that Libby, like her friend Tallulah Bankhead, blossomed when surrounded by a court of admiring attendants. Tallulah called her coterie her "caddies," while Libby called hers "my bright boy pages." Lloyd willingly became one of them.

Lloyd soon learned that between Libby and those who loved her, there existed a kind of subtle and insidious cult worship. She was, he believed, the only true femme fatale he had ever met. An artless hedonist with little sense of sin or shame, she was both innocent and amoral. She was not a beauty, but Libby's charms were stronger, more obscure.

The young men gathered about her because Libby made them laugh and because she caused them to feel more important than they had ever believed themselves to be. She responded to them by pouncing on their defects and weaknesses, purring at their witticisms, playing with their affections in a manner that was at once both cruel and sensuous. She had suffered, and seemed to understand their sufferings—the tortures of being homosexual, the absurd precautions they were compelled to take in order to conceal it. In Libby's presence, they could be themselves. They could be, as George Lloyd observed, "naughty, giggling girls together"; and with each of them, Libby was something of a romantic thug. One loved her in her way or suffered the consequences.

33

ARLIER THAT YEAR, THE PHILADELPHIA *EVENING BULLETIN* announced that the "slumber-eyed, raven-haired, petulant-lipped, husky-voiced" Libby would return to Broadway in the autumn, playing the lead in a new musical comedy composed by Howard Dietz and Arthur Schwartz. Nothing else was known about the project, but Howard Dietz declared that, although no mean-spirited irony was intended or implied, the show would be called *Revenge with Music*.

Libby, after denying the press reports, signed her contracts in September. Remembering Maine, she had been reluctant to return to Broadway so soon, but George Lloyd persuaded Libby that her fears were exaggerated. This was New York, after all. Libby was uncertain. "As Maine goes, so goes the nation," she said.

Howard Dietz considered *Revenge with Music* an operetta. Based on an old Spanish folktale, which had been turned into a novel called *El Sombrero de Tres Picos* by Pedro A. de Alarcón, the improbable plot concerned an elderly but amorous provincial Spanish governor who coveted the favors of the lowly Maria (played by Libby). Maria was in love with Carlos, the town miller. Much to the governor's distaste, he is obliged to marry the pair, but later that day contrives to have Carlos, the bridegroom, arrested. The rapacious rake then invades Carlos's home in order to seduce the innocent Maria. Meanwhile, Carlos escapes from jail and, convinced of the worst, rushes inadvertently into the willing arms of the governor's wife. The usual musical-comedy mix-ups ensued.

The operetta featured Libby, Charles Winninger, George Metaxa, Rex O'Malley, Imogene Coca and Ilka Chase. Seventeen colorful Spanish sets followed one another pellmell on a revolving stage, and the songs included "That Fellow Manuelo," "If

There Is Someone Lovelier Than You" and Libby's showstopper, "You and the Night and the Music."

In the wake of Smith Reynolds's death, the producers considered Libby a questionable asset. But Howard Dietz insisted on hiring her, and his opinion prevailed. It was not only Libby's reputation that concerned them; they fretted also over her performance. During the tryouts, she was nervous and difficult. She had recently taken operatic singing lessons and now she not only sang operatically, she talked that way. Steve Wiman, Dwight Deere Wiman's wife, warned Dietz: "If Libby doesn't stop acting so goddamned piss-elegant, she's going to wreck our show. For God's sake, tell her to speak American."

During the opening night intermission in Philadelphia, Arthur Schwartz was assigned to mingle with the crowd to eavesdrop on any criticisms or comments concerning the performance of their benighted star. Schwartz lingered in the lobby while members of the audience talked tiresomely of the Dionne quintuplets, the recent shooting of John Dillinger, their golf scores, the rise of Nazi Germany, and the interminable Depression. No one mentioned Libby. Schwartz was about to return to his seat when he overheard Libby's name. Unobtrusively, he backed up to the woman who had spoken of her; but she was not commenting on Libby's performance. In tones of pure and unmistakable conviction, she was saying: "I *bet* she killed him. I just *bet* she killed him."

Revenge with Music opened at the New Amsterdam Theatre on Forty-second Street on November 28, 1934. Despite running for 158 performances, it received lackluster reviews. Dietz and Schwartz's book was considered routine, the lyrics disappointingly uneven. Most of the critics thought the show was dire and, in one way or another, said so. Nevertheless, *Revenge* went on to make a return of $45,000 on a $120,000 investment, and Libby's hit song, "You and the Night and the Music," was temporarily banned on the radio. The lyrics of the song, particularly the manner in which Libby sang them, were considered risqué and immoral, and did much to support her already notorious reputation.

Although Dietz was never to regret his decision to cast Libby, he attributed a portion of the blame for the show's failure to her.

She had been miscast, and her singing lessons, rather than improving her voice, had ruined it. In Dietz's view, Libby now lacked the ability to project her lyrics, and worse, her voice had lost its raw, untrained sensuality. It had become merely grand, pretentious.

During the twenty-week run of *Revenge*, Libby, Topper, his governess and a detective moved into an apartment at 325 East Seventy-ninth Street. Formerly owned by John Barrymore, the duplex contained four bedrooms, a sumptuous wood-paneled bar, a library, and a badminton court on the upper terrace.

Libby was to be seen everywhere in the city. In the company of Clifton Webb, Noel Coward, Woolworth Donahue, Tallulah Bankhead, Louis Bromfield and Lucius Beebe, she had become a prominent member of what was now being called café society. Following the repeal of Prohibition, café society flowered in its purest form in New York and in what New Yorkers liked to call their nearest suburb—Hollywood. The familiar diversions of its members were tirelessly chronicled by such gossip columnists (or paragraphers as they were known) as Walter Winchell in the *Daily Mirror*, Leonard Lyons in the *Post*, Ed Sullivan in the *Daily News*, Louis Sobol in the *Journal* and, most effusively, by Lucius Beebe in the *Herald Tribune*.

Each evening after the show, Libby met her friends at one or another of Manhattan's chic nightclubs. She drank at the Chapeau Rouge, where the owner, Pepy d'Albrew, wore a live white mouse in his lapel. She went to the Rainbow Room to hear her friend Bea Lillie sing. She dined at the Colony, at "21," or at the Central Park Casino. Afterward, she stopped by the Stork Club, owned and operated by Sherman Billingsley, a former Oklahoma farm boy and bootlegger. More frequently, Libby went to John Perona's El Morocco, the zebra-striped, cellophane-palmed club that, although only two years old, had become the most fashionable nightery in town.

One evening, Libby appeared unexpectedly at Tallulah's suite in the Elysée Hotel. Tallulah and a few friends were playing a game called Murder in the Dark when the doorman announced Libby's arrival. Seeking guidance, Tallulah's friends asked if they should stop or play on. Before Tallulah could answer, the doorbell rang. When Libby walked in, Tallulah embraced her and said: *"Darling*, we're playing Murder in the Dark. *Do* join us. We could use a professional." Libby laughed. Looking over at the bar and then back to Tallulah, she said, "I'll just kill that bottle of Scotch . . . for now." The game was abandoned.

Libby's most devoted fan and friend during the mid-thirties was the gossip columnist Lucius Beebe. A year older than Libby, Beebe considered himself a social historian of café society. With a pronounced distaste for bad manners, casual dress, mornings, foreigners, foreign places, and for those who lived on what he called "the purlieus of magnificence," Beebe was the consummate snob, a connoisseur of trifles and baroque effects.

A Boston Brahmin, Beebe had attended both Yale and Harvard where he was often seen wielding a gold-headed walking stick and wearing gray, orchidaceous trousers. While he was at Yale, one of his professors complained that the college was infested with women and, spotting Beebe in the distance wearing pantaloonlike white-linen knickers, the professor observed: "Here come two of them right now."

Beebe was thought to be the most unreliable reporter in New York. Tallulah claimed that he must have a great respect for the truth since he very rarely used it. Yet Beebe became one of the most successful and outlandish columnists of his time. In the midst of the Depression, he permitted himself an allowance of one hundred dollars a day for food and drink. He covered fires in white tie and tails and claimed to brush his teeth each morning in a light Chablis. Much later, he traveled around the country in his private railway car, which contained a gold-and-crystal-chandeliered drawing room, an ornate fireplace, and brocade tapestries in the Venetian Renaissance style.

Beebe and Libby were devoted to one another. He admired her wit and style and Libby called him Luscious. On one occasion, hearing that Beebe was to undergo minor surgery, Libby assured a group of his stricken friends over lunch at "21": "Don't *worry*, boys. They're bound to open Luscious at room temperature."

Beebe escorted Libby everywhere—to the theater, to select nightclubs (which he called "plush puddles" in his column) and to openings at the Metropolitan Opera. For the opening of *Tosca* that year, Beebe wore his favorite dress coat, lined in mink and collared in astrakan, and Libby, barefooted, had painted exotic pumps on her feet. During the first act, Beebe lost the diamond orchid he normally wore on his lapel. At intermission, Libby and Beebe rushed to a nearby police station and Libby demanded the police bar the doors of the Met so that no one could spirit the diamond away. After a heated argument, the police refused. When the opera ended, Beebe discovered his diamond orchid in Libby's bushy hair.

In his curt, inconsequential style, Beebe recorded Libby's antics in his daily column— her comings and goings, her affectations. He reported Libby and Noel Coward's arrival at his apartment at five o'clock one morning, demanding his specially prepared chili con carne. He told of the evening he escorted her around Manhattan, watching as she changed into three different and progressively more costly wraps, which he called "her phalanx of furs." Libby began the evening in a simple mink, which, over drinks at the Colony, she discarded in favor of an ermine, which she wore to the theater and as far as dinner at Monte Carlo, where she donned a sable before hurrying on to El Morocco. Beebe explained that Libby wearied of her furs and dispatched her maid with a new one to whatever club she intended to visit next. When he claimed that the sable had cost $42,000, Libby retorted: "That item belongs in the *Wall Street Journal*, not a gossip column."

Revenge with Music closed in early April of 1935, and Libby was relieved when the producers decided against taking it on tour. There had already been too much lurid publicity and she didn't want any more.

That summer, however, MGM released a film called *Reckless*. Written by David O. Selznick under a pseudonym, the film was based on the Smith Reynolds tragedy, and starred Jean Harlow in the Libby role, Franchot Tone as Smith Reynolds, William Powell and Rosalind Russell. The similarities were unmistakable and the New York tabloids alluded to them again and again. The New York *American* said: "Obviously the plot was concocted from the experience of a Broadway star whose tragic romance with a wealthy waster was stranger than fiction." In the film, Tone, the troubled young southern socialite, goes to New York and falls in love with Harlow, a Broadway chorus girl who aspires to become a singing star. Within weeks of their marriage, Tone shoots himself. Harlow returns to Broadway and the film ends with her singing *Reckless* to an unruly first-night audience.

Libby was outraged and threatened to sue. The film was not successful, but on opening night in New York, when the intoxicated Harlow informed Franchot Tone that she was "just a Big Sister out on a spree," the audience tittered over the obvious ironies. Libby did not see the film. Closing down her Manhattan duplex, she retreated to Montchanin, where she spent most of the rest of the year with Topper and Louisa Carpenter.

That autumn, the New York *Times* was filled with rumblings of war and racism: Italian troops had invaded Ethiopia; Germany's Nazi Party had deprived the Jews of German citizenship and, to prevent "racial pollution," decreed that intercourse between "Aryans" and Jews was punishable by death. Ordinarily, whenever Libby considered her Jewishness, she bristled with repudiation, but this was too monstrous to ignore. For months thereafter, she considered giving up her married name, deciding against it in the end. Nonetheless, for the first time, she began to engage herself in Jewish causes and Jewish charities.

In the evenings, after Topper and Sunny had been put to bed, Libby and Louisa listened to *Fibber McGee and Molly* on the radio; they saw *Anna Karenina* with Greta Garbo at a Wilmington cinema and played the popular new board game Monopoly. They traveled for a fortnight to Cuba—attending Havana's exotic revues and lying tirelessly on the sunny beaches, where Libby read *Appointment in Samarra*, her friend John O'Hara's first novel, published the year before. Topper and Sunny were left behind at Montchanin in the care of nannies, governesses and bodyguards.

For the moment, Libby relinquished all thoughts of returning to the stage; but she continued taking singing lessons—from Theresa Armitage, a well-known teacher of concert artists in Manhattan. She was determined to improve her voice. "I had a voice I liked," she said, "and it was distinctive, but it didn't have range. I told Miss Armitage I wasn't a lieder singer, that I didn't want the quality of my voice changed, I just wanted it stretched." Libby was to work with Theresa Armitage for nearly a decade and, contrary to her original wishes, her voice did change. Most of her critics and many of her fans agreed that Libby had trained out what had been natively hers, that her voice had become cautious and correct.

Libby would not have concurred. She felt that, musically, she had made vast strides. Eager to sing in public again, not on the stage but in the more intimate environs of a club, she arranged to appear at the Club Versailles in New York—an engagement for which she was paid $2,500 a week. It was Libby's first nightclub date in nearly five years.

On opening night, Libby arrived in the company of several of her pages. The club was crowded with what the next day's newspapers would call "gobs of the socially prominent." Libby and her friends sat down at a table next to the piano. At midnight, the house lights suddenly dimmed. Without any introduction, Libby stepped up onto the small raised stage and into the glare of a single, piercing pin spot. She wore a black velvet gown, embellished with tiny clusters of ornamental white gardenias. An enthusiastic burst of applause prevented her from beginning, and she stood by the piano, a slight smile on her face. As was her custom, Libby did not use a microphone. She extended her long, prehensile fingers into the light like a benediction. Her fingernails were painted a deep rose red and the women in the audience craned forward to get a better look at her.

Libby sang for more than an hour. Her repertoire included such popular lamentations as "Am I Blue?," "In the Dark," "You Let Me Down" and "A Woman Is a Sometime Thing." Her initial nervousness quickly gave way to a powerful performance, and by her third number, she had conquered the crowd. She gave no bows or encores; as the applause began to build, she returned to her table and sat down, and each of her pages slurped at her cheeks enthusiastically.

Afterward, in her dressing room, Libby was interviewed by tabloid reporter Michael Mok, who had intended to ask several bold and pointed questions until Libby's manager, Bud Williams, warned: "Remember, the cigarette angle is out. The kid's out. The money's out. Winston-Salem, North Carolina, is off the map as far as you're concerned. Got it? Good. Then she'll talk to you."

In his article, Mok concluded that the audience was little more than a curious mob. He had not liked her voice. Although

Walter Winchell was to call her "the chartreuse chanteuse," and Lucius Beebe, "the high priestess of the love-lament," Mok felt that Libby had been self-conscious and apologetic.

He himself had not introduced the subject of money, but Libby seemed inordinately concerned with it. "The rewards are very generous," she said, "but so much is eaten up by over-head—my six specially designed evening gowns, the salaries of my accompanist, my arranger, my personal representative, my press agent, my secretary, my maid, my manager, and my agent's commission. I only take home about fifty percent. And, on the road, it's even less. Then I have to pay my own traveling expenses and transportation and hotels for most of these people. It's a real circus.

"Singing satisfies me," she said, "though it isn't what I want to do eventually. It's my ambition to become a good dramatic actress." Libby hesitated. "But I'll sing just so I keep on working. Just so I'm not forgotten."

34

ONE OF THE MEN IN THE AUDIENCE THAT NIGHT AT CLUB Versailles was actor Phillips Holmes. Like Smith Reynolds, he was mesmerized by Libby's sultry voice. The twenty-six-year-old looked as though he had stepped from the pages of a John Held cartoon in *Vanity Fair*. He was the ideal of what American men of the thirties were supposed to be—overly tall, incredibly blond, unimaginably handsome, impeccably Anglo-Saxon. Within a week, Phillips contrived to meet Libby and they began a love affair that would last, precariously, for two years.

Phillips Holmes was born in 1909—the eldest child of actor Taylor Holmes, "the prince of farcical comedy," as he was known. Phillips was educated at the Newman School, an institution in Lakewood, New Jersey, for wealthy Catholic boys. Among his classmates were the sons of the British ambassador, George M. Cohan, and William Vanderbilt, who referred to boys who couldn't afford to attend the Newman School as "N.Q.'s"—"Not Quites."

Phillips was school president in his senior year and graduated with honors but was best remembered for a single episode: One evening, while emerging from the local brothel, Phillips was apprehended by his French teacher. The French teacher, who was just going in, affected shock and said, *"Well,* Mr. Holmes, I suppose I shall have to report you." "Likewise, I'm sure," the impudent Holmes retorted.

Phillips attended the University of Grenoble in France and spent a year in England at Cambridge. In September 1927, he returned to America and entered Princeton as a sophomore shortly before his eighteenth birthday.

The following June, a Paramount-Famous-Lasky production crew was shooting scenes on the Princeton campus for a film called *Variety.* Spotting Phillips in a crowd of onlookers, the director offered him a screen test, and Phillips was ultimately given a featured role. *Variety,* a turgid tale of collegiate jazz-age hijinks, eventually opened to scathing reviews, but Phillips Holmes, as the young dissolute in training for a life of aristocratic abandon, was considered a discovery.

He decamped for Hollywood and during the next three years, appeared in more than a dozen films, invariably playing the urban sophisticate, the college boy, the suave man of action, or the British gentleman. In 1931, he co-starred with Sylvia Sidney in *An American Tragedy.* During filming, the Hollywood scandal sheets reported a torrid romance between Phillips and Miss Sidney. But the affair was fictitious—drummed up by the studio's publicity department in order to promote the film. Miss Sidney, in fact, rarely saw Phillips off the set and, privately believed him to be a repressed homosexual, "a perfectly nice, perfectly charming, perfectly weak young man." Phillips's most successful film was *The Man I Killed,* directed by Ernst Lubitsch in 1932. Libby despised the title, but adored the movie. It was the first time she had ever seen Phillips Holmes and she was smitten by his haunted style.

Now, in 1936, Libby was in love with him, and Phillips, as Libby liked her men to be, was obsessed with her. He loved her slender form, her boyish bob, the striking way she applied her lipstick in a kind of inverted bowl. She wasn't merely fashionable and Phillips liked that too. As he told his sister, Madeleine, "an awful lot of Libby is just plain Libby." Most of all, he admired her worldliness, her authority. In turn, Phillips fulfilled many of Libby's prerequisites: He was not rich, but he was more than five years her junior; he was pliant and beautiful, and he had, albeit briefly, attended Princeton. Phillips seemed too good to be true and, in the end, he was.

From the beginning, Louisa Carpenter sensed that Libby and Phillips's love affair was too emotional, "too hot not to cool down," as Louisa, quoting Cole Porter, liked to say. She considered it just another of Libby's vain caprices. She felt no jealousy; her sexual affair with Libby had ended some time before and Libby was free to dally with whomever she pleased—just as Louisa was. Still, Louisa was emotionally involved with Libby and felt obligated to tell her that she considered Phillips little more than a silly jackanapes. Libby wouldn't listen. Louisa shrugged: She could do what she liked in Manhattan, but Louisa refused to entertain Libby's "limited engagements," as she called them, at Montchanin.

Libby, heedless as always, proudly told George Lloyd that she was "going straight." Within a month of their meeting, Phillips moved into Libby's Manhattan duplex. The young actor was impressed that the lavish apartment had once belonged to John Barrymore, and he was devoted to the four-year-old Topper, whom Libby now referred to as "my only sun." During the first weeks of their affair, Phillips introduced Libby to his sister, Madeleine, and to his handsome younger brother, Ralph, both of whom were then performing in Broadway plays. Libby, in turn, introduced Phillips to café society, escorting him to parties and restaurants, to first nights and openings, "showing him off," as George Lloyd observed, "like some bright badge of sexual achievement."

There were problems, however, and although Libby chose to ignore them at first, they were obvious to her friends. Phillips was utterly dependent on Libby and, when left to his own devices, drank excessively. Whenever Libby was out of town, Phillips was often seen at Manhattan nightclubs in a state of somnambulant intoxication. From the outset, he had pleaded with Libby to marry him. He had an old-fashioned concept of marriage, quaint even then—believing the man was the unassailable head of the household, that he would perform and provide while the workless woman remained at home. Phillips would be no more fortunate in converting Libby to his prejudice than Smith Reynolds had been. Moreover, Phillips was often in Cape Cod or London or Hollywood acting in plays and films, and romance at long distance was not one of Libby's specialties.

During one of Phillips's absences, Libby discovered she was pregnant. At first she was overjoyed, as was Louisa. But Libby quickly became disillusioned. She had almost certainly concluded that she would never marry Phillips. There had been too much scandal already and a misbegotten child could jeopardize her guardianship of Topper. In August 1937, therefore, Louisa took Libby to the Manhattan Hospital for Rectal Diseases, where she had a clandestine abortion. Libby never told Phillips. It had been too shattering an experience: She had given life and taken it away. She didn't know that she would never have another child of her own.

On Phillips's return, they quarreled increasingly. Phillips did not understand her outbursts, her venomous denunciations, nor did he seem to realize that Libby, a strong, tyrannic woman, was attracted to weak, subservient men whose weaknesses she initially exploited and, in the end, did not forgive.

During the late spring of 1938, Libby suddenly ordered Phillips from her home and, despite his pleas, refused to see him again. She had her reasons—the long absences, the drinking, his hangdog dependency. But above all, there was the aborted child. Libby seemed to feel that if Phillips had been different—stronger, braver, more resolute, then she would not have had to give up her child. She blamed him entirely; and Phillips, who did not know about the abortion, was unable to understand her wrath. Libby felt no regret and gave no lengthy explanations. Nor did she mention that, in Phillips's absence, she had begun to see his younger brother, Ralph, or Rafe as she called him.

Ralph Holmes was twenty-three, some eleven years younger than Libby and six years Phillips's junior. Like his brother, he had graduated from the Newman School, but he had not attended college. A tall, extremely handsome youth, he was, in early 1938, performing in a Broadway play called *Thanks for Tomorrow*.

Ralph admired his older brother but they had always been fierce rivals. When Phillips left for Hollywood to make a film called (ironically, Libby thought) *The Dominant Sex*, he asked Ralph to "look after his girl," and Ralph, already enamored with Libby, seized his opportunity. They soon became inseparable.

That summer, Phillips traveled to London. Clifton Webb and his friend Joseph J. O'Donahue IV were also there. Hearing that Phillips was staying at the Ritz, they went round to see him and found him in bed—unshaven, drunk and terribly ill. His bedsheets were steeped in bile and urine. Sitting up, Phillips drank nervously from a bottle of gin. He pleaded for recent reports of Libby, how she spent her time and in whose company. Some minutes later, he fell asleep. As Webb and O'Donahue left the room, they noticed for the first time an entire wall covered with photographs of Libby—snapshots of her and Phillips's romantic days together, publicity stills from *The Little Show* and *Three's a Crowd*, newspaper photos of Libby in North Carolina, and one of the naked Libby when she was a babe. Phillips blubbered in his sleep—drunk, discarded and unaware that he would never see Libby again.

35

THE YEAR BEFORE, LIBBY HAD BEGUN CONSTRUCTION ON what she called "a suitable and attractive home for Topper," midway between Greenwich and Stamford in Connecticut. Designed by a friend, the architect William Ballard, the neo-Georgian house sat in the midst of a fifty-five-acre estate, bounded on the east by the Mianus River and on the north by four hundred acres of natural parkland. Because the white brick and shingled house had been built on a knoll, looking out over the tops of the surrounding trees, Libby called her new home Treetops.

Treetops had three stories and contained sixteen bedrooms, nine bathrooms, a large living room, a wood-paneled library and a formal dining room. The lower floors were constructed of pegged oak and all the main rooms had fireplaces—eight in all. There were a solarium, powder rooms, a flower room, a vast kitchen and butler's pantry. The lower floor had been designed as a playroom and three sets of French doors opened onto the terrace and the twenty-by-forty-foot oval swimming pool. The servants' quarters occupied the entire east wing and included a wood storage room, a humidifier room, a workshop and a large laundry.

Another friend, Mimi Durant, decorated Treetops; but Libby, awash with ungovernable pretensions, knew precisely what she wanted. The main floor was almost completely Sheraton and Chippendale. The floors were covered with imported Austrian carpets, which Miss Durant had managed to smuggle out of Vienna shortly before the German invasion. The formal dining room was an exact replica of the dining room at the Governor's Mansion in Williamsburg, Virginia—the windows of which were adorned with pale-green satin draperies with crystal fringes. Still concerned with the safety of Topper, Libby installed a solid steel door to his second-floor bedroom. Outside the door was a control panel for opening and closing it, as well as an elaborate alarm system.

Beyond the house, the grounds would ultimately contain a four-car garage, a red-clay tennis court, a caretaker's cottage, two greenhouses, kennels, a potting shed, an emergency generator and a five-hundred gallon gas pump, a studio and a huge treehouse for Topper. Treetops was magnificent, grander, Libby liked to believe, than Montchanin or even Reynolda. Libby and Topper moved in during the early autumn of 1938. She felt at home, at last, and would live at Treetops for the rest of her life.

Four years had passed since Libby had last appeared on Broadway. She thought of herself as a dramatic actress now and continued to nurture reservations about performing in musical comedy. But when the opportunity arose for her to star in Cole Porter's *You Never Know*, Clifton Webb persuaded Libby that it would be the perfect vehicle for her. How could one fail by singing songs composed by Porter, Webb argued, and besides, he had already agreed to be her co-star. Reluctantly, Libby gave in.

The plot of *You Never Know* was lifted from Siegfried Geyer's *Candlelight*, a Viennese musical that had flopped on Broadway in 1929. In the story, the Baron Ferdinand de Romer exchanges places with his butler, Gaston, so that he may more conveniently court Mme. Henri Baltin, played by Libby. Maria, Mme. Baltin's maid, takes to wearing her mistress's clothes and, before long, a second romance ensues between her and Gaston, whom she mistakenly believes to be the baron. The Shuberts, who produced the show, retained two of the original songs, entrusting most of the new material to Cole Porter.

Porter had been working on the score for more than a year. On October 24, 1937, while he was riding at the Piping Rock Club in Locust Valley, Long Island, Porter's horse suddenly slipped, threw Porter, then fell on top of him, smashing both his legs and causing severe damage to his nervous system. The story was told that the dazed, though conscious, composer, while waiting for assistance, took out pencil and paper and reworked the lyric of "At Long Last Love," one of the songs in *You Never Know*.

He traveled to Cuba to recuperate, returning to New York in early 1938. His legs had still not healed (they would eventually be broken and reset seven times) and it was impractical for him to attend rehearsals at the theater. The Shuberts, therefore, dispatched the entire cast and the eighteen-member orchestra to the Waldorf Towers, where for weeks the stars—Libby, Clifton Webb, Rex O'Malley and Lupe Velez—performed the show in Porter's suite. The convalescing composer, still ill and drugged with pain pills, believed that it was almost certainly his finest show—a score that included such songs as "At Long Last Love," "From Alpha to Omega" and the title song.

During the thirties, musicals customarily had out-of-town tryouts in the spring, closed for the summer, and opened on Broadway in the autumn. Thus, on March 3, *You Never Know* commenced its circuit in New Haven, drawing the largest opening-night crowd since pre-Depression days. The reviews, however, were mediocre. The local critic said the show was "possibly most notable because it brings Miss Libby Holman back to a stage which for sufficient reasons she has of late eschewed. On the whole, this reappearance may be said to have been auspicious."

But the show was another matter. Libby thought the production cumbersome; she disliked the bumptious Shuberts; and she did not, as yet, have a decent song—having been saddled with a melancholy ballad called "I'm Yours," which had not even been written by Porter. But these were trifles compared to her intense hatred of Lupe Velez, who played the part of her maid.

After a career in films, Lupe Velez was making her Broadway musical debut in *You Never Know.* A tempestuous beauty, known in Hollywood as the Mexican Spitfire, Lupe was famous for her affairs with John Gilbert and Gary Cooper, and for her brief marriage to Johnny Weismuller, the former Olympic swimming champion who had achieved fame by portraying Tarzan on the screen. By all accounts, Lupe was a horrific woman. Libby thought she was little more than a vulgar Mexican peasant and, whenever she could, she said so.

In New Haven Lupe traveled between the theater and the Taft Hotel dressed only in slippers and a mink coat. She owned six cacophonous chihuahuas, two of whom were called Chips and Chops, and she carried them with her wherever she went. She antagonized everyone, screaming at the director, at the stage manager, and particularly at Libby: "You bastard, you son-a-beech, I *keel* you with *thees*"—brandishing the huge diamond ring given to her by Johnny Weismuller. Occasionally she would show the ring to Clifton Webb, saying, "Thees is the ring I'm going to murder that Jewish beech with." Following these outbursts, Lupe would kneel down in the wings, cross herself and pray.

The two actresses fought continually, and one night in New Haven during a curtain call, they came to blows, Lupe blacking Libby's eye. Libby limited her revenge to witty, vitriolic imitations of Lupe's accent and coarse behavior, on one occasion coming to rehearsal wearing a huge, shiny rhinestone ring, which she claimed resembled Lupe's nose. By the end of the New Haven run, members of the company had begun to refer to them as the Mexican Spitfire and the Jewish Witch.

The production itself had more serious troubles. After New Haven, it moved to Boston where it fared no better, then to Washington where the book and the score were altered, but to no avail. When *You Never Know* reached Philadelphia, J. J. Shubert claimed he didn't understand what the show was supposed to mean, contending it would be much improved by the addition of several chorus girls. Clifton Webb persuaded him to bring in

George Abbott to doctor the musical. Cole Porter was so distressed by the turbulent and continual changes that he likened the show to being married to the wrong woman seven times.

By May, when the production closed for the summer, Abbott had improved it by cutting scenes and tightening dialogue. When the cast returned in late August, however, they learned that J. J. Shubert had eliminated all of George Abbott's revisions, had added a bar scene, a swimming-pool scene, and nearly a dozen chorus girls—one of whom, Marriane O'Brien, was later to marry Smith Reynolds's older brother, Dick.

As *You Never Know* approached New York, the cast was disconsolate, and relations between Lupe Velez and Libby had deteriorated to such a degree that the stage manager, who took seriously Lupe's threats of murdering Libby, insisted on escorting Libby from her dressing room to the stage. The outraged Lupe, knowing that Libby was nearsighted, took to urinating in the wings. Since Libby followed her onstage, Lupe hoped that she would slip in the puddle and fall—a hope that was never realized. Finally, on August 30, Rowland Leigh, the director, walked out, swearing he would not return until the ladies settled their differences. Libby was intractable; she knew Lupe wouldn't change. "But you've got to give her credit," she told Clifton Webb. "Lupe aspired and succeeded in becoming little more than a cheap whore."

You Never Know opened at the Winter Garden Theatre on Broadway on September 21, 1938. The first-night crowds were described by a reporter as "a chatting, smoking melange of bejeweled, befurred and perfumed women wedged between the black and white phalanx of their escorts." They liked the show a good deal more than the critics did.

John Mason Brown in the New York *Post* expressed the prevailing opinion. "You might think," he wrote, "that with Cole Porter on hand to supply music and lyrics for such performers as Webb, Velez and Holman, the results would have to be sprightly, but in spite of what you may have thought, permit me to report that you are wrong."

Brown was somewhat more enthusiastic about Libby. "Miss Holman is as deep-throated as ever," he wrote, "a songstress who is always willing to serve jazz as its Lady Macbeth. She wanders through a script which gives her little to do with terrifying poise. No singer in Grand Opera could have more manner. She can be effective, too, in a sultry way that is uniquely her own. Although she is a great one for arranging her draperies . . . and striking an arrogantly forlorn pose, her skill with a certain limited kind of song cannot be disputed, even by those who may not count themselves among her warm admirers."

Brooks Atkinson of the New York *Times*, who had once praised "the dark purple menace" in Libby's voice, wrote: "Miss Holman's singing, which had the town at her feet some years ago, has more recently become mannered. She is not Mr. Porter's best spokesman just now."

Cole Porter did not attend the opening night party and, revising his initial opinion, admitted that *You Never Know* was the worst show with which he had ever been associated. After a month, certain economy measures were taken and a few of the cast accepted salary cuts. One night in late November, J. J. Shubert appeared in Clifton Webb's dressing room. "Clifton," he said, "if we put things back the way they were, don't you think we could get a run out of it?"

"Not with me," said Webb. The next day, after only seventy-eight performances, *You Never Know* closed.

The cast believed the Shuberts were at fault. They had changed the format of the show behind the director's back. They were notoriously mean. On tour, for example, in order to save overtime, the Shubert brothers would often order the stagehands to begin packing up the props while the actors were still onstage. One night in Philadelphia, Libby made her entrance late in the second act to discover that all the pictures and some of the furniture had been removed from the scene. As the play progressed, Libby looked around the barren set and then ad-libbed to Rex O'Malley: "I'm terribly sorry you lost your inheritance and had to sell all your pictures." The audience missed the point, of course, but O'Malley, the actors and the stagehands in the wings broke into raucous laughter.

Libby had not done badly by the show. Her reviews, for the most part, were good, and in spite of the fact that Cole Porter had not composed a single song for her, she had emerged from what many of her fans considered a lengthy and unnecessary retirement.

Up until the final night, Libby and Lupe Velez continued to squabble. Libby claimed that she had never met a woman she disliked so much. She told Clifton Webb that she had put a hex on Lupe. "You'll turn into a witch yet, m'dear," said Webb.

"She already has," said Mabelle.

Six years later, in Hollywood, the thirty-six-year-old pregnant Lupe Velez arranged bouquets of colorful flowers in her bedroom and, having lighted several large candles, lay down beneath the great crucifix she kept above her satin bed and swallowed seventy-five Seconals. It was there that Lupe hoped to be found—dead, but immaculately composed in her chapel-bedroom.

But the dose was not immediately fatal. At some point during the night, violently ill, Lupe Velez revived and lurched to the bathroom. She was found the next morning by her Mexican maid, dead, her head in her specially designed toilet—her Egyptian Chartreuse Onyx Hush-Flush Model Deluxe.

When the show closed, Libby threw herself into the night life of Manhattan with the frenzy of one who believed she would not have the opportunity to do so again. She was seen continually at galas, first nights, Harlem honky-tonks and Eastside supper clubs, always accompanied by Rafe Holmes, whom Libby referred to as "the sexiest man on *both* sides of town." She particularly liked Café Society Downtown and the little jazz joints on West Fifty-second Street—"Swing Street," as it was known. Her favorite club was the Famous Door, where, once or twice a week, she stopped in to hear Teddy Wilson play intermission piano and Billie Holiday sing "Easy Living" and "Billie's Blues."

During the late thirties, Libby's name continued to appear regularly in the newspapers—most ostentatiously in Lucius Beebe's column in the *Herald Tribune*, where her dress and eccentricities were reported with unabashed pride and partiality.

Beebe escorted her to the opening of *Tristan and Isolde* at the Metropolitan Opera and wrote: "If anything were needed to illustrate the decline into comparative obscurity of old-time formal society in Manhattan and the complete dominance of what has come to be known as café society, it was the stir that Libby Holman Reynolds made at the first night of the opera.

"This year, great names, great personages and great entrances were all relegated to anonymity and oblivion by La Belle Libby, who arrived in a bale of white fox furs, enormous red camelias in her hair and no stockings at all. To say that she was the sensation of the opera is to put it mildly. She was at once a paragrapher's pride and a photographer's heaven. Front page names that once commanded a hundred flash bulbs for their grand entry were forgotten or left unsnapped by the lensmen who followed Miss Holman wherever she went, fashion experts who sketched her in a score of poses and society reporters who jotted down the last detail of her hairdress, sandals and lacquered toe nails."

For years, Beebe reported, Libby had attempted to give up tobacco and had managed to limit her smoking to Saturday nights, when she preferred cigars. At one Saturday night party, Libby asked her host, the novelist Louis Bromfield, for a cigar and Bromfield was reluctant to give her one. Appealing to Bromfield's well-known sense of literary snobbery, Libby said, "Well, Amy Lowell *always* smoked cigars." "That is true," said Bromfield, "but Amy *always* brought her own."

Libby was now thirty-four and, through fastidious dieting, had become extremely thin. Claiming it was good for her voice, she subsisted on steak tartare with a raw egg. Libby had become so emaciated that her friends were concerned. "You're *too* thin, Libby, you're *too* thin," the actor Ray Dennis warned. "You're *thinner* than Constance Bennett exhumed."

Attending a party at the Elysée Hotel, Libby walked into the elevator where she encountered Ray Dennis and Tallulah Bankhead. Suddenly, Tallulah began screaming obscenities at Libby and cursing her in a drunken growl. Libby was startled, but said nothing, getting out on the next floor. When the doors closed behind her, Dennis said, "*Tallulah,* why were you so rude to Libby?"

"I *don't know,*" said Tallulah. "I thought she was deaf and couldn't hear."

"She's *not* deaf," said Dennis. "She's *blind.*"

"Oh, I *knew* it was *something,*" said Tallulah.

On January 9, 1939, Libby gave an extravagant party in her Manhattan duplex to celebrate Topper's sixth birthday. Topper had recently developed a keen interest in jazz and, at his instigation, Libby hired Benny Goodman, Teddy Wilson, Gene Krupa, Lionel Hampton, Helen Ward and Billie Holiday to perform. Topper dressed for the party in a sailor suit and vowed, as it began, that he would try to stay awake till midnight.

As the party progressed, Jimmy Donohue performed a hilarious striptease; Mrs. Clark Gable cried continually because Gable had deserted her for Carole Lombard; taking Topper as his partner, Clifton Webb executed a sinuous apache dance, leaping and twisting onto the sofas, the tables and chairs. At ten o'clock, backed by the band, Libby, Helen Ward and Billie Holiday sang an upbeat version of "Happy Birthday"; and then, as Rafe Holmes carried an enormous birthday cake into the room, the lights were dimmed, and Libby sang "You Are My Sunshine" to her little boy, who finally fell asleep as she finished it. Topper was put to bed, but the band played on and, at nine in the morning, when the party ended, Lionel Hampton was found asleep in Libby's bedroom, embracing what Billie Holiday described as "a big-assed bottle of vintage champagne. That was one hell of a party," she said, "the way a party's supposed to be."

36

TOPPER WAS AN INTELLIGENT BOY, TALL FOR HIS AGE, AND HE closely resembled his father. Libby worried constantly about his education: Should he be sent away to school or tutored at home? She didn't know what to do with him. Louisa Carpenter suggested sending him to sea, a facetious alternative for which Topper feigned great enthusiasm; but the joke was lost on Libby. Concerning her son, she worried about everything.

Later that year, she explained to a bemused reporter that she was attempting to teach Topper the value of money. "I had to learn it for myself the hard way," she said, "and I feel it's necessary for everyone to learn. Money comes from work, and life without work would be pretty unhappy. I don't want him to be spoiled. He is given twenty-five cents for carrying mown grass from off the lawn. He has no idea he is a rich boy. In fact, Clifton Webb heard him say that he hoped mama would get a job on the stage because we needed the money."

Already, at six, Topper had his mother's malicious sense of humor. Shortly after Libby's new house was furnished, she gave a lunch for some friends to ask their opinions about what it should be called. Treetops, she felt, sounded rather too botanical. Clifton Webb, Joseph J. O'Donahue IV and Lucius Beebe arrived and, over a three-course lunch, suggested catalogs of grand and stately appellations. As the three men talked, Topper interrupted and, alluding to Ralph Holmes and other men who had traipsed through the front door, he suggested they call it Cathouse. "That's hitting below the belt, young man," said Libby, and dispatched Topper to his room.

Libby had been seeing Ralph Holmes continuously for eighteen months, and when Treetops was completely furnished, the young actor moved in. For weeks, she had debated the wisdom of marrying Rafe. He was eleven years younger; he was having difficulties coping with her homosexual friends; and she knew it would devastate Phillips. Such intimates as Louisa Carpenter, Clifton Webb and Lucius Beebe cautioned her against it. Louisa thought Rafe "a piece of fluff, a pretty whippersnapper." Webb and Beebe agreed that the only serious reason for marrying Holmes was that his initials approximated Libby's and, since all the towels and linens, the silver and china at Treetops were monogrammed LHR, Libby would not be forced to alter them. But Libby had convinced herself that she was in love with the handsome young man. More important, she wanted another child.

Libby had a penchant for pretty youths; she could not resist them. Only a few months before, Theresa Helburn of the Theatre Guild had invited her to attend the opening of a new play called *Dame Nature* in Westport, Connecticut. The production required urgent funds to reach New York and Libby had been invited in the hope that she would provide at least a portion of them. Rafe was away and Libby's friend George Lloyd was spending the week at Treetops. Since this was business, Libby decided to attend the opening alone and the chauffeur drove her to nearby Westport.

Libby didn't like the play—she thought it "lacked balls"—but she sat through the performance because of a young actor portraying a fifteen-year-old boy who has just discovered he is to sire a child. He was mesmerizing and exuded a palpable sense of masculinity that overpowered her. Afterward, she went backstage to meet him. When she returned to Treetops, she was terribly excited. "George," she shouted, "I've just seen the most divine young actor in the world. He's even more gorgeous than Rafe. He's seventeen, much too old for me, but I'll get him if it takes the rest of my life." The young actor's name was Montgomery Clift.

On March 27, 1939, Libby and Ralph Holmes were secretly married in an Episcopal church in Alexandria, Virginia. Libby's friend, the interior decorator Mimi Durant, acted as both maid of honor and best man—carrying the ring for Rafe and giving Libby away. Topper, who sanctioned the alliance, remained behind at Treetops. The couple pledged eternal love and fidelity, and Rafe swore he would cherish the thirty-four-year-old Libby as no one had done before—an extravagant assertion for a man of twenty-three.

News of the wedding was not released for several days, by which time the couple were honeymooning at Treetops. In order to repel the curious, Libby hired two special constables to guard the gates. Several reporters and photographers turned up. "Sorry, pal," said the chief constable to one of them, "but the lady give us orders not to let nobody by. We'll have to toss you out on your panties if you try and get in." The reporter withdrew, and Libby and Rafe remained in seclusion for nearly two weeks.

That summer, Libby and Clifton Webb performed in a road show called *Burlesque*, portraying the roles created on Broadway by Hal Skelly and Barbara Stanwyck. *Burlesque*, an unashamedly sentimental piece about a clown who makes good in a Broadway revue, opened in June at the Chapel Theatre in Great Neck, New York, then moved to other playhouses along the eastern shore before beginning its final two-week run at the Ogunquit Playhouse in Maine. Ogunquit audiences treated Libby more respectfully than they had five summers before.

The play was primarily a vehicle for Libby and Webb to

amuse themselves. Rafe and Topper tagged along, driving leisurely from town to town in Webb's blue-and-white Rolls-Royce.
Libby had recently originated a verbal game in which she added
"uary" to the names of people she loved. She called herself Libu-
ary. Webb was Cliftuary and Rafe was Rafuary. Young Topper,
however, disliked the appendage. He thought it silly and juvenile—not the sort of witty raillery he had been taught to expect
from clever adults.

In early 1940, the thirty-one-year-old Robert Lewis, who with
Harold Clurman, Lee Strasberg and Cheryl Crawford had been
a founding member of the Group Theatre nine years before,
was conducting a scene class for professional actors in a studio
on Manhattan's West Side. A bald and jovial teacher, Lewis, behind his back, was known as "the Buddha," but everyone called
him Bobby to his face. Among his students were Montgomery
Clift and Ralph Holmes. Lewis attempted to teach his pupils how
to discover an acting style without sacrificing inner truth; he was
having problems with Ralph. A straight leading man, Ralph was
not as sensitive an actor as his brother, Phillips, and he possessed
an exceedingly limited range. But Lewis persevered. One day,
Ralph asked him if he could bring his wife to the class. Lewis
consented and the next day Libby arrived.

In order to give Lewis some idea of her dramatic skills, Libby
performed a drawing-room-comedy scene with Ralph. Lewis
thought it was fine, but told Libby that it had seemed too easy
for her, that the point of acting was to stretch one's self, to ex-
ceed one's limits. Unwittingly, he suggested that Libby portray
someone *in extremis*, a woman, perhaps, who kills her husband.
Libby said nothing, but narrowed her eyes, and Ralph looked
wildly around him. Lewis was terribly embarrassed. He began to
stutter and, finally, his voice trailed away.

Libby, however, seemed unperturbed and decided to do a
scene from Somerset Maugham's *The Letter,* in which a woman
shoots her husband. When she had finished, Lewis patiently explained that while Libby was holding the gun, she had looked
most unconvincing. "You've got to *convince* the audience," he
said. "You've got to make them *believe* you're about to gun your
husband down." Realizing what he had said, Lewis began to stut-

ter again. But Libby laughed and said she would reenact the scene, this time with greater intensity.

Libby remained in Bobby Lewis's acting class for less than a fortnight. Only once did she encounter Montgomery Clift. As she left the studio late one afternoon, Monty was coming in, and they bumped into one another. The nineteen-year-old actor smiled and apologized, then moved away. Libby couldn't speak; she just turned and stared. As she later told George Lloyd: "I was burning up. Just looking at him made me feel like I'd caught an incurable fever."

The next day, Libby left the acting class. Bobby Lewis was not surprised. Libby had exhibited certain undeveloped acting skills, but Lewis felt that she had been in love with the idea of theater, not the theater itself. Her enthusiasms were greater than her talents, and like most enthusiasts, she did not have a long attention span. George Lloyd believed that Libby had involved herself in Lewis's classes because she loved humorous intellectualizing about the theater, and Bobby Lewis was both bright and funny. In the end, however, all his talk of inner truth was too abstract, too insubstantial for Libby. About this time, she began to employ what would become one of her fondest phrases. She used it about café society and torch songs, about lovers she would soon dismiss, and she used it now in reference to Bobby Lewis's theatrical disciplines: "It's not good enough," she said. "It's just not good enough."

The collapse of Europe was imminent: Germany had conquered most of the continent, it had invaded Russia, and the Luftwaffe was bombing Britain. America, meanwhile, continued to pursue a policy of nonintervention. That summer, Ralph and Phillips Holmes, who were half-Canadian, joined the Royal Canadian Air Force. Ralph enlisted in Ottawa on July 9 and would receive his commission the following year. Libby tried to dissuade him, but Ralph felt duty bound. He was to spend the next three years in Hamilton, Ontario, training pilots and was permitted two days leave every fortnight. He always traveled to Treetops to see Libby; not once did Libby go to Canada.

On December 26, almost three weeks after the Japanese attacked Pearl Harbor, Phillips Holmes was inducted into the RCAF in Toronto. Assigned to the Initial Training School in Regina, Saskatchewan, he ultimately obtained the rank of leading aircraftsman. Both brothers were determined to see action and contrived unsuccessfully to acquire European assignments.

Libby would see Ralph infrequently during the next four years, and although she missed him in the beginning, she soon accustomed herself to the loss. There would be other lovers during the war years, too many, she admitted, but they were cursory, transient affairs. Her real obsession was with a new career, the singing of blues and folk songs—a repertory of which she would ultimately call "Americana."

Libby was especially enamored with the music of the black singer and guitarist Josh White. She had first heard him at the Village Vanguard in New York, singing duets with Leadbelly, the great blues singer and self-styled "King o' the Twelve-string Guitar," and persuaded a mutual friend, Nicholas Ray, to introduce them. The twenty-nine-year-old Ray, a fledgling theatrical director, would not begin his Hollywood career as a film director for another eight years. With Stan Lomax, Ray had presented the first American folk-song program on radio in 1939. Libby desperately wanted to work with Josh White, but both White and Ray were reluctant. White believed that white women could not sing black songs; they couldn't even understand them. And Ray, although he admired Libby's voice, didn't like it personally. She displayed, even flaunted, certain vocal affectations that although perfect for torch songs, were not compatible with the blues. But Libby persisted and Ray arranged an audition. If anyone could temper Libby's affectations, Ray surmised, that man was Josh White.

Josh White was born in Greensville, South Carolina, on February 11, 1908. When he was seven, he helped a blind black singer home. The singer, Joel Taggart, asked Josh's mother if the boy could accompany him to Florida for the winter. Josh liked Taggart and was eager to go. He hated South Carolina where he had seen his father beaten to death and his uncle lynched by the Ku Klux Klan. His mother, who believed that leading the blind was performing God's holy work, allowed him to leave. For four years, the blind singer and the young boy wandered from South Carolina to Florida to Texas to Chicago. It was from Taggart that Josh received his early musical education.

While in Texas, Taggart introduced Josh to Blind Lemon

Jefferson, the nomadic black blues singer, who had been Lead-belly's chief influence, and Josh learned to sing the songs that only Blind Lemon knew—pre–Civil War songs he had heard old people sing, rare spirituals, work songs, field hollers, and rural ballads that the early English and Irish settlers had brought to America and sung down the generations. Blind Lemon taught young Josh these songs and how to master the twelve-string guitar.

In 1932, the American Standard Recording Company brought Josh to New York to catalog a definitive collection of American folk songs, blues and spirituals. Josh ultimately obtained a recording contract and his own radio show and, as a studio guitarist, sat in on sessions with such great blues singers as Leadbelly and Bessie Smith. He looked forward to a splendid career, but one night in a Harlem brawl, he put his right hand through a glass door and three fingers were severely damaged. His doctors told him he would never perform again.

From 1934 to 1939, Josh worked as a janitor, a building superintendent and elevator operator. He lived in a three-room Harlem walk-up with his young wife, two children, his brother and mother-in-law. One night, while he was playing whist, life suddenly, inexplicably, returned to his withered hand and he found he was able to play again. The strange occurrence made him uncommonly superstitious, and for the rest of his life, he never went anywhere without his guitar.

In 1940, Josh portrayed Blind Lemon Jefferson in the musical, *John Henry*, which starred Paul Robeson. His song, "One Meatball," sold a million records, and by 1941, he was one of the most famous folk singers and guitarists in America. The big, husky, handsome singer, who always sang with a lighted cigarette behind his ear, was called, when Libby met him, "a rare repository of black Southern music."

Libby's audition with Josh White was held at her Manhattan duplex. "It was worse than any audition I ever had on Broadway," she said. "It was winter and my palms were wet. His approval meant more to me than a million dollars." Despite Nicholas Ray's apprehensions, Libby performed admirably. Josh was impressed, but cautioned Libby that, should they work together, she would have to forget everything she had learned before. "I'm prepared to forget even more than that," she replied.

Under Josh's tutelage, Libby learned the blues and ballads of New Orleans and the Mississippi Delta, of Louisville, Memphis and Kansas City—the true blues sung by a people who had never heard of Broadway.

Libby felt reborn. With Josh accompanying her on guitar, they performed at the Village Vanguard, the Café Society Downtown, La Vie Parisienne and the Blue Angel in New York. She wore clothes designed by Mainbocher—gingham blouses embroidered with cabbage roses and paillettes and wide tobacco-brown skirts spreading four to six inches upon the floor, which she handled artfully, swirling them about her legs like a cape. Her repertoire of early American blues included such songs as "Evil Hearted Me," "Hard Times Blues," "The Lass with the Delicate Air," "'Buked and Scorned," "Got a Head Like a Rock and a Heart Like a Marble Stone," "Strange Fruit" and "House of the Rising Sun."

One New York critic described them as "a cast of one, an orchestra of one." And somewhat later, in Chicago, Claudia Cassidy, the prestigious and notoriously difficult music critic for the *Sun-Times*, wrote: "A kind of molten mesmerism hung tingling in the throbbing air. They sang as Negroes sing, a native gift to Mr. White (the man with the Svengali guitar), an acquired one of Miss Holman, and in their voices were the quavers, the curious cadences, the shadows, the sorrows, and the joys of a race superbly articulate in improvised song. . . . Miss Holman was singing the songs she was born to sing, the songs that waited for years for the husky, quavering, sudden deep velvet magic of her voice."

"The Negro of the South," Libby told a New York reporter, "long ago discovered that the throbbing story of his life could best be told in words and music. Sometimes the result bites into your flesh and leaves you feeling raw inside, but it is dynamically true. It is life. Tin Pan Alley is still writing the white man's blues, while the real blues call out for emancipation. 'Strange Fruit,' for example, is typical of the blues sung in the cotton fields, share-croppers' hovels and Southern kangaroo jails.

"Despite the fact that the composers are mostly unknown, almost every song tells a story—of love, conflict, hate or ambition. That's what is needed in the theater today, a new form combining the acting art with song and music. These are the kinds of songs I've always wanted to sing, the ones I was meant to sing. It's the kind of music you can feel—the lusty, earthy kind that doesn't come from Tin Pan Alley."

———————————————— **37** ————————————————

D ESPITE THE OPINIONS OF TEACHERS AND FRIENDS, LIBBY continued to believe she had a genuine talent for the dramatic theater. Confusing artistry with desire, she decided to back a play called *Mexican Mural* provided she be given one of the leading roles. Her real motivation, however, was that she knew the star of the play was Montgomery Clift. It was Libby's first venture—and, indeed, her last—into what she considered her real future, the legitimate stage.

Mexican Mural, a series of four sketches, or panels as they were called, was set on Ash Wednesday, the day after a carnival in Veracruz. An experimental production, the play was intended to dramatize the religious superstitions, the poverty and desperation of the Mexican people. In addition to Libby and Montgomery Clift, the performers included Kevin McCarthy and William Le Massena. The play was written by Ramon Naya and directed by Libby's former dramatic teacher, Bobby Lewis.

In 1942, Monty Clift was twenty-one and already a star in the Broadway theater. *Mexican Mural* was his tenth play. Libby had not seen him for two years and she found him even more beautiful now. As she told George Lloyd: "Monty has the voice of a siren, the face of an archangel. Just looking at him makes me cry."

Edward Montgomery Clift was born in Omaha, Nebraska, on October 17, 1920. His father was a vice-president of the Omaha National Bank. For the first ten years of Monty's life, while his father remained in Omaha, his mother, Sunny, moved Monty, his brother and twin sister to Chicago, New England, Bermuda, to Paris, St. Moritz, to America and back to Europe again. Nothing was too good for the little boy. He rarely attended school, but was tutored in French and German and learned to speak both languages fluently. He was given piano, singing, swimming, photography, golf, tennis and ice-skating lessons, and attended classes in ballet and elocution.

By the time he was eight, Monty was so handsome that strangers turned to gape at him in the street. He began his career as a male model and appeared on Broadway for the first time when he was fourteen. He was very much the son of Sunny, his domineering mother, who prodded and pampered him. During his early teens, Monty was attracted to both men and women and by seventeen was thought to be a spoiled and conceited sissy. His few friends thought him aloof and guarded, a young man set apart, with what seemed to them a heightened sense of his own superiority. As *Mexican Mural* went into rehearsal, he was still living at home with his mother.

The cast rehearsed for more than a month, the nonunion production being almost an extension of Bobby Lewis's acting classes. Since there was so much movement onstage, Lewis organized elaborate improvisations designed to liberate the actors physically. There was considerable hugging and clutching during rehearsals and the atmosphere became increasingly sensual—even though many of the actors thought the play pretentious and tiresome.

Bobby Lewis instructed his players to treat Libby as they would any other actor; but when she entered the rehearsal hall for the first time, they turned and stared. Wearing a pale Mainbocher dress that accentuated her deep tan and slender legs, Libby seemed to pose at the top of the center aisle. Her black hair tumbled wildly to her shoulders, and as she moved down the aisle, she smelled strongly of her favorite scent—Jungle Gardenia. She reminded Augusta Dabney, Kevin McCarthy's wife, of a black-widow spider.

Libby played the part of Celestina Ruiz, a Mexican peasant woman. As rehearsals began, Kevin McCarthy could not fail to notice that she had extraordinary presence, but he thought it a curious piece of casting "to take Libby, this child of café society, this Reynolds mystery woman"—and attempt to turn her into a Mexican earth mother. At the same time, he sensed that Libby had guts and a peculiar style; and, as he would come to know, she did not abide by anyone else's notions of how one should live. She was conspicuously singular.

As opening night approached, a predictable tension and excitement welled up among the players. They continually discussed the significance of their lines, the importance of truly becoming their characters—although, in the end, the play would serve to enhance only Montgomery Clift's career. Indeed, most of the excitement revolved around him. As an actor, he was mesmerizing; and offstage, he was even more beguiling. His colleagues tended to cluster around him and Monty accepted their admiration easily and without arrogance.

Monty flirted indiscriminately with Libby, Kevin McCarthy, Augusta Dabney and the diminutive Mira Rostova, a Russian émigré who played a minor role in the show, and the flirtations were conducted in an eerily similar manner. Augusta Dabney remembered seeing Monty and Mira walking down Forty-second Street, their arms linked, talking softly, with utter concentration. They seemed to be speaking a special language she was unable to understand. Two days later, she saw Monty and Libby walking toward Libby's car. Their arms were linked and they talked softly, with utter concentration. Miss Dabney approached them, but they ignored her. They seemed to be speaking a special language she was unable to understand.

The other actors knew that Libby was attracted to Monty. And Monty was genuinely, though guardedly, attracted to her. Libby would have been impressed with Monty's dramatic talents; she would have been aroused by his youth, his beauty, his androgynous nature. In turn, Monty responded to Libby's wit, her strong, quirky intelligence, and to the fact that she seemed not only to understand but to sympathize with the odd, mercurial qualities in him. But Libby was still in love with Rafe, and Monty was too consumed with himself, with chorus boys and ingenues. And so a delicate truce was fashioned, a harmless flirtation ensued—the implication being that one day, perhaps, a genuine passion would be declared.

When *Mexican Mural* opened at the Chanin Auditorium on April 27, 1942, Brooks Atkinson wrote in the New York *Times*: It "is a strange, wild, evocative sketch of an undisciplined civilization. Some of the acting is excellent, especially Montgomery Clift's superlative portrait of a brooding beaten youth who cannot endure the coarseness of his environment." Atkinson neglected to mention Libby. Other reviews were mixed and some were blatantly bad, but later that year Tennessee Williams in the New York *Times* declared that it was one of the ten best plays he had ever seen. Toward the end of the run, there was encouraging talk of moving the play to another theater, but nothing came of it. Three weeks after it opened, *Mexican Mural* closed and the actors and actresses drifted apart. Libby would not meet Monty again for nearly nine years.

Phillips Holmes had not seen Libby since she had ordered him from her home four years before. Tormented by her marriage to his younger brother, Phillips had managed to forgive Rafe, but he felt, as he would always feel, that Libby had betrayed him. In her wake, there had been other women, but none of them had been able to supplant her. It was curious: Phillips no longer cursed Libby nor drank himself to sleep beneath her photographs; and, whenever he thought of her, it was not with longing. He wished only that life could once again be rich with possibilities, as it had been before the war, before her perfidy.

In early August of 1942, Phillips passed his RCAF flying examination. Thinking he would be posted to the European front immediately, he telephoned Libby at Treetops to say good-bye. The maid informed him that Mrs. Reynolds was not receiving calls that evening. Phillips left his name. On the afternoon of August 12, shortly after takeoff from Armstrong, Ontario, an Anson aircraft in which Phillips was a passenger collided with another military plane. There were no survivors. Phillips was thirty-three years old.

Libby and Phillips's sister, Madeleine, flew to Toronto to collect his body. Six days later, following a service in St. Patrick's Cathedral, Phillips was buried in Mount Pleasant, New York. After the funeral, Libby drove back to Treetops with Rafe and George Lloyd. Over drinks in the library, she told Lloyd that she felt somehow responsible. It was absurd of course; what had Phillips's death to do with her? "Nothing," Lloyd assured her, but he, too, sensed Libby's guilt. She almost welcomed it. The next day, she hung Phillips's photograph in the foyer outside her bedroom—on the wall next to the one of Smith Reynolds.

Throughout the war years, Libby appeared occasionally in

summer stock. She played the lead role in *My Sister Eileen* at the Bucks County Playhouse in Philadelphia and repeated the performance at the Strand Theatre in Stamford before appreciative audiences and critics. But she spent the majority of her time touring America with Josh White.

She and Josh had recently released their only album, *Blues Till Dawn*, a classic of early American blues. On this one album, Libby overcame the vocal mannerisms and affectations she had learned before she met Josh and which she would employ again when their partnership ended. Her voice was low and vibrant, the pulsing and seemingly untrained voice of her early torch songs. The album included "When the Sun Goes Down," "Good Mornin' Blues," "Baby, Baby" and "House of the Rising Sun."

A New York reviewer wrote: "Miss Holman and Mr. White are offering a program of early American blues. Up to now, Libby Holman has never been one of my great passions. She was a star, of course, and more than that, a symbol of an era. You thought of Libby Holman and you thought of the days of plenty and the nights of giddiness when the theater was the 'thittuh.' You thought of her and you thought of Prohibition and raccoon coats and million dollar gates. But this is a new and I think better Libby Holman."

In September, they opened at La Vie Parisienne, a fashionable supper club at 3 East Fifty-second Street in New York. Their show was a critical success and the audiences were enthusiastic, but the racial prejudice that accompanied it was dispiriting, and would give Libby a cause for which she would fight for the rest of her life.

At their first rehearsal, Josh, because he was black, was not permitted to enter La Vie Parisienne by the front door. Libby was livid, but insisted that Josh accede to the management's wishes. "Don't degrade yourself," she said. "I'll take care of it." Libby waited until La Vie had secured advertisements in the Manhattan papers. The day they were scheduled to open, she suddenly announced that she refused to sing unless the club altered its racial policies. Surprisingly, the management relented.

But it was a recurring problem. When they appeared at the Balinese Room in Boston's Hotel Somerset, the management refused Josh accommodations. In the crowded lobby, Libby became indignant and screamed: "You should take down the

American flag outside and put up a swastika." Libby and Josh were asked to leave.

They made numerous attempts to travel overseas with the USO, but were continually told that the USO did not accept what they called "mixed shows." "What do you mean by mixed shows?" ranted Libby. "Boys and girls?" Libby went so far as to write to Eleanor Roosevelt, offering to head a committee to rectify the problem. "I can get to more important people more quickly than you," Mrs. Roosevelt replied, "but I don't think it will help. There are many who will give lip service, but there are few of us who will stand up and be counted."

Referring to the war abroad and to domestic racial prejudice, Libby wrote to a friend: "I am fed up to the teeth with humanity. Any race of bipeds that can get itself into this mess deserves extermination. Jesus, I have washed my hands of all of it."

But Libby could not contain her fury; she was committed now. She spoke long and eloquently against racial discrimination; and she and Josh spiked their songs with ironic rebuke for the plight of the American Negro. They were particularly appalled with the discrimination black soldiers were forced to endure in American army camps. The clubs of the white soldiers were always more elaborate than those of the blacks and, by unwritten rule, blacks were not permitted to enter them. In these clubs, Libby and Josh often ended their show with a song of Josh's entitled "Southern Exposure," which included the lyric: "I think democracy is fine/but I mean democracy without the color line."

They toured black servicemen's clubs at army bases up and down the east coast. In Fort Meade in Maryland, Libby sang not only the blues but many of her early torch songs. The black servicemen began to sing along with her, stamping their feet, clapping their hands and rocking their chairs to the primitive melodies. Libby had brought Topper to Fort Meade. It was the first time the nine-year-old boy had heard his mother sing publicly, and as the black crowd keened and moaned, Topper became distressed and began to cry—thinking the audience was angry with Libby.

Afterward, Libby took Josh and Topper and three black servicemen into Baltimore to the Hotel Belvedere for drinks and dinner. As they entered the bar, Libby shouted to the bartender: "Double Scotches and raw meat for everyone."

"You're raw enough already, lady," said the bartender.

38

L IBBY AND RALPH HOLMES HAD BEEN MARRIED FOR FOUR years. But since he had enlisted in the RCAF, they had seen one another infrequently. Only once in two years had Rafe been given an extended leave; in early 1943, he contracted viral pneumonia, was hospitalized in New York's Doctors Hospital and recuperated at Treetops.

During his convalescence, Rafe was transferred, as he had long wished to be, to England as a flight lieutenant. Just before he was scheduled to leave, Libby decided to give a party for him. She wanted it to be extravagant, a momentous occasion. Because of rationing and the shortage of staff, Libby had closed down most of Treetops and thought it more practical to stage the event in a Manhattan hotel. George Lloyd agreed to make the arrangements, but whenever he mentioned Libby Holman Reynolds to hotel managers, there was a short and agitated pause, followed by a polite refusal. Finally, the Waldorf Astoria consented to rent Libby rooms for the night, the manager explaining that the Duke and Duchess of Windsor had vacated their suite unexpectedly the week before. He hoped it would be satisfactory.

That very afternoon, Libby and George Lloyd drove down to New York to inspect the premises. The hotel manager ushered them in and they wandered excitedly through the Windsor suite. Separating, Lloyd went into the living room, while Libby withdrew to the master bedroom. Some moments later, Lloyd heard Libby shouting for him to join her in the bedroom. As he walked in, Libby pressed her hands down on the large double bed and, looking up with a grin, she said: "The Windsors were here all right. The bed's still cold."

The party for Rafe was a great success, lasting till eight in the morning. He left for England the following day. Rafe was to spend the next fifteen months ferrying high-ranking military personnel between England and the Continent. But desperate to see action, he transferred to the American armed forces—flying bombing missions over Germany. For the last two years of the war, Libby did not see Rafe at all.

While Rafe was overseas, Libby busied herself with old lovers and acquired numerous new ones. Louisa Carpenter often visited Libby at Treetops or dispatched her plane to Westchester Airport in order to fly Libby down to her new house in Rehoboth Beach in Delaware. Their relationship was platonic, but they continued to love one another and share their deepest feelings. There was a real and touching bond between them, and they told friends that they intended to spend their old age together, nattering in ornate rocking chairs, at one or another of their country homes.

Libby missed Rafe intensely at first, but she craved the excitement of an affair at hand. She was drinking excessively (Dewar's and water) and whiskey made her uppity; when drunk, she preened and strutted. On her frequent sorties to Manhattan nighteries—to Reuben's, the Stork Club, the Blue Angel, and the Barberry Room in the Berkshire Hotel—Libby began, quite suddenly and indiscriminately, to pick up strange men—waiters, maître d's, bartenders—conveying them back to Treetops for the night. Like her friend Tallulah Bankhead, Libby's carnality was unbridled and obstinate. Men, to them, were little more than rash adventures. They thought of themselves as experimentalists, explorers. If "limited engagements" seemed dangerous, unusual or, best of all, amusing, then Libby passionately embraced them; and when they had ended, she and Tallulah described their abbreviated amours to one another, thrilling at the novelty of it all.

George Lloyd thought Libby's transient affairs were wholly dangerous. He remembered Libby leaving the Blue Angel late one night, climbing into the front seat of a Mack truck and driving off. Tallulah, who had previously had a fling with the handsome young trucker, had told Libby he was "literary." Between runs to Wheeling and Harrisburg, he claimed to be writing the great American novel. At Treetops, Libby fed and clothed him, gave him bubble baths in her sumptuous gold-flecked bathroom, equipped him with a desk and yellow scratch pads, and waited patiently for inspiration to come. But as the days passed, he didn't work. At last the trucker explained that he suffered from a particularly virulent form of writer's block, and about a week after he arrived, Libby threw him out. "He didn't inspire me either," said Tallulah. But the two friends agreed that he had looked remarkably like Jack London.

Normally, Libby wearied of her lovers in a day or two, dismissing them with scant deliberation. But when they had gone, she was filled with remorse. She would sit in the library at Treetops with George Lloyd, drinking Dewar's and water, and as the night wore on, would mutter over and over again: "It's not good enough, George; it's just not good enough." Lloyd attempted to console her, but Libby interrupted him, saying: "*Jesus*, George, I'm becoming just like Fanny Ward"—an allusion to an aging actress continually surrounded by questionable young men.

Rafe was kept informed of Libby's escapades. Before leaving for England, they had agreed to relate their indiscretions to one another—believing it to be advanced, sophisticated, a sloughing off of old-fashioned taboos. And so, writing from London, Rafe meticulously explained that English girls were more sexually adept than Americans, or that the Italians were more imaginative and less constrained than the Swedes, or that French girls were nonpareil. In turn, Libby dutifully informed Rafe of her limited engagements and one-night stands. They believed they were being liberated when in fact they were doing little more than destroying an already precarious marriage. The revelations ended, however, when Libby received a letter from a French girl called Lili, who claimed that Rafe was in love with her. Lili asserted that Libby was much too old for Rafe, that he didn't require a mother, and that, when the war ended, she intended to keep him in Paris. Rafe had failed to mention Lili in his letters, leaving Libby both shocked and hurt.

In consequence, Libby neglected to tell Rafe of an affair she had initiated with a journalist called Chinky Collins. A Texan, the twenty-eight-year-old redhead held a master's degree in constitutional law from American University in Washington and had become a prominent free-lance journalist in New York, specializing in opera and ballet. Chinky was young, attractive, educated, successful and a woman.

When Libby and Josh White opened at Le Vie Parisienne, Chinky interviewed Libby for *Theatre Arts*. She was not familiar with Libby or her work, knowing only that Libby Holman had been notorious many years before. But she dutifully watched the show and, when it was over, met Libby in her suite at the Berkshire Hotel. It was a complicated interview, since Libby asked Chinky so many questions about herself that Chinky felt that *she* was being interviewed.

Chinky would subsequently write a brief, inocuous report about Libby's singing folk blues instead of Broadway blues. But during the interview, she sensed that Libby was attracted to her and when Libby invited her to Treetops for the weekend, she accepted. After the Saturday night show, they set off for Connecticut in Libby's fashionable English Ford town car. Libby chattered all the way to Stamford, and Chinky was astonished at her disclosures. "I suppose you've heard all these wicked stories about me," she said. "Well, I've lived my life as it came. And I've done bloody marvels with a bad hand." Libby then alluded to Smith Reynolds's death, claiming she remembered very little about it; to her friendship with Louisa Carpenter; to Topper; and to her marriage to Rafe Holmes and the tragic death of his older brother. Chinky had not expected Libby to be so open: It sounded like a confession.

That night after dinner, the two women went upstairs to bed. As they walked into Libby's bedroom, Libby laughed loudly and whispered, "Rafe is going to *kill* me for this." Chinky didn't understand what Libby meant; but knowing this was not her first extramarital affair, she assumed that Rafe had made Libby promise to go straight—that is, not to sleep with women.

Their affair would last for more than a year. In the beginning, they usually met when Libby had finished her last show at La Vie Parisienne—in the Barberry Room, the elegant bar designed by Norman Bel Geddes in the Berkshire Hotel. But when Libby's engagement at La Vie ended, Libby spent most of her time at Treetops and Chinky saw her only at weekends. Chinky was busy; she had a job—covering openings at the Metropolitan Opera, the Ballet Theatre and the New York City Ballet—and this was something of an anomaly in Libby's life. Libby was accustomed to having her lovers at her beck and call. On at least two occasions, she pointed this out to Chinky, who patiently explained that her work came first, that to spend more of her time at Treetops, in a vacuum, was unacceptable.

But it was, for Chinky, a fortunate affair; and she would always remember it with joy and satisfaction. She and Libby had much in common. They had both considered entering the legal profession; they shared a love of music, particularly of the opera and of Kirsten Flagstad; and both of them had conducted too many thwarted relationships with men.

Chinky believed Libby preferred women, observing that she was uncomfortable with men, that she chafed at their struts and swaggers, their strident insistencies. And because she still had a certain celebrity, they expected her to live up to a reputation she could not live down. Normally, Libby became maternal with men, and when she allowed those relationships to become sexual, they almost always ended violently—as none of her relationships with women had done.

Libby and Chinky also shared a genuine sexual predicament, one felt by many women of their generation. To begin with, almost every able-bodied man was away at war. But even before the war, the men they had known were incompetent lovers, "seeking sex and self-seeking," as Libby liked to say. Their most passionate conversations were limited to the worlds of business, sports and squalid sex, and as a result, many intelligent women were attracted to homosexuals, men who could speak fluently and without embarrassment of music, literature, opera and the ballet. Both Libby and Chinky believed that heterosexual men just weren't as interesting as women, nor were they as interesting as homosexuals.

And yet Libby had married twice, for reasons Chinky never completely understood. The marriage to Smith Reynolds made a certain sense—an irresistible combination of weakness, youth and wealth. But Rafe Holmes was a riddle. Chinky attributed the marriage to a desire on Libby's part for conventionality. Affairs were not so casual then and marriage was a convenient disguise, enabling one to conduct clandestine sexual sorties while maintaining an irreproachable air of respectability. But Libby regretted neither marriage. Indeed, she claimed to regret almost nothing. Whenever Chinky voiced regret or shame over something she had done, Libby barked: "Don't ever say that again. If you're ashamed, you dishonor yourself. Just don't do it twice."

Libby was obsessed with youth. Those, like Chinky, who were fresh, unspoiled, trusting and trustworthy inflamed her. In January of 1944, she invited Chinky to a revival of Thornton Wilder's *Our Town* at the City Center, a play featuring Montgomery Clift. Following the performance, Libby claimed to have swooned in her seat and, after telling Chinky that they had met several times before, she said: "Isn't he the most beautiful youth you ever saw? I'm a cot case over that boy."

One of Libby's favorite lines at the time was "I'm giving him to Gigi [her friend Gigi Gilpin]; he's much too old for me"—the youth in question being twenty-four. Age unsettled Libby, made her vexatious. She considered it a kind of hideous disease. Much later, referring to Tallulah Bankhead, to Tallulah's face gone flaccid with drink and drugs, Libby said: "Tallulah looks like she went down on the *Titanic* . . . twice."

Chinky would always feel that being in love with Libby had been a kind of enraptured paradox. In the beginning, she had been overwhelmed with titillating visions of some intangible wickedness, smitten as she was with Libby's scandalous reputation. But that wasn't Libby at all. Almost at once, Libby had become an affectionate and intelligent friend. She was also, Chinky knew, both spoiled and bossy and could, when opposed, become violently abusive.

There were other drawbacks. Libby didn't like sex and was inept and awkward in bed. She was a shrewd and inventive seductress, but the sexual act itself bored her. Rather, it was the emotional bond that mattered. Libby adapted herself to her lover so successfully that, often, she seemed not to exist except as a more perfect mirror image. When talking, she had an unaccountable ability to make it seem as if her lover were the only person alive. She anticipated thoughts and feelings so uncannily that she might have provoked them herself. As a result, Libby made her lovers feel important, not only to her but to themselves. She was also extremely possessive and Chinky didn't want to be possessed. They never argued, but they made no attempts to hold on to one another and, in time, drifted irreparably apart.

Long after they had stopped seeing one another, Chinky encountered Libby by accident at the Cape Playhouse in Dennis, Massachusetts. She asked her how she had been. Libby said that life was tolerable, that she was driving too fast, drinking too much and sleeping with too many men. Not bad, all things considered. Libby did not elaborate, but she implied that Chinky would not approve. Chinky never saw her again.

39

B Y THE TIME TOPPER WAS ELEVEN, HE WAS GROWING MORE and more to resemble his father, and the boy thought about him increasingly. Now and again, Libby surprised Topper searching through her scrapbooks for photographs of Smith Reynolds. Tall and well-mannered, with his father's high cheekbones and prominent aquiline nose, Topper was quiet, introspective and rather frail. At Treetops, he spent much of his time in his workroom, a huge second-floor area with a sun porch, doing woodwork and making model airplanes. At eleven, Topper would not have been aware of the real extent of his wealth; and Libby would not have told him. Libby received an allowance from Topper's trust of $6,944 a month for the boy's "support and education," but she continually complained about the wretchedness of being rich. That year, she increased Topper's allowance to fifty cents a week.

During the war years, Topper spent most of his time at the New Canaan Country Day School or at summer camp, but his relationship with Libby remained a close one. He called her Lib, and Libby claimed that they were more like sister and brother than mother and son. But she held strict views on how children should be raised. She insisted, for example, that Topper, when referring to his genitals, should avoid the silly euphemisms of little boys; rather, she urged him to use the formal, accurate names of penis and testicles.

Libby was contemptuous of anything that smacked of childishness, going so far as to ban allusions of childish heroes and heroines. When one of the gardeners gave Topper a kitten, he decided to call it Shirley Temple. Learning of the name, Libby summoned Topper to the library and said: "You're not going to call anything in *this* house Shirley Temple. From now on, the cat's name is Shirley Rosenblum." Topper called her Rosenblum till the day she died.

On another occasion, Libby was told that Topper had been seen at the Stamford railroad station handing out pamphlets urging discontented conductors to strike for higher wages. Libby was pleased and proud. She considered Topper's actions wonderfully adult, and asked him where he had learned to promote good causes. "At home with a club," said the little boy, referring to the fact that Libby had hectored him with radical principles for as long as he could recall. Libby blatantly ignored Topper's youth; and this attitude served only to reinforce the boy's sense of his own isolation. He had no real friends of his own age and, increasingly, longed for their company.

Topper loved his mother, although he seemed embarrassed not only by the opulence of his surroundings, but by Libby herself. He disapproved of her histrionic poses, her bluster and brashness, and showed his displeasure by retreating to his workroom. The workroom had become a symbol of his disapproval. He left his tools and half-completed model airplanes littered everywhere. Ordinarily a tidy boy, he became increasingly slapdash and seemed pleased whenever Libby reprimanded him. He held secret conversations with Rosenblum and, as early as eleven, nursed arcane ambitions: He was never specific, but he yearned to achieve something magnificent, something for which he alone had been responsible. He didn't want to be just someone else's rich boy.

Shortly after his eleventh birthday, Topper wrote George Lloyd a typed letter thanking him for a birthday gift:

Dear George.
    The things I have here to tell you may be boring, but if it gets too boring, why read this dull manuscript of mine. A lot of people ask how was school today and I answer, "today school was just like school any other time and school was just as tiring and boring as it was every other day of the week and the days

between those other days were just as boring as school was today. In other words, school is just the same every day." (Tell this paragraph to your friends as a tongue-twister.)

Now this next paragraph is very secret. It is a new code I invented. Now if I wanted to say "will meet you at 2:00 near railroad station," the first thing I would write would be the number which would tell the number of words to skip. For example: if I put the number 2 down I would have to say—"I will not meet you at the 2:00 train near our railroad crossing station." Now cross out every other word like this:

~~I~~ will ~~not~~ meet ~~you~~ at ~~the~~ 2:00 ~~train~~ near ~~our~~ railroad ~~crossing~~ station. Catch on? (Don't I explain the most difficult things?)

Talking about crowded weekends, I am the one you just better sit down and talk with. The weekend before last, I slaved on my cabin and last weekend I went to a boy's party, saw a movie, "It Ain't Hay" and went to a concert. Tomorrow, Sunday, I am going to the circus and next weekend I'm going camping.

Everybody sends their love to you including Rosenblum.

Love, Topper.

One evening, Topper stunned Libby by asking unexpected questions about the mysterious demise of his father. His classmates had been gossiping, and Topper was confused and troubled. "We'll talk about that tonight when you go to bed," said Libby firmly. That evening, she told George Lloyd: "Fix me a stiff drink, George. Tonight's a night of reckoning." Lloyd never knew what Libby said to the boy, how she solved the delicate problem of her innocence or guilt, but the next morning, Topper informed Lloyd that Libby had told him a fairy tale the night before. It had been, he said, "mythological."

In early 1944, Libby advertised in the New York *Times* for a new secretary. Among the applicants was a twenty-three-year-old woman named Nancy Overland. A pretty blonde, Miss Overland had graduated from the Neighborhood Playhouse in New York where she had studied theater and dance under Sanford Meisner and Martha Graham. She had been hesitant about applying for the position—having been cautioned by friends that Libby was a lesbian, that her political views were "rather liberal."

The interview was conducted in the library at Treetops. After settling such matters as salary, her duties, days off and holidays,

Libby said, "Now, I hope you won't make the mistake of falling in love with me." Libby smiled, but it was a serious remark, a warning. Miss Overland was shocked; she started to speak, stuttered, blushed, but said nothing. Libby did not elaborate, and they agreed that Nancy would move into Treetops the following week.

Libby became very fond of Nancy Overland. She admired her spunk, her fresh midwestern looks and, within days of hiring her, began to call her Nancy Overboard and, occasionally, Miss Hap. The title *secretary* was something of a misnomer. Libby intended that Nancy become Topper's friend and companion. At eleven, Topper was too old for a governess and he refused to have a tutor; he didn't want a companion either, so to disguise Nancy's true role, she posed as Libby's secretary.

She longed to become a writer, and the job was supposed to provide her with ample time in which to write. But for the two years Nancy worked for Libby, she did no writing at all. Libby simply demanded too much of her. When she was not with Topper, she was expected to supervise and pay the four members of the staff, to balance Libby's checkbooks and keep the household accounts. She reviewed all manuscripts of plays arriving at Treetops with a view to potential investment; and from the beginning, she became involved with Libby's most recent obsession.

Libby wanted another child. Encouraged by Topper, who wanted a baby brother, she was also influenced by Louisa Carpenter, who had recently adopted two more orphans whom she had found walking down a country road near her house in Rehoboth Beach. When Nancy joined Libby's employ, Libby was adamant. However it could be accomplished, she would have another child.

That spring, during Topper's Easter vacation, Libby, Topper and Nancy traveled to Mont Tremblant, a ski resort near Quebec. Topper loved skiing and was already devoted to the search for what he would later call his "magic mountain."

Returning to New York by plane, Libby fell into conversation with a young girl sitting across the aisle. By the time they reached the city they had become fast friends. The girl's name was Vonnie Richards. Having become pregnant from a brief encounter with a ski instructor, the hapless girl was now faced with a choice of disgrace or abortion. In no time at all, Libby persuaded Vonnie to accompany her to Treetops, to have the baby and give it to her. She would pay for everything. It was, she felt, a masterful solution. Vonnie was enthusiastic, but when the baby girl was born, she decided to keep it, and Libby was heartbroken.

Libby persisted—going so far as to pester her friend Gigi Gilpin, who had recently married, to have a child and give it to her. It became something of a joke; at least Gigi thought of it as such, and that exasperated Libby. "All *you* have to do is to get pregnant," she said. "*I'll* take care of everything else." Finally, Gigi refused.

Libby did not discuss her plan in her letters to Rafe, who she knew, was displeased with the prospects of another child. He was close to Topper, felt that the boy was family enough for the moment, and in any event, there was nothing he could do to alleviate Libby's problem three thousand miles from home. But Libby needed children, required them even more than lovers now, and she was determined to have one.

That spring, following a series of interviews with the Children's Aid Society, a voluntary adoptive agency in New York, Libby took in not one but two foster children—a fifteen-month-old half-Caucasian, half-Chinese toddler named Bobby, and a four-year-old half-Caucasian, half-Filipino named Douglas— both of whom were casualties of World War II. Bobby, who had spent his entire life in a hospital crib, had not learned to walk, not even to crawl, and he was terribly overweight. But Libby and Topper adored him. From the beginning, however, it was understood that this was to be a temporary arrangement. Adoption laws in 1944 stated that adoptive parents must be of the same race as the adopted child; the law had not yet taken into account the offspring of American soldiers who fraternized with Asian women.

Libby, however, agreed to the arrangement—and just as quickly forgot it. She was capable of enormous warmth and it was most apparent in her relationship with the little boys. Initially, she had been concerned about what her behavior should be toward them, and the social worker had said, "Love them, feed them, and let them be." Libby followed the advice verbatim. She decorated and furnished each of their rooms; she taught them games and shopped for toys and clothes; she escorted them to Sunday school, played with them in the pool, and took

Douglas on long walks through the grounds with her Irish wolf-hounds, Various and Sundry.

When Libby was not involved with the children and their activities, she rehearsed on the grand piano in the living room; she took a nurse's aide course at nearby Stamford Hospital, and worked, as a form of exercise, in her extensive vegetable garden. Libby had no gardening skills and no real interest in agriculture. Mimicking Tallulah Bankhead, she liked to say that she was interested only in "chives for the vichyssoise, mint for the juleps."

She was active politically. With her friends, the novelists Dawn Powell and Katherine Anne Porter, she joined the committee of Women for Roosevelt. She also joined the New York chapter of the CIO Political Action Committee, a radical branch of the labor movement, devoting time and money to it. She espoused liberal views and her detractors often accused her of being a Communist. During this period, Libby was not, as some of her more conservative friends suggested, merely passionately foolish; she was outspoken and well informed and believed, as she always had, in extravagant beaux gestes.

But it was the children who obsessed her and inspired her most ardent feelings. She was utterly devoted to them. About a year after they arrived at Treetops, Libby and the boys were summoned to the offices of the Children's Aid Society in New York. The boys were taken into an adjoining office and one of the staff informed Libby that they had been placed elsewhere, in homes with parents of their respective races. The staff member was sympathetic, but there was no point in argument or in discussion; the law was the law. Libby was not even allowed to say good-bye.

Libby was disconsolate. She had given too much of herself to the orphaned boys. Returning to Treetops, she dismantled their rooms—"like destroying a world," she told Nancy Overland—and dispatched all their belongings, all the toys and games and clothes she had lovingly purchased, to the Children's Aid Society. She refused to go into their rooms again, but she did not intend to surrender either easily or gracefully. Putting her arm around Nancy, Libby said: "We'll just have to get another one."

Within weeks of the boys' departure, Libby returned, as she said, to "the thrust and parry of decadent society." She began entertaining lavishly at Treetops. Given the difficulties of finding suitable staff during the war, she had shut down most of the house, moving into the servants' wing. And so, at weekends, the ample servants' quarters were crowded with such friends as Constance Collier, Lucius Beebe, Gigi Gilpin, Steve Wiman, Louisa Carpenter, Tallulah Bankhead, Tamara Geva, Imogene Coca, Auriol Lee, Ruth Chatterton, Clifton Webb and Mabelle. Libby's friends often spent several days at Treetops—eating, drinking, cavorting in Libby's home movies, recording discs such as "the laughing song" (a five-minute track of Libby, Bobby Lewis and Dawn Powell laughing hysterically), dancing, playing tennis and charades—pretending, if only fleetingly, that the war did not exist.

At Treetops, Libby reigned like an absolute monarch, exercising supreme authority over what her friends had come to envisage as Libby's court. They even imagined themselves in the roles of ladies-in-waiting, courtiers and jesters (all of them pages as far as Libby was concerned); and if any of them challenged her unnecessarily, he was banished from Treetops forever. A willful woman, Libby wore a gold whistle around her neck in order to herald her commands, and her devoted court, with joyous shrieks and titterings, dutifully fell into line.

For as long as they were favored, Libby had a remarkable ability of appearing utterly fascinated with the most trivial details of their lives. Her conversation was sprinkled with staccato questions such as where did you go, what did you wear, what did you eat, what did you say? Her listeners were always flattered. Once, on meeting the composer David Diamond, Libby questioned him relentlessly concerning his childhood, his education, his musical ambitions, and ended by asking: "Is counterpoint manufactured or inspired?" The young composer was very impressed.

Libby had developed an ulcer the year before, a malady that would plague her for much of the rest of her life. A fellow sufferer and casual friend, Harold Ross, the editor of *The New Yorker*, wrote her a cautionary note: "Next time I see you, I'll give you the Ulcer Club grip," he said, "which is done with an amphojel tablet in the palm of the hand." Ross advised circumspection, adding, "But I know being careful isn't up your street."

Libby's ulcer worsened in 1944 and it began to impair her

capacity for drink; after two or three Scotches, she tended to fall asleep, "phasing out," as she called it. One night at Treetops, Libby gave a formal dinner party for twelve. Midway through the meal, it became obvious to everyone that she was drunk. She seemed neither to know nor to recognize any of her guests, and she reminded George Lloyd of some exquisite female Gatsby surrounded by strangers, by butlers and maids, by the extravagance of her possessions. She sat at the head of the table drinking—withdrawn, dispassionate, and a little appalled, as though she had stumbled into the wrong affair.

The push bell to summon the servants was on the floor near Libby's chair. When the second course was finished, she reached for the bell with her foot. At first she was unable to find it, and as she searched, she sank, like a drowning woman, beneath the table. The last Libby's guests saw of her, as she disappeared, was her hand delicately fluttering good-bye. A hush fell over the table and, moments later, George Lloyd carried Libby upstairs and put her to bed.

In the morning, she remembered nothing and questioned Lloyd as to whom she had insulted, whom she had banished from her home the night before. It grieved Lloyd to do so, but he always told her the truth. Lloyd knew that Libby's passions were short-lived. She embraced almost everyone, befriending some, nurturing others, drawing them seductively to her; and then, suffering from some imagined slight, Libby would sneer and bully the bewildered friend until, after several Scotches, she would shake her head imperiously and say, "It's not good enough; it's just not good enough." And the friend would be gone forever.

Only once was Libby forced to sample someone else's dismissive scorn. That summer, she drove over to Tantallon, Steve Wiman's Greenwich home, for cocktails with Steve and Clifton Webb, her oldest friend. By ten that evening, the three friends were exceedingly drunk, and Webb began to blubber about his tyrannic mother, Mabelle—how she abused him, how she schemed and pried and meddled. Libby, who had listened to Webb's maternal lamentations for fifteen years, became exasperated. "Cliftuary, Mabelle's *ruined* your life," she said. "Why don't you chloroform the old cunt."

Webb glared at Libby, his eyes glistening with surprise and

pain. Putting down his glass, he rose to his feet and in a clipped, reedy voice said quietly, "Libby Holman died tonight." He tossed his head and strode briskly from the room. Libby and Webb would never see one another again. Webb went so far as to forbid the mention of Libby's name in his presence; and if some unsuspecting stranger referred to her, Webb always stiffened, explaining that Libby Holman, whom he had once known long before, was "a black angel of death."

Nancy Overland had been in Libby's employ for eight months and accompanied her everywhere—on skiing holidays near Quebec; to the theater and supper clubs in New York; to the weekly sessions with Libby's Swedish masseuse in Greenwich; and to Rehoboth Beach for weekends with Louisa Carpenter. She drove Topper to school each day in a new Ford convertible, which, though owned by Libby, had been given to Nancy for her exclusive use.

The two women shared a love of children, of liberal politics, of Henry Miller and D. H. Lawrence, of music and opera. After dinner, in the library, they talked incessantly, divulged old secrets, immediate plans and future aspirations. Libby, Nancy knew, longed to have a real career, and somehow it continued to elude her. Libby explained that she had never understood the wellsprings of her stardom, how it had come about, precisely how it had slipped away. As she grew older—and Libby had just turned forty—she preferred to pretend that it had never existed, that her days of glory were still before her. For this reason, she disliked singing her early torch songs, and railed against critics who reminded her that she had once been a star.

They discussed their lovers (old and new), Libby alluding to Louisa, to Smith and Phillips, and the absent Rafe. Nancy mentioned her young fiancé, a Manhattan-based novelist. Gradually their relationship had ripened from that of employer-secretary into one of close camaraderie. Nancy was in awe of Libby. She admired her wit and intelligence, and although Libby was seventeen years older, Nancy began to think of her as a rather older contemporary—a woman in whom she could trust and confide, and from whom she could learn. At the same time, Treetops itself was becoming more important to her; it had become, in fact, her whole life.

It must have been obvious to the more experienced Libby that the young girl had fallen in love with her. One morning, Nancy went up to Libby's bedroom as she usually did, to open and discuss the daily mail. It was a bright, beautiful day. Nancy sat down on a small silk-covered chair at the foot of Libby's huge double bed.

Nancy was unusually nervous that morning, and as she sorted through the letters and circulars, Libby, throwing the white satin sheets and the vicuña coverlet aside, rose from her bed and walked to the window. She wore a white silk negligee and a white silk ribbon in her tousled hair. The sun streamed into the room behind her, and Libby turned to the girl and said, "You know, Nancy, I've fallen in love with you." Nancy became giddy; she was overwhelmed. It was everything she had hoped to hear. They embraced and for Nancy, at least, it was an extraordinary event. She had never been to bed with a woman before; but Libby was sensuous, soft and feminine, her lingering looks hypnotic, her expressions of love imaginative and moving.

As the weeks passed, they loved to lie in Libby's double bed, to stare at and to touch one another's bodies. Because Libby always lay naked in the sun, her body was completely bronzed. The two women loved one another passionately, but it was never to be an intense sexual affair. Despite Nancy's inexperience with women, she soon learned what Chinky Collins had learned before her: Libby was indifferent to the sexual act itself, and she never had an orgasm. As with Libby's nonsexual relationships, there was about her, as Nancy observed, "an air of *noli me tangere*. Incapable of real intimacy herself, she neither sought nor expected it in return. She had to be in control."

Their relationship would last for nearly a year, and they were as discreet as possible. Louisa Carpenter knew and approved of it; but they maintained separate bedrooms and tried not to be affectionate publicly, so that no one in the house, they hoped, neither the servants, Topper nor weekend guests, suspected they were more than friends.

Libby was a generous lover, plying Nancy with innumerable gifts, with gold pins and diamond rings and, for Christmas that year, an expensive striped-beaver fur coat. Libby's generosity, however, was accompanied by an intractable streak of possessiveness. She refused to allow Nancy to travel anywhere beyond Treetops without her, and demanded that she sever all relations with her fiancé, who, in Libby's view, was an inferior novelist and, as such, unacceptable as a man. Gradually their relationship disintegrated. All the ties that had bound them were unraveling. The two children had been taken away; Libby's career was aimless, unsatisfactory; and, finally, Nancy had a cursory fling with one of Libby's gardeners. When Libby found out, she was furious. Nancy had committed the unpardonable blunder: She had left before Libby had sanctioned her leaving.

Just before Christmas, Libby gave a party at Treetops for a crowd of her New York friends. After dinner, the guests wandered through the house, drinking and dancing to music emanating from a custom-built Capehart record player. The music throbbed loudly through a series of intricate monitors and speakers that Libby had installed in every room. Toward midnight—Libby had already gone to bed—Nancy decided to retire. But the music was deafening and Nancy did not (as Libby did) use earplugs for sleeping. The longer she lay awake, the angrier she became. At about one o'clock, she rose in a rage and marched downstairs. Grabbing an ice pick from the bar, she hacked at the record player and smashed several records. Returning upstairs, she disengaged the monitors from every room and hurled them out the windows.

The next morning, assaying the damage, Libby was apoplectic. She could barely speak. She summoned Nancy into the library, berating her for destroying her record player, for insulting her guests, for behaving like a shrew and a vulgarian. "Who . . . who do you think you are?" she screamed. . . . "Me?" Nancy Overland laughed. That very morning she was fired.

40

AT THE END OF THE YEAR, LIBBY BEGAN WHAT WOULD BE her final tour with Josh White. They opened at the Civic Theatre in Chicago, and, in the spring of 1945, traveled to Los Angeles, where they performed at Ciro's on Sunset Boulevard, staying at the Garden of Allah—the legendary hotel that had become an uninhibited home-away-from-home for eastern writers, Hollywood stars and European émigrées. There, on April 12, Libby heard the news that President Franklin Delano Roosevelt had died of a cerebral hemorrhage.

The hotel residents sat outside on the steps of their bungalows commiserating, some of them weeping openly. The movie studios closed early that afternoon, and Robert Benchley returned to the hotel and suggested to Libby that they spend the rest of the day in the bar. Little Ingrid Herman, Woody's daughter, walked around the garden telling anyone who would listen: "My best friend died today." Libby sat on the steps of her bungalow drinking Dewar's and water. She was on the verge of hysteria. "Oh, my God," she screamed. "*Anything, anybody*, but Harry Truman." Overcome by Roosevelt's death, she was unable to perform that evening, and George Lloyd went on in her place.

Libby and Josh drove north to San Francisco where they played for a fortnight at the Geary Theatre. But now, after more than three years together, their relationship was becoming strained and complicated. There seemed to be more racial prejudice in California than there had been in the East. Josh became increasingly agitated and Libby was in a continual temper. Moreover, rumors began to circulate that they were having an affair. The old myth of Libby's Moorish blood cropped up again, and during one performance, they were booed. Josh was depressed and argumentative, Libby tense and disagreeable. They fought and, finally, at the end of April, canceled the rest of the tour.

Libby always denied having an affair with Josh White. "I was tempted," she said. "I won't deny it, but it was difficult enough without that." The rumors, however, persisted and were even given a kind of spurious credence by a malicious remark of Eugenia Bankhead, Tallulah's older sister, which was bandied about at the time. When asked her opinion of the alleged affair, Eugenia said: "Well, darling, one can't be sure, but Josh was always known as Libby's basic black."

Ralph Holmes had been overseas for exactly twenty months. "He's not coming back yet, either," Libby told a Manhattan reporter, producing a snapshot of her handsome husband in uniform. "I hoped, naturally, that he'd be sent back to this country so that we could see each other and have a little time together, but the present plan calls for him to go directly from Europe to the Pacific war and that means another long indefinite wait. He's been in so long, five years. If it were not that I could keep busy every minute, in summer theaters, in politics, and working on my concert program for next season, I'd really be badly off. As it is, I keep trying not to remember how when Rafe was in the country, we would at least talk together every night and how unbelievably lonely it is to have him so far away."

Shortly after V-J Day, August 11, 1945, Ralph Holmes came home at last. He had not been transferred to the Pacific after all, and for the last five months of his European tour, he had flown P-51s on combat missions over Germany. Discharged from the Army Air Force as a captain, the twenty-nine-year-old returned with the Clasp War Medal for bravery, white sideburns, and battle fatigue. Libby was with her friend Gigi Gilpin when Ralph called from New York's Idlewild Airport; Libby almost swooned in her arms; she seemed happier than Gigi had seen her in years.

To celebrate Rafe's return, Libby gave a series of gala parties at Treetops. Rafe had decided to do nothing for a year in order to get reacquainted with his wife; but Libby proved elusive. Within weeks of his homecoming, he began to complain to his sister, Madeleine, that there were all-night parties at Treetops, that Libby filled the house with people he had never seen before, with homosexuals, so-called celebrities. He wished to be alone with her, and that, it seemed, was impossible.

Rafe intended to give up acting in order to enter Wall Street or politics. Despite several business offers, however, he took none of them. He brooded. He began to drink, often as much as a fifth of Scotch a day. He grew fat. He took eight to ten sleeping pills a night, rarely rising before early afternoon. His skin had broken out into a rough rash which Libby found repulsive. Because of her ulcer, Libby had stopped drinking, and when Libby stopped drinking, she expected everyone around her to stop; but Rafe was uncontrollable. Libby became irritable, impatient. They rarely made love. Rafe was either too tired, too distracted or too drunk. He needed sleep, he said; he wanted to forget.

Libby was not sympathetic. Paraphrasing a remark of Clara Bow's, she began to say: "Poor Rafe. Poor Rafe. He's got the biggest cock in Connecticut, but no ass to push it with."

For five years, the war had torn Libby and Rafe's marriage apart; now, there were other, more immediate reasons. Libby detested his drunkeness, she couldn't tolerate him physically, and there remained her unabated desire to have another child.

Even before Rafe came home, Libby had been consulting doctors, interviewing unwed mothers—wooing them in the hopes of obtaining a baby boy. Nothing but a boy would do; and she was finally successful. Shortly before its birth on October 18, 1945, Libby arranged through a Stamford doctor to preadopt a child, whom she had already decided to name Timmy. She had created a nursery on the second floor, bought vast quantities of expensive presents and hired a foreign nanny. Rafe tried to become enthusiastic, but viewed the child as just another obstacle in his attempts at reconciliation with Libby, just another intruder.

Within a week of Timmy's arrival, Libby ordered Rafe to leave Treetops. He was stunned, but Libby was unyielding. Whatever dream she had nursed of him had been sullied and the marriage was over. Rafe retreated to Manhattan, leasing an apartment on East Sixty-sixth Street. He continued to drink and was often seen after midnight at the Stork Club, his favorite nightery. He planned to leave New York, he told a friend. He had secured a job as a pilot with a West Coast airline and would be leaving the next week or the week after. In a hoarse, uncertain voice, Rafe said he was looking forward to living in California.

On November 15, Ralph Holmes's body was found in his Eastside apartment by the building superintendent. Clad only in underwear, he had been dead for five or six days. His body was bloated and the odor was horrific. Near the sofa on which he lay, the police discovered an empty bottle of sleeping tablets.

Libby was with her sister, Marion, in Cincinnati, where they had gone to visit their sick seventy-eight-year-old father. She hurried back to New York. The tabloids reported that she was suffering from severe shock, but, privately, Libby told George

Lloyd: "How could Rafe have done this to me?" An autopsy failed to disclose the cause of Ralph's death and a chemical analysis was ordered. Ultimately, the New York medical examiner revealed that Rafe had died of barbiturate poisoning. But no one knew whether the overdose had been deliberate or accidental.

Ralph Holmes was buried at the Gate of Heaven Cemetery in Mount Pleasant, New York, next to the grave of his brother, Phillips. The next day, Libby wrote to Bobby Lewis: "The funeral was yesterday and now we go on with our life. As you know, Rafe and I had been separated for a month and I hadn't seen him. It was purely accidental, we know that, no notes or anything—just tired and wanted to go to sleep."

"Good God," retorted Lewis. "Rafe was only twenty-nine. How *tired* could he have been?" And Hassard Short, who had staged *Three's a Crowd*, quipped, "*Well*, Libby certainly seems to be in a rut."

Libby was forty-one and her second marriage had ended as unnaturally as her first. Certain ominous precedents had been set, she knew, but they were unaccountable accidents, the terrible but fitting destinies of weak, fainthearted men. Libby had loved Rafe in her fashion; she had loved them all. But she, at least, remained intact, unbroken, and would remain, she believed, unbreakable.

41

LIBBY'S YOUTHFUL DREAMS OF FAME AND RICHES, OF BECOMING an actress "in big-time dramatic roles," had sustained her through the years, and she refused to relinquish them. It was as if she had created a catalog of potential errands and, one by one, had crossed off the accomplishments, transferring the oversights and failures to some bright new list of urgent and solvable ambitions. In this, she was obstinate. Despite the counsel of friends, her inexperience, her age, Libby would become, because she wished to be, a legitimate presence of the Broadway stage.

During the summer of 1946, Libby performed in a new musical, *The Best of Friends*, at the New England Mutual Hall in Boston. The musical, written and composed by Andrew Rosenthal, was expected to open in New York, but because of bad reviews and a lack of funds, it closed. Within weeks, however, Libby was offered another role—one, she was convinced, that would restore her Broadway reputation. The show was called *Beggar's Holiday* and, more than any other in Libby's career, seemed destined for certain success.

The musical was a contemporary version of John Gay's *The Beggar's Opera*. The book and lyrics were written by John Latouche, the music was composed by Duke Ellington and the show was co-directed by John Houseman and Libby's old friend Nicholas Ray. Oliver Smith designed the sets and Valerie Bettis created the choreography. Fresh from his Broadway successes in *Oklahoma!* and *Sing Out, Sweet Land!*, Alfred Drake was hired to play Mack the Knife. Zero Mostel, in his Broadway debut, was cast as Mr. Peachum and Avon Long as Filch. The chorus included such talented new dancers as Paul Godkin, Herb Ross and Marge Champion. Libby was to play the role of Jenny Diver.

Latouche's plan had been to update John Gay's eighteenth-century London underworld, transferring it to a modern urban slum. Latouche, or "Touche" as he was known, was a squat, dark, twenty-nine-year-old Virginian; although he had written the lyrics for the cantata *Ballad for Americans* and, with Vernon Duke, had composed the music for the successful Negro musical *Cabin in the Sky*, he considered himself a serious poet.

Beggar's Holiday was the first show in the history of the Broadway stage to have a wholly integrated black-and-white production. Libby had not been so excited since *Three's a Crowd*, and considered the part of Jenny Diver, the perfidious whore, the best role she had been offered in years. At first, John Houseman harbored serious misgivings about hiring Libby, considering her too mature, too jaded for the role. She was much older than Alfred Drake, her leading man; her voice was not as great as it had been, not as brilliant or as sultry; but Houseman thought it interesting casting and hired her.

During rehearsals, Libby became increasingly nervous. Her performances were tentative and she was unable to immerse herself in her role. She was drinking again and during bouts of rampant uncertainty, withdrew to her dressing room for nips of Dewar's and milk. Libby's doubts concerning her dramatic abilities were not relieved by an affair she had begun with Nicholas Ray. Some nine years away from his first real fame, as the director of such films as *Johnny Guitar* and *Rebel Without a Cause*, the thirty-five-year-old Ray was a difficult, disturbing man, whose drinking often reduced him to states of rambling unintelligibility.

Ray's friend and mentor, John Houseman, thought him a handsome and complicated man. "Reared in Wisconsin in a household dominated by women, he was a potential homosexual with a deep, passionate and constant need for female love in his life. This made him attractive to women, for whom the chance to save him from his own self-destructive habits proved an irresistible attraction of which Nick took full advantage and for which he rarely forgave them. He left a trail of damaged lives behind him." Ray was the perfect adversary for Libby. "You've got quite a reputation, Nick," she said. "I daresay you didn't come by it honestly."

The New York rehearsals went surprisingly well. The quality of Ellington's music and the energy of the mixed cast almost made Houseman forget the dire inadequacies of Latouche's book, the absence of a structured score. Whenever additional music was required, Billy "Sweet Pea" Strayhorn, Ellington's arranger, rushed up to the Duke's apartment; from a drawer crammed with unperformed music, he extracted whatever tune seemed to fit the scene.

By the middle of the second week of rehearsals, the cast was mired in a nonexistent second act. The producer's checks began to bounce. Because of a lack of funds, the costume and scene shops threatened to suspend fittings and building. But at the eleventh hour, as John Houseman said, "a new angel was unearthed in the person of a small, ill-favored, timid alcoholic, who, in a series of desperate scenes of blackmail and tears, was separated over the next few weeks from a substantial part of his inherited wealth. Unfortunately, the money never seemed to arrive in time to reestablish our credit or to assure the smooth progress of the production." The company arrived in New Haven just before Thanksgiving. Opening night was calamitous, the final twenty minutes being virtually improvised before an au-

Libby and Lucius Beebe in the cocktail lounge of the Metropolitan Opera in 1937 at the opening of *Tristan und Isolde*. Libby appeared without stockings, her toenails painted scarlet, wearing a gold lace gown bestrewn with brilliants.

George Lloyd, Libby's longtime friend, whom she described as looking like a "corrupt choirboy." Lloyd used this Marcus Blechman photograph as his Christmas card during the late thirties. The caption read: "Freud by Lloyd. (Tongue in Cheek.)"

The forty-year-old composer Alec Wilder, who would become Libby's lifelong friend.

The twenty-six-year-old actor Phillips Holmes and his favorite Sealyham, Peter.

Libby, her new husband, Ralph Holmes, and the six-year-old Topper attending a preview of Walt Disney's *Pinocchio* at New York's Radio City.

The novelist and composer Paul Bowles reflecting in the bottom of Libby's oval swimming pool at Treetops during a scene from Hans Richter's *8 × 8*, which Libby called "the Richter Picter."

Libby's favorite photograph of her friend Jane Bowles taken by Karl Bissinger. As a joke, Jane arranged for a tear of mascara to roll down her cheek.

Treetops, the neo-Georgian house Libby built in 1938 between Stamford and Greenwich in Connecticut. It is opened every spring for the blooming of Libby's million daffodils.

Libby dressed in Mainbocher with her friend and accompanist, Josh White, singing a number from her vast repertoire of black blues and ballads, which she called "Americana."

Montgomery Clift and Libby talking on the set of *Raintree County* in 1956.

Louisa Carpenter, her adopted daughter, Sunny, and Topper.

CAUGHT ABOARD THE
REEF CORSAIR
WITH
Capt. HUGH BROWN

Tony and Timmy Reynolds, Libby's adopted boys, following a day's fishing in Key West. Their catch hangs above them.

Three generations of Holmans: Topper, Libby's mother, Rachel, and Libby, taken in 1948.

Libby and the fifteen-year-old Topper arriving in New York on the *Queen Mary* following their five-week holiday with Jane and Paul Bowles in Morocco.

Libby with her lawyer, Benet Polikoff, in Lone Pine, California, moments after she had been told that Topper was dead.

A Hirschfeld caricature of Libby and her pianist, Gerald Cook, done in the midfifties. In her one-woman show *Blues, Ballads and Sin-Songs,* Libby's favorite prop was her kitchen chair.

Louis Schanker, Libby's third husband, sitting in front of one of his abstract paintings.

Libby in 1966 following a concert she gave at the United Nations. On her right is Gloria Vanderbilt and on her left is Dorothy Parker.

Libby, at fifty, holding what she called
her "witch's fan."

dience that included, as Houseman observed, "the usual number of vulturous ill-wishers from New York."

Following the performance, the alcoholic angel, Houseman, Latouche, Duke Ellington and Nick Ray adjourned to a suite in the Taft Hotel. Over whiskey and sandwiches, they shouted and screamed till dawn. Their arguments were gorged with acrid contradictions: Libby was too old; the ingenue was too young; the choreography was too sexy; it wasn't sexy enough; Zero Mostel was a ham; he was the best thing in the show; there were too many blacks in the cast; there were not enough. Everything was discussed and torn apart except for the obvious failing that the show lacked a book and a score. For some hours, Duke Ellington sat and nodded and smiled until his wife finally dragged him to bed. John Latouche passed out. John Houseman brooded; he considered the play an unspeakable mess.

During the early rehearsals and the disastrous tryout in New Haven, Libby's "age" and her "reputation" became favorite topics of conversation among members of the production. Alfred Drake dismissed her age as inconsequential; rather, he equated Libby with a line from Don Marquis's *Archy and Mehitabel*—"toujours gay, kid, toujours gay." He thought of her as a light-hearted, vulnerable woman who had learned to disguise her tragedies with a chic and cheerful facade.

Oliver Smith believed that the insecurities of Libby's performance grew from her long absences from the stage. Libby, he knew, loved the camaraderie of the theater, and though she thought of her talent as an aberration, she desperately missed displaying it. Libby lived a spoiled and self-indulgent life, and whenever she attempted to return to the real world, she was unable to comprehend it. In order to survive, she felt she had to control everything—people, places, events—and this self-protective urge drove her into unreckoned difficulties. Even so, Smith continued to think of Libby as a remarkable woman. She had the incalculable savvy of a survivor; a lesser woman would not have come so far.

Nicholas Ray envisaged Libby in much the way he envisaged himself—as little more than star-crossed. There was something about her that was both seductive and dangerous. For Ray, Libby was a sexy Jewish Medea who longed to become a laughing girl.

Ebullient and attractive with a jaded elegance, she was also a kind of moral vulgarian with strict, unwavering standards—driven but honest, and unfortunately all too willing, when life went awry, to cry *mea culpa*. More significantly, she was afflicted with the Midas touch, except that, in her case, everything she touched seemed to wither and die. "Libby would have had a very bad horoscope," he said. "I once suggested that she consult a fashionable clairvoyant in New York and Libby shuddered. She already knew too much about herself, she said, and she didn't wish to know any more."

Beggar's Holiday moved to Boston and was panned even more bitterly than in New Haven. Following the reviews, John Houseman quit and George Abbott, the eminent play-doctor, was summoned to remedy matters. When Libby heard that Abbott had been brought in, she told Alfred Drake that she would almost certainly be fired for what she explained were long-standing personal reasons. She neglected to mention that she and Abbott had fought eight years before when Abbott had been hired to doctor *You Never Know*.

The fifty-nine-year-old Abbott, a former actor, director and producer, was considered America's preeminent play-doctor. Tall, thin, bald and magisterial, he was a well-known teetotaler. Libby disliked him and Tallulah Bankhead referred to him rather nervously as "skilled." The day after Abbott arrived in Boston, he let it be known that he disapproved of Libby's voice and thought her much too old to play Jenny Diver. He told Libby he was scrapping two of her songs.

"What does that leave me?" said Libby.

"Not much, really," said Abbott.

"What does the show do for me, then?"

"Not much, personally," said Abbott.

He instructed Nick Ray to deal with Libby and that night, after they had made love, Ray told her that she had been fired. Libby took it calmly, even gracefully, Ray thought. Lying in bed, she took a drink of Dewar's and milk, turned her face to the wall, and cried. "I had too many polka dots too soon," she said. "Everything I touch turns to shit."

"Not me, old girl," said Ray, putting his arm around her. "You've still got me."

"Not anymore, you son-of-a-bitch," said Libby. "You just fired me, and I don't mean sexually." She ordered him from her room. The next day, Ray himself was fired.

Libby withdrew to Treetops. Less than two weeks later, she became seriously ill with another ulcer, one she promptly named for *Beggar's Holiday*'s play-doctor. Whenever any of her friends asked her how her ulcer was, Libby would smile and say: "George is rather better than he deserves to be."

Beggar's Holiday opened at the Broadway Theatre in New York on December 26, 1946. It was greeted with despicable reviews and, much to Libby's satisfaction, died after fourteen weeks.

42

T HAT WINTER AND THE FOLLOWING SPRING, LIBBY LIVED AL-most exclusively at Treetops, entertaining a variety of friends for brief holidays and long weekends. These friends were a close clique of loyal Libby Holman fans, and that season, Libby's favorites included director Bobby Lewis, dancer Paul Godkin, lyricist John Latouche, set designer Oliver Smith, British director Peter Glenville, writers Jane and Paul Bowles and, occasionally, the fledgling dramatist Tennessee Williams, then in the process of struggling to write *A Streetcar Named Desire*.

Paul Godkin, a tall, muscular, thirty-one-year-old, who had been *Beggar's Holiday*'s leading dancer, was Libby's particular favorite; and Godkin was enthralled with what he called "Libby's all-enveloping persona." Shortly after they met, Godkin, Libby and John Latouche lunched together in New York. "I just love Paul," Libby told Latouche, running her fingers through Godkin's hair. "I think we're going to have to get married." Godkin, amused with the preposterous joke, exclaimed, "Oh, Libby, you *kill* me." Latouche gasped and after lunch reprimanded Godkin for his lack of tact. Godkin did not understand until Latouche described the fate of Libby's two husbands; then he was mortified.

Godkin was invited to Treetops the following weekend. During the next few months, he went again and again, and the house became for him, as it was for Libby's other friends, a sumptuous sanctuary in which he could eat, drink, laugh and, within elaborate limits, do as he pleased. The coterie usually gathered on Friday afternoons for cocktails in the wood-paneled library or, occasionally, in Libby's extravagant bathroom. The gold-flecked, domed bathroom was the most ostentatious room at Treetops. It contained custom-built mirrored cupboards, a copper sink, white fur rugs, an elegant chaise longue, and a wood-burning fireplace. The shower had nine brass jets protruding from the ceiling and the Italian-tiled wall. But the most resplendent feature in the room was Libby's mirrored tub with brass dolphin-shaped spouts and recessed glass shelves cluttered with bottles of fragrant soaps and exotic perfumes. While Libby bathed and dressed, her friends lounged about the room drinking and gossiping.

At forty-two, Libby retained her splendid figure—the long shapely legs, the gorgeous hands and breasts. She was inordinately proud of her breasts, so proud that Louisa Carpenter had taken to calling her "T. P. Holman"—meaning tit proud. Many of the young men who now surrounded her employed the name privately, with Libby's tacit approval.

Over cocktails and hors d'oeuvres in the library, the adults were usually joined by Topper, now a tall, slender fourteen-year-old. Topper was always reserved and polite, as Libby had taught him to be. Indeed, except for one occasion, Libby's coterie that year barely remembered him at all. Every January, Topper received a birthday gift of a silver goblet from his godfather, Clifton Webb. But in January of 1947, Libby and Webb were no longer speaking, and the goblet did not arrive. When Topper commented on its absence, Libby announced, somewhat vehemently, that it was unimportant, adding: "I don't even know if the old faggot is still alive." Topper was shocked, but all the lank young men in the room hooted uproariously.

Dinner at Treetops was always served in the large formal dining room—the table's centerpiece a handsome bouquet of multicolored orchids grown in Libby's greenhouses. There were often so many orchids that the guests had to peer around them in order to see one another. The food was superb, the conversation brilliant, malicious and witty. On Saturdays, the guests, following Libby's example, slept late in their allotted rooms on the third floor—the strawberry, the cherry and the raspberry rooms, so-called because the wallpaper, the sheets and the pillows were decorated in those motifs. The rest of the weekend was usually devoted to drinking, to strolls through the woods and the daffodil-covered hills or, when the weather was warm, to leisurely swims in the large oval pool.

Libby's coterie looked upon Treetops as a second home, a haven free from the complicated concerns of the Broadway theater, and they anticipated their visits as children look eagerly forward to their summer holidays. They would have done almost anything for Libby; they thought her warm and loving, generous to a fault. She took them in and made them laugh. She could be bawdy one moment, imperious the next; but in either mood, she exerted a private and powerful glamour all her own.

Of all the people who gathered at Treetops that year, the only two who would not, as Paul Godkin observed, "be banished to Coventry one day," were Jane and Paul Bowles. Libby and the Bowleses had been introduced by John Latouche at the Heublein Hotel in Hartford, Connecticut, during tryouts for *Beggar's Holiday*. The Bowleses lived in Manhattan, in Greenwich Village, but they made numerous trips to Treetops that year, occasionally for weekends but more frequently for extended periods of two or three weeks. The thirty-five-year-old Paul Bowles seemed as reserved and separate as he had been in childhood—having not spoken to another child until he was five. Bowles attended Jamaica High School in New York and the University of Virginia, but left before graduating. He aspired to a career as a composer and, failing that, a poet. In Paris in 1931, he met Gertrude Stein who informed the impressionable youth that he was "delightful and sensible during the summer, but that he was neither delightful nor sensible during the winter." Miss Stein blithely explained that Bowles was not a poet, that he should concentrate on his music instead.

Paul Bowles believed her. Some fifteen years later, he had composed successful songs and sonatas, scores for plays, ballets and operas, the most important of which was *The Wind Remains*, which had been conducted by Leonard Bernstein at the Museum of Modern Art in New York in 1942. But literature was never far from his mind. Within months of meeting Libby, Bowles would sail for Morocco to begin work on what was to become his first novel—*The Sheltering Sky*.

Bowles's wife was Jane Stajer Auer, whose father, like Libby's, had been born in Cincinnati. Again like Libby, she was Jewish— of Hungarian-Jewish descent with vague family claims to Gypsy blood. The twenty-nine-year-old woman looked, in her happier moods, like a pixilated elf with large, luminous dark eyes. She had a turned-up nose and hennaed hair that twirled around the top of her head like a nest. Her friends thought her imaginative, bright and zany. She was also given to turbulent moods that bordered on depression. During her teens, she developed a series of phobias that were to haunt her for the rest of her life—fears of dogs, sharks, mountains, jungles, elevators, and of being burned alive. John Latouche, who did not take them seriously, called her "Complications Janie."

Jane attended Julia Richmond High School in New York and the Stoneleigh School for girls in Greenfield, Massachusetts. As a young girl, she developed a series of crushes on women, particularly torch singers, among them Frances Williams and Helen Morgan. Listening to their records for hours, she learned to imitate their voices with eerie accuracy.

From birth, Jane had suffered from a bad knee, which was later broken when she fell from a horse. The bone was set but the knee failed to heal. After a series of complicated operations, Jane developed tuberculosis of the knee, which was finally ankylosed so that she was never able to bend it again, and she would always wear a patch of adhesive tape in order to conceal the scars. At seventeen, she left school, having decided to become a writer.

During the mid-thirties, Jane frolicked in the clubs and bars of Greenwich Village, mixed in the uptown art-literary-music circles and wrote a novel in French, the few copies of which were lost. She met Paul Bowles in 1937 and they were subsequently married. Prior to the marriage, Paul had conducted affairs with both men and women, and Jane solely with women. Nonetheless, they would remain married until the end of Jane's life, and it was a relatively happy, if eccentric, union.

Jane published her first novel, *Two Serious Ladies*, in 1943. The book attracted dispiriting reviews but a small and passionate circle of admirers, one of whom was Libby. Jane wrote desultorily thereafter. When she met Libby, she had published only three short stories and, in early 1947, while living at Treetops, she worked on her abortive novel *Going to Massachusetts*.

Libby and Jane struck an odd and immediate rapport, understanding one another swiftly and completely. They shared much in common: both disliking their cloying effusive mothers, preferring instead what Libby called the noble restraint of their fathers. They disliked being Jewish, considering it some tragic accident of birth which, if they could not correct, they could at least ignore. And yet their letters to each other were filled with exaggerated glee whenever they came across common Yiddish words they had never heard before—such words as *shlepping, schnorrer, yenti, tsouris,* and Libby's favorite Yiddish expression *ganze megillah,* which she translated with some bravado as "miles and miles of woes."

The two friends were nearsighted and occasionally affected lorgnettes. They were flirtatious and seductive with almost everyone they met—both men and women. Although Jane remained in love with Paul, relied on him as a husband, a father, a companion, she was sexually attracted only to women. Both Libby and Jane respected men considerably more than women but sexually agreed that men lacked mystery, whereas women, Jane believed, were "profound, mysterious, obscene."

When Paul sailed for Morocco, Jane remained behind at Treetops with Libby, and the two women initiated an intimate, though not sexual relationship. Buoyed by their mutual enthusiasms, bound by their reciprocal fears and prejudices, they became kindred spirits. They mocked everything, including themselves. With typical self-deprecating humor, Libby, when talking of herself, would say: "The major tsouris in my life is me," and Jane, alluding to her stiff knee, her Jewishness and her predilection for women, called herself, "Crippie, the Kike Dyke."

43

B ECAUSE IT WAS SPRING, PERHAPS, A SEASON OF GAMBITS AND suppositions, Libby decided to procure a playmate for Timmy, her adopted son. She made arrangements with her Stamford doctor to adopt another child, and the boy, subsequently born in Port Chester, New York, on May 19, 1947, was christened Tony. Now, all three of her sons, as well as her house, possessed names beginning with the same letter.

Three weeks later, Libby's elderly father wrote to her from Cincinnati: "Your three T's no doubt are under one roof by now, what? And thriving and happy, well, contented anyhow; and their lovely mater, too, I trow. Treetops must be idyllic this June time of the calendar. How's les chiens—well and dog-busy, we hope. Ma and I o.k. Ma a bit tired today account helping the maid with house cleaning yesterday. She doesn't know moderation; actually, the only virtue there is in life."

Alfred Holman looked forward to his eightieth birthday in August, but wrote: "To me, personally, the 80th is no different from the last B day; both of them just phases in the human cycle." The next day he died of a heart attack in his home in Avondale, the unsavory Cincinnati suburb in which Libby had been raised. Libby had not seen much of her father in recent years, but his death was a terrible blow to her. She had admired him, and he had been the one real anchor in her tumultuous life. She told Paul Bowles that if she ever married again, an improbable event, it would be to someone who reminded her of him.

Accompanied by her mother, her sister, Marion, and her nephew, Michael Kahn, Libby attended his funeral at the Cincinnati Crematory. Alfred Holman was buried in the United Jewish Cemetery, and Libby and Marion inscribed a quotation from *Hamlet* on his gravestone—"Now Cracks a Noble Heart." Remembering how her father had read those lines to her as a child, Libby wept.

*   *   *

That summer, through John Latouche, Libby was introduced to the German painter and experimental film maker Hans Richter. Richter had just completed a new film, the first feature-length avant-garde film ever produced in America. Shot in a Manhattan loft for $25,000, it was called *Dreams That Money Can Buy*. Richter asked Libby if she and Josh White would be willing to sing a song in it. Libby was hesitant; she knew nothing about the film, but loved the title. "Isn't it terribly *me*?" she said to Latouche. When Latouche said that he would write the lyrics of a song he intended to call "The Girl with the Pre-fabricated Heart," Libby agreed to sing it.

The music of *Dreams That Money Can Buy* was composed by Paul Bowles, John Cage, David Diamond, Louis Applebaum and Darius Milhaud. The film told the story of Joe, a young poet in desperate straits who, in order to make money, decides to capitalize on his unique gift for interpreting dreams. He becomes a dream salesman, a "heavenly psychiatrist," as he calls it, settling into a fancy Manhattan office in order to sell his clients whatever dreams he divines from their unconscious—each of which he sees as a vision of wish fulfillment.

Joe's clients include a bank clerk—an inept lover who doesn't make enough money and doesn't understand why but hopes a dream will make everything clear—a girl who doesn't wish to buy a dream, but suffers from an organization mania and feels impelled to collect signatures; the wife of the bank clerk in search of her lost youth; a gangster who wishes to buy a prophetic dream with the name of the next Kentucky Derby winner in it; and finally, Joe himself, who, because business is bad, is left alone—in effect, his only client. The seven surrealistic dreams were shaped after visions by such contemporary artists as Max Ernst, Fernand Léger, Man Ray, Marcel Duchamp and Alexander Calder.

Libby and Josh White sang "The Girl with the Pre-fabricated Heart," Latouche's lyrics based on an idea contributed by Fernand Léger. The song told the story of a misbegotten love affair between two department-store mannequins, whose automated appearance resembled the figures in Léger's paintings.

Dreams That Money Can Buy did little more than baffle film critics when it opened in New York in March 1947, but it went on to win the Venice Film Festival award for the best original contribution to the progress of cinematography, and is still considered the classic film of the experimental cinema. For years thereafter, Libby concocted bizarre analogies between the film and her own life, quipping that had she been born with a prefabricated heart, her life would have been considerably less chaotic.

44

FOLLOWING THE DEATH OF HER HUSBAND, RACHEL HOLMAN, accompanied by a private nurse, moved from Cincinnati to Los Angeles. Now in her late seventies, Rachel suffered from a variety of bronchial ailments and had been advised that the desert air was more suitable for her health. She took up residence in the Ambassador Hotel on Wilshire Boulevard, where, dressed in diamond rings and secondhand clothes, she spent her days prowling through the vast lobby gawking at the guests and visitors. Occasionally, she would inveigle one of them into conversation and, by degrees, turn the talk toward her infamous daughter. When these encounters were reported to Libby by Rachel's nurse, Libby was always mortified. She disliked her mother's "making hay on my name"; she disliked, in fact, almost everything about her. Libby thought her mother was vulgar and loud, a meddlesome Jewish shrew. She reminded Libby of her own Jewishness, her impoverished youth; and now that her father was gone, she made few efforts to conceal her disapproval.

Rachel visited Treetops infrequently—arriving once a year and cautioned, in advance, that her visit would be limited to ten days. On these occasions, Paul Godkin or George Lloyd would receive a call from Libby complaining: "Drive up for the weekend and help me out. My mother, as she calls herself, is coming." At Treetops, Rachel was kept as far as possible from Libby, incarcerated in the servants' quarters on the ground floor. Even so, Rachel was always "interfering," as Libby told her friends. Libby, for example, owned some twenty fur coats, her favorite of which was a $55,000 baby sable. During one of her visits, Rachel became chilly and borrowed the sable to wrap around her legs. Libby was furious, snatched it away, and warned her mother not to touch it again.

Rachel had become completely deaf. At dinner in the formal dining room, Libby, if she talked to Rachel at all, employed a crude form of sign language. Much to the amusement of her friends, Libby would wiggle her hands slowly and subtly, moving them gradually from above the table until, in midsentence as it were, they disappeared in her lap. Unable to see Libby's hands, Rachel would sit up, crane her neck, and shout from across the table: "What did you say, Libby, what did you say?" And Libby's friends would turn away, concealing their laughter behind their napkins.

Libby took continual advantage of her mother's malady. At dinner, she would declaim in a loud voice, "Pass the cauliflower, you old battleaxe," and the guests would cluck and titter. On one occasion, with Rachel in residence, Libby invited Paul Bowles, Tennessee Williams and Tennessee's grandfather, the Reverend Walter Dakin, for the weekend. The Reverend Dakin, an Episcopalian minister, wore clerical garb; he was ninety-four, suffered from cataracts in both eyes and, though Libby was unaware of it, was nearly deaf.

Williams had recently completed his new play, *A Streetcar Named Desire*, which was scheduled to go into production that autumn. He liked Libby, thought her bizarre and elegant, and adored her voice, describing it as "the sound of a siren in heat." After dinner on Saturday night, Libby, Bowles, Williams and the Reverend Dakin played cards. As the game progressed, Rachel kept interrupting the others with inconsequential queries. Libby detested the sound of her mother's voice. When Rachel asked a particularly banal question for the second time, Libby, embarrassed for the Reverend Dakin, went stiff and crimson. It was the only time Paul Bowles had ever seen her blush. When Rachel interjected again, Libby shouted, "*Shut up*, fuckface." Williams burst into laughter, and the two elderly relatives glanced round the table with startled looks of incomprehension.

"In the years after Rafe died," Libby told a friend, "I sang sad songs in saloons and sewers." That, at least, is how she remembered it; but in fact, during the late forties, Libby sang, for the most part, in small college theaters. She no longer liked performing in public, by which she meant nightclubs; moreover, she had convinced herself that her perfect audience was an audience of one. Following the dissolution of her partnership with Josh White, she claimed to be dissatisfied with the guitar. "I require a piano now," she said, "so I can hit the audience on two levels. I want a dialogue between voice and piano, between the lyrics, which are beautiful poetry, and the melody line."

To that end, Libby acquired a new accompanist, a young black pianist named Gerald Cook. Cook was born in Chicago, attended the University of Illinois and won a scholarship to the Longy School of Music in Cambridge, Massachusetts, where he studied composition with Nadia Boulanger. He went on to Columbia, Hunter College and the Manhattan School of Music, attaining a BA and an MA in music. Cook would be Libby's accompanist for the rest of her life. A slim, dapper musician, he tended to intellectualize Libby's music, and as the years progressed, her songs, in the view of many critics, became stilted, mannered and precious.

Libby and Cook performed at college theaters in Washington, Baltimore, Chicago, Milwaukee and Detroit, driving from town to town in a gray pickup truck. Oliver Smith designed the screens for the show, and Libby's friend Gus Schirmer created the lighting. Libby now used a plain kitchen chair as a prop in her act—a chair she described as "an executioner's block in one song, as a cradle or a jail in others." Exclusively attired in Mainbocher, she continued to sing the American songs she had learned from Josh White, but, as a sop to her fans, she closed her show with "Moanin' Low" and "Body and Soul."

The sole "saloon" in which Libby sang was the Café James, a small club operated by an ex–New York detective named James Reardon, on East Fiftieth Street. On February 10, 1948, opening night, a glamorous audience crowded into the little club, including such well-wishers and old friends as Leonard Sillman, Lucius Beebe, Louisa Carpenter, David Diamond and actresses Nancy Walker and Judith Anderson.

Appearing in a striking yellow sequin-embroidered blouse and a brown crepe skirt, Libby sang her now familiar repertory of Americana, including "House of the Rising Sun" and "Evil

Hearted Me," but there was also much new material—written by Paul Bowles and Tennessee Williams—"Sugar in the Cane," "Heavenly Grass," "Cabin" and "Lonesome Man." Even so, the audience reserved their loudest ovation for "Moanin' Low" and "Body and Soul."

Following the performance, Libby told Earl Wilson of the New York *Post*: "Tennessee's words have the same quality of authenticity that you find in the centuries-old songs from the southern hills, and Paul Bowles's music has done the same thing in its own form.

"When I made my first success," she said, "I really didn't know what I was doing. I suppose my voice had a natural quality that was appealing and I was lucky in the songs I sang. They seemed destined to be great. But it was pretty much chance. Today, I have studied and really feel I understand the kind of thing I'm doing. I think so few people know anything about the music that is indigenous to their own country. Perhaps I am helping to educate as well as entertain."

Libby explained that she had amassed a repertoire of nearly a thousand songs. "Some people will be outraged," she said, "but it's fun to be in something controversial. Some of our arrangements use dissonance a lot. Gerald plays G's; I sing F's. But his G's may be expressing overtones of emotion and meaning that the words I sing on F don't even approach. Our goal is a marriage of voice and piano for subtlety and completeness."

"Where did you get Gerald Cook?" asked Wilson.

"From heaven," said Libby.

At the conclusion of the six-week engagement, Libby and Topper flew down to Maryland to spend the Easter holidays with Louisa Carpenter at her new home, Rock Farm. One night, Louisa gave a dinner party for twelve and one of the guests was Libby's old friend the journalist Jennings Perry. During dinner, one of the male guests told a virulently anti-Semitic story. There were a few titters, but Topper lost his temper and rushed from the dining room. Jennings Perry and Libby followed him outside and tried to soothe the boy, but Topper refused to be placated.

Perry had to return to his home in Nashville the next day and Libby drove him to the airport. They sat outside the terminal building in Louisa's Cadillac convertible talking for nearly an hour. Libby was depressed. She agonized over Topper's future, her wayward career, the men in her life. Perry asked her if there had been many men and suddenly Libby burst into tears. "Oh, *God*, Jennings," she cried, "I can't even remember their names."

Sobbing fitfully, Libby explained how much she regretted the past eight years—the war, the long absence from Ralph Holmes, the loneliness, Rafe's suicide, the men she had sought out, hoping that they would fill the void. But the void had remained— darker, more unfathomable than before. She was almost forty-four, she said. What was she to do? Perry shook his head. He didn't know. He consoled her as best he could and caught his plane.

But Libby's passionate period of promiscuity was over. That night, she became exuberant, almost defiant. Laughing, she said to Louisa, "I've cast my pearls before swine, you know, but not *all* of them."

The adopted boys, Timmy and Tony, were now two and one. Since the arrival of Tony the year before, Timmy had begun to suffer from hyperactivity and had extreme difficulty in speaking; but he was a beautiful little boy and Libby and Topper were partial to him. Tony, on the other hand, was a fat and amiable child—so fat, in fact, that Libby dubbed him "Little Farouk," after the elephantine Egyptian king.

Topper was fifteen. As Libby had hoped, her friends thought they seemed more like friends than relations. That Hallowe'en, Topper disguised himself as a tramp and went to the Stamford railroad station to meet Libby's train. Libby failed to recognize him, and as the boy badgered her for a dollar, Libby impatiently waved him away until, at last, she penetrated his disguise, and they fell laughing into one another's arms. At home they jabbered together in faulty French, laughing loudly at their implausible accents.

That summer, Topper asked Libby why he had to attend the terrible school to which he had recently been sent, when his few friends attended another, much nicer school. Libby explained that it was because he was rich and his friends, unfortunately, were poor. "Then why don't we give our money away," suggested Topper. "Then we'd all be poor together. That would be much nicer, don't you think?"

"I don't think there would be anything nice about that at all," said Libby.

The "terrible school" was the Putney School near the village of Putney in Vermont, where Topper had matriculated in 1946. The school had been founded eleven years before by Mrs. Carmelita Chase Hinton, whose husband, Sebastian, had made a minor fortune by inventing the jungle gym. A graduate of Bryn Mawr, Mrs. Hinton believed that the revolution John Dewey had wrought in the elementary schools should be extended to secondary schools; she wanted to experiment, to break through some of the traditional ideas of education for adolescents. The Putney School was one of the first integrated coeducational boarding schools in America and was situated on about a thousand acres of farm, pasture, sugarbush and woodland. Self-reliance, manual labor, farm work, athletics, the arts and social conscience were stressed along with academics. Because of its avant-garde reputation, the Putney School attracted the children of some of America's most influential liberal families.

Carmelita Hinton's son, William, had worked in China in 1937 and returned there, as a tractor technician, at the end of the war. Her daughter, Joan, who would become a physicist, also lived in China, making four-wheeled carts in an iron factory in the mountains of Shensi Province. In a letter published in *People's China*, she wrote: "The Chinese with their bare hands are building up a new nation; while the Americans are preparing to destroy mankind"—sentiments Libby would soon espouse.

First and foremost, Carmelita Hinton advocated communal effort among her wards. She believed that individual excellence flourished best in a collective, rather than a competitive, environment and sought to create an atmosphere of mutual respect and trust by abolishing grades, even while engaging youngsters in a rigorous intellectual life. Libby and Mrs. Hinton became friends, and as a result of her sway, Libby went through what her friends described as "a communistic period" during the late forties: that is, she talked a giddy line of socialism—a source of some hilarity among her friends. That summer, three or four of them lay by the oval pool at Treetops. Suddenly, a dozen planes flew overhead and Paul Godkin said, "It's the Russians . . . looking for Libby." Libby was not amused. Attempting, perhaps, to minimize her own opulent life-style, she began employing the phrase "All you dirty capitalists" with her wealthier friends. She embraced the belief that everyone with money was frivolous, greedy and superficial. Her more impecunious intimates humored her. They realized that Libby adopted new beliefs like lovers, convincing herself that they were just and true. And, like too many other passions in her life, they knew this too would pass.

45

TOPPER RETURNED TO TREETOPS FROM THE PUTNEY SCHOOL in June. At fifteen, he was too old to attend his regular summer camp, but Libby did not know how else to occupy him. "Where would you like to spend your summer holidays?" she asked finally. Topper did not hesitate. "I would like to go to Africa with Paul Bowles," he said, "and have my tongue cut out." The line was a reference to the fate of one of Bowles's characters in a story called "A Distant Episode," which Topper had read and admired in *The Partisan Review*.

They flew to Lisbon at the end of the month. Libby looked forward to seeing Jane and Paul Bowles again, and she had never been to Africa. Jane had sailed for Morocco some five months before. Already, she had begun to study Arabic and had fallen in love with Tangier and a wild Arab girl named Cherifa. Their relationship did not disturb Paul, though the unpredictable Cherifa would always mystify and concern him; and Jane, of course, was free to do as she wished. He had just completed his first novel, *The Sheltering Sky*, which he modestly described as "a novel like any other: a triangle laid in the Sahara." Oliver Smith, the scenic designer and Paul's second cousin, had joined the Bowleses for a holiday that June. When Libby and Topper arrived in Tangier by boat from Algeciras, Paul and Jane Bowles and Oliver Smith were at the dock to greet them.

Libby and Topper checked into the El Minzah, the great sprawling stone and tiled hotel in the center of Tangier. Libby loved Tangier immediately, and for the first few days, Jane guided her around the bustling city, through the Casbah and the medina, to all her favorite souks and bars, pointing out the most impressive mosques and minarets. Paul showed Libby the little house he and Oliver Smith had bought near the Place Amrah. Paul had not yet moved in, and in any event, the house had no plumbing and the ceilings were so low that visitors were forced to stoop when moving from room to room. From the roof, however, there was a magnificent view of the medina and the Straits of Gibralter beyond.

On the third night, it was decided that everyone would make a long leisurely trip through the mountains and the desert. Jane refused, citing her fear of heights. Five years before, she had taken a trip to Mexico; returning to Mexico City from Taxco by train, she was in the dining car when the train crossed a bridge over a river. Without warning, the train jumped the tracks, plummeting from the bridge. Jane passed out. When she regained consciousness, she was half in and half out of the water with a dead man in her arms. Jane now avoided mountains and trains and, although Libby attempted to persuade her to change her mind, Jane was intractable, electing to remain in Tangier with her friend Cherifa.

Libby and Topper, Paul Bowles and Oliver Smith set off for the southern town of Tafraoute in the Anti-Atlas in Paul's ancient Kaiser automobile. The six-week trip would take them to Fès and Marrakech, to Taroudannt and Tiznit and back to Tangier again. They had to pass through the *Zone d'Insecurité*, in which there were military road checks, and from the outset, they looked upon their trip as an adventure, as a romantic and possibly dangerous expedition.

Before coming to Morocco, Libby had read Federico García Lorca's play *Yerma*. She believed it would make an excellent vehicle for her and suggested that Paul compose the score. During the trip, Libby and Paul discussed the play's possibilities *ad infinitum*—while dallying in oases, basking on beaches, while driving through the infernal landscapes of the Anti-Atlas. Paul finally agreed to compose the score and to translate the play from the Spanish himself.

The trip was made during Ramadan, the period during the ninth month of the Islamic calendar when fasting is rigidly enjoined from dawn until sunset. Food, therefore, was difficult to find, and because they had employed a Muslim driver, they were unable to drink in the car.

They spent their nights in small roadside hotels. On the first night in Ksar-el-Kebir, Topper was informed that he would have to share a room with Oliver Smith. With some embarrassment, he demurred. Libby demanded an explanation, and Topper muttered, "Isn't he supposed to do things in the night?" To which Smith replied: "*Yes*, I go to the toilet."

It was a fine trip. They visited the Palais Jamais in Fès. In Marrakech, they trooped through the ocher palace of El Glaoui and wandered late one night through the Djemaa al Fna (the Place of Death), Marrakech's main square, gawking at the camel traders, the snake charmers, the fire-eaters, and the *chleuh*, the boy dancers. They visited the high cascades of Ouzoud, where Libby stripped and jumped into the freezing water, screaming, "Come on in, Topper, come on in; this is better than sex." Topper complied, but said in a disappointed voice, "I don't feel anything *at all*."

Although Libby knew that Paul Bowles was sexually indifferent to women, she was attracted to him nonetheless. She admired his intellect, his musical and literary abilities. As she had done in the past, she now confused admiration with desire. At Treetops some months before, Libby and Jane had discussed the possibilities of Libby's having an affair with Paul, and Jane had quipped, "Well, you'd better hurry; you're losing your boyish figure."

Now, in Morocco, in Ksiba at the leopard-hunter's lodge, while lying on the rocks in the moonlight, Libby proposed marriage to the astonished Bowles. She told him she had discussed it with Jane and that Jane had been agreeable should that be what Paul preferred. She assured him that Jane would always be welcome to live at Treetops with them, that it would not be a problem. Paul stared at the moon and said nothing; he had no intention of becoming involved with Libby beyond being her houseguest and close friend. After a while, Libby laughed and said, "I don't think Jane likes the idea *really*. I think she really wants to be Mrs. Bowles herself." Paul said nothing, and Libby never mentioned it again.

*   *   *

For most of the trip, Libby was in an ebullient mood. She loved the imagined danger, she loved the cliffs and precipitous curves, she loved taking her chances. Before leaving New York, she had purchased a number of chic, colored dresses, each of them with a circular hole cut out at the stomach. She wore them now, a different color for every day, and her arms were completely covered with gold bracelets. Libby was, she knew, a Jewish woman traveling in an Arab country, and she seemed almost to flaunt it. Wherever she went, she attracted small curious crowds who stopped to stare at her. The revealing frocks both fascinated and shocked the Arabs and their disquiet appealed to Libby.

It was obvious to both Bowles and Smith that Libby and Topper were closer than they had ever been; and yet a rift was becoming evident. Libby was a possessive mother; she fussed, she scolded, she upbraided, and Topper was beginning to rebel. Once, near Agadir, he wandered off by himself. He was not missed for some time and Libby, Bowles and Smith began to search for him. As it grew dark, Topper was discovered atop a forty-foot-high pinnacle, which he had climbed only to find he could not get down. As Libby approached, he brandished his fist and seemed, in some way, to be challenging her. Looking up, Libby rebuked the boy, then relented and made light of it. But she wasn't pleased. Bowles and Smith helped him down. It seemed to Smith that Topper yearned to be like any other teenaged boy—ordinary, anonymous—but he had a mother who was a celebrity and, worse, a notorious one.

Libby could help neither Topper nor herself. She gave in to all her inclinations. One night in Rabat, she dressed up as a Moroccan peasant woman and disappeared from the hotel. Topper, Bowles and Smith searched everywhere, but were unable to find her. Late that night, Libby returned to the hotel. She wouldn't tell them where she had been, admitting only that her purse had been stolen. Later, Libby, still flushed with her adventure, claimed that, like a character in one of Paul Bowles's stories, she had allowed herself to be picked up by a young Berber.

On the drive back to Tangier, the dust swirled continually into the old Kaiser, and everyone looked ashen. Suddenly, near Toubkal, Libby began to cry. She cried silently, the tears streaming down her pallid face. Topper reached for her hand, but she continued to cry. Oliver Smith asked her what was wrong. Libby shrugged and, staring at the lunar landscape of the Anti-Atlas, replied, "I just don't feel *connected* to anything. What's *wrong* with me?"

46

I N EARLY AUGUST, LIBBY AND TOPPER LEFT MOROCCO, RE-turning via Lisbon and New York to Treetops. Topper began his junior year at the Putney School the following month, and Libby spent more of her time in New York, where she had recently purchased a house at 121 East Sixty-first Street. The five-story brownstone would be her Manhattan residence for the rest of her life.

In New York, Libby decorated and furnished her new home, shopped, attended openings and went, by her own reckoning, to the theater four times a week. *A Streetcar Named Desire* had opened the previous December and Libby had seen it a dozen times.

One evening, she invited her friends George Lloyd and Marcus Blechman to see the play. During the intermission, as they walked to the bar, Libby drew the two men aside and said, "Well, boys, how do you like the story of my life?" Lloyd and Blechman were puzzled, but Libby reminded them of a particular speech in the play, a speech, she said, that had hypnotized her. The next day, Libby gave the two men copies of *Streetcar*, referring them to Blanche DuBois's soliloquy:

He was a boy, just a boy, when I was a very young girl. . . . There was something different about the boy, a nervousness, a softness and tenderness which wasn't like a man's, although he wasn't the least bit effeminate looking—still—that thing was there. . . . He came to me for help. I didn't know that. I didn't find out anything till after our marriage when we'd run away and come back and all I knew was I'd failed in some mysterious way and wasn't able to give the help he needed but couldn't speak of. He was in the quicksands and clutching at me—but I wasn't holding him out, I was slipping in with him. I didn't know that. I didn't know anything except I loved him unendurably but without being able to help him or help myself. Then I found out. In the worst of all possible ways. By coming in suddenly into a room I thought was empty, but had two people in it . . . the boy I had married and an older man who had been his friend for years.

The boy and the older man were making love and, ultimately, when the boy realizes that Blanche has seen him, he shoots himself. Libby, Lloyd knew, was making obvious allusions to the death of Smith Reynolds and to his close friendship with Ab Walker. But Lloyd also knew that Libby liked to dramatize her past, that she had not actually known what had happened the night Smith Reynolds died, and that her story changed according to whom she told it to. Even so, this new version haunted her.

Libby went so far as to mention the soliloquy to Tennessee Williams, who admitted that he had been aware of the Smith Reynolds tragedy but had not, at least consciously, made any use of it. Williams sympathized with Libby. He sensed she desperately required a truth, an answer to the question that had baffled her for more than fifteen years, and he had plucked one possible solution from what he called "my dandy box of tricks." On the other hand, Williams knew that Libby had survived her tragedies; like Tallulah Bankhead, she was one of the strongest of all the lost and broken women he had ever known.

George Lloyd, who had been one of Libby's closest friends for more than ten years, moved to California in 1949 and Libby rarely saw him again. In typical fashion, she cast about for substitutes and, within months, had become enamored of two other men—Alec Wilder and Marcus Blechman.

The forty-two-year-old Wilder had composed hundreds of popular songs such as "The Sounds Around the House," "Blackberry Winter" and "Who Can I Turn to?" He was one of the first composers to attempt to break down the barrier between jazz and formal music by writing a series of eccentrically titled octets—"Jack, This Is My Husband," "Sea Fugue Mama" and "The House Detective Registers"—for oboe, clarinet, bass clarinet, bassoon, flute, harpsichord, string bass and drums.

Wilder had lived at the Algonquin Hotel in Manhattan for nearly twenty years, and Libby rang him unexpectedly one day; she wanted to sing one of his songs and insisted on meeting him. Flattered, Wilder agreed. Libby said she was coming right over and thirty minutes later, over cocktails in the Algonquin lobby, they became immediate friends. During their long relationship, they would never see one another more than three or four times a year; but when the daffodils were in bloom at Treetops, Libby always invited him up for the day. She loaned her house to him for auditions and commissioned him to write an opera based on the life of Aimee Semple MacPherson, which he never completed.

Their relationship was almost exclusively telephonic. Libby had recently become obsessed with Yoga, an exercise in which Wilder was only mildly interested; but Libby would call up Wilder regularly, opening the conversation by saying: "Alec, I'm sitting in the lotus position. Let's croak, like frogs." Wilder found it difficult to accept Libby's passion for Yoga. She was an aggressive Western woman with nothing of the passive, the yielding or the Eastern in her being. He chided her about it, but nothing would deter her. Libby was to practice Yoga, and subsequently Zen, for the remainder of her life.

Like Wilder himself, Libby had an instinctive flair for what was excellent in life. And so, during their long telephone conversations, usually conducted late at night, they discussed their common distaste for "cant, snobbery, fakery, egocentricity, fawning, pomp, social climbing, cleverness and fashion." They believed that the twentieth century was, in general, trivial and mindless—beneath their standards.

Marcus Blechman, on the other hand, was Libby's personal court jester. With her penchant for cute names, Libby called him Mar. A wry and witty homosexual, the thirty-nine-year-old Blechman was Libby's official photographer—photographing her for all her publicity stills whenever she toured. He claimed not to photograph his subjects but to celebrate them, and so his shots of Libby were warm and flattering. Their friendship was to last until Libby's death, and he, among all of her friends, was the only one permitted to disagree or contradict her. Once, when Libby complained that one of her photographs was too realistic, Blechman said: "Madam, should you continue to carp, I'll have little choice but to retouch my retouches."

Libby and Gerald Cook gave a concert at the University of Cincinnati that year and Marcus Blechman accompanied them. Before the show, Libby was introduced by a voluble master of ceremonies to an enthusiastic audience of old friends and acquaintances, high school and college classmates: "And now, ladies and gentlemen," he said, "here is the person you have all been waiting for, that splendid singer, that universally famed actress, the favorite of millions, a person whom you all know and love, and whom it is my great pleasure and highest honor to introduce to you tonight—Miss Lipsy Colmar." The audience grew silent and then began to laugh. Libby was mortified. For years afterward, Blechman introduced Libby to strangers as Lipsy Colmar, and eventually Libby began to refer to herself by that name.

Throughout most of early 1949, Libby conducted an erratic affair with Blechman. It was not, as Libby knew, an ideal alliance. Blechman preferred the favors of young men, but he had fallen in love with Libby, and Libby returned, if not his love, his affection. Blechman was a lost soul, a society photographer with few real friends, but Libby admired his wit and intellect, and more important, he amused her—the highest attribute in Libby's personal pantheon of virtues. Moreover, she thought of Blechman as she thought of herself, as star-crossed, and she liked to joke about it. Laughing at herself, she would say: "I'm *Doom, Doom, Doom*," punctuating the words like the resonant thump of a drum.

One sunny morning at Treetops, Alec Wilder accompanied Marcus Blechman on a walk through the surrounding woods. Blechman was photographing the trees and the daffodils, and toward noon they came upon a magnificent magnolia tree. The bright sunshine streamed through its branches, and just as Blechman photographed it, an oriole lighted on a branch, its wings fluttering, the sun glinting from its golden breast. It had arrived unannounced, almost magically, and Alec Wilder laughed and said, "*Well,* Libby can't be all bad."

*   *   *

Libby and Gerald Cook began their third concert tour that summer, performing at such venues as the YMHA in New York and Pierce Hall in Washington, D.C. Libby now called her music "Earth Songs"—"because that's what they are," she said. "They're earthy, lusty, gritty. They don't have a bit of morality. They just spring right from the earth themselves; they've grown out of the hearts of the people, in their joys and sorrows. These are simple songs, the kind you'd sing sitting on the back porch of a shanty, looking out over a cotton field.

"You see," she added, "torch songs are all the same. I love a man and he don't love me. Poor sobbing me. And that's it. Folk songs are so much broader in scope. I always wanted to sing them for I felt I had that type of voice. Trained singers shouldn't attempt them. They must come from the heart."

Libby's reviews were excellent, the most glowing of which was written by Tom Donnelly in the Washington *Daily News*:

> Miss Holman possesses a generously rounded face, a pair of narrow eyes, a mass of passionately black hair, and a voice that suggests a mixture of sugar, graphite and raw whiskey. Attired in a simple, sequin-encrusted blouse and a voluminous brown skirt designed with all the artless innocence Mainbocher has at his command, Libby opened her show with "Good Morning, Blues."
>
> Once that loud throbbing slightly erratic voice has been in operation for a moment or two, the most sceptical concert-goer realized that Miss Holman knows what she's about. She makes gestures, but they are invariably the right ones. And she does more with that chair of hers than Alfred Hitchcock does with a penthouse or lifeboat. She sits on top of it and moans. She sits beside it and sobs. She turns it into a rocking horse and she turns it into a divan.
>
> And always, her voice rises and falls, hardens and softens, expands and contracts. It is not, of course, a noble instrument, but Miss Holman uses it nobly, and if she does not quite achieve the piercing melancholy which still lingers in the frayed records of a Bessie Smith, she manages something that is very fine in its own way.

When the tour ended, Libby returned to Treetops where Marcus Blechman awaited her. Their affair was now in its fourth month and Libby had wearied of it. She adored Blechman, but he was much too foppish for her; he made her nervous, and his assignations with itinerant young men had begun to appall her. One night at dinner, Libby told him that it was all over. She wanted his friendship, relied on it, in fact, but more than that was more than she could tolerate. "Mar," she said, before going to bed, "it's just not good enough." Blechman took it badly. At some point, long after Libby had retired, he packed his few belongings and drove to New York.

In the morning, Libby awakened and ordered breakfast. When the maid arrived with her tray, Libby instructed her to ask Mr. Blechman to join her. The maid left and, some minutes later, returned to say that Mr. Blechman had not slept in his bed, nor was he to be found anywhere on the premises. He had simply disappeared. Libby, remembering the dark conversation of the night before, sat up in bed, a look of horror in her eyes.

"Drain the pool," she screamed. "Drain the pool."

47

At the Putney School, everyone called Topper Chris. Topper, a diminutive of Christopher, was used exclusively by Libby and her close friends. Topper detested the nickname and implored his mother not to use it anymore, and Libby, in her fashion, capitulated. She called him "T."

Topper intended to become an engineer and hoped to attend the Thayer School of Engineering at nearby Dartmough College. But in late 1949, there was a hazing incident at Dartmouth involving a Jewish boy, and Libby became apprehensive about allowing her son to apply there.

Topper was now nearly seventeen and already six feet tall. A good student, a lackluster athlete, he was courteous, determined, introspective, an unquestioned leader, and during his senior year, he was elected president of the student council. He also played the lead in almost every school theatrical production—

possessing an excellent stage presence and a marvelous sense of character, inherited, his classmates felt, from Libby.

A talented writer, he composed plays, poetry and essays for the Putney literary magazine, as well as short stories, many of which, with exotic Arabic backgrounds, had been influenced by Paul Bowles. Secretly, Topper also labored over a novel, inspired, in this instance, by another of his heroes, Norman Mailer, who had published *The Naked and the Dead* two years before.

At the beginning of his senior year, Topper met a dark pretty seventeen-year-old girl named Lynda Williams. Lynda had been born and raised in Pine Bluff, Arkansas, and had entered Putney as a sophomore in 1947. She had met Topper then, but was unimpressed. Not until their senior year, working together in the school's theater workshop, did Lynda begin to sense that Topper was a remarkable young man.

He displayed a kind of restrained self-confidence, she felt, restrained because it was important to him that he not be conspicuous in any way. He longed to grow, to work and to succeed without fireworks or fanfare. He wanted to be normal and that was one of the attractions Lynda held for him: She was such a normal girl from such a normal American family.

As Lynda grew to know Topper better, she realized that despite his charm and mischievous sense of humor, he was also a fatalist. He talked to her continually of death and separati~~. In this context, he invariably referred to his father—to his :arly demise, what sort of man he had been and, by extension what sort of man he, Topper, would become.

That autumn, they fell in love and began an affair, the first sexual involvement for either of them. No other student at Putney was having a love affair, and it was considered amazing, extraordinary, particularly since Carmelita Hinton was strenuously opposed to cigarettes, alcohol and sex. Lynda believed that their affair was tolerated because Mrs. Hinton held Topper in such high regard. But no one—not Mrs. Hinton, not the teachers and, most surprisingly, not even Libby—would interfere.

Although Lynda had met Libby briefly at Putney, they were not formally introduced until just before the Christmas holidays in New York. Initially, Topper had been concerned whether

Libby would like Lynda, but Libby's warmth and graciousness soon quelled his doubts. Lynda sensed that Libby had decided that if she were to keep her son, she had better like whom he brought home. Even so, Lynda felt that she was somehow stealing Libby's lover and that Libby would retaliate. But she had worried needlessly. Libby liked her and encouraged their relationship to the point of allowing them to share a bedroom whenever they came to Treetops. She placed no obstacles in their way.

Lynda saw Libby frequently during her senior year. With Topper, they spent weekends together in New York, and Libby accompanied them to restaurants and the theater. At Treetops, they played tennis and swam and filmed home movies around the oval pool. On one occasion, they enacted the voyages of Ulysses—Topper starring as Ulysses, Lynda as Penelope, and Libby, singing siren songs on a rubber mattress in the pool, as Circe.

Topper loved heights. As a teenager, he had studied maps and Alpine guides in search of what he had always called "my magic mountain." He had become obsessed with mountains and the mystique of scaling them. During his senior year at Putney, he wrote a short poem called "The Mountain," and an essay entitled "None but Ourselves," in which he attempted to examine the psychology of mountain climbers:

> What manner of men are these whose eyes are ever straining upwards, whose legs cannot be content to walking on the level, and whose bodies yearn for the dry thin air and the higher ground where any normal man would never dare to tread? . . . The frontiers of latitude and longitude are gone, but not the frontiers of altitude. . . . There will always be men born with adventure in their blood, who will want to get away from civilization and the dull monotony of a life full of peace and security. . . . They will have to look to the mountain. To make one's self turn back when to go on is suicide, is as difficult as it is to stagger upwards with only a slight chance. A mountaineer goes through all this not to reach the summit or to break a time record, but to overcome his weaknesses.

Topper spent the Christmas holidays of 1949 with Libby and his adopted brothers at Louisa Carpenter's house in Palm Beach,

Florida. He talked incessantly about climbing a mountain the following summer, a venture in which he would be joined by his classmate Steve Wasserman, the son of a prominent Philadelphia financier. Sunny, Louisa's adopted daughter, who had always thought of Topper as something of a sissy, told him he was not only foolish, he was mad. Libby considered the proposal too dangerous and refused to sanction it. "For Christ's sake, T," she screamed, "you *can't* go. Do you *hear* me? You *can't* go."

Topper had confided his summer plans to Peter Caldwell, his best friend at Putney, but he was vague and contradictory. Caldwell didn't know precisely what it was that Topper had in mind; he knew only that Topper envisaged something grand—some daft and dangerous caper such as robbing Fort Knox or swimming the Dardanelles.

Neither Topper nor Steve Wasserman was an experienced climber. Wasserman had once been on a guided tour of the Matterhorn, and three years before, Topper had walked through the Dolomites. But Topper had read all the literature of mountain climbing, and had come to envisage his proposed adventure in terms of some romantic tale by Richard Halliburton. It represented, as Lynda Williams observed, "the quintessence of all his early poetic reading, *Everyman* and *The Waste Land* rolled into one."

Topper told Lynda that the symbolism was extraordinary. The two seventeen-year-old youths wished to fulfill their manhood, to conquer the West, to live alone. The trip was to be the realization of all their adolescent fantasies—to prove their rites of passage, to ascend the highest peak—leaving mothers, families and lovers behind.

Topper pleaded for permission but Libby continued to balk. To placate her, he promised to take the appropriate precautions—to dress warmly, to study the terrain, to climb, if he actually climbed, with experienced mountaineers. Didn't she realize that this was to be the greatest adventure of his life? And then, playing perhaps his finest card, Topper said: "My father would have understood." And finally, Libby, who in any event believed that Topper was capable and conscientious, relented, and let him go.

A month before, at Louisa Carpenter's Maryland farm, Libby had met a thirty-three-year-old college professor named Luke

Readdy. A tall, lean redhead, Readdy taught Greek, Latin, literature and mathematics at St. John's College in Annapolis. He had graduated from the University of Virginia in 1939, winning a Rhodes scholarship to Christ Church at Oxford, but the war had intervened, and now, ten years later, he intended to matriculate in the autumn of 1950.

Luke Readdy was immediately taken with Libby. He found her bright and attractive and the fact that she was more mature than most women he had known appealed to him. Midway through the long Thanksgiving weekend, Libby invited Louisa to Treetops and, almost as an afterthought, invited Readdy too. He accepted and they flew up to Stamford in Louisa's plane. That autumn and throughout early 1950, Readdy visited Treetops frequently. Libby was alone and lonely, Topper was completing his senior year at Putney, and during Readdy's second visit, he and Libby began a love affair that would last for more than a year.

Readdy would always think of it as an improbable alliance—a college professor earning $4,600 a year dallying with a notorious millionairess eleven years his senior. But he was more than a little in love with Libby; he liked and admired her, was sexually enthralled, but didn't, as he said, "spend his nights composing odes on her behalf." Libby, on the other hand, fell completely in love with Readdy. Discussing her sexual liaisons with women, she admitted they had been tense and unfulfilling, that it required a man to satisfy her. More important, Readdy was stable, well educated, an intellectual—qualities Libby lacked but admired. She explained that she had plumbed the depths of debauchery and they had left her tremulous, adrift. She didn't want respectability; rather, she required a rudder, a sense of firm and knowledgeable purpose. And, for a time, Readdy was to give her that.

In June of 1950, having already been accepted at Dartmouth, Topper graduated from the Putney School. He and his friend Steve Wasserman had considered spending the summer at a ranch in Wyoming's Grand Tetons; but the two youths decided to journey instead to the foothills of Mt. Whitney near Lone Pine in California. Wasserman's father owned a portion of the Cerro Gordo mine and they were given summer jobs mining silver and lead. Topper spent his last weekend at Treetops with Libby and

Lynda Williams and, in late June, he and Wasserman drove away in his secondhand Studebaker in order, as Topper told Lynda, "to challenge the Gods, to chart the unknown."

That summer, Libby decided to travel to Europe, and Luke Readdy, due to enter Oxford in October, agreed to accompany her. Libby was now passionately devoted to the idea of producing and performing in the García Lorca play, *Yerma*. Paul Bowles had already translated it from the Spanish and was composing arias at his home in Tangier. In order to immerse herself in the Spanish atmosphere and to gather additional research for the play, Libby planned to motor through Andalusia with Bowles and Readdy. She wanted to return to the earth, she said, to hear flamenco and castanets, to dance through the night with wanton Gypsies.

As Topper and Steve Wasserman drove across America, Libby and Luke Readdy flew from New York to Paris. Readdy owned a black 1947 MGTC, which he had previously shipped to Le Havre. They picked up the little open car, spent two days in Paris at the Lancaster Hotel, then drove slowly down the western coast of France—to Bordeaux, across the Pyrenees to San Sebastián, to Burgos, where they visited the great cathedral in which El Cid was buried, then on to Madrid and Málaga, where they met Paul Bowles.

Then, with Libby and Readdy in the front seat and Bowles crouched in the back, they circled through Andalusia, to Seville and Córdoba, to Granada, Ronda and on to Algeciras, where they boarded the ferry to North Africa and Tangier. Throughout their Andalusian travels, Libby and Bowles talked incessantly of *Yerma*, and whenever they could find a piano, they rehearsed the completed arias.

Readdy had never before spent so much time in Libby's company. Now, after two continuous weeks together, he felt even more strongly that she was somehow detached from life, fragmented. One night in Córdoba, she told him that during the early thirties, at the height of her fame, she had had to make an important holiday decision: whether to meet Clifton Webb in Monte Carlo or to sail to London with Noel Coward. Her life, it seemed to Readdy, had been fraught with such frivolous quandries and imbroglios. He believed that the glamour, the fatuous trappings of celebrity, had diverted Libby at too early an age, and that she had not been able to find her way back again.

A scholar, Readdy recognized (and accepted the fact) that Libby was intellectually pretentious. There was nothing wrong with her mind; she had excellent instincts, but no rigorous mental disciplines. It was tragic, he felt, to have been catapulted to fame at twenty-five without having achieved anything beyond being able to sing a song. Libby was better than that and her tragedy was that she knew it. She was intellectually ashamed of the tawdry theatrical world she inhabited, embittered with her errant career. But what exactly *was* her career? Being Libby Holman, he presumed.

In late July, Lynda Williams, who had taken a summer job in the White Mountains of New Hampshire, received a letter from Topper from Holbrook, Arizona:

> I am sitting on a trunk jack in a desolate garage. This town is located in the Painted Desert and it is one of their hottest days. Steve's French typewriter is sitting on the jack—my only table. Two mechanics and about three fluctuating hot rod experts busy themselves about us. The car, my great Studebaker, sits silently in the corner. It has sprung a leak and the cooling system is shot to hell. Caldwell was right. He said I would never drive home in the same car.
>
> I am writing on some of Steve's drawing paper. He is sitting over in the corner of the garage drawing a picture of me. The handle of the jack makes a cross above my head so he's making the portrait very symbolic.
>
> It's sort of a good experience to have to drive across country in a beat-up car instead of the usual Cadillac convertible. Now we are really getting the feel of the country and having really to work and sweat it out to get anywhere.
>
> I love you. I love you. I love you.
>
> No one is working on the car now. We drink Cokes and read "Lady Chatterly's Lover" to each other. It's the pocket edition and when we get to the good parts, they stick in some *** and it skips. Hell. This doesn't help our frustration.
>
> Don't worry about me. I'm having the time of my life. Always in love with you. Chris.

In early August, Lynda heard from Topper again, this time from the Cerro Gordo mine in Lone Pine, California.

> Lynda, darling. Now to clear you up. Lib didn't enter a race with Luke. I said a veritable road race; which means (if that word is indistinguishable either because of your vocabulary or my spelling) that they had to travel so fast across France and Spain to get to Gibraltar in time. She got to Gib but Paul wasn't there and I still don't know if they found him. There is no address. They are roaring around Europe so fast the mail can't catch up.
>
> Now clear up again. When do you quit your job? And when do you leave for home after that? You see, I'll be back East the first week of September, probably around the third.
>
> We're climbing Mt. Whitney definitely at the end of the job. I got some close-up photographs of the East face and have mapped out a route up the cliffs on this side. It ought to be pretty good. Lots of love. Chris."

On August 6, Topper and Steve Wasserman set out from the mine at Lone Pine to ascend the eastern peak of the 14,496-foot Mt. Whitney, the highest mountain in the continental United States. The eastern peak had been scaled only twice before by parties of two and only a few times by larger groups.

Most experienced mountaineers used a trail on the western side of the peak. Topper and Steve, however, parked their Studebaker at Whitney Portal, at the foot of the precipitous eastern side. They carried supplies for about two days. They told Ralph Adams, the Cerro Gordo mine operator, that they had previously climbed the Swiss Alps and were convinced Mt. Whitney would not prove to be as formidable. Topper looked eagerly ahead to the climb. It was to be the apogee of all his youthful dreams—conclusive proof that he was the man his father would have wanted him to be. His grand adventure had begun.

Libby and Luke Readdy spent less than a week in Tangier. They sunbathed, took abbreviated trips to the outlying towns, and drank with Jane Bowles in the local bars. Almost every night, they dined at Paul Bowles's little house in the medina, and were usually joined by Oliver Smith and Oliver Messel, the British set designer.

On August 10, they embarked by boat to Marseilles, intending to drive leisurely up through France, through the Loire valley, to Paris. The next day, plying between Mallorca and Marseilles, Libby received a radiogram from Benet Polikoff, her lawyer. It was vaguely worded; there was nothing definite; but Topper, while climbing Mt. Whitney three days before, had simply disappeared. Libby took it calmly; she didn't cry. But Luke Readdy could see she was distraught, and he embraced her.

From Marseilles, they flew to Paris, boarded another plane and flew on to New York. At Idlewild Airport, Jack Clareman, Libby's junior lawyer, and a host of rowdy reporters and photographers awaited them. They drove into Manhattan to Libby's Eastside brownstone where they were joined by Mike Kahn, Libby's nephew. Leaving the car, they were besieged by reporters. Kahn told them to go away, but the reporters continued to mill outside the house on the sidewalk.

There was no further news. Search parties had been dispatched several days before, but the two boys had not been found. Mike Kahn maintained an optimistic air. Clareman, however, took Luke Readdy aside and, cautioning him not to tell Libby, said that he had given up all hope of finding them.

Later that night, Libby, Luke Readdy and Mike Kahn chartered a plane and flew to Los Angeles. They arrived the next morning and immediately chartered a smaller plane to take them to Lone Pine. Flying north, Libby was weak and withdrawn. She slumped in her seat and Readdy sensed she had given up. It was as if she had always known it would come to this, that what awaited her had always been absurd and unavoidable.

Steve Wasserman's frozen body was found in a crevasse on the eastern peak just over twelve thousand feet up the mountain. He had fallen some eight hundred feet. A ten-foot nylon rope, frayed at the end, was tied around his waist, indicating that the rope had been severed by a jagged cliff as the two friends, linked together, edged ever higher.

Topper's body was found a day later, just three hundred feet from the top of Mt. Whitney. He had been dead for two days. The American Alpine Club attributed the deaths of the two boys to inexperience, overconfidence and a lack of proper equipment.

They were wearing tennis shoes and clearly had had no real conception of what such a climb entailed.

The Alpine Club conjectured that high above the sheer buttress, the two friends had been afraid to descend and thought it less dangerous to press on, to attempt the top. And then, the rope had snapped. It would not have taken long: a winded cry, a breathless fall, unconsciousness. And then, as Topper had ended one of his last works, a story entitled "Mountain Scene," "the valley was rocked by fog and storm, but we were in the stars."

Libby, Luke Readdy and Mike Kahn were staying in a small motel at the foot of Mt. Whitney. When Libby was told that her child was dead, she began to sob, her hand clenched to her mouth, the tears welling down her face. And then, referring to the reporters and photographers who had gathered in Lone Pine, she cried, "I don't want his body shown to those people. I'll pay anything, just so his poor body's not exposed to those people."

Libby never saw Topper's body. His .22 pistol, his pack and sweater were returned to her, and both boys' bodies were shipped back east. The next day, Libby, Luke Readdy and Mike Kahn flew to New York. Libby said nothing, she felt nothing, but she cried all the way home, biting her lower lip, and clutching Luke Readdy's arm.

In his daily column in the New York *Herald Tribune,* Libby's old friend Winsor French paid tribute to the dead boy:

> No one I can think of, has been so goaded by tragedy and risen so courageously above it as Libby Holman. Twice married, both of her husbands died violently and now her only son, Chris, has fallen off a mountain, bringing the relentless saga to full circle.
>
> I knew Chris all of his brief seventeen years and it is easy to understand why he would want to scale dangerous, snow-clad peaks. Few youngsters had such sheltered lives. Threatened by kidnappers from the instant of his birth, he was protected twenty-four hours a day by bodyguards who were later replaced by tutors—all in an enormous, remote house in Connecticut that was fortified with burglar alarms.
>
> Burglar alarms and bodyguards breed their own particular dreams. Chris's was a soaring character and like the suddenly

un-caged eagle, once free, he had to climb a little higher and a little more recklessly than anyone else ever had.

He had his mother's utter disregard and contempt for risks of any sort and he deserved something far, far better than such a tragic, wasted ending.

Topper's death was Libby's crucifixion. Never again was she to love so yieldingly, so spontaneously. All that remained was remorse and endless recrimination. Her friends agreed that when Libby returned from California, she wasn't Libby anymore. She lay in a state of collapse for weeks, buried in her big satin bed, sobbing uncontrollably. She refused to do anything or to see anyone. She sorted through Topper's belongings, touching them, picking them up and putting them down, keeping them in order, almost as if she expected him to come home again. But Libby knew better. She had always believed that Topper would do something splendid with his life, that his would be some bright and singular destiny, "but not *this*," she cried, "*anything* but *this*."

Lynda Williams was shattered by Topper's death, although she believed it had been symbolic, a macabre and somehow fitting end for the dream-driven boy. Topper had been cremated and, that August, Libby told Lynda she had decided to scatter his ashes over Mt. Whitney, that that is what her child would have wanted. There was no question in Libby's mind that it was the proper thing to do. A few days later, Lynda and Mike Kahn flew to Los Angeles. They hired a small plane, which Kahn piloted himself, and high above Mt. Whitney, Lynda Williams scattered Topper's last remains into the clear and turbulent air.

Libby now decided to spend a year in France in a villa she had leased on the outskirts of Paris. She shut down Treetops, packed all the household effects, the linen, the china, the silverware, into enormous cartons and dispatched them abroad. The entire staff was dismissed. Before leaving for France, she donated the Reynolds Building for Science to the Putney School and one full tuition scholarship each year. It was Libby's final salute to her son. In the years to come, except with her most trusted intimates, she never referred to Topper's death again.

BOOK THREE:
THE SMART OLD WITCH

48

F LIGHT INVARIABLY FOLLOWS FAILURE: OR THAT, AT LEAST, IS how one of Libby's banished friends envisaged her abrupt departure for Europe. For twenty years, Libby had dreamed of maintaining a villa in France; now, in order to put Topper's death behind her, she intended to fulfill that dream. She did not conceive of it as flight, any more than she considered that she had failed. Rather, it was a kind of emotional mutiny, a new beginning.

And yet, after only three days in Paris, Libby felt an oppressive sense of alienation; although Topper's death had not been her responsibility, she was overcome with tortured feelings of delinquency and guilt. Her grief remained ungovernable. Libby was forty-six years old: "But I feel like a hundred," she said, "and, every day, I feel a little older."

Libby rented a large house called the Château Bellevue in Louveciennes, a village some thirty miles west of Paris on the Seine. The chateau was in execrable taste—having been built in the 1890s by an arriviste two hundred years after chateaux had been in fashion. The current owners were charging an exaggerated rent, but Libby took it anyway; she was too spent emotionally to haggle.

Libby would pass the next ten months in Louveciennes in the company of her pianist, Gerald Cook, and Timmy and Tony, now five and three. Tony remained a fat and merry child and Libby continued to call him Little Farouk. She kept him on a permanent diet; while her guests dined on lobster bisque and *paupiettes de veau*, Tony was given curds and whey. Timmy, on the other hand, was a source of serious concern to Libby. A cute and winsome boy, he had idolized Topper, and Topper's death seemed to have traumatized him. That October, Timmy suddenly ceased to speak. Libby procured special tutors and doctors, but Timmy remained absolutely mute for the next two years. Then, just as suddenly and inexplicably, he began to speak again. He would remember nothing of that time and, much later, called those years his "cold, dead period."

Earlier that year, Libby and Gerald Cook had created a one-woman show entitled *Blues, Ballads, and Sin-Songs*—a compilation of songs that Libby had sung throughout the years. While in Europe, Libby brought the show to Paris, Rome and Milan. In order to advertise it, the artist Fred Koester painted an *affiche* of Libby; and it remains her most dramatic portrait. Drawn primarily in black-and-white, the poster depicted Libby standing on a stage. Her back is arched, her head thrown back, and she leans on a tiny kitchen chair, a Spanish fan at her feet. The only other color, a violent shade of pink, illuminates Libby's sweeping gown and the downward melancholy turn of her lips. It was a confident theatrical pose and Libby adored it.

Blues, Ballads, and Sin-Songs was meant to be a different kind of blues performance. Prior to Topper's death, Libby had spent weeks in the Library of Congress in Washington, D.C., studying its collection of early American songs. She was fascinated with the recordings made by Alan Lomax and his son, who had taped unwritten songs sung to them by the back-country inhabitants of southern Appalachia, and would sing many of them in her show.

"I've been working backwards from where I began as a singer of torch songs," she told a French reporter. "The torch song is a song of unrequited love. It's a modern thing. Nobody carries a torch in the early American songs. If the one they love doesn't love them, then, the hell with it, they can get themselves another girl or man. People in early American ballads just don't feel sorry for themselves."

Libby's engagements in Milan and Rome were not successful. Italian audiences were baffled by her deployment of the kitchen chair and by her voice, which Italian critics considered too masculine for a lady. But the Parisian performances were an unqualified success—with both audiences and critics. One of her warmest admirers was Alice B. Toklas, to whom Libby had been introduced after the last of her Parisian shows. Miss Toklas's friend Gertrude Stein had died four years before and she was still in mourning. But she attended Libby's performance and, afterward wrote her a letter:

"Dear Miss Holman," she said. "You have given me so much pleasure—your concert—then meeting you and now the lovely flowers. They come at a very black moment and immediately cast a spell of encouragement, comfort and courage. So you see, there are many reasons why I am your grateful, appreciative, cordial A. B. Toklas."

Libby received a continual flow of visitors at the Château Bellevue that year—the novelist Dawn Powell, the actor Louis Jourdan, and Jane Bowles, who had come to Paris earlier in the year to work on the ending of her first play, *In the Summerhouse*. Jane lived in a pleasantly shabby hotel on the Rue de Bac where her neighbor was the novelist Truman Capote, then twenty-six years old. Libby's old friend Paul Godkin was performing with the American Ballet Theatre at the Palais de Chaillot. She attended his opening night, and Godkin remembered particularly her kinky black hair, the long black eyelashes, the smeared pink lipstick, all of which were accentuated by a black trench coat lined with white ermine. Libby's appearance caused a sensation and her photograph appeared in many of the next day's newspapers. Dining with Libby afterward, Godkin sensed that she had pulled herself together, and throughout the meal, she maintained an air of bright insouciance. They alluded to Topper only in passing. Libby had cried all she could, she said. "There are no more tears."

Luke Readdy visited Libby at Louveciennes just once. He had flown with her from New York to Paris and, after spending a few days at the Château Bellevue, took the boat train to England in order to enroll at Oxford. Libby visited him there, staying at the home of one of Readdy's friends, another Rhodes scholar, and they punted on the Cherwell, strolled along the Meadows, drank stout and ate beef patties at the Trout and other river pubs.

Their love affair continued (and sexually it flourished), but the emotional intensity had gone. As Readdy knew, Libby was floundering, and she sensed a calm in him, an anchor. She proposed marriage repeatedly, suggesting they live together wherever he preferred. She neither wanted nor needed Treetops anymore, she said, and, concerning her money, added: "Why don't you just take over and manage it for me." Readdy declined. He did not envisage Libby living as a teacher's wife on a teacher's salary in a small southern town. Her proposals were more romantic than passionate, and she never insisted, but Readdy felt she mentioned it more often than she should have.

At the end of Libby's stay at Oxford, Readdy put her on the London train; walking back to Christ Church, it occurred to him that he would never see her again. He was surprised at how easily he accepted that. He would miss her, but concluded it was just as well. He was a scholar, a man of solitude; and Libby, despite her hankerings for privacy, would always be a performer, a woman who not only wanted but required public acclaim. As far as Readdy was concerned, her longing for marriage was as futile as her desire for fame: Libby's teeth were sharp, but she had no appetite.

Meanwhile, in America, an acrimonious squabble over Topper's estate was taking place. The Reynolds family contended his entire estate should revert to them; but Connecticut state laws provided that any monies left in trust for minors reverted to the parents or surviving parent. Thus, Topper's share of the R. J. Reynolds cigarette fortune, which now amounted to $6,502,000 was awarded to Libby.

She was greatly relieved. Although claiming that Topper's money was unimportant, she also felt that it was rightfully hers. Since she did not wish to wrangle publicly, she remained abroad until the issue was settled, but already the additional wealth had begun to make her suspicious. She now believed that strangers and even old friends courted her solely for her money, that *she*, Libby Holman, was of little consequence. "I feel like a sacrificial lamb," she said, "but at least I have the wherewithal to keep the wolves from the door." Libby had, in her way, come through, and in August of 1951, a year after Topper's death, she returned to America.

49

REETOPS HAD BECOME LITTLE MORE THAN A GHOST HOUSE now, lonely, unoccupied—a testament to a portion of Libby's life she no longer wished to recall. Like the dust and the dank smell of disuse, the memory of her dead son was everywhere. Almost immediately, Libby packed up Topper's clothes, his tools, his childhood toys and model airplanes, all of which she gave to local charities. She saved only four mementos: his short stories, poetry and essays, which she collected and bound into a large black folder; a ceramic bust of the boy, which she displayed above the fireplace in the library; and a large oil portrait of Topper dressed in the foppish guise of Fauntleroy. The painting was a joke that only she and Topper had shared. It was, in fact, a nineteenth-century portrait by an unknown painter of an unknown boy. They had discovered it in Tangier and were so amused with its eerie likeness to Topper that they had purchased it. The painting did not arrive at Treetops until after Topper died, and because her son had loved it so, Libby placed it prominently in her all-white, formal living room.

Libby also saved a black-and-white photograph of Topper taken during the last year of his life. It was her favorite likeness of her son and she hung it in the foyer outside her bedroom next to the photographs of Smith Reynolds, of Phillips and Ralph Holmes—her dead lovers, or as Libby bitterly referred to them—"the gallery of all my romantic homicides."

Because she had fired her staff the year before, Libby arranged interviews with prospective maids. One of the first applicants was a thirty-two-year-old black woman from North Carolina named Alice Byrd. Alice had been directed to the rear of the house and Libby, wearing a red bikini, was rising from the oval pool. Timmy and Tony sprang forward to grab her hands.

Libby's tan was dark and deep and, momentarily, Alice believed she was in the presence of some ancient Mayan princess; it was all she could do to keep from genuflecting. After only a few minutes of conversation, Libby hired her. Alice Byrd would remain at Treetops for the rest of Libby's life, becoming her personal maid, her friend and confidante. Libby called the young woman Owl, and in time, and only in private, Alice called her Cuddles.

Timmy and Tony were seven and five. In 1951–1952, Tony attended the New Canaan Country Day School and would be sent the following year to board at the Poughkeepsie Day School. Timmy had regained his speech, but had considerable difficulty learning to read and he was dispatched first to numerous reading clinics, then to the New Canaan Day School, and finally to the North Country School in Lake Placid, New York.

Libby treated the boys like fragile and valuable possessions. Should any of her friends refer to them as adopted, she became outraged, screaming that the word *adopted* was forbidden. Privately, however, she made a point of telling the boys that if they ever wished to meet their real parents, she would happily arrange it. Libby was not an easy mother. She was strict and bossy, bossier even than her own mother had been, and she tended to project her personal problems onto her sons. She disapproved of any manifestation of idiosyncratic behavior, and Timmy and Tony were given interminable batteries of complicated tests in order to substantiate their "normality"—though precisely what Libby meant by that, they were never to comprehend. From the time they were tots, they were sent to psychologists and psychiatrists—sessions Libby considered both healthy and constructive.

When Tony was seven, he was sent to a psychiatrist—the problem (nail-biting) not even his, but Timmy's. Tony, however, was elated. He detested school and the twice-weekly psychiatric appointments gave him an opportunity to escape his studies. The consultations were an hour long, during which time Tony and the doctor sat side by side on a Victorian settee. The doctor seldom spoke; rather, he stared and fiddled with his spectacles, waiting patiently for Tony to reveal his juvenile fears and inadequacies. But Tony remained silent, and when the hour ended, the doctor drove him back to school.

As time passed, Tony began to anticipate these sessions as one looks forward to an exciting game. Because he refused to speak (even to tell the doctor how old he was), the psychiatrist concluded that the boy was morbidly inhibited and advised Libby to give him everything he wanted. Tony thought this a splendid prescription and, that evening, devised a lengthy list of arcane desires. Libby, however, was dubious and, much to Tony's chagrin, decided to ignore the doctor's advice.

Libby had given Timmy Topper's old bedroom, and, although it occurred to her that Tony might have felt slighted, she considered it unimportant. Libby tried to be impartial, but it was obvious to most of her friends that she favored Timmy—a cute and charming boy who was something of a hellion. Somewhat later, as an adolescent, Timmy deliberately set two fires—one in his school chemistry laboratory and another at Treetops, where, one evening, he placed a lighted candle in a rolled-up carpet, calculating that it would catch fire during the night. The candle eventually went out, but not before the house was charged with smoke. Libby was furious, but she did not punish Timmy. In this, as in other instances, Timmy could do no wrong. Rather, it was Tony, sweet and slow and overweight, who bore the brunt of Libby's fulminations.

Both boys had numerous extracurricular appointments and activities and, in order to keep track of them, Libby maintained a book she called her "tsouris" book—*tsouris* being the Yiddish word for grief or trouble. The journal contained detailed times and dates of Timmy's and Tony's school holidays, Timmy's reading clinics and Tony's diet, their tutoring, riding and swimming lessons, the consultations with psychiatrists and psychologists, the tennis lessons from Lloyd Budge, Don's younger brother, and the piano lessons from Gerald Cook. Libby kept it by her bedside, referring to it constantly, fretting and clicking her teeth over just how much there was to do, and what there was yet to be accomplished. "There's more tsouris in this slender volume than in all of the Bible," she liked to say.

In February of 1952, Frank Williams, a sophomore at Columbia University, placed an advertisement in the *Saturday Review* in the hope of obtaining summer employment. The ad stated: "Columbia student would like to travel abroad with family as tutor-companion." Libby, who regularly completed the acrostics in the

Saturday Review, responded on her blue stationery, her initials, LHR, embossed in gold on the top.

When the letter arrived, Williams, an eighteen-year-old from Seagate in Brooklyn, was studying for his examinations and neglected to answer. Not until his roommate told him who Libby Holman Reynolds was ("an old-time blues singer, a millionairess and, possibly, a murderer") did the dazzled youth reply. A few days later, he was interviewed by Libby at her Manhattan brownstone, and was subsequently hired for the summer at a salary of $750. The lodging and the food were free, but Benet Polikoff, Libby's lawyer, stipulated one additional condition: Topper's name must never be mentioned in Libby's presence.

That Easter, Williams drove up to Treetops to meet Libby's sons. As he got out of the car, Timmy smiled and took him by the hand, and Libby said, "Don't let him charm you . . . or he'll charm you."

Williams, who had come from a modest middle-class background, was amazed at what he described to his roommate as the "magnificence" of Treetops. The impressionable youth was completely seduced by the spacious grounds, the views, the fifty-six rooms which he counted meticulously. Libby now maintained a permanent staff of six—a gardener, a personal maid, a cook, a butler-chauffeur, a governess and a secretary. But she refused to call them servants. "We don't have servants," she explained. "We have friends and helpers." Libby considered them an extension of her own family; and as in any other family, the staff members vied for Libby's favor and spread tart rumors about the others.

Williams's favorite room at Treetops was the library, where Libby's numerous weekend guests invariably congregated. The wood-paneled room contained row upon row of leather-bound volumes—the works of such authors as D. H. Lawrence, Giorgio Vasari, Mark Twain, Théophile Gautier, Alexandre Dumas and Charles Dickens. It was here that Libby held court, curled up on the sofa beneath a vicuña lap rug, punctuating her comments and commands with lighted Kools in disposable white-plastic cigarette holders.

Treetops was at its most beautiful during the spring and early summer. The narrow Mianus River wended through the extensive property and the grounds were blanketed with lush patches of strawberries (Libby's favorite fruit), with azalea bushes, laurel, andromeda, hybrid rhododendron, black and white birch, red oak, pine and pin oaks, sycamores, beech, dogwood and Japanese flowering cherry trees, through which ran Libby's Irish wolfhounds.

Libby despised developers and whenever she could purchase additional acreage adjoining Treetops, she did so, "to keep," as she said "the bulldozers at bay." Twice a week, fresh flowers were carried up to the main house from her two greenhouses—tulips, hyacinths, orchids, snapdragons, stock, carnations, sweet peas and six separate varieties of roses.

Daffodils were Libby's abiding passion. Every year, some ten to twelve thousand daffodils, between three and four hundred varieties, were planted at Treetops. Libby even had one named after her, a dainty pure-white flower, presented to her by a Dutch horticultural society. Each spring, Libby gave an elaborate garden party to celebrate the blooming of her favorite flowers. It was a spectacular sight—literally a million pink, yellow and white daffodils which seemed to flood and shine and ripple like an illuminated lake across the hill.

Frank Williams spent the summer at Treetops, returning to Columbia in the autumn. In New York, he moved into Libby's Eastside brownstone and, for the next four years, commuted between Manhattan and Treetops in the 1947 De Soto sedan Libby had given him. Much later, he came to believe that he had not had a normal young adulthood. The teenager envisaged his life with Libby as the fulfillment of some fantastic fantasy, the kind of life he had never known and would never know again. For years, he was drunk with the sense of it.

Libby, Williams learned, was a woman of conflicted passions—an extremist, who was either up or down, drunk or sober, silent or verbose, impassioned or unmoved. She hated or loved, despising anything or anyone who was gray or bland or in-between. Her mood swings were profound and instantaneous. Much later, when someone called her schizophrenic, Libby laughed and said, "Darling, you couldn't be more wrong. The truth is, I'm *multi*phrenic."

These contradictions were reflected in Libby's religious observances. She continued to despise her Jewishness; and when she adopted Timmy and Tony, who were from Protestant families, she found it necessary to join a Protestant church, subsequently choosing the First Presbyterian Church in Stamford. Somewhat later, she attended the Friends Meeting House in Stamford and considered becoming a Quaker for a time, but nothing came of it. She was passionately involved with Zen and gave everyone her favorite book, *Zen and the Art of Archery*. Libby's whimsical beliefs were passed on to her children. Thus, Timmy and Tony, while growing up, attended the Presbyterian Church, the Quaker Meeting House, Zen Buddhist sessions and the Stamford Catholic Church, which, to Libby's delight, they called "Our Lady of the Holy Mackerel."

Frank Williams believed it was these very contradictions that set Libby apart, elevated her from the run of practical, even-tempered women. She read incessantly, although she never thought of herself as well-read or intelligent, and one of her favorite expressions was "I'm such a stupe." Having forsaken academe for the theater, she considered herself an intellectual imposter and always deferred to such friends as Paul Bowles and Tennessee Williams.

She never wore a bra. She remained inordinately fond of her breasts and took intramuscular shots to keep them firm. She despised being photographed, even in her own home, and only Marcus Blechman was permitted to take pictures of her. She hated television, except for Imogene Coca's weekly appearance in Sid Caesar's *Show of Shows*, which she watched religiously. She was also a compulsive organizer and if one of the maids had cleaned the floor improperly, Libby dropped to her knees and scrubbed it herself. And yet, in spite of her contradictions, Libby had a keen sense of who she was and how she wished to be seen in others' eyes. As she once said: "I'm a lady and, whether I'm drunk in public or swear in church, I expect to be treated like one."

Libby continued to think of herself as something of a sorceress, a woman possessed of potent and fearsome proclivities. "I used to be a black witch," she told Louisa Carpenter, "but now I'm a white one," by which she meant that age had tempered her talismanic powers. For more than twenty years, one of her favorite poems, which she could recite by heart, was Robert Service's "The Harpy," the first stanza of which Libby was particularly fond of quoting: "There was a woman, and she was wise;

woefully wise was she/She was old, so old, yet her years all told were but a score and three/And she knew by heart, from finish to start, the Book of Iniquity."

In late 1952, before going on a fishing trip to Key West, she left Frank Williams a note: "The keys to the Jaguar are on the library desk. Don't take any shit from Timmy. See you in a week. Love. The Witch."

In the first few years after Topper died, Libby displayed little of her fabled energy, but she continued to amuse. One evening, she took Frank Williams and a young Colombian friend of hers to the Broadway opening of Leonard Sillman's *New Faces*, a revue that would make a star of an unknown singer named Eartha Kitt. Throughout the play, the Colombian youth continually caressed Williams's arm. Afterward, at a party, Williams told Libby that the South American had seemed like a nice young boy, but he was unable to understand why the youth had caressed his arm. "Are *all* Colombians like that?" he wished to know.

"*All* Colombian homosexuals are like that," said Libby.

50

LIBBY HAD NOT SEEN MONTGOMERY CLIFT SINCE THEY HAD worked together in *Mexican Mural* nearly ten years before. But she had attended most of his Broadway performances—Thornton Wilder's *The Skin of Our Teeth* and *Our Town*, Lillian Hellman's *The Searching Wind* and Tennessee Williams's *You Touched Me*. She had also seen three of the films that had brought him his early fame—*The Search, Red River* and *A Place in the Sun*, which had opened to widespread praise in 1951.

At thirty-one, Monty was at the height of his fame, "the idol of millions," as the Hollywood fan magazines observed repeatedly. The beautiful young man had already established his cinematic image—that of the loner, the outsider, the man of conscience who is both vulnerable and sensual, determined and disillusioned. A generation of bobby-soxers had fallen in love with him. But Monty detested their adoration. He didn't wish to be what he derisively called "a pubic figure." He was no longer able to walk in the streets of New York without unruly groups of oglers crowding round, demanding photographs and autographs, mementos, attention, time. Paramount Studios was promoting him as its latest sex symbol, "the most eligible bachelor on the silver screen." Monty not only loathed the publicity campaign, he did not even feel sexual, nor did he comprehend what sexuality had to do with his work.

Unknown to his fans, however, Monty was a desperate, tormented youth, whose friends compared him to Jekyll and Hyde. He was sexually confused, attracted to men and women, and guilty about his transient involvements with both of them. "I don't understand it," he used to say. "I love men in bed, but I *really* love women." In addition, he suffered from a complicated variety of diseases and complexes, among them colitis, insomnia and hypochondria, and in his jacket pocket, he carried a motley of vitamins and phenobarbitals. His huge medicine cabinet at home contained pain relievers, antibiotics, anticonvulsants, antidepressants, antispasmodics, antinauseants, decongestants, muscle relaxants, tranquilizers, and such sleeping pills as Tuinal, Nembutal and Seconal. Monty was also an alcoholic; his drinking disturbed him to such a degree that he had sought the aid of two psychiatrists, neither of whom was able to help him.

Only his intimates were aware of these problems. For anyone else, to associate briefly with Montgomery Clift was to fall in love with him, and all manner of men and women did. He was famous, he was stunningly handsome, intelligent and wonderfully funny. He was perceptive and well-read. He spoke both French and German fluently and thought of himself as more European than American.

In the early spring of 1952, Libby met Monty Clift again through their mutual friend, the director Bobby Lewis, and within weeks their long-lapsed relationship was transformed into a love affair. Their closest friends thought it a preposterous alliance, but Bobby Lewis considered it a natural mingling of their separate needs. "Libby wanted to own people," he observed, "and Monty wanted to be owned."

*   *   *

In the beginning, they met surreptitiously in Manhattan, at bars and restaurants, or at Monty's new duplex apartment at 207 East Sixty-first Street, less than a block from Libby's brownstone. Occasionally, Monty would drive up to Treetops, often staying for weeks at a time. Observing the proprieties, Monty slept in the strawberry room on the third floor, soon known among Libby's staff as "Monty's room," and it was always kept in readiness.

During the first flush of their affair, Libby's influence colored almost everything that Monty did. He consulted Libby on his diet, his doctors, his career. They studied the scripts he was being offered—Lillian Hellman's script of Norman Mailer's novel *The Naked and the Dead,* a script of *Look Homeward, Angel* and a draft of a new western called *High Noon*—all of which Libby advised Monty to reject.

They were a curious couple—the "dark Adonis," as Monty was known, and Libby, more than sixteen years his elder, her face prematurely wrinkled by the sun. But these unlikely lovers shared much in common. They were both passionate dieters, each of them favoring milk and raw meat. They doted on doctors and prescription drugs. They were intense interrogators, demanding detailed replies to their incessant queries. By nature, they were both deceptive, yet despised deception and deceit in others—particularly Monty, a self-loathing homosexual, who realized that unless his sexual proclivities were concealed, his career would almost certainly be jeopardized. They tended to compartmentalize their relationships so that one of their friends might not necessarily know another. They both adored the theater and shared a passion for literature, especially the works of D. H. Lawrence and Marcel Proust. Mischievous lovers of puns and practical jokes, with a keen sense of the absurdity of life, they thought of themselves as artists, rebels, committed to the precept of violating accepted rules.

Monty was the abiding obsession of Libby's middle life; indeed, he was practically an occupation. From the very beginning, however, Libby's intimates felt their entanglement was doomed—"a match made in hell," as Alec Wilder said. But Libby was willful. She exhibited an unquenchable greed for that which could never be satiated; and she genuinely believed that, given her love, her admiration, her beneficial ministrations, she could change Monty, heal him, enable him to somehow transcend his homosexuality.

Paul Bowles felt that Monty was one of the least happy people he had ever known, and it made him uncomfortable to be in his company. Libby told Bowles that she could sense the torture in her young lover and longed to alleviate it. But when they were together, there was, in Bowles's view, too much drinking, too much self-doubt, too much introspection, and it was bad for both of them. He concluded that Libby, who had hitherto suffered only for others, began now to suffer as Monty suffered—for herself and herself alone.

Jack Larson, who had achieved a certain fame by portraying Jimmy Olsen, the cub photographer for *The Daily Planet* in the successful television series of *Superman,* was a close friend of Monty's and, through him, had come to know Libby. He believed that her romantic obsession with Monty was purely masochistic. "Just as rats sense a sinking ship and rush ashore," he said, "Libby always rushed to get aboard."

When they were separated, which happened frequently because of Monty's film career, each of them drifted into brief, passionate liaisons with other men and women. Neither Libby nor Monty had been or ever would be faithful to anyone. But while they were both in the New York area, they talked frequently on the telephone and saw one another almost every day. The long separations appeared to be little more than trifling parentheses. Even so, it remained an extraordinary alliance: a young homosexual who claimed to love women, and a middle-aged millionairess with a latent penchant for other women. And yet they were devoted to one another, both of them zany and preposterous—lovers who often seemed more like accomplices committed to pulling off a romantic swindle just to prove that it might be done.

During the summer of 1952, Libby traveled to England with her one-woman show, *Blues, Ballads, and Sin-Songs.* The show was a critical success, but much to Libby's consternation, priggish authorities refused to allow her to use the word *Sin-Songs,* on the marquee of the Lyric Theatre in Hammersmith. She remained abroad for nearly a month and, in her absence, Monty and his friends Jeanne and Paul Green moved into Libby's brownstone.

Monty had begun extensive renovations on his new Manhattan duplex and had enlisted the aid of the Greens, friends from California. Paul Green, a builder and designer, was to spend four months on the renovations, tiling, plastering, demolishing rooms. While Green worked, Monty and Green's wife, Jeanne, spent their afternoons in Libby's living room, drinking brandy and listening to Monty's favorite song—the Sinatra recording of "I've Got the World on a String."

Although Jeanne and Monty were only friends, Jeanne was aware that Libby disapproved of their relationship. When Libby returned from England, Jeanne became disgruntled, uneasy. Often, while she and Monty sat in Libby's living room, Libby just materialized, hovering like a sentinel in the background, then disappearing, and Monty would curtly conclude their conversation and scurry after her.

Jeanne soon came to detest Libby's house, considering Libby little more than a stern and vigilant housemother; only her devotion to Monty kept her there. Wherever she walked in the four-story house, she smelled the pungent fragrance of Jungle Gardenia, Libby's favorite perfume—even on Monty's shirts and skin. But, most significant, whenever Libby was in residence, Monty was a different man. He became pliant and obsequious and seemed completely mesmerized by Libby.

Jeanne believed that Libby exerted some strong and malevolent influence over the young actor. One afternoon, Jeanne and Monty were sitting on the sofa in Libby's living room, listening, for what seemed the hundreth time, to Sinatra singing "I've Got the World on a String." Suddenly, a figure, partially obscured by a huge spray of flowers, appeared in the doorway. It was Libby who had arrived unexpectedly from Treetops. Monty became palpably nervous. Getting down on the carpet, he crawled over to Libby, muttering repeatedly how gorgeous, how wonderful, how strong, she was. Libby said nothing, accepting Monty's homage as her due, but she stared balefully at Jeanne, and Jeanne Green was horrified.

In the wake of his success in *A Place in the Sun*, Monty entered what for him would be an uncharacteristic period of intense industry. Throughout the autumn of 1952 and during the first six months of 1953, he performed in three films, shot on locations in Quebec, in Rome, and in Hawaii, and in his absence, Libby initiated a desultory affair with a handsome youth named Ted Benedict. The twenty-six-year-old Harvard graduate had met Libby through her nephew, Michael Kahn, who had been his Harvard roommate. Following a two-year period in the army, Benedict seemed unable to find himself or to make much use of his liberal Harvard education. Employed as a dancing instructor at the Arthur Murray School of Dance in Manhattan, he specialized in foxtrots and tangos. He had not intended to become involved with Libby—indeed, his mother had warned him against it, alluding to Libby's fatal charms and witcheries—but they drifted together because Benedict was alone and because Libby, he surmised, was too.

Although Libby was twenty-two years older, she was an original, a woman who believed that all her behavior was without precedent. Libby called him her beau, a term she thought cute and old-fashioned. But there was nothing old-fashioned about Libby. As their affair began, she told Benedict: "I'm a seductress with standards, but I'll make an exception with you," and she said it so charmingly that he was not offended. But Benedict soon learned that the sexual act itself was not what captivated Libby. She sought instead its ensuing intimacy, its friendship and camaraderie. For Libby, making love was an act of solidarity, and for all her bravado, she was sexually insecure. If a lover failed to perform, Libby took it as a personal slight, an indication that he thought her unattractive, or worse, unworthy. Few alibis were acceptable, and fortunately Benedict had little cause to make them. Their romance, a convenient and casual affair for both of them, would continue for nearly a year, and not once, during all that time, did Libby mention Montgomery Clift.

One Saturday morning, during the first weekend he spent at Treetops, Benedict strolled through the large all-white formal living room and stopped to admire the oil painting of Topper hanging over the fireplace. Somewhat later, over breakfast, when he pointed out that the painter had managed to capture Topper remarkably (Benedict had seen photographs of the boy), Libby burst into tears and whimpered, *"Jesus,* it's not even him." She threw down her napkin and rushed from the room.

At dinner that evening, she drank a bottle of chilled Chambertin and attempted, for the first time, she said, to describe Topper's tragic demise. Haltingly, she spoke of her love for the boy, and her guilt for having allowed him to climb "that goddamned mountain"—a guilt, she explained, she would never be able to overcome. Not even her adopted children, whom she loved, could compensate for his loss. His death had been pointless: "Not good enough," she said, staring blankly out of the dining room window, "just not good enough." She began to sob uncontrollably and eventually passed out. Benedict carried her up to her bedroom.

Several weeks later, in memory of her son, Libby created the Christopher Reynolds Foundation, a charitable institution, which she intended to be actively involved in the advancement of human rights, with specific emphasis on the environment, civil liberties, race relations, peace and disarmament. Other than Libby, the foundation's Board of Directors included her nephew, Michael Kahn, her lawyer, Benet Polikoff, and her friend Jack Neustadt. Under Libby's aegis, the foundation would ultimately contribute more than three million dollars to universities, hospitals, race-relations councils and institutes, refugee relief and community-relations programs. Libby considered the foundation her proudest achievement.

Of all the numerous endowments and grants the foundation awarded, Libby was most pleased with one that was not bestowed until 1959. For several years, she had followed the tempestuous career of Dr. Martin Luther King, Jr. King, espousing the principle of nonviolent resistance, was emerging as the leader of the American civil-rights movement. He greatly admired Mahatma Gandhi and wished to visit India in order to talk with those of Gandhi's associates who were still alive. When Libby learned of this, she instructed the foundation to award Dr. King a five-thousand-dollar grant.

In February 1959, Dr. King and his wife, Coretta, traveled to India where King spoke with Prime Minister Nehru and other veterans of the Indian independence movement. "To other countries I may go as a tourist," he said, "but to India I come as a pilgrim." King spent four weeks on the subcontinent and returned to America "more convinced than ever before that nonviolent resistance is the most potent weapon available to oppressed people in their struggle for freedom." He was always grateful to Libby for giving him the opportunity of visiting India, and King, Coretta and Libby would eventually become friends.

51

LIBBY WAS ALONE AGAIN. TIMMY AND TONY WERE AWAY AT school. Ted Benedict had entered the Harvard Law School and Monty was in Hawaii shooting *From Here to Eternity*. In their absence, Jane and Paul Bowles spent a substantial portion of 1953 at Treetops or at Libby's brownstone in New York. Jane was Libby's particular intimate—"my playmate, my confidante, my zany Janie." The two women may have sensed that an affair between them would have endangered their friendship and so agreed to suppress any sexual desires either of them may have had. But they genuinely loved one another, and the bond between them would prove to be unbreakable.

Libby loved Paul also and, in his detached and introspective fashion, Bowles reciprocated those feelings. Whenever he came to America, she took considerable care to make his life as comfortable as possible. Libby was superb at giving what Bowles called "schizophrenic parties"—a tight core of intellectuals and, dotted around them like colorful balloons, her absurd theatrical friends—operating on the sound if extravagant principle that her guests could have all they wanted, whenever they wanted it; they had only to ask.

She was a brilliant conversationalist, a charming raconteur, who talked in a kind of excitable hyperbole. Everything was in millions and trillions. But she didn't care for hyperbole in others. As she instructed her sons: "I've told you a *million* times—*never* exaggerate."

Paul Bowles had come to New York in order to compose the score for Jane's play *In the Summerhouse*, scheduled for a Broadway production later that year. He was accompanied by a twenty-four-year-old Moroccan painter named Ahmed Yacoubi and Libby invited them to stay at Treetops.

Paul and Jane had elected long before to lead separate sexual lives and it was, in the main, an amiable arrangement. But Jane was unexpectedly jealous of Paul's relationship with Ahmed, disapproving both of its intensity and its duration. She never spoke directly to Paul about it. Once, when Paul asked her what she thought of Ahmed, Jane replied, "He has holes for eyes." When she mentioned Ahmed to her friends, Jane always said, "Yacoubi, *ech!*" Paul stayed at Treetops for only a few days, leaving with Jane for Washington, D.C., where *In the Summerhouse* was in rehearsals. Ahmed Yacoubi remained behind at Treetops.

In the beginning, Libby tried to befriend the young painter. Through Benet Polikoff she arranged to extend his six-month visa and she helped arrange exhibitions of his work in New York and other eastern cities. She adored Ahmed's painting, particularly one entitled "The Man with the Green Head," influenced by Francis Bacon, and she later purchased it. But she was also taken with the man himself, his exotic clothes, his unctuous charm, his hard and wily countenance and, by degrees, she fell in love with him.

Born of a poor family in Fès, Ahmed had never before experienced such wealth and sophistication as Libby possessed. For him, it was a splendid fling, neither constricting nor complicated. Libby was weak, of course, like all Western women. She was imperious and spoiled. She was also too old for him and overly concerned with getting older. She darkened her hair, put strange drops in her eyes, took vitamin injections and, in order to keep fit, performed Yoga exercises each morning. But no matter, she had her compensations. She was so rich, so generous.

Although Libby preferred Ahmed in his native attire, she bought him expensive Western shirts and suits and shoes. Whenever he rode with Libby in her new Mark VII Jaguar and saw something he desired, he had only to say so. Libby's secretary dutifully wrote the item down and it was delivered the following day. During one brief heady moment, Libby may even have proposed marriage and Ahmed may have accepted. He was never sure. His English had not been very good at the time, and he tended to smile boyishly and nod at almost anything she said.

Some weeks later, when Paul returned to Treetops, his old friend the director Hans Richter arrived to shoot a sequence for his new experimental film, "a surrealist commentary on chess," entitled *8 × 8*. Libby called it "the Richter Pichter." For a set,

Richter chose Libby's oval swimming pool, emptied it, put in an organ, Libby's *affiche,* and the old furniture from the playroom, all of which was placed upside down. Libby's brief role was shot in reverse, the pool, at the end, filling up with water. Paul's head was "cut off." There was a gun that shot talcum powder and Ahmed Yacoubi emerged from a grotto in the pool dressed in a colorful djellaba. He twittered delicately on the flute and Libby thought he resembled an Arabic Pan.

During the shooting of the film, it was obvious to Paul that Libby and Ahmed had become involved. In his view, Ahmed had simply been overwhelmed; Libby, on the other hand, was a masochist. She longed to be overpowered, to be subdued, yet invariably chose men whom *she* could dominate. It was a continual and difficult battle for her and, unfortunately, she almost always triumphed. But Ahmed was a powerful man. Libby told Jane Bowles that it was the best sex she had ever had, barbarous and brutal.

Paul decided to return to Tangier, to complete, he said, the still half-finished score of García Lorca's *Yerma,* which he had begun for Libby five years before. Just before leaving, at the beginning of May, Libby came to Paul and said: "Paul, I've fallen in love with Ahmed. I feel so guilty, but I couldn't help myself." Paul was not angry, and in a curious way he understood, but he left Treetops immediately. Ahmed chose to remain with Libby.

One Friday at Treetops, only Libby and Ahmed were in residence, although Libby was expecting Ted Benedict to come down from Cambridge for the weekend. Ahmed knew that Libby had conducted a sporadic affair with Benedict, but it didn't concern him. Ted Benedict was nothing, a trifle, and Ahmed called him "Dead" Benedict. That evening, after Benedict arrived, the three of them had dinner. Ahmed wore his yellow, braided djellaba. Over dinner, they became very drunk on vintage champagne, and at some point, when Benedict had disappeared, Libby went into a closet between the library and the drawing room, returning with two small loaded pistols.

Handing one of the pistols to Ahmed, she suggested they make a suicide pact. "You shoot yourself and then I'll shoot myself," she said tipsily. Ahmed was drunk but he wasn't crazy. He hastily explained that he didn't think it was a good idea. "Okay," said Libby, "I'll shoot myself and then you shoot yourself." This seemed, at first, more sensible, but then Ahmed envisioned the next day's newspaper headlines. He saw them quite vividly. They said: MOROCCAN IMMIGRANT MURDERS MILLIONAIRESS. He refused to have anything to do with the plan and took Libby's gun away.

In early June, Jane Bowles returned to New York from Ann Arbor, Michigan, where a production of *In the Summerhouse* had been performed. That very evening, she received an agitated telephone call from Libby. There had been an incident involving Ahmed. Libby was extremely angry and intended to call the police. What had happened was never to become entirely clear. Ahmed told Paul Bowles that Libby believed he had tried to drown her seven-year-old son, Timmy, in the swimming pool, but that it had been a misunderstanding. Whatever had happened, Ahmed was subsequently expelled from Treetops, and Timmy was dispatched to his psychiatrist.

Ahmed would always deny that his affair with Libby had ended that way. It was *he*, he insisted, who had decided to go. After three months with Libby, he felt he had been entrapped by sex and riches. All he had ever wanted was his art, and he had been seduced by baubles and pagan clothes. On that last day, he collected the countless suits and garments that Libby had given him, cut each of them into tiny pieces, and threw them into her large bathtub. Libby screamed that he was crazy. Ahmed slapped her, calling her an "infidel, a camel." Wearing his yellow, braided djellaba, he left Treetops in Libby's Jaguar.

Libby did not call the police. Jane Bowles persuaded her to keep Ahmed in her Manhattan brownstone until he could be returned to Morocco. For three days he was locked in an upstairs room where he moaned and keened, emitted garbled Arabic imprecations and continually called out Libby's name. But it was too late. He had lost her friendship and, more important, her protection. As for Libby, she wanted only to be certain that Ahmed Yacoubi was gone for good; and she behaved, in Paul Bowles's view, "magnificently"—shipping the young painter to Morocco first-class on the U.S.S. *Constitution*.

52

Monty Clift continued to drift in and out of Libby's life, an itinerant and lazy lover. When he needed rest or advice or sustenance, he would go up to Treetops for the weekend or for several weeks, leaving often without warning for some unspecified and perhaps unfixed destination. Throughout the early fifties, he came to Treetops frequently, bringing with him such friends as actors Bill Le Massena, Roddy McDowall and Jack Larson.

Monty was not involved with anyone at the time and, now that Ahmed Yacoubi had been deported, neither was Libby. When they were together, they seemed very much in love. In Libby's presence, Monty gave an impression of extreme masculinity and there were many of Libby's friends who had no inkling that he was homosexual. They held hands and kissed openly and were utterly devoted to one another. Alec Wilder remembered seeing Monty and Libby one Sunday afternoon at Treetops standing by the oval pool. Each wore an abbreviated bathing suit, and each revealed a browned, emaciated body, and Wilder said to Marcus Blechman, "*Look,* there's Mahatma Gandhi and her disciple."

For the most part, Libby accepted Monty for what he was and remained immune to his outrageous behavior. Because of his excessive drinking, Monty suffered from periodic blackouts. Occasionally, over dinner at Treetops, he became so drunk that his head fell into his soup, and Libby would yank him up like a marionette and wipe his face without interrupting the conversation. The British director Peter Glenville attended several of these dinners and was always impressed that Libby presided over them with considerable dignity and grace, ignoring the fact that her guest of honor was, in his view, "*hors de combat.*"

*   *   *

On May 23, 1954, Libby turned fifty, but continued to falsify her age, hovering insistently at forty-eight. She seldom left Treetops anymore and rigorously adhered to her programs and schedules there. On Tuesday afternoons, she rehearsed with Gerald Cook on the grand piano in her drawing room—an exercise one of her friends described as "a kind of therapy." Although she weighed just over a hundred pounds, she continued to diet, subsisting mainly on milk, raw meat, bland broths and fruit. Each morning, she practiced Yoga, and swam and played occasional tennis in the afternoons. She usually retired at ten o'clock.

Libby read continually and indiscriminately—*The Nation, The Observer, The New Statesman, The Saturday Review,* Kafka, Faulkner, and any literature pertaining to Zen. Because of her ulcers, which were becoming worse, she drank modestly—milk, a little Chambertin—but she remained addicted to Seconal. She was an enthusiastic player of bridge. She was partial to low lights and strawberries, to roses, white satin sheets and the formal dancing of Merce Cunningham. She was violently opposed to the policies of President Eisenhower, Vice-President Nixon and Senator Joseph McCarthy, whom she called "the gray assassin."

Libby, among her friends at least, remained a legend—and she was both desperate and determined to perpetuate the appropriate myths and exaggerations in order to support that reputation. She continued to surround herself with effete young men, sycophants who praised her genius while reaching for the gin. And increasingly she looked upon the world beyond Treetops as unbalanced, chaotic, a crass and barren land of scheming autocrats and warring factions. That summer, Libby told Alec Wilder that when her children were grown and she could no longer sing, she would almost certainly kill herself.

Libby took her one-woman show, *Blues, Ballads, and Sin-Songs,* on the road again in June—to the New England Mutual Hall in Boston and to Sarah Lawrence College in Bronxville, New York. The show opened in Boston on a bright, beautiful day, and the Ritz-Carlton glimmered in the noonday sun. As Libby walked into the hotel, it suddenly grew dark and began to rain. A bolt of lightning crossed the summer sky. Libby laughed and said to her secretary: "Lightning is my calling card." For the duration of her engagement, it rained torrentially.

At Sarah Lawrence, Libby was interviewed by the intense young editor of the college newspaper. The girl asked Libby if she searched for meaning in her songs. "Yes, I do," she said, "and when I find it, Gerald plays it and then I vomit around it." Unperturbed, the girl asked Libby why she had substituted folk songs for the torch songs that had made her famous. "I've turned against Tin Pan Alley," she said. "It's been romanticized. I want to sing about the kind of people we all know—whores, drunks, pimps and drug addicts." The editor nodded and dutifully reported what Libby said. Libby was amused enough to save the interview and was fond of showing it to friends as a particularly fine example of collegiate irony—just the sort of piece she would have written had she attended Sarah Lawrence.

Libby had taken *Blues, Ballads, and Sin-Songs* to colleges and recital halls across America for more than four years, receiving enthusiastic ovations and exceptional reviews, but she had failed to obtain the recognition she felt she deserved. After much deliberation, she finally decided to bring the show to Broadway— arranging a six-day booking for the fall and electing to finance the limited engagement herself. But she remained apprehensive. She had not performed on Broadway for sixteen years. As a final dress rehearsal, she decided to export the show to Europe.

"I'd sing my songs in English," she later told an American reporter, "except when I got to Paris. You know how the French are; they think you're out of the zoo if you don't speak French. So I threw them a fish, if I'm not mixing my metaphors, by giving them a group of Louisiana Cajun ballads. I sang them in a Creole dialect.

"The show uses all the magic I know is in the theater," she said. "Most of the songs are dramatic incidents done in song. There are lights, and I'm in costume, moving around the stage and impersonating various characters in the same song. I'm not a trained singer any more than were the people who originated the songs. When I'm singing, I let 'er rip. I go all out—flamenco fashion. At times, I make harsh sounds that aren't music at all, tearing clear across my vocal cords. I sing against my vocal cords, and often against my better judgment."

Libby's reviews in Paris were excellent, all she had hoped they would be, but her favorite came in the form of a letter from Alice B. Toklas, who had seen the show on opening night. "You brought to Paris what I was dying to go to New York for," she wrote. "You have given me intense pleasure. What a delicate instinct you have. Even after having heard you before, your concert was a surprise. Impossible to say what there was to improve, but there is certainly more mastery, greater ease, and a total sense of perfection. If perfection is good, more perfection is better. So all my felicitations and thanks."

Before her Broadway opening, Libby granted her first real interview in ten years, to J. P. Shanley of the New York *Times*. Shanley asked her if she thought her career had been altered by the tragedies that had marred her life.

"My professional life," she said, "has been going a certain way and no matter what happened to me, I think it would have taken the same turn. I may have acquired another dimension, but my course would have been the same. I'm really of the Maude Adams school. Private life is one thing and professional life another.

"I know it's awfully out-dated, but that's what I believe. I'm not a very gregarious person. I lead a kind of quiet life. It's always been that way. I love being on the stage and I'm a bit of a pig about it. In fact, audiences learn more from watching me perform than they ever could from seeing me outside the theater."

Blues, Ballads, and Sin-Songs opened at the Bijou Theatre in New York on October 4, 1954, to considerable fanfare and disrespectful reviews. *Time* said that Libby just wasn't enough of an actress or a sorceress. "She manipulates herself and the kitchen chair that is her only prop, in all sorts of bold, mannered, ingenious ways; but they call too much attention to themselves, or seem too cute, or wear thin too soon, or don't really blend with her songs." Walter Kerr in the *Herald Tribune* felt "there was a private studied quality to the program. . . . Holman seems to be listening to something the audience can't quite hear."

But the greatest blow came from New York's most prestigious drama critic, Brooks Atkinson of the *Times:* "Sixteen years having gone into the trash basket," he wrote, "Libby Holman is appearing on Broadway again. . . . In the years since those torch songs were new, Miss Holman has learned so much about singing that the old vulgarity has gone out of them. She sings them artistically now, which is a pity. But it is comforting to hear that deep, sultry, fluctuating voice again in some practical Broadway music. . . . Miss Holman's voice was never one of the marvels of the world in comparison, for example, to Marian Anderson's. But it did have a quality of broken-hearted passion that convinced you she had suffered. It is less convincing with the material she is now choosing. . . . Miss Holman is a pleasant lady with a dedication to her art. But her earnest throaty tussle with her blues, ballads, and sin-songs last evening set one playgoer to musing on an occasion twenty-six years ago when Miss Holman did her suffering in the midst of a gutsy show.

"The show was *Rainbow*. Charles Ruggles played a dirty mule skinner. Brian Donlevy played a romantic captain. Miss Holman played a wretched outcast who was about the unhappiest female in California during the brawling days of the gold rush. She smoldered fiercely and she sang vividly. *Blues, Ballads, and Sin-Songs* is more elegant and cultured. But it lacks the common touch."

Across the street from the Bijou was the Morosco Theatre where Tallulah Bankhead and Patsy Kelly were starring in a comedy entitled *Dear Charles*. Over the years, Libby and Tallulah had maintained a distant but amicable rivalry, punctuated by sudden outbursts of latent animosity. Tallulah's house, Windows, was in Bedford Village, New York, only a few miles from Treetops. Libby had not seen Tallulah for several years, but whenever she drove by Windows, she would pull a shawl over her head and shout:

"There's the *awful* house of that *awful* harridan."

The day after *Blues, Ballads, and Sin-Songs* opened, Tallulah said to Patsy Kelly, "*Darling,* do slip across the road and ask her *Highness* if she'd like to have a cup of tea."

"Oh?" said Miss Kelly. "Is Libby working again?"

"*Yes,* darling," said Tallulah. "She's in between murders."

When *Blues, Ballads, and Sin-Songs* closed, Libby and Monty flew to Havana for a holiday, staying at the Hotel Nacional. They spent two weeks in Cuba, lying on the beach, attending the

Havana strip shows and nightclubs. One afternoon, in the lobby of the Nacional, Libby was accosted by an American reporter, who blatantly asked her if she was having an affair with Montgomery Clift. Libby waved him away. Unperturbed, the reporter then asked if she had had an affair with Montgomery Clift. Libby glared, then laughed and said: "Yes. *Several* times."

The next day, in order to avoid the press, Monty flew to New York alone. Libby remained in Havana for two more days. She was exhausted, and claimed that her bad reviews had been irrelevant. "I never read the hatchet men," she said. "You can't change what you're doing just because some people don't like it. No retiring to a chicken farm for me. I'm going to keep on singing for as long as I have a voice."

But the reviews had disturbed her deeply. Libby had wanted a triumph, she had wanted, after so long an absence from Broadway, a kind of vindication for all the reversals and failures, the wasted time, the wayward career. And now, in Havana, she wanted only to forget. On October 21, Libby flew back to New York and drove up to Treetops. She would never return to Broadway again.

53

AUTUMN PASSED, AND LIBBY REMAINED LISTLESS, DEBILI-tated. She continued to brood about the critical failure of *Blues, Ballads, and Sin-Songs*. Given her prejudices against Tin Pan Alley and her distaste of "the hatchet men," she gradually convinced herself that her music was too good for Broadway, that it was neither crass nor commercial. But she found no real solace in these convictions. She was haunted, she believed, by hallucinations not entirely of her own making. She became withdrawn and melancholic and, if that was not enough, no medication could alleviate the pain of her ulcers.

Two months after returning to Treetops, Libby tried to commit suicide by taking an overdose of Seconal. But the pills succeeded only in making her violently ill. She retched for days and, under Alice Byrd's gentle ministrations, gradually recovered. When she was well enough to walk around the house, Libby summoned her young black maid into the library one afternoon and told her she had burned her pills. Taking Alice by the hand, Libby said, "Owl, I'll never do this to you again."

When Libby told Monty what she had done, he was furious. She had seemed so surefooted, so strong to him. Libby apologized, but warned him that she was a threat not only to herself but to anyone she loved. "Be careful," she said, "or something terrible will happen to you, too." Monty laughed. "Shut up," he said. "I think you're fantastic."

Libby was the one fixed element in Monty's life and, despite her maladies, his single source of solace. They spent the Christmas holidays of 1954 together in Key West fishing and sunbathing, and would spend the summer of 1955 in Europe, drifting through Italy, avoiding friends and public places, sequestering themselves in small hotels, attempting to keep, as Libby said, "the vulgar world at bay." They were, for the moment, inseparable and gave one another the strength to ignore their separate weaknesses.

Monty displayed an X ray of Libby's skull in a shadow box in his Manhattan apartment and, when asked what it was, would laugh and say, "It's my steady girl." They exchanged Zippo lighters which they invariably misplaced or lost. On one of them, Monty had inscribed: GO AHEAD AND LOSE IT. They liked to make frivolous wagers, the loser paying with a pound of caviar. Libby called such escapades "royal madnesses." Their antics were regularly reported in the Manhattan gossip columns—how they had behaved boisterously at a Museum of Modern Art opening; how they picked their teeth at "21"; how they had been seen entering an Eastside cinema drinking whiskey from a milk carton. During the summer of 1955, a comedy based on their affair, *Single Man at a Party* starring Ruth Merrick, was briefly performed at the Theatre Manqué in New York.

If the gossip columns were to be believed, Libby and Monty were a capricious couple, devoted to innocent hijinks and careless pursuits, a bright, indulgent pair, who envisaged the world as little more than a luxurious rumpus room. In reality, Libby continued to nurse her private disappointments and public defeats; and Monty, at thirty-four, was a desperate man, fluctuating between moods of forced exhilaration and frantic melancholy. Alec Wilder called them "Flotsam and Jetsam—the tortured twins, whose capsized dreams cast them adrift."

By late 1955, instead of healing, as she had hoped it would, Libby's ulcerous condition was deteriorating. She consulted her psychiatrist five times a week and, in order to ease the physical pain, took to chewing Gelusil. Alice Byrd was so concerned (not only for Libby but for herself) that she began to chew the little pills as well, hoping they would prevent her from getting ulcers. Libby was placed on a strict diet of bland foods and skimmed milk. Her doctor advised her to avoid stress, and Alice attempted to ensure that Libby's life at Treetops was smooth and uneventful.

But Libby continued to suffer. In moments of extreme discomfort, the tears poured down her face, and Alice would rub Libby's stomach for hours at a time. On at least two occasions, driving back to Treetops from New York in her convertible, Libby was forced to turn the radio's volume to its highest pitch so that her screams of anguish would not be heard by passing motorists. Every four hours, while she was awake, Rose Minor, Libby's new secretary, administered shots of Probanthine. But nothing helped, and Monty only made the situation worse.

When in residence, he tended to pace his bedroom floor at night, which was just above Libby's bedroom. He tramped continually between his bedroom and bathroom seeking pills to alleviate his insomnia. Hearing him and unable to sleep, Libby would dispatch Alice Byrd upstairs to put him to bed. Night after night, Alice explained that Libby was in pain, that Monty was disturbing her, and that she would have to lock him in his room till morning. It was always the same: Alice led Monty to his bed, put him under the covers like a little boy, and stroked his brow—until he fell asleep muttering, "Yes, dear. Yes, dear. I won't bother her anymore." The next night, it would happen all over again.

By late December, Libby's condition had become so intolerable that Monty drove her to the New Haven Community Hospital for emergency surgery. So that Timmy and Tony should not know just how ill she was, they were sent to the Hanover Ski School in New Hampshire for their Christmas holidays.

On New Year's Day, 1956, Libby underwent a six-hour operation, during which seven eighths of her stomach was removed. Alice thought it a miracle that she survived at all. Following the operation, Libby was never the same—even her thick black hair began to thin. Jane Bowles was so upset that she told Libby that Libby was going to die and leave Jane "alone in her Jewishness." Shirley Stowe, who had married Libby's nephew, Michael Kahn, wrote and said: "I think, by now, even God must admit that you deserve a break and let you have a quieter, painless time of it."

But Libby maintained her sense of humor. Visiting Libby at the hospital, Rose Minor asked her if she had finally forsaken smoking. "Yes, I have," said Libby, "but everytime the doctor puts a thermometer in my mouth, I'm tempted to light it."

Libby left the hospital in late January and Monty drove her back to Treetops. He was particularly attentive to Libby now, and Libby's staff thought him charming, delightful, an exuberant clown. He was equally devoted to her two boys, especially Timmy, who was nine. Despite the difference in their ages, Monty and Timmy were oddly alike—wild, childlike, unpredictable, even sharing the same birthday, October 18.

Timmy idolized Monty and often wished that Monty could have been his real father. While Libby recuperated, they played hide-and-seek in the house, frolicked in the oval pool, and Timmy was Monty's enthusiastic accomplice in many of his escapades. One morning, rebelling against Libby's rigid and (in Monty's view) absurd sense of order, they went around Treetops tipping every picture and painting just an inch or so askew. Then, giggling deliriously, they hid downstairs. When Libby came down for lunch and realized that she was not suffering from vertigo, but that all of her pictures were crooked, she was furious.

That evening, Monty told Libby that he had decided to take the leading role in a film called *Raintree County,* based on Ross Lockridge's best seller about the Civil War. Although Monty described the screenplay as resembling "a soap opera with elephantitis," he thought he would be a coward not to do it. He had not worked in films for nearly three years; he was broke and MGM was offering him $300,000 for the role; moreover, it would give him another opportunity to work with his old friend Elizabeth Taylor. In March of 1956, Monty flew to California and Libby would not see him for nearly two months.

Monty had remained close friends with Elizabeth Taylor, or Bessie Mae as he liked to call her, since they had performed together in *A Place in the Sun* five years before. They exchanged notes and talked to one another on the telephone for hours, holding what Monty called "Elizabethan discussions." When in Los Angeles, Monty stayed at the home of Taylor and her second husband, Michael Wilding, and when Taylor came to New York, she often moved into Monty's duplex while Monty stayed at Libby's. They were not lovers, but Taylor considered Monty her dearest, most devoted friend.

On May 12, the Wildings gave a dinner party at their home on Beverly Estates Drive off Benedict Canyon in Beverly Hills. That evening they invited Monty, Kevin McCarthy, Rock Hudson and Phyllis Gates, Hudson's secretary and future wife.

The dinner party bored Monty. He ate meagerly, drank several glasses of warm rosé, and announced he was leaving early. He was tired and a little concerned about driving down the serpentine hill in the fog and the dark. Kevin McCarthy agreed to guide him to Sunset Boulevard.

Winding down the precipitous road, McCarthy suddenly saw that Monty's car was much too close to his. At first, he thought it was one of Monty's practical jokes, that Monty intended to nudge the rear of his car, so McCarthy sped up. But Monty accelerated too, and soon both cars were swerving down the hill at forty miles an hour. Looking in the rearview mirror, McCarthy saw Monty's headlights shifting from side to side. And then the mirror went dark, and he heard a loud crash. He looked in the mirror again and a cloud of dust appeared.

McCarthy reversed back up the hill. Monty's car was crumpled against a telephone pole and Monty was curled up under the dashboard, his face bloody and torn away. McCarthy thought he was dead.

He drove back to the Wildings' house and pounded on the door, urging the couple to call an ambulance. He wanted to re-

turn to Monty, and Taylor said she was coming too. Both Mc-
Carthy and Wilding attempted to dissuade her, but Taylor was
adamant.

The front door of Monty's car was impossible to open, so
Taylor crawled through the back door and over the front seat.
Crouching down, she cradled Monty's head in her lap. Monty
moaned and began to choke, weakly indicating his neck. Several
teeth had been knocked out and two front teeth had lodged in
his throat. They were choking him. Taylor immediately shoved
her fingers down his throat and pulled them out, an act that
almost certainly saved his life.

When Monty reached Cedars of Lebanon Hospital in Hollywood, he was bleeding profusely; his nose and sinus cavity were
broken; both sides of his jaw were crushed; and he was suffering
from a severe cerebral concussion. Even so, the doctors determined that no plastic surgery was required, and the most la-
borious task would prove to be the reconstruction of his teeth.

At 11:30, Dr. Nathan Hiatt was summoned to operate on
Monty's upper lip, which had been split in two. It was not, he
felt, a major operation, merely a question of aligning the ver-
milion line—the thin red line that separates the lip itself from
the skin. Realizing that Monty was drunk, Hiatt used no anes-
thetic and, at about two in the morning, completed the operation.

Monty was placed in Room 516 on the fifth floor of Cedars of
Lebanon—"the fancy floor," as it was known among the staff, for
actors and other celebrities. He did not regain consciousness until late the following day. No one, not even the doctors, were able
to predict what Monty's face—"the most beautiful face in Hollywood"—would look like once the layers of bandages were finally
removed.

Libby did not hear of Monty's accident until the next morning when Jack Larson telephoned from Los Angeles. She made
immediate plans to fly to California. It was a sweltering Mother's
Day weekend; the Long Island Expressway was crowded with
stalled or overheated cars, and Libby missed her plane. She and
Rose Minor spent the night at a hotel in Queens and Libby flew
to Los Angeles in the morning. Libby was calm, but she was always imperturable in times of trouble.

In Los Angeles, Libby was driven directly to Cedars of Lebanon Hospital and spent the next few nights curled up on a couch at the foot of Monty's bed. Some days later, when his bandages were removed, Monty looked grotesque. Libby burst into tears when she saw him. Above the eyes, he was just the same, but his lower features were swollen and distorted. "He looked as though he'd been stuffed," Jack Larson said.

Moreover, a gaggle of MGM executives gathered around Monty's bed, attempting to persuade him to return to work as soon as he was well. At five million dollars, *Raintree County* was the highest-budgeted domestic film in MGM history. Only half the film had been shot, and the MGM hierarchy were frantic that unless Monty completed it, they would lose about two million. Libby advised Monty to ignore them. He needed rest, not for weeks but for months, if his health and his looks were to be restored. She implored him to return with her to Treetops in order to recuperate properly. She would obtain the best nurses, the finest medical practitioners; she would attend to his every need. But much to Libby's consternation, Monty would not commit himself.

Libby detested the movie executives who simpered and fawned at Monty's bedside, but reserved the brunt of her rage for Elizabeth Taylor. She had long been jealous of the twenty-four-year-old actress. Libby thought her "sensual and silly— rather like a heifer in heat. There's no telling," she said, "where her lust will lead her next." She was furious that Taylor had allowed Monty to leave her home when it must have been obvious that he was drunk. Dr. Nathan Hiatt walked into Monty's room one afternoon while Libby and Taylor were inside, and the room resounded with Libby's execrations.

Monty eventually decided to complete the filming of *Raintree County.* Libby was resigned; she had lost him, she believed, and she elected to go home. Jack Larson attempted to convince Libby that Monty needed her, that she should remain in California. But Libby was adamant. She felt Monty was being duped by MGM. "As long as I can help him, I'll do it," she said, "but he's acting foolishly. I've got two little boys. They need me more than Monty does. I love Monty, but the boys have first call." The next day, Libby retreated to Treetops in a fury.

*   *   *

Monty would take more than nine weeks to recuperate. Gradually, the swelling disappeared. There were no serious scars, his missing teeth had been replaced, and his broken jaw was wired. But he was never to look the same again. The perfect facial angles were askew; his mouth was twisted; a nerve in his cheek had been severed, so that the left side of his face looked frozen; his nose, once so wonderfully precise, was misshapen; and because of his damaged teeth, even his voice had changed. The sole feature that remained the same were his eyes, still dark and glittering, but filled now with a sense of inexhaustible pain.

54

Although they had corresponded regularly, Libby had not seen Jane Bowles since the late spring of 1956 when she had spent several weeks at Treetops. On February 22, 1957, Jane turned forty—"always, however long one had prepared for it, a shock," she wrote to Paul, who was in Ceylon. She had been given an advance to complete a new play, but for weeks at a time was unable to write at all. And worse, "failure follows me into my dreams," she said. She suffered from severe depressions, and cried continually. Terrified of being left alone, of being unable to write, of turning forty with no work behind her, she was also anxious about her marriage, and incapable of escaping what she called "obsessive thoughts."

On April 4, Jane suffered a stroke, which caused partial paralysis of her limbs, partial blindness, and an odd form of aphasia, as a result of which she confused genders and used the antonym of a word instead of the word she intended. She asked a friend to write to Libby.

Libby replied immediately: "I am so worried about you because I know how hard it is for you to have anything wrong with you, more so than any of us because you get so wildly imaginative about everything. I want you to call on me for any help you need. . . ."

Jane's medical bills were prohibitively high, more than she and Paul could afford, and Libby, with what Paul called "one of her typically gorgeous gestures," offered to assume the brunt of them. She wrote to Jane from Treetops on June 1: "The typed letter I received from you yesterday was absolutely miraculous. You will kill me for this, but it was better than some of your letters before you were ill. . . .

"Janey, the financial end will be taken care of to your satisfaction. $175 a month as you asked. I will ask Polikoff to send you a check monthly if that is the way you want it. I suppose you already have the $500 I sent last week. So I shall send the monthly amount beginning July 1st. If that is not enough, please don't hesitate to let me know.

"I feel so yenti talking about *my* glooms—but they are very, *very* bad—I won't go into it—I have no physical pain—just black, black, black outlook all the time. I know it doesn't make sense, but there it is."

Libby's "glooms," her "lows" as she often called them, were uncontrollable now. She spoke to almost no one. She claimed that she had domestic problems, that Treetops was deteriorating, that she just might clear out and "close the joint." She considered going to Tangier to visit Jane, but decided she didn't have the strength. The world, she said, held little meaning for her anymore. It was "just not good enough."

Through most of 1957, Libby rarely ventured farther from Treetops than Manhattan. She continued to rehearse with Gerald Cook, but gave no concerts. Timmy and Tony, twelve and ten, attended separate boarding schools in New York State, and Libby was alone for much of the time. Since Topper's death seven years before, Libby had come to despise Christmas and this year would prove to be no exception. As the day approached, she wrote to Jane, who was still recuperating in Tangier: "The absolutely revolting Christmas is descending on us and we are trying to pretend it isn't happening, although I have got everybody else doing all the necessary chores. I can't touch it because after all I am a Jew, am I not?"

Just before the holidays, Libby fell into a catastrophic depression. That Christmas, her repressed rage over Topper's death exploded suddenly and, on Christmas Eve, she knocked over the Christmas tree, shouting, "Fuck Christmas, fuck Christ, fuck everybody."

*   *   *

Monty spent several weeks at Treetops that year. Except for his altered features, he seemed much the same—"the old Monty in disguise," as Libby generously described him. But Monty *had* changed. He loathed his new face, and found it difficult to understand that often he was not recognized in the streets of New York, that old friends reacted to him with shock or embarrassment. He had recently seen a private screening of *Raintree County* and predicted that audiences would attend the film in order to guess which was the genuine Monty Clift. Monty had liked being beautiful and now, as he said, "I'm catching up on the pain."

But he had agreed to do another film, playing the role of Noah Akerman in the Twentieth Century-Fox version of Irwin Shaw's successful novel *The Young Lions*. Libby and Monty spent long afternoons and nights reading the screenplay, making elaborate notes in the margins. They both agreed that the real Noah Akerman had been lost between the book and the screenplay. "What else can one expect from men with a genius for mediocrity," said Libby.

In May, Monty flew to Paris and then to Hollywood for the filming of *The Young Lions*. And Libby, as she had done so often before when abandoned by her phantom lover, initiated an affair with another man—this time a writer named Ross Evans. Evans was forty-one, twelve years younger than Libby, and as if to compensate for Monty, he was wonderfully handsome, "a beautiful hunk of Victor Mature," as one of his friends called him. Others, skeptical of his intelligence, called him Li'l Abner.

Ten years before, Evans had conducted a long affair with Dorothy Parker. Once, when leaving a Hollywood party, someone had complimented Miss Parker on Evans, alluding to his gorgeous suntan. "Yes," said Parker, "Ross has the hue of availability."

But Ross Evans was a moody man, a writer who thought of himself as a hack and, worse, an unsuccessful one. He was also a heavy drinker, and in Monty's absence, he came increasingly to Treetops, often going on rowdy binges that lasted for weeks at a time. But, as he had done for Dorothy Parker, he made himself available to Libby. He admired her wit and intelligence. He loved her, amused her, attempted to alleviate her accelerating moods of melancholia. And, for a time, Libby was grateful.

*   *   *

After ten years of false starts and haphazard industry, Paul Bowles finally completed the musical score for García Lorca's *Yerma*. Libby was jubilant and, within weeks, arranged for it to open at the University of Denver Theatre in Colorado, where it was billed as the world premiere. The opera starred Libby and Rose Bampton, and Libby brought along Ross Evans, who claimed to be in between projects, as her publicist. From the very beginning, however, Paul Bowles sensed that *Yerma* was doomed.

Bowles felt that Libby should have performed the role in 1947 when they had first envisaged it. But he had taken an unconscionable time to compose the score, and though spurred on by Libby, who would write with the warning "I won't be young forever," Bowles had dallied. Now, in July 1958, Bowles knew he should have heeded Libby's warning. *Yerma*, he believed, was a perfect example of how an opera should not be produced. At a party Libby gave prior to the opening, Bowles looked depressed and Libby said, "What's the matter, Paul? Aren't you happy with *Yerma*?" And Bowles replied, "Oh, yes. I worship the ground it crawls on." He had intended to express his discontent, but Libby heard only the humor of the remark.

"I think of myself as an actress as well as a singer," Libby told a reporter from the Denver *Post*. "I've always wanted to do both. I'm tired of the slick, commercial things that Broadway does. *Yerma* is drama with its own earthy, honest content. It is original and vivid for a theater mossy with clichés." Libby added that she intended to bring the opera to Broadway in the autumn.

But the reviews did not reflect Libby's optimism. "In *Yerma*," said the New York *World-Telegram* and *Sun*, which had sent a critic to Denver, "García Lorca has written a brooding, passionate drama of a Spanish peasant woman whose unfulfilled yearning for a child becomes a consuming obsession. The flame that gnaws within her is as hot and dry as the Andalusian country where the action is set.

"Paul Bowles, who translated the drama from the original Spanish, has created an outstanding musical score. His music is haunting, weird, mystical. The score is modern, but strongly flavored with the compelling music of Spain's Arabic background. . . . Miss Holman appears to advantage when singing, but displays uncertainty in her acting. She got off to a slow, stiff start in Act One, but warmed to the job as the show went on. Her portrayal of Yerma is a sincere one and there were moments in the play when she reached across the footlights with the strong emotion of the peasant woman."

But the moments were few and far between. *Yerma* played for four days in Denver, and although it was performed once again in Ithaca, New York, it never reached Broadway. Libby was disconsolate. She fired Ross Evans for reasons of drunkenness, and when the opera closed, she told Jack Larson, "Well, there goes two hundred and fifty thousand dollars down the drain."

Shortly after *Yerma* closed, Libby changed her mind and invited Ross Evans to Treetops for as long as he cared to remain. Evans was a churl, of course, but an amusing one, and Libby required diversion. Within days, however, she had tired of his drinking, his sloth, his repentent charm. But she concealed her reservations.

One early autumn evening, Libby and Evans drank vintage champagne and had, for a change, a convivial dinner, during which Evans proposed the possibilities of Libby's backing a comedy he intended to write. Libby said she would consider it seriously. Toward midnight, they went up to bed. Libby was tired and Evans, as usual, was, as Libby said, "higher than an elephant has a right to be."

Late the next morning, Evans discovered that all of his belongings had been neatly packed; his suitcases and typewriter awaited him in the downstairs hall. Tucked into a pocket of his briefcase was a one-way ticket to Acapulco (where, coincidentally, Evans had deserted Dorothy Parker ten years before), and two hundred dollars in cash. Libby was sitting at the breakfast table; she was charming, unruffled, intractable. She told Evans to eat his breakfast and go, that if he hurried, he would just be able to catch the afternoon plane. Her chauffeur would drive him to the airport. Evans was meek and tremulous and, over bacon and eggs, made ostentatious promises.

After breakfast, Libby kissed him good-bye. She hoped he would have a wonderful time. Winter was coming and Acapulco, she understood, was a balmy place where one might happily spend a long, long time. Evans protested, but Libby put her finger to his lips and said: "Darling, you're sweet, but you haven't been a gentleman long enough to have become a cad."

55

N LATE 1958, A NEW MAN ENTERED LIBBY'S LIFE—HER nephew, David Holman, the only son of her younger brother, Alfred. Libby and Alfred had never been close, not even as children, and they rarely saw one another although Alfred lived in nearby New Jersey, where he was a professor of English at Trenton State Teachers' College. David, who was nineteen, had seen Libby infrequently over the years, but that autumn he sought her out at Treetops, and they became immediate friends. Libby called David "Da" and David called her "Lipsy"—a humorous allusion to the time when she had been introduced as Lipsy Colmar.

David was a student at Bucknell University in Lewisburg, Pennsylvania, but he commuted to Manhattan every weekend in a bright red MG sport car that Libby had given him. He had also been given a key to Libby's Eastside brownstone, and whenever he was in New York, he stayed there. Given Monty's continual absences, there would be no serious man in Libby's life for more than a year, and David Holman became Libby's closest confidant. He and Libby were kindred spirits, outsiders who happened to belong to the same conventional family. One of David's friends likened them to Violet and Sebastian, the doomed mother and son in Tennessee Williams's play *Suddenly Last Summer.* They were bound together—romantic, careless, extravagant. But David insisted that theirs was a perfectly ordinary familial relationship.

David Holman was sartorially outrageous, a brazen youth who wore tight T-shirts and short-shorts into New York bars. On weekends, he threw opulent parties in Libby's brownstone—parties given for no particular reason and for almost anyone who cared to come, and the house was often filled with more than a hundred revelers. Libby rarely visited New York on weekends and was unaware that David had converted her home into his personal club. One weekend, however, David went too far. Someone, a complete stranger, performed a rowdy tap dance on Libby's Steinway. It collapsed and could not be mended. Libby was livid. She told David that her house was to be redecorated immediately and he would have to leave. The parties were over, but their relationship endured.

Libby was the most complicated woman David had ever known, and the most possessive. She talked volubly about how money had ruined her life, by which, David supposed, she meant her career; and yet, she would not have had it any other way. Over the years, money had become more than mere currency to her. It symbolized an attitude, a way of looking at the world. It was a shield, a source of perpetual wonder. Whenever Libby didn't wish to do something—to travel, to shop, to perform—she always said it was because she was "too old, too tired, and too rich." During this period, she continually changed her will, adding new beneficiaries (including David), revoking others who had offended her. Libby referred to it as her "musical comedy will," and was always saying in her low, singsong voice, "I'm going to change my codicils today."

David thought of Treetops as Wonderland. The house was spacious and light and there was always the pervasive aroma of flowers—fuchsias, roses, spray orchids, the flowers changing according to the season. He loved Treetops's understated elegance, its sparseness, its formality; and all of Libby's personal touches— her linens and perfumes, her monogrammed satin sheets and towels, her Persian carpets, Venetian lace and English silver; the gold-domed bathroom with its fireplace, the brass, dolphin-shaped fittings, and the antique telephone with an unlisted number that only Monty had; the white sable lap robe with satin borders in Libby's bedroom; the vicuña lap robe in the library; and, most of all, the bedroom cupboards, which David called "Libby's Gloria Swanson closets"—chock-a-block with clothes and shoes and scarves and furs, a Persian lamb, a Russian sable, a black trench coat lined with snow-white ermine. In David's view, the clothes and the cupboards resembled the wardrobe department at MGM or, more incongruously, the trappings of a deposed monarch in exile. It was "so outdated," to him, "so ancien régime," particularly in view of the fact that Libby was "intellectually, so progressive." Yet Libby prized her possessions, her "relics" as she called them. They had taken on some mysterious and propitious meaning above and beyond their actual worth: They represented a position in life that was not only becoming but unassailable.

Two of Libby's most cherished possessions were Smith Reynolds's gold wristwatch and his diamond wedding ring. That summer, Libby lost the ring. Using the insurance money she received, she designed a circular drive in front of Treetops in honor of the wedding ring and planted it with tall birches. When asked by Marcus Blechman why the birches were so large, so fully grown, Libby grinned and replied: "Darling, I'm *much* too old for saplings."

What would become Libby's most coveted possession was her Rolls-Royce. She had always wanted a steel-blue convertible, but the Manhattan dealership was out of stock and Libby was forced to settle for an $18,000 green Rolls-Royce sedan. When it arrived one rainy afternoon, Libby telephoned David Holman in New York and screamed: "The *god-damned* Rolls came today and, can you believe it, it *leaks*. You call those pricks in New York and tell them I want a rainproof convertible *immediately*. Steel Blue." The new Rolls was delivered the following day.

Because Libby had always been an incompetent driver, she employed a full-time chauffeur. But occasionally she drove herself. Years later, in her early sixties, she drove the Rolls to New York. The next day, after too much wine at lunch, Libby returned to Connecticut. Driving up the Merritt Parkway at seventy miles an hour, she was stopped by the police. But before the police officer had time to ask for her driving license, Libby said: "Officer, *please, please* don't give me a ticket. Mummy and Daddy don't know I have the car." The bemused officer let Libby go.

In mid-April of 1958, Jane Bowles arrived in New York. Paul had remained in Europe—in Funchal in Madeira, where, because of the new, oppressive, military regime in Morocco, he had temporarily taken residence. Jane continued to suffer from aphasia and the loss of half her vision; she had extremely high blood pressure and was subject to convulsions; she missed Paul desperately and was terrified of being left alone. Still unable to write, she believed that God was punishing her for not doing so. "Do I really have any (work)?" she had written to Libby. "Can I ever have any again?"

Jane moved into Tennessee Williams's vacant apartment for a time, and then into a larger flat near Park Avenue and Seventy-ninth Street with an old friend, Dione Lewis. Libby paid Jane's share of the rent.

In early May, Jane wrote to Paul: "Libby is drumming up money from scarse and another—some from Oliver—and some John Goodwin and some from Katherine and twenty-five dollars from Natasha. . . . She herself has contributed the sum you're already familiar with and will continue to for life. I think this is very sweet of her and the work she is doing with my passport and calling up these people to ask for a small sum of money from each for as long as I need it is invaluable. . . . Libby does not think I should be in fact (alone) she says it is out of the question and thinks there will be enough money for medisons and rent and a maid between the groupe. She is writing you all about it very soon, but she is terribly busy and I do not see her very much. . . . I cannot live with Libby and she will explain that to (you) herself. She had been sweet and making great efforts collectin the Jane Bowles fund, which I started telling you about earlier in the letter. I feel better than I did when I hit the 'lows' as Libby calls them."

Libby's lows, although not as extreme as Jane's, were becoming longer and more pronounced. "The poets lied," she told Alec Wilder. "*Everything* is shit." In such moods, Libby usually retired to her dark bedroom, where the curtains were always drawn, retreating there, as she liked to say, "to have the vapors." At fifty-four, she talked increasingly of suicide.

One evening at Treetops, Libby told David Holman how she had once tried to kill herself. Some months before, one of her favorite Aubusson carpets had been returned from the dry cleaner's. When it arrived, Libby lighted a cigarette, rolled herself up in the carpet, and went to sleep contentedly. She fully expected to inhale the carbolic acid from the cleaned carpet, to become unconscious and die. Two hours later, Libby awakened. She had an unpardonable headache and, worse, she was still alive.

*   *   *

That summer, Paul Bowles, who had come to America, introduced Libby to the brilliant young composer Ned Rorem. Rorem, an excessively handsome homosexual, who once described himself as "sweet as a violet cream pie," was immediately smitten with Libby, and they became fast friends.

As a child in Chicago, Rorem had heard lurid tales of Libby's legend, replete with an aura of evil and mystery. For as long as he could remember, he had collected Libby Holman records. He remembered her stage appearance in a Chicago production of *You Never Know*—an appearance accompanied by the sound of subdued hisses, while Libby sang "One Step Ahead of Love." Scandal, he believed, was both her cross and her glamour. Libby once said to him: "People told me that the Reynolds trial would be forgotten like yesterday's newspapers, but it's hounded me now for nearly thirty years." She alluded to Smith Reynolds continually, and his death was at the heart of her legend—both ominous and unexplainable. On another occasion, Libby told Rorem that a decade after the Loeb-Leopold murder trial, she had encountered Richard Loeb in the halls of a Chicago law court and a look of mute understanding had passed between them.

Pencil-thin, Libby continued to have a complex about her looks. But for Rorem she emanated physical beauty. She had wonderful posture, a stylish stride, a hearty laugh, and her speech and gestures were exaggerated, flamboyant. He once asked her why she had never appeared in films and Libby laughed and said, "What? With *my* mug?"

Rorem believed that Libby, like so many other wealthy performers, lacked the patience for discipline. Should a Broadway show or a concert fail, she could always withdraw to her money; and in order to safeguard that retreat, she had developed a kind of self-protective parsimony. But in every other facet of her life, Libby was magnificent, full-blown.

His admiration for Libby was reflected repeatedly in his "New York Diary": "Libby Holman, whom I love and when I grow up I'd like to marry"; the thirty-five-year-old composer wrote: "Libby Holman, who's lately been trying to convert me to Zen—except that I've always 'had' it; it's just that now it's been given a title." "Libby Holman is not only the world's one real female baritone capable of sustaining a consonant (and it cannot be done), but the world's thinnest lady with a plump character: joie de vivre of Sarah Bernhardt. I think I love her."

*   *   *

Monty Clift, David Holman and Ned Rorem were the three fragile fulcrums supporting Libby's unwieldy emotional life throughout 1958 and early 1959. Holman was the youngest and most malleable; in many ways, he reminded Libby of Topper and he fulfilled many of her maternal needs. Rorem was Libby's resident intellectual, an original composer and writer, a worldly man consorting with the likes of Jean Cocteau, Virgil Thompson, Leonard Bernstein and the young Edward Albee—a man, in fact, who claimed to know almost everyone. Libby loved them both, but it was Monty for whom she continued to reserve her deepest affections.

Both Holman and Rorem met Monty for the first time during the summer of 1958. Rorem thought him a spoiled, cantankerous drunk, while Libby seemed more like a nurse than a lover. David Holman liked Monty, was captivated by his raffish ways, but in the end, David found him embarrassing, silly. Moreover, at thirty-eight, Monty was preternaturally thin and hunched. There was a kind of translucence to his skin, a sickly sheen. The former pretty boy looked like a sexagenarian.

In late 1958, Monty flew to Hollywood to film an ill-fated version of Nathanael West's *Miss Lonelyhearts*. Libby visited him briefly there, and they spent the Christmas holidays fishing in Key West. But Monty was conducting a separate affair with a young Frenchman named Giles, and Libby had just met a new man. By early 1959, their long liaison had, for the most part, ended. Libby continued to think of Monty as "the grand passion" of her life, but she began to speak of him in the past tense, nostalgically, as one speaks of an old lover one hasn't seen in years.

56

L IBBY HAD AN OBSESSION FOR IMPROVING HERSELF, FOR "GET-
ting off my ass and seeing the light," as she liked to say. In
early 1959, she began to attend Charlotte Selver's weekly classes
on sensory awareness in Manhattan. While there, she became
friendly with a young sculptress named Risa Sussman. Libby was
also taking courses in Zen Buddhism at the New School for Social Research in Greenwich Village, and one evening she invited
Risa Sussman to accompany her.

Miss Sussman had studied at the New School two years before under painter and sculptor Louis Schanker. Before attending Libby's Zen course, she stopped in to see her former teacher
and told him she would like to introduce him to Libby Holman.

"Who the hell is Libby Holman?" said Schanker.

"Well, she's *quite* famous and *very* rich," said Miss Sussman.

"I guess I'd better meet her then," said Schanker.

They were introduced in Schanker's classroom at the New
School the next evening. They met again the following week at
an uptown exhibition of Risa Sussman's sculpture, and attended
the subsequent party together. Schanker would always claim that
he had never heard of Libby Holman, that he had no idea who
she was or who she had been, but they began to see one another
regularly.

Born in a cramped, cold-water apartment in the Bronx on
July 20, 1903, Louis Schanker was a year older than Libby. His
family were Orthodox Jews who owned a modest store off
Bruckner Boulevard, selling tailor's trimmings. When Schanker
was fourteen, he ran away from home to join the army and go to
war. He altered the date on his birth certificate to prove that he
was eighteen, but army officials did not believe him.

At fifteen, Schanker quit school and began a series of romantic peregrinations—working as a harvest hand in the wheat fields

of the Dakotas and Canada; as a gandy dancer on the Erie Railroad; as a stevedore on Great Lakes steamers; as a shipfitter in the Federal Ship Yard; and as an animal hostler and canvas man in a traveling circus, performing menial chores for the acrobats and clowns.

In the course of their courtship, Libby told Schanker a story that had taken place at the University of Cincinnati in 1924. Bored, she had been sitting in a classroom when she noticed a passing circus in the street outside the window. She leaped out the window and followed the circus into town. Schanker, it turned out, had been working in that very circus, and Libby and Schanker liked to believe that they had seen one another thirty-four years before they were actually introduced.

Eventually, Schanker returned to New York, where he studied painting at Cooper Union and subsequently at the Art Students' League and the Educational Alliance, a settlement house. In the early thirties, he spent two years traveling in France and Spain. In 1935 he made his first woodcut, a technique not widely used in America at the time, and ultimately Schanker would be considered by many critics as the grand master of the American woodcut. In 1943, he began teaching a course in the technique of woodblock color prints at the New School and, for many years, taught painting and sculpture at Bard College.

By the fifties, Schanker was considered an important abstract expressionist. He lived and worked in a large, cluttered studio on West Twenty-third Street. He was celebrated, sought after by women, and treated deferentially in the local bars. With his white hair and flowing mustache, his burly figure and flamboyant style, Schanker was often mistaken for Ernest Hemingway, and he was not displeased.

But the fifty-five-year-old painter remained a rough, unworldly fellow from the Bronx with little taste or charm or conversation. Risa Sussman considered him an attractive guttersnipe. But Libby found him forceful, brash; and it was, for her, a sexual debut of sorts. Schanker was neither young nor gay, not Gentile, nor pretty. But he seemed to Libby a romantic figure, an artist of consummate quality, and she pursued him with characteristic zeal.

*　　*　　*

That July, Libby wrote to Jane and Paul Bowles in Tangier, enclosing a photograph of Schanker. "I did want you to see what Louis looks like," she said. "He is the first beau I ever had who is not only older than I am but isn't twenty years younger. Do you think I'm slipping? Apropos of him and of your saying in your letter that you are getting older, but you are sure I'm not, I wish to announce to you here and now I am letting my hair go gray. I am doing it in a kind of trashy way, though. I brush a lot of silver paint all over the hair so you can't tell where the gray ends and the dye begins. Do you get the picture? I have it cut short too."

Libby continued to worry about Jane's health (which had not improved) and felt rather guilty that she had not seen more of her when she had been in America the year before. "I love you both very much," she wrote, "and really miss you in my life. The older I get the more I realize how few the really precious ones in my life are. Did you ever hear such a yenty statement in your life, but it's true."

Libby and Schanker saw one another three or four times a week, sometimes at Treetops but more often in New York, where they attended lectures and exhibitions, and dined at neighborhood Italian restaurants. Schanker was thrilled with the new romance and described his feeling for Libby to his friend and neighbor John CuRoi, a fellow abstract expressionist. The two artists often dined in CuRoi's studio, drinking vast quantities of Italian wine and discussing women and art with tedious regularity.

Schanker told CuRoi that Libby was one of the most extraordinary women he had ever met and, narrowing his hooded eyes, admitted that he had known some. He described Libby's love-making as "fantastic, beyond your imagination." He was, he said, consumed by her. Their early erotic relationship inspired Schanker to create a series of paintings based on the Hindu Tantra; and CuRoi arranged an exhibition of them at the Willard Lucien Gallery on Christopher Street.

CuRoi never met Libby. She was not, in the beginning at least, permitted to visit Schanker's studio—his private, inviolate domain, he told her. But Schanker's real reason for banning Libby was that he was living with a much younger woman. When Libby found out, having arrived unexpectedly at the studio one afternoon, there was an angry, violent scene before the younger woman was dispatched.

For about six months during early 1960, Schanker accepted a teaching position at a midwestern university, where he openly consorted with other women. When his affairs were reported to Libby, she bristled with jealousy, telephoning Schanker nightly, her tirades glutted with rage and accusation. One night, Schanker told her that he would curtail his philanderings, but only if Libby agreed to marry him. Schanker was a forceful, dominant man, an unabashed bully, and curiously, Libby tended to submit to his demands. On this occasion, Libby, who had hitherto been hesitant, agreed to his proposal. She resented the emotional blackmail, however, and was never to forgive him. But Libby was fifty-six and love, she feared, might not come around again.

Ned Rorem met Schanker only once at Libby's brownstone in New York. He considered him a gruff and stolid man, "a burgher with airs." But it was obvious to him that Libby was smitten and he said nothing to upset her. In his "New York Diary," Rorem wrote:

> Tomorrow I return to Manhattan where (since my apartment's sublet) Libby will let me use her top floor and piano for a couple of weeks. . . . Libby has become a loyal and hospitable friend—just at a time when I was convinced I'd never allow more people into my life. Naturally, like anyone not born rich she's unclear about that money beyond cultivating the widest variety of daffodil in America and sponsoring her own recitals which are more stimulating than anyone's in this dead day of the voice. Eventually, she'll turn away from the crippled, the lost, the vain, and get solidly married. Then, I shall lose her, as one loses most of one's men friends and all of one's women friends with weddings.

For two successive years, Libby had rented a cottage in Montego Bay in Jamaica for the Christmas holidays. Coolie Point Cottage, as it was called, contained three bedrooms and a glassed-in living room cantilevered out over the shimmering, blue Caribbean. On December 27, 1960, Libby and Louis Schanker were married on the cottage's terrace by a local justice of the peace. Timmy and Tony, thirteen and eleven, attended, as did Benet Polikoff and Rose Minor. Libby smiled throughout the simple ceremony; she seemed happy, but retained grave doubts as to the wisdom of her betrothal. That morning, she had told Miss Minor: "Well, we're getting married today, and after the wedding, the honeymoon will be over."

The marriage baffled most of Libby's friends. Few of them approved of Schanker, considering him little more than an opportunist. But Libby felt she had come "full-cycle" and told Paul Bowles that Schanker reminded her of her father. Her friend Gigi Gilpin thought that Libby had learned, at last, to relax, to accept her age, that there would be no more gallivanting, no more fey young beaux, that she intended to settle down and become a proper bourgeois Jewish lady, as her mother had always wanted her to be. Oliver Smith was more pointed: "Libby wanted to marry someone solid," he said, "and she succeeded in marrying cement." Libby wrote to Luke Readdy, explaining that Schanker was not the sort of man she would even have looked at ten years before, but he was nice and secure and seemed to have a stronger grip on life than she did. "Besides," she said, "I want a husband who will leave me alone." Ned Rorem noted in his diary:

> When I first met Libby, she was flailing about emotionally and she chose to marry Schanker. I've known many women to do that. Libby must have thought of herself at that stage in her life as a bohemian, a painter's mistress. But, they certainly liked each other. There must be a rule. Women of this kind tend to choose abstract expressionists. They *appear* to be steady and safe.

There were immediate difficulties. When the Schankers returned to Treetops, Alicy Byrd greeted them, calling Libby Mrs. Schanker.

"Alice," retorted Libby with a smile, "you may call me Libby. You may call me Mrs. Reynolds, but *never* call me Mrs. Schanker again." And so Alice continued to call Libby Mrs. Reynolds. Roger McStocker, Libby's head gardener, avoided the problem altogether by calling her "the Mrs."

A week after their marriage, Louis Schanker turned to Libby over dinner and thinking, perhaps, of the LHR monograms visible everywhere throughout the house, he said, "Now that we're married, dear, don't you think you might use *my* name?"

Libby was astonished. "That's *ridiculous*," she said. "Would *you* exchange Reynolds for *Schanker*?" She laughed, almost jeeringly, but it would prove not to be funny.

57

IN EARLY 1961, LIBBY PURCHASED ANOTHER HOUSE, HER third, in East Hampton on Long Island at the edge of the dunes above the Atlantic Ocean. She called it Dune House. As she wrote to her friends, Peter Caldwell and his wife, Susan (Peter, a doctor, had been Topper's best friend at the Putney School): "I have a new address in East Hampton. Did I tell you about the Glass House I was hoping to buy? I think we got it. Oh, you'll like it next year when you're living here. One glass room." For the rest of her life, Libby would summer there.

Libby redecorated the little house. Some years later, a local civic society described it thus: "As one approaches down a flowered path, one looks through the house directly to the sea. So integrated is this glass and wood dwelling with its surroundings, it seems to have been dropped among the beech, plum and cherry trees that hide it. Screens designed and made in Japan divide living quarters; low swung-wooden platforms, gay with pillars, form conversation areas. Louis Schanker's sculpture in bronze and wood and a dramatic poster portrait from Libby Holman's European tour add both interest and a decorative quality. A free-form miniature swimming pool shaded by a wild cherry tree that is bedded in rose granite stones sent from Colorado gives an exotic touch. A dining terrace opulent with trailing fuchsia and begonias contrasts with the simplicity of the interior."

Libby had decided to spend time in East Hampton because Schanker wished to mingle with the artists who congregated there during the summer months. For some years, he had owned a ramshackle house in nearby Sag Harbor, which he liked to describe as "early Federal, modern earthy." But Libby hated the house; and it reminded Alice Byrd of a pigsty. When Libby first visited it, she told Alice to bring a shovel "so we can dig our way in."

Through Schanker, Libby met many of the artists who lived in the Hamptons. She liked them, invited them to her home, but Libby had no real interest in the visual arts and would never become a collector. She admired such men as Larry Rivers and Willem de Kooning, identifying with their errant ways, "their unfettered spirits," as she called them, but their work remained obscure and complicated and, for Libby at least, peripheral.

That summer, Libby gave a party for some two hundred people in her little house, a practice she would continue at least once each summer for the rest of her life. She called them "sardine squeezes." The local celebrities had not heard of Libby Holman in years, and many of them had not heard of her at all, but they flocked to her parties, to gawk and meet their friends, to eat and drink and dance, and Libby, in turn, knew less than half of them. Usually, she sat by herself in a corner, watching the loud proceedings with an enigmatic smile, and was occasionally introduced to strangers as "Libby Holman. She owns this place." On the other hand, Louis Schanker knew everyone and strutted through the crowds with the jaunty air of a man who had recently staged a successful coup d'état.

The house was always glutted with notables: Manhattan gallery owners; minor European counts with unpronounceable names; successful businessmen who dabbled in the arts; gaggles of elderly writers, painters and their mistresses; actors, actresses and their retinues. Each summer, they trekked to Libby's house as to the shrine of some ancient worthy: Eli Wallach and his wife, Anne Jackson, came. Edward Albee came, almost always accompanied by his mother. Stella Adler came, as did Saul Steinberg, Lucia Chase, Vladimir Horowitz, Carlos Montoya, Dorothy Schiff, Lillian Ross, Mrs. Sara Murphy and Willem de Kooning—and they were always flattered to have been asked; but Libby, when they were introduced, seemed remote, unknowable. Eli Wallach, who didn't know her very well, thought of Libby as a lonely woman, sitting unobtrusively in a corner of the room like a gate-crasher at her own party.

The fact that Libby knew almost none of her guests did not disturb her; she knew almost no one anymore. Indeed, her closest friends had become her employees—her personal maid, Alice Byrd; her secretary, Rose Minor; and her butler, William Hill. Hill, a wry and humorous Scot, adored Libby. He thought of her always as "that gorgeous hussy." Hill called her Mrs. Reynolds, except when she annoyed him, when he called her Mrs. Schanker. In his view, Libby was the funniest woman he had ever known, and one of the saddest. His chief regret was that he had not known Libby earlier in her life. Now (and it happened with alarming frequency) Libby would turn to him and say, "It's no good getting old, William. There's no elegance in it."

Libby's youth disturbed her as much as her age. She felt she had not been allowed to forget her tragedies or that she had once been a Broadway star. Chuckling, she would say to Hill, "They'll never forgive Libby Holman and her ill-gotten minks." But there were too many other occasions when Libby muttered with resignation: "They can say what they like about me after I'm dead."

In the second year of their marriage, Libby and Schanker had their palms read by someone whom she described as "a very reputable palmist." The palmist told Libby: "Yours is a remarkable hand because it shows that in one way, you have managed to use even your imperfections to your profit. Your hand is moody, restless, and shows an acutely delicate nervous sensibility. But, because you also have a strong will, powerful ambition and pride in your accomplishments, your sensitivity and emotional turbulence can enlarge your talent, even while they probably have often made it difficult for you to come to terms with yourself.

"You are extremely complicated. You are both highly emotional and analytical. You must feel a thing deeply and then analyze it carefully before you come to terms with it. Sometimes this must cause a conflict when feeling and reason cannot easily reach the same conclusion.

"You are independent, can think on your feet, and extemporize the right course of action in an unexpected emergency, though you prefer to plan ahead. Strangely enough, when there is no immediate emergency, you are less sure of yourself, and inclined to worry and stew about the future.

"Perhaps your hand has changed tremendously over the years, but as of now, you are a temperamental worrier, and would tend to worry even if there were no serious difficulties to justify it. Your hand suggests that this may be because you have to be more careful than most people to avoid physical and mental poisons. It is harder for your system to rid itself of the effects of food and drink that disagree with you, or the effects of depressing surroundings or unpleasant company or unhappy events.

"You and Mr. Schanker are both very determined people. You are more self-analytical and, therefore, his very decided opinions are a foil for your inner civil war which produces sure opinions more slowly."

Libby considered this an accurate portrait of at least a part of her—that is, a profile, illustrating a single side of herself. Subsequently, she liked to joke about her "civil war," which, depending on her fluctuating moods, she had either won or had only recently lost.

Libby's public protestations of love aside, she and Schanker were squabbling, "not communicating," as she told her accompanist, Gerald Cook. In her letters, Libby referred to Schanker as "my beautiful and famous husband" or employed other extravagant forms of endearment. To her old college friend Roberta Nicholson, she wrote: "Just because you were once the head of a V.D. hospital is no reason for you to mis-spell my husband's name. I know your theme song was 'Shankers Away,' but my famous husband spells his name 'Schanker.'" Privately, however, Libby feared she may have made "a terrible mistake."

In the beginning, it had been odd but charming to observe an elderly couple publicly holding hands. She continually talked of all the headlocked men she had known in her life—"headlocked" being Libby's new portmanteau word for intellectual. But as she told her friend Susan Caldwell, Louis Schanker "was different. He has *real* gut reactions. He's not hidebound by brains. He's a *genuine* primitive." Mrs. Caldwell believed that Libby had romanticized those qualities, transforming Schanker into something he had simply never been—a great man, a great artist, whatever it was she currently required.

Louis Schanker was not an articulate man. He talked exclusively of his tennis, his fishing, his work. At Treetops, he often remained until two or three in the morning in the studio Libby had constructed for him. During the summers in East Hampton, he went surf fishing every day in front of Dune House, trolling for blues and blowfish, which he stored in two upright freezers in the backyard. Libby's closest friend in East Hampton, the fabric designer Jack Lenor Larsen, thought of Schanker as Libby's consort, her attendant. He was her inferior in every way—intellectually, socially, financially—and although Libby admired his work, Larsen felt that Schanker would finally come to bore her.

As an artist, Schanker was simply not as well known as he had been during the forties and fifties. Since marrying Libby, he had had only one exhibition, and there were those who believed that his marital ease and luxury had corrupted the talent he originally possessed. It was so much more interesting to get drunk, to go fishing, to lollygag in the Rolls. Risa Sussman suspected that Schanker had not only ceased to grow as an artist, he had become moribund.

Libby's friends had never liked him. Louisa Carpenter had taken to calling him "the hairy ape." Alice Byrd found him snide and sarcastic, "the nastiest man I ever knew." Paul Bowles thought him a gruff, ill-tempered man who treated Libby abominably, rattling the newspapers over the breakfast table and, when Libby demurred, adding: "What the fuck do you want now?" "It's hard to say what you didn't like about him," said Eugenia Bankhead, "but you didn't like him." William Hill thought Schanker egotistical and arrogant and had it not been for Libby, he would have handed in his notice. Whenever his friends asked Hill about Libby, her past, the death of Smith Reynolds, he would grimace and say: "I don't know whether she killed Smith Reynolds or not, but the husband she ought to kill is Louis Schanker."

Timmy and Tony were mortified by Schanker's presence. Treetops, for them, had been a place of fun and merriment, but following Libby's third marriage, it had become dark and cheerless. Tony disliked Schanker's smelly Italian cigars and his preference for blue cheese and Bermuda onion sandwiches. In his view, Schanker overplayed the role of the bohemian, rarely dressing for dinner, and often arrived at the table splattered in paint and turpentine. Tony also disliked the fact that Schanker drank too much, believing that it was bad for him but terrible for Libby.

One evening, Libby invited Ethel and Paul Tishman and Olga and Joseph Hirshhorn to dinner. They had been at the table for several minutes when Schanker strode in from the studio, completely disheveled and intoxicated. He became even more drunk as the dinner progressed, muttering to himself, and making veiled, but lewd, remarks to the ladies.

Following dinner, Libby served her favorite dessert—a kind of cherry mousse, consisting of canned Queen Anne cherries. The cherries were pitted and filled with a walnut stuffing, and cherry syrup and crème Chantilly were added to make the gelatin. It was usually served in a silver tureen and, as Tony recalled, boasted "some fancy and incomprehensible French name." Schanker, as a rule, served the portions. On this occasion, the drunken painter slapped the serving spoon into the dessert, causing sections of it to fly around the table, one of which struck Libby in the face. No one said anything. Schanker looked around the table belligerently and then, quite suddenly, he dropped the spoon to the floor, crumpled forward, his face falling into the dessert, and passed out. Libby wiped the mousse from her face. "Would anyone like coffee in the library?" she asked. She made no reference to her comatose husband, nor even looked at him, but escorted her astonished guests into the library, leaving Schanker behind, his head submerged in the cherry mousse.

Libby was only too willing to overlook what she called "Louis's eccentricities," but she did not seem to realize that her marriage to him had done little more than emphasize her isolation. Gradually, her old friends began to feel that they were unwelcome at Treetops. Schanker detested homosexuals, and he refused to have them in the house, no matter how famous they happened to be.

Monty was the first to go. Schanker had met him briefly in New York, and when Libby invited him to Treetops for the weekend, Schanker became enraged and ordered Libby to cancel the invitation. Thereafter, Libby's other friends were banished one by one—David Holman, Paul Godkin, Oliver Smith, George Lloyd and Ned Rorem. Jennings Perry, who had known Libby for forty years, telephoned her at Treetops in the early spring of 1963, and Libby said: "Jennings, you'd better not call me here again. My husband is terribly jealous of other men, particularly of men I knew before I met him. Let me call you in the future." Perry never heard from her again.

Libby did not discuss her marriage openly, explaining to her few remaining friends that Louis was "a beautiful, sensitive man with the troubled soul of a great artist." Only Libby's employees knew that the marriage had become a torment to her. By early 1963, Libby's depressions were deepening, and her psychiatrist insisted that she take a holiday. That May, accompanied by Schanker and Alice Byrd, Libby traveled to Italy, Greece, Spain, and to Morocco to visit Jane and Paul Bowles. They were abroad for three months.

Alice, who had never been to Europe before, thought it a splendid trip. But Libby, concerned that Alice might be unhappy so far from home, suggested she could return to Treetops whenever she chose. Alice insisted she was having "the time of her life," and even had she hated it, she added, she would not leave Libby alone. Looking directly at Schanker one day, Alice assured Libby that should she decide to return home, she was taking Libby with her. Libby had never heard Alice so outspoken before and laughed openly. Schanker was furious. But Alice was indifferent to Schanker's displeasure. Libby was recuperating; she was under doctor's orders and Alice felt responsible for her.

They spent ten days in Tangier. Libby was not well, her lows enveloped her, and she began to argue with Schanker. Somewhat later, Jane Bowles wrote to a friend: "I had not seen . . . anyone . . . for ten days because Libby Holman was here with her abstract painter fisherman husband and she did not want to meet anyone or go anywhere—so we stayed closeted for ten days. I did not write either letters or plays of course as you know. Her departure left me feeling sadder even than I had felt when she came and I am still trying to recover."

One night after dinner in the medina, Libby fought with Schanker again. She told Alice that she had had enough, that when they returned to America, she intended to get a divorce. Alice smiled; she couldn't help herself. "I thought you'd approve of that," said Libby. "I *do*. I do," said Alice. But on returning to Treetops, Schanker became uncommonly attentive and clung to Libby, as Alice said, "like a leech to a log." Libby never mentioned divorce again.

Sometimes, toward the end of her life, Libby had a look of mild astonishment in her face, almost as though she had discovered some new form of suffering, one she had not been forced to appreciate before. Her bouts of melancholia seemed not only to depress but to enlighten her, and she was always astonished at their infinite complexity. She had talked with Jane Bowles about them in Tangier, but Jane had jeered at Libby's fanciful conjectures. *Her* glooms were merely gloomy; there was nothing to be gleaned from them. Their depressions were yet another bond between the two old friends, and they related their causes and effects to one another with a kind of morbid glee. On July 30, Libby wrote to Jane from East Hampton:

> Dearest Janie,
> Naturally, I had tsouris and gonzamagillah from the minute we arrived home. There was mail a mile high and most of it was about my children's problems, both of whom have more than Profumo and Christine Keeler put together. Tony has to repeat the Tenth grade at Putney. Tim has to change schools and doesn't like the one I have chosen for him. Tony is in Japan, as Tim says, "on a hiking trip," and Tim is out on a ranch in Wyoming buying pistols, fireworks, and girls. I was absolutely inundated with all their problems when I came home. Finally, we got to East Hampton hoping to have a calm summer. Louisa and Tamara Geva came out for the 4th of July weekend. That was very pleasant. Louisa talked in very warm terms about you and told Geva you were the funniest person she knew. We had then planned to go visit Tim on his ranch and his pistols and his fireworks and his girls, but before we got started, I had word from California that Polly, my lawyer, had had a second heart attack. That put me down in more doldrums than you can imagine. We spent a week with Tim at his ranch, Louis came home to work on his sculpture and Rose and I went out to, God help us, Los Angeles. Have you ever felt that you had

to be a Rock of Gibraltar when you knew you were nothing except a wet rubber sponge? Well, that's the way it was.

When we came home, I collapsed, but good. I have been sleeping twelve hours every night and wake up as if I have been beaten to death.

Louis is working like a mad thing on wood sculpture, the thing I love the best he does. He stays up until three or four or five in the morning, and when he is not working in the Studio, he is fishing. However, it is a joy to be in East Hampton in our very simple house.

As you once said to somebody at somebody's dinner party, "you live for the hearts of your friends." I feel that is very apt for me, so please do write to me soon, even if I don't understand what you are writing about. I miss you very much.

Over the years, Libby and her elder sister, Marion, had not remained close. On Marion's infrequent visits to Treetops, Libby tended to defer to her, continuing to believe, as she had as a child, that Marion was more beautiful, more fortunate. In the mid-twenties, Marion had married Myron Kahn, a successful Cleveland businessman, and moved there from Cincinnati. Kahn died, however, of an early heart attack and Marion remained in Cleveland, raising her two children and working as an actress at the Cleveland Playhouse. In 1940, she married John Tuteur, a wealthy businessman, and they moved to San Francisco where Tuteur owned and operated a flag manufacturing company. Other than giving occasional dramatic readings, Marion confined her activities to civic and charitable pursuits, to running her townhouse and her ranch in the Napa Valley. The local papers described her as "a talented socialite."

Taller and more handsome than Libby, Marion rarely went into the sun, believing it was bad for her skin. A vain woman, she took herself very seriously, considering herself a patron of the arts, a *grande dame*—a pose Libby thought pretentious, "San Franciscan."

There was about Marion a kind of ungovernable grandiloquence. When she met Louis Schanker for the first time, she climbed up to his loft, collapsed on a chaise longue, and viewed his work. "My *God,*" she exclaimed, waving her elegant arms in the air, "this one reminds me of Rembrandt and that one reminds me *terribly* of Titian. They're so *beautiful.* Louis, I must have *everything.*"

Like Libby, Marion was manic-depressive, but her depressions were deeper, her peaks more volatile than Libby's, and they continued for longer periods of time. During the autumn of 1963, Marion went through a prolonged, acute depression. On Friday, December 13, in the bedroom of her San Francisco home, she committed suicide by taking an overdose of sleeping pills. She was sixty-two. Before dying, she had written notes to her three children and her husband asking each of them to forgive her.

Marion's ex–daughter-in-law, Shirley Stowe, telephoned Libby with the news. At first, Libby thought Miss Stowe was referring to her mother, then, realizing it was Marion, was incredulous. She flew to San Francisco immediately. Libby felt Marion's death deeply, but she rarely spoke of it, and as the weeks passed, she came to look on it as an act of love. Libby told her old college friend Roberta Nicholson: "It was a generous and selfless gesture. Marion's torment must have been intolerable."

Marion Tuteur was the eighth of Libby's relatives or intimates to have disappeared or died unnaturally—her uncles Charles and Ross and Wallace, Smith Reynolds, Phillips and Ralph Holmes, and Topper. In 1964, there would be another. Libby's close friend, Jack Neustadt, an assistant professor of psychiatry at the Johns Hopkins University School of Medicine and a director of the Christopher Reynolds Foundation, hanged himself in a basement room of the Phipps Psychiatric Clinic in Baltimore.

Libby was distraught, convinced that it was she who inspired her tragedies. She thought of herself as a kind of medium, a conduit, through which death not only quickened, but radiated to others. And there was something else. Marion and Jack Neustadt had seemed so much more fortunate than she. And yet they had achieved surcease of pain, deliverance, while she remained behind—compelled to soldier on, to suffer, to endure.

58

L IBBY DID NOT CELEBRATE HER SIXTIETH BIRTHDAY. SHE RE-
fused to acknowledge it and, in any event, was posing as fifty-
eight. Although infirm and agitated, beset by depressions she
now described as "having the jitters in spades," Libby busied herself, shuttling between the four homes she and Schanker maintained—Treetops in Stamford, the brownstone in Manhattan,
the early Federal house in Sag Harbor, and Dune House in East
Hampton. She worked industriously with Gerald Cook on a
huge repertory of new musical material and would, during the
next eighteen months, give six separate concerts, which, for
Libby at least, constituted prodigious activity. And she appeared,
momentarily, content. As she told Alec Wilder: "The moment of
my career I've enjoyed the most is the present." But neither
Wilder nor anyone else believed her.

Libby intended to give a concert that summer in East
Hampton. "I'll do what I call Libby Holman's grab bag of musical comedy," she said, "because people want that, but I also plan
to sing several songs based on speeches and put to music by
Gerald Cook. They are all speeches on civil rights and women's
rights that a former slave named Sojourner Truth made around
the country in the early eighteen hundreds. I'm not trying to
stand on any soapbox or put across any messages. If there's any
message at all, it's simply the great salty humor and the fact that
it's wonderful a woman could write those speeches long before
the Civil War broke out.

"When I sing," said Libby, "the thing I want to do is to estab-
lish communication with the audience. I look for a dramatic pos-
sibility or a comedy situation in a song, something that gives a
vignette of life or tells a story. I let that song get into the marrow
of my bones. I want it to be so much a part of me that if I died
while singing, rigor mortis wouldn't set in until I finished every
last word of it."

Libby gave her East Hampton concert at the John Drew Theatre on July 30, 1964. She was particular about whom she invited, asking such old friends as Leonard Sillman, Dennis King,
Gaby Rodgers, Burton Lane, Kermit Bloomgarden, Tamara
Geva and Louisa Carpenter. She didn't want those with whom
she had fallen out to come, and dispatched polite notes of repudiation. To Bobby Lewis, she wrote: "I am asking the few
close friends I have *not* to come to my opening night. I wish to
have the audience as *impersonal* as possible. I hope you will understand. Love, Libby."

That evening, Libby stepped out on the darkened stage of
the John Drew Theatre, a black velvet curtain behind her. A
single blue spot picked out the piano and, as Gerald Cook played
"Good Morning Blues," Libby, sporting a deep tan, a new silver
hairdo, and a long black Mainbocher skirt, shouted, "Good
morning," and began to sing. Her repertoire included "Barbara
Allen," "Evil Hearted Me" and "House of the Rising Sun," all of
which were warmly received, but it was the old Libby, the torch
singer, whose voice had been described as "a mixture of sugar,
graphite and raw whiskey," that the audience wanted. During
her first encore, Libby sang "Body and Soul" to boisterous applause and, as *Newsweek* proclaimed: "The 'Moanin' Low' girl of
the 30's was back."

"Welcoming her return," continued *Newsweek*, "was a small,
elite audience of Long Island's cultural summer set including
painter Willem de Kooning, sculptor Frederick Kiesler, playwright Paul Osborn, pundit Max Lerner, flamenco guitarist Carlos Montoya, and theologian Paul Tillich. These people, who had
spent most of a lifetime in creation and thought, had come to
hear a unique artist. But they were also anticipating one of the
great human pleasures—nostalgic recreation of their own emotional high tide." Libby concluded her program by singing "Love
for Sale," "in which Cook's Oriental-like accompaniment seemed
like the voice of a Tangier pusher whispering, 'Sell it. Sell it.'
And when she came to the word 'surrender,' you heard the melt-
ing blur of surrender itself."

The concert took in $2,215, which Libby donated toward the
refurbishing of the Guild Hall auditorium. She believed that it
was the finest concert she had ever given. Afterward, Max
Lerner called her "indestructible," Paul Osborn thought she was
"as moving as she has ever been," Willem de Kooning sent her

roses. Libby herself was jubilant. "I can't tell you how much I love it," she told *Newsweek*. "I'm a performing woman. The audience is my partner—I feel them out as they feel me out. If they give, I give them back, and that was a warm wonderful audience."

"That accounts for her expressive little musical grunt," the reporter wrote. "'I call it my vomit,' she laughed. Libby Holman is a tough survivor who expresses survival poignantly. When she sings the phrase 'true love' in 'Love for Sale'—'that's the only time I get schmaltzy and sentimental,' Libby said, 'because I've never known it.'"

Libby believed it was her most luminous summer in years, and she intended to bask in it for the rest of the season. Writing to Jane and Paul Bowles, she said: "I have had a wonderful time in East Hampton this summer. I think I told you about my concert. At least I told you I was giving it. Anyway, it happened and it was very successful and fun. I am doing some more. Gerald and I made all new arrangements of the songs and we have new costumes and the whole works. I am starting an entire second career. I get the craziest offers now. My new record album will be out on October 15th. If you have a phonograph that plays Hi Fi, I'll send you one."

Libby's album was entitled *The Legendary Libby Holman* and was divided equally among her blues, ballads and torch songs. Libby hated the title, specifically the use of the word *legendary*. "It makes me sound like I'm dead," she told her husband; and when Schanker did not reply, Libby added: "But I'm not posthumous yet. Or hadn't you noticed?"

This was to be Libby's most productive period in years. She busied herself with correspondence and causes. She had become a member of the National Committee on U.S.-China Relations. Her foundation supported seminars on world law and helped produce an award-winning political cartoon entitled "The Hat." She and Gerald Cook were preparing an album of new songs and old standards, and they gave another concert at Elmira College in Ithaca, New York. "I have never had such a reaction from an audience," she said. "They really dug it. You know where I belong, old as I am? Singing in colleges." She was asked to join the National Social Directory and wrote on the back of the invitation: "Boy, did I ever not answer this. Ix!" And despite her considerable wealth, she worried continually about money, claiming, when some innocuous new expense arose, that she would have "to rob Fort Knox in order to pay for it."

Nothing dampened her ebullience, not even the ongoing depression of Jane Bowles. In a cheerful letter to her, Libby wrote: "It is very important that I hear from you. I understand what you are going through. You know I am the Master of Melancholy if of nothing else." During the early summer of 1965, she wrote to Jane again: "Are you really in a black state? I hope not and, if so, I hope it doesn't last too long. My state of mind is alright. . . . I don't like at all what is going on in the USA or in the world and, so far as that goes, my state of mind is troubled."

But not overly, since she added: "Romances are flowering around here like mad things." She had just met "a Catholic priest whom I am now in love with. If you are interested in that subject I will tell you more, but not until you evince interest."

Jane, apparently, was uninterested, but Libby's friends in East Hampton were agog. Libby had developed a new (and perhaps dangerous) passion, and they watched it unfold with the rapt expectation of children at a Punch and Judy show.

At her annual summer "sardine squeeze," Libby had been introduced to a thirty-five-year-old Roman Catholic priest named Terence Netter. Netter—although taller and fairer than Monty Clift had been as the priest in Alfred Hitchcock's 1953 film *I Confess*—had the same look of concentrated intensity, of what Libby later described as "a kind of passionate purity." The handsome priest had been a member of the Jesuit order for thirteen years, having been ordained in Innsbruck, Austria, in 1960. He had received his MFA degree from George Washington University only weeks before. Netter was also a talented painter and had had his first one-man show in Washington, D.C., that year. In order to paint and perform his ministry, he had been given leave to spend the summer in East Hampton, residing at the Parish of St. Philomena (now Trinity Church), painting, preaching and hearing confessions. As a painter-priest, Netter was an oddity in the summer resort and he rapidly became well known.

He had never heard of Libby before, knew nothing of her. Over the course of the summer, however, they developed a fervent friendship. It was never a flirtation, at least on Netter's part, and he was unaware that Libby had fallen in love with him. He, after all, had taken a vow of celibacy long before and liked to think of himself as a good Jesuit. Their friendship was based on what Netter called "a mutual fascination," and on such mutual interests as politics and the civil-rights movement. Netter was even interested in show business—his father having once been a vice-president of Paramount and his mother a former dancing partner of Fred Astaire's.

Libby was sixty-one, but Netter thought she looked considerably younger. She had no illusions about herself and he liked that immediately. She was cosmopolitan and bright and exhibited what Netter liked to think of as "a man's mind." On the other hand, he felt that Libby might have been afraid of herself, that given her life and her constricting marriage, she might have been seeking a kind of salvation from him. But Libby was an idealist; she was drawn to serious-minded people, to those with intelligence and purpose. She was both stimulated and stimulating; and Netter was so fascinated that he never allowed himself to see her alone, not even for a meal.

He never understood her relationship with Louis Schanker. Schanker was unrefined, a brash, ignoble man, who appeared to perform the role of protector. He reminded Netter of a mastiff, prowling aimlessly before the palace gates.

It was a summer of protest and violent change. One hundred twenty-five thousand American combat troops were entrenched in Vietnam and the first real tremors of domestic dissent were heard. It was a summer of "teach-ins," "love-ins" and "flower power." Martin Luther King, Jr., had recently led large civil-rights demonstrations in Selma and Montgomery, Alabama (and had invited Libby to join him), and Malcolm X had been gunned down in Harlem. Ten thousand impoverished blacks burned and looted Watts. Given her long championing of black ballads and blues, Libby saw a connection between these events and herself, and her friends attempted to persuade her to speak out, to sing more frequently.

Terence Netter offered to arrange two concerts for Libby at Georgetown University in Washington and she agreed at once— provided they were benefits for the university's black students. Before Netter returned to Washington, Libby commissioned him to create a collage, based on significant events in her life; she gave him numerous old newspaper cuttings, many of which concerned Smith Reynolds's death and the subsequent inquest more than thirty years before.

Libby gave two concerts in the Dag Hammarskjold Auditorium at the United Nations that autumn, both of them benefits for UNICEF, the United Nations Children's Fund. She became only the second artist to perform there, the first being Pablo Casals. In an interview with the New York *Times*, Libby said: "I've been doing Americana for twenty-four years now and I'm still thought of as a torch singer. Gerald and I work like this because we keep growing with our material. We want these songs to always be contemporaneous musically and dramatically. Carl Sandburg knew this was how it should be: 'Sing it anyway you want to,' he said, 'but keep it alive.'"

Following the second concert on November 4, Libby threw a lavish party for some sixty people in her brownstone on East Sixty-first Street. Dorothy Parker attended, as did Terence Netter, who had come up from Washington for the occasion. About an hour after the party began, Netter, because the house was overheated, took off his coat and clerical collar; he wore a sports shirt underneath. He sat down on the sofa with Libby, and told her how impressed he had been with her concert.

As they chatted, the young priest placed his arm around Libby's shoulders. Immersed in their conversation, they failed to notice Louis Schanker striding purposefully across the room. Suddenly Schanker began to scream. The other guests fell silent, pivoting around to listen. "I'm *sick* of this," shouted Schanker. "You two. It's been going on *too long*." He was apoplectic. Not wishing to embarrass Libby, Netter put on his clerical collar and coat and left the party. Libby sat back on the sofa, a blank, impassive look in her eyes. She said nothing, but she would never forgive her vulgar spouse.

As she had promised, Libby gave two concerts at Georgetown University's Trinity Theatre in early February of 1966, the proceeds being donated to Georgetown's Civil Rights Committee.

Terence Netter, now on Georgetown's faculty as an art professor, had arranged the concerts, and by the time Libby arrived in Washington, he had also completed the work of art she had commissioned. He liked his multi-colored collage, although it was not a happy picture. Composed of paper cutouts of Libby singing, cracked faces (including a faded impression of Smith Reynolds), scissored newspaper cuttings and jagged headlines, it was overlaid with sharp, glittering stars. Behind it all was the faint, tragic image of a broken heart.

Netter showed the collage to Libby in his studio. She stood mute before it for a long time. "It's *very* good," she said finally. "You've captured *everything*," but there was a look of horror in her face, the look of a woman who had never seen her shattered life so fixed, so synthesized before. When Libby left Netter's studio, the picture remained behind. She didn't ask that it be shipped, she didn't pay for it, and she never mentioned it again.

That evening, during her second concert, Libby sang three or four songs to an enthusiastic audience that clapped more loudly with each successive number. Suddenly, the entire bank of ceiling lights fell to the stage, missing Libby by inches. She didn't move. And then, expressionless, she walked slowly into the wings. Backstage, Libby said, "Don't worry, don't worry, I'll go back on," and when she returned, there was a great ovation. Libby never alluded to the accident, but it was an omen, Netter believed, and Libby, despite her composure, had been terrified.

When the concert ended, Netter hosted a reception for Libby at his parents' Georgetown home. The convivial evening was marred by one peculiar circumstance. For as long as Netter had known Libby, he had never seen her drink alcohol. In his presence, at least, she had always drunk Perrier. That night, he was unable to discern whether she was calm or agitated, happy or forlorn; but as the evening progressed, she consumed glass after glass of wine, drinking with savage determination, and eventually, Schanker, her vigilant castellan, helped her out to a waiting limousine.

Netter did not see Libby for several months. The next summer, they met by chance at a party in East Hampton. They did not speak. Both of them knew that, although their friendship had been platonic, it was over, that it could not continue without arousing Schanker's wrath. They smiled and nodded across the crowded room, and Netter never saw her again.

59

EEKING RESPITE FROM HER MOODY SPOUSE, LIBBY DROVE into New York just before Christmas to see the actor Roddy McDowall. McDowall was the only one of Monty's friends with whom Libby had remained friendly. She called him Roduary and McDowall called her Lipsy. She admired his acting and photographic talents and was vastly amused by his sense of humor, referring to it as his "witty bitcheries."

That evening, they had arranged to meet at Arthur's, the chic Manhattan discotheque owned by McDowall and Sybil and Christopher Burton. Because McDowall valued his time with Libby, they dined alone in the club's Pub Room. The Pub contained only twenty tables and it was crowded, the music was live and loud, and Truman Capote waved delicately from across the room. It was the first time McDowall had seen Libby with silver hair and he thought it suited her. Libby was in high spirits that evening. The two friends giggled hysterically, and afterward, Libby thanked him, saying it had been just like old times.

On New Year's Day of 1966, Libby wrote McDowall a letter:

Dearest Roduary:

This was supposed to be a simple Seasons Greeting card and a belated thank you note for a gloriously hateful time with you at your dump. I loved every minute of it.

(A) Being with you.
(B) Seeing Truman (Capote)
(C) Having my ear drums cracked
(D) The only fun I missed was the opportunity to refuse to meet your partner.

I am late because I am busy. I will now stop to compare your busyness with mine (not according to ages because neither the new mathematics nor Einstein could figure that one out).

RODDY'S ACTIVITIES
(All of which, naturally, I don't know)

1. Distinguished actor of stage, screen, TV and, oy!! opera, yet.

2. Part-owner and Considerate and Efficient Manager of "Most Successful Joint in Town."

3. Photographer of the Great and the Famous.

4. Chief Photographer to Her Royal Highness, Bessie Burton.

5. Author and Publisher of Book (or Books?).

6. Musician of Note.

7. Saver of Everything.

8. Keeper-Upper with the Joneses.

9. Graceful and Intellectual Friend of the Great and the Lowly.

10. Giver of Scintillating Parties.

11. Receiver of Pianos and English Decca Phonographs (Crippler of my nephew).

LIPSY COLMAR'S ACTIVITIES
(All of which, naturally, I won't mention)

1. Wife of (and in love with) Artist Husband (you can never know what this involves).

2. Mother of Two Draft-Age Sons!!! Attending Schools.

3. Daughter of Beautiful Ninety-three Year Old Mother. (If in your leisure time in Los Angeles, you want to do research on this, I will give you the address of her Nursing Home. You can then see for yourself where my vitality and dictatorship come from).

4. Singer.

5. President of Christopher Smith Reynolds Foundation. Member of the Board of Directors of American Foundation on Non-Violence. Honorary President is Martin Luther King, Jr.

6. Owner and Manager of four houses. (In regard to this, I am a Manic-Compulsive. Only by living with me twenty-four hours a day—God help you—could you understand the agony of the people around me).
   (a) Directress of large daffodil stand which is shown yearly (for charities and friends).

7. Thrower-Awayer of Everything (taking time and elbow grease). This must now be changed to your number 7. She must now preserve, itemize, identify and cross-file *EVERYTHING* for "Lipsy Colmar Collection" for Boston University.

8. Violent Champion of Left-Wing causes (which somehow now must be done "Sous Cloche" because it is "chic").

9. Refuser of Have Anything to do with Mechanical Devices as much as possible. (Meditate for a moment on this).

10. Addict of Crossword Puzzles and Double Crostics (no time no more for this fix!).

11. Teller of My Life History to Biographer (Oy! Vey!).

12. Avoider of Cliches which takes more vocabulary and energy in getting around them than I have time for which (never mind the grammar). A Few Examples:
    I must say:
    (a) "within" and "without" for "Inside" or "Outside".
    (b) "Airplane" instead of that new, faster kind.
    (c) Will you play a "round" of tennis? Or, will you "put the places on" the table for dinner?
    (d) It's a "sage" owl.
    (e) Will you have a little "smidgeon" of ice cream?
    (f) This one I can only *write, never say*—When I am enjoying myself "I am having a bawl!" As you know, I always cry when I am ecstatic.
    (g) I shall use the "rising staircase" at Bloomingdales.

    As you can see, this portion of the list can go on forever. So could each of our lists.

                                        Love,
                                        Lipsy

EPILOGUE

There are many interesting people, Roddy, in both our

lives. The ones of long-standing *value* must never be neglected. The older I grow, the more important this feeling becomes to me. We must never let as much time lapse between our trysts again.

———————— **60** ————————

A S THE REBELLIOUS VOICES OF THE SIXTIES BECAME MORE strident, Libby felt a growing sense of alienation. She seemed muddled, adrift, teetering precariously between absurd extremes. When a friend advised her not to worry about a thing, Libby replied, "I don't. *It's everything.*" She loathed Broadway and protest songs; she detested hippies, drugs and politicians; the burgeoning war in Vietnam enraged her. In a letter to Jane Bowles she said: "Both of my boys have decided that we will go to jail until they take us up to the Supreme Court of the United States before they will go into the Vietnam War. Maybe the next time I write to you, I will give you a jail address."

And if this was not enough, in a span of less than five years, those who had once been Libby's intimates, one after the other, began to die—Lucius Beebe, Clifton Webb, Tallulah Bankhead, Josh White, and finally, Benet Polikoff. Libby felt as though she had lost her father all over again. It was, she said, "like having your right hand severed when your left had already been paralyzed." Libby withdrew to her bedroom, closed the curtains, and cried off and on for several weeks.

Libby's mother, Rachel, had lived in a Los Angeles nursing home for eight years. She was deaf, and she was going blind. She had had pneumonia and numerous strokes, but not until April 23, 1966, at the age of ninety-three, did she die. Rachel's death distressed Libby and, oddly, left her with a nagging sense of guilt. She flew to Cincinnati for the funeral, later describing it in a letter to Jane Bowles: "It will be a Christian Science ceremony," she said, "and then her ashes will be put in a Jewish cemetery next to my father's, who didn't believe in any religion anyway." Rachel Workum Holman's tombstone read: MAY FLIGHTS OF ANGELS SING THEE TO THY REST.

Before going to East Hampton for the summer, Libby considered calling Monty Clift. Given Schanker's ban on homosexuals, she had not seen him in nearly six years. Libby thought about Monty more often than she cared to admit and, now and again, considered risking her husband's displeasure by dropping in on him. But Libby procrastinated and, on this occasion, did not telephone.

She would not have recognized Monty now. His glittering reputation had faded and he was defensive about being unemployed. Although he had just completed filming *The Defector* in Germany, prior to that he had not worked for four years, not since *Freud* in 1962. He suffered from racking cramps in his back and legs, a direct result of his car accident, and, to ease the pain, took repeated injections of Demerol. His once beautiful face was ravaged, gaunt. Like Libby, he was almost skeletal. His hyperthyroid condition was deteriorating and he suffered from a calcium deficiency. There were varicose veins all over his body, he was losing his hair, and his hands had become ugly and gnarled. Both physically and psychologically, the forty-five-year-old Clift seemed, as one of his friends observed, like an open wound.

On July 23, Roddy McDowall telephoned Libby in East Hampton to tell her that Monty had died in his sleep. Because of the Demerol injections, he had been hallucinating for the past few days and had been trying, unsuccessfully, to stop drinking. His death was officially diagnosed as occlusive coronary artery disease; but Bobby Lewis may have been more accurate in calling it "the longest suicide in history."

For Libby, Monty's death was the last insupportable sorrow. Three days later, she drove into New York to attend his funeral—a simple Episcopalian service at St. James's Church on Madison Avenue. The funeral attracted tourists and teenagers, housewives and movie fans, and such celebrities as José Quintero, Jerome Robbins, Mel Blanc, Lauren Bacall, Dore Shary and

Nancy Walker. There were two bouquets of white chry-santhemums from Elizabeth Taylor and her husband, Richard Burton, and wreaths from Roddy McDowall and Myrna Loy.

Libby sat at the back of the church with Tim and Tony. She was stupefied. When Monty's casket was carried down the aisle, she rose to her feet and started toward it, then hesitated, her hand to her mouth, watching helplessly as Monty was taken away. She could not bring herself to go to the cemetery.

In Monty's memory, Libby made a substantial contribution to the Motion Picture Relief Fund. She also wrote to Monty's mother, Sunny. "We are grieved that Monty is not with us any-more," she said. "It was a great pleasure and a deep gratification to have known a human being like him. He will always be like a bright shining sun to my family and me. I send you my sympa-thy and gratitude for having made it possible for us to know him."

Somewhat less formally, Libby wrote to her mother's last nurse in Los Angeles: "It was *very* sad about Monty dying. He was a very dear friend of mine. He died too young, but he had lived too hard."

Although Libby was only sixty-two, Monty's unexpected death had set off ominous signals of her own mortality. She had reached, she felt, a point of no return, and she longed to be free, transformed. She wanted peace and dignity. For nearly ten years now, she had studied Zen, and Monty's demise and the numer-ous deaths of other friends spurred her into a more obsessive involvement with that Eastern discipline.

That autumn, she visited Japan, spending eight days in Ryutaku-ji (Temple of the Swamp Dragon), a Buddhist monas-tery in the foothills of Mt. Fuji. When she returned, stricken with pneumonia, the daily life at Treetops was rearranged to accom-modate the mechanics of her new philosophy. In the mornings, Libby practiced hatha-yoga, a form of breathing and exercise; she meditated in the lotus position for at least two hours every afternoon, and whenever she was "sitting" and the telephone rang, the servants explained that Mrs. Reynolds was engaged and could not be disturbed.

Libby's favorite book had become *The Three Pillars of Zen* by Roshi Philip Kapleau. Her own volume was worn and dog-eared and she sent other copies to almost everyone she knew. The fifty-four-year-old Kapleau, an ordained Zen monk, had spent thirteen years studying and working under three illustrious Zen masters in Japan. In 1966, he returned to America to found the Zen Center in Rochester, New York.

Libby called him. She was troubled, she said, suffering from an uncontrollable angst, and she wanted desperately to meet the venerable roshi and discuss her problems. Kapleau told Libby that everyone desired to know who they were, but he sensed that Libby was driven, that she had "a felt need and profound pain— a very heavy karma."

Subsequently, Kapleau invited Libby to attend a series of "sesshin"—a retreat conducted in silence from two to seven days in duration. Libby, thrilled, accepted immediately. From the start, she was devoted to Kapleau and gradually came to regard him as a great man. Moreover, Zen represented the most important and enlightening experience in life, she believed, but typically Libby would not commit herself to it entirely.

"I am a singer, Philip," she wrote, "and I never know when my concert dates and radio interviews and everything involved with being a performer will take place. That is why I am not certain I can attend all ten weekend Sesshins, as much as I should like to come to all of them. Again, thank you for being in this country, and for being my friend."

In the course of the next year, Libby attended three separate sesshins at the Zen Center in Rochester and another in the little town of Wyoming in western New York State, to which she dragooned Louis Schanker. But Schanker, Kapleau realized, was not a serious student, nor did he possess Libby's need. At their first meeting, Kapleau was astonished at the litheness of Libby's body, an attribute he ascribed to the practicing of Yoga, and he reckoned that she was in her early fifties. From his days as a young student in Manhattan many years before, Kapleau remembered Libby's torch singing, and he thought of her still as a child of the twenties, a freewheeling showgirl. On the day she arrived in Rochester, Libby confirmed those prejudices by producing a flask filled with whiskey.

For many years, Libby had been partial to sandals and simple Mexican frocks, worn over a skin-colored body stocking, which, because of her deep tan, gave the illusion of uncovered flesh. In a letter to a friend, Libby had written: "You know those Mexican dresses I wear over a body stocking so when I am sunburned, and I was and am sunburned, I look kind of naked? One day a man in the town told me that I created a sensation. I asked him how he knew. He said the priest had told him. One of the priest's parishoners had come to confess, and had confessed that he had seen me and that it was so shocking and exciting to him that he had to confess. Louis said that I am getting to be a big show-off and exhibitionist in my old age, but when I look back, I think I have always been a big show-off and exhibitionist."

At the sesshins both in Wyoming and in Rochester, Libby lived up to these assessments of herself. She wore patterned miniskirts to accentuate her legs, and several of the older female participants expressed their indignation to the roshi, while some of the men were both shocked and sexually stirred. During sesshin, nothing is permitted to distract the mind from meditation, and because of Libby's dress and flamboyant behavior, she was at times a serious distraction.

Libby rarely wore undergarments and the same female objectors claimed that the cushions, after contact with her bare skin, were unhygienic. Kapleau was obliged to post a notice forbidding such behavior. Because alcohol and drugs violated the fifth precept of Zen Buddhism, Libby was reprimanded for drinking. Smoking and talking indoors were not permitted either, and as a compromise, Libby limited herself to these indulgences outside the center.

During the seven-day sesshins, the students were awakened at 4:30 each morning; and for the next seventeen hours, with infrequent breaks, they concentrated, meditated, chanted and exercised in what Kapleau described as "a honing of the mind." Unless one rested long and well when these periods ended, a strong sense of depression usually ensued, a process Kapleau likened to "having the bends." Students were permitted to speak with their teachers only during "dokusan"—a private encounter with the roshi in his teaching chamber. It was here that Libby discussed her psychological problems with Kapleau, her most urgent question being: "Who am I?" Kapleau attempted to give Libby guidance and enlightenment.

During the course of the sesshin, Kapleau gave Zen talks, technically known as "teisho" to his students. During one of these lectures, he created an analogy between the teaching of Zen and climbing a mountain, explaining that the higher one climbs, the more one must cast off excess baggage—one's superfluous prejudices and preconceptions. Libby, obviously distraught, suddenly leaped to her feet and rushed from the room. That evening, during dokusan, she told Kapleau of Topper's death, admitting that she had never been able to allay her guilt, and that she never would.

When the sesshin ended, the joyous students gathered around Roshi Kapleau in order to touch and hug him. Although short and bald, Kapleau was a powerful, attractive man; and many of his female students fell in love with him—thinking, perhaps, that they would become enlightened on contact, that he was, in some mysterious way, a source of power. Kapleau himself liked the attention of women and was as responsive to them as he could be without titillating them sexually.

During Libby's final sesshin, she attempted, unsuccessfully, to seduce the venerable monk, literally throwing herself upon him. She told her nephew, David Holman, that she had not understood why she had acted so brazenly, that she had been both shocked and shamed, but that the desire had been uncontrollable. Philip Kapleau remembered nothing of the incident, but considered it both possible and amusing. He himself failed to notice such behavior anymore.

In the teaching of Zen, a strong emphasis is placed on enlightenment, or "satori." Satori is possible at any time, but students are cautioned that they may have to wait for five or ten years. Libby, of course, wanted enlightenment immediately. Following her last sesshin, Kapleau spent a weekend with Libby and Schanker in East Hampton, during which time Libby ordered Schanker about like a servant, and spoke passionately of her problems—her dead son, her dead friends, her dead life. Kapleau had tried to help her in the limited time she had spent with him, but, in his view, Libby was spiritually afraid and obstinate.

During the late sixties, Libby was searching not only for herself, but for a release of some kind; and she seemed, however momentarily, to find it in Zen. But in the end, the discipline was destructive. The very precepts of Zen—denial, restraint, submission, control—were contrary to her nature. Her few remaining friends believed that Zen was just another of Libby's masochistic drives, that instead of providing the promised peace, it contributed to her eventual decline.

Louis Schanker had an exhibition of his carved wooden sculptures at the Dorsky Gallery in Manhattan that summer. Because they were meant to be touched, Schanker had dubbed them "feelies." Based on the theme of the circle, the voluptuous sculptures varied from one to nine feet in height and were carved from mahogany, walnut, oak and birch.

Marcus Blechman attended the opening and later wrote to a friend: "Schanker is obsessed with testicular forms. They leer at you from various nooks and crannies and the crowning masterpiece is called 'Woman and Man' and guess what it is? A breast (over-ripe) and the entire male apparatus just below. I would like to know if that is necessary? Will it contribute to my spiritual fulfillment or will it remind me that even in wood the sexual organs look very foolish?"

To celebrate her husband's opening, Libby threw a party at the gallery, serving corned beef and beer. Just as the party began a friend of Libby's arrived with her miniature cocker spaniel. In order to drink her beer, she put the spaniel on the floor. As she talked to Libby, the tiny dog scurried about the room, finally lifting its leg and urinating on one of Schanker's wooden sculptures. "Darling, *naughty, naughty,*" shrieked Libby. "We have come to *admire,* not to *criticize.*" Everyone but Schanker laughed.

Libby wanted to spend the Christmas holidays in Italy. As she wrote to Jane Bowles: "I feel I need to see the Pope on Christmas Day and get some ecumenical advice from him. What the hell does 'ecumenical' mean? They are always having Ecumenical Councils. What I am really going for (but please don't tell Louis) is in the hopes that I can meet Marcello Mastroiani." In the end, however, Libby and her husband spent Christmas with Louisa Carpenter in Ft. Lauderdale—an abbreviated visit, since Louisa felt that Schanker, "that hairy parvenu," was Libby's inferior. And so, on December 29, Libby and Schanker traveled to the Yucatán for three weeks. Libby's depressions deepened and she found the Yucatán "tedious," but admitted, on her return, "It's good for my compulsive nature to be slapped down like this."

At Treetops, Libby found a belated Christmas present from

Tangier, an anthology entitled *The Collected Works of Jane Bowles,* which had been published recently. It contained an introduction by Truman Capote. "I do owe you thanks from the bottom of my heart for your Anthology," Libby wrote to Jane. "I love it. I think it's a beautiful book and I love every word in it. There are several of the stories I had never read. They are marvelous."

But Libby took exception to Capote's introduction, particularly a reference to Jane in which he said that she was "a spookily accurate mimic and can re-create with nostalgic admiration the voices of certain singers—Helen Morgan, for example, and her close friend, Libby Holman."

"Now about that preface by Truman Capote," wrote Libby. "He says you mimic me or imitate me perfectly. Why do you do it behind my back? I have never heard you do it. I have heard you imitate Helen Morgan and you have a high lyric soprano the way Helen Morgan had, but how do you get to my bass voice? I might even come to Tangier to hear you."

Libby, in fact, had been planning a surprise visit to Jane for weeks, and in the spring of 1967, she and Schanker flew to Tangier to see her. Jane was at the airport to greet them. When Libby deplaned, she screamed with pleasure, running to throw her arms around Jane. Jane smiled vacantly. For the next few days, Jane took to her bed, suffering, she said, from melancholia. Paul, who had been in Thailand for several months, writing a book on Bangkok, arrived in Tangier a week later, and Libby came to him in tears. "I can't take another hour of Jane," she said. "It upsets me too much. We're leaving on the first plane." The next morning, Libby and Schanker returned to New York.

From Treetops, Libby wrote to Paul: "The first evening I saw Jane," she said, "she was so completely depressed and seeming to want to get away from Tangier that I offered her the hospitality of Treetops when and if she could make the trip. After being with her the amount of time I was, I have had to reconsider this seriously and must withdraw the invitation for a long stay at Treetops and/or East Hampton.

"Jane's effect on me was devastating, both physically and emotionally. I didn't realize it until the night before I left Tangier when I was violently ill. Also, the next day on the plane, for the first time in my life, I traveled very badly. I had to have oxygen and I also vomited whatever I ate. This, you must remember, was when I was with her only a short time and had no responsibilities of my own.

"My life at home is too eventful and busy to be able to take care of her, or even to be able to be with her for long periods of time. . . . She has her two maids in Tangier who wait on her hand and foot. I have no one to do that who would have the time or the energy.

"Naturally, I don't want to sadden Jane any more than she is, and I don't want her to feel that I am pulling out as a friend. I love her very much. That is why her condition is so painful to me. . . . I send you very much love, darling, and am sure you can make some sense and peace out of our poor Janie."

Libby added: "I must also talk a little bit to you about Louis. He is just coming out of a deep state of depression. He began to get nervous and go back into his depression when he was around Jane those last few days in Tangier. Naturally, I must think of him first."

Libby neglected to mention that Schanker had never liked Jane and Paul Bowles and, although his "depression" may have coincided with his trip to Tangier, he had no intention of allowing either of them to visit Treetops. Libby was never to see the Bowleses again.

Tamara Geva, the actress and dancer who had performed with Libby in *Three's a Crowd,* had not seen her in nearly four years.

In early 1968, prompted by their mutual friendship with Louisa Carpenter, they began to meet once or twice a month, usually on Wednesdays when Libby drove into Manhattan. Geva was shocked at the dramatic change in Libby: Her hair was white, her face rough and wrinkled, and she looked like a secondhand scarecrow. In Geva's view, Libby was no longer tragic but pathetic; and many of her old friends and acquaintances tended to avoid her as they might circumvent a once beautiful but now dingy part of town.

One Wednesday evening, they went to the Cherry Lane Theatre to see *Corruption in the Palace of Justice* by the Italian playwright Ugo Betti. At the first intermission, as they walked into the lobby for a cigarette, Libby suddenly fell to the floor. A small crowd formed. Geva knelt beside Libby gently slapping her face. Her eyes opened, but they were glazed, and Geva decided to take her home. As she helped Libby through the front door of the brownstone, Libby's butler, William Hill, appeared. Hill clucked and, wagging his finger, said: "Mrs. Reynolds, have you been drinking again?" Libby said nothing, and Hill assisted her upstairs.

For Libby, alcohol represented the last escape. Faced with the absolute meaninglessness of her life, she drank incessantly. Soave Bolla was her favorite libation—she drank two or three bottles a day—but she had also begun drinking vodka, and Alice Byrd had taken to concealing the unopened bottles. When Libby drank, she was unable to walk and usually fell asleep on the sofa in the library. Both Alice and Rose Minor felt that Schanker, instead of deterring Libby, encouraged her to drink. Nor did he set an admirable example.

That spring, Libby invited three Russian diplomats to dinner at Treetops. She had met them at a reception at the Russian Embassy and, assuming they were spies, KGB perhaps, looked forward to the dinner for days. The diplomats brought imported Russian vodka, and before dinner, Schanker matched them drink for drink. They drank several bottles of wine with dinner, then, switched to champagne with cognac chasers. Throughout the meal, Schanker related salacious and increasingly drunken stories. Although the Russians laughed, they found him vulgar and tedious. While her guests drank coffee and talked, Libby, embarrassed by her husband's inelegance, retired to the library to read.

Eventually, Schanker became violently ill and vomited on Libby's newly upholstered, handloomed-damask couch. He became so nauseated that he coughed up his false teeth which clattered to the floor and slid under a chair. When one of the diplomats told Libby what had happened, she shrugged and told him to take Schanker outside. Schanker became sick again on the lawn and Libby instructed the Russian to close the door and leave him there.

61

ALTHOUGH RARELY SEEING LIBBY, CORETTA AND MARTIN Luther King considered her a friend. They admired Libby's long crusades for civil rights in America, her substantial donations to black causes and, specifically, her foundation's generous award to the young Baptist minister, which had enabled him to travel to India nine years before. They called Libby several times a year, and Coretta wrote occasionally, urging Libby to join her husband on civil-rights marches in the South. But Libby, usually claiming that Coretta had not given her sufficient warning, always declined. Even so, they maintained a mutually respectful and admiring relationship.

On the afternoon of April 4, 1968, Martin Luther King, Jr., stepped out on a balcony of the Lorraine Motel in Memphis, Tennessee, and was murdered with a single shot from a 30.06 Remington rifle. He was thirty-nine. In one of his last public addresses, King had said: "I've been to the mountaintop. . . . I would like to live a long life. Longevity has its place. But I'm not concerned about that now. I just want to do God's will. And He's allowed me to go up to the mountain. And I've looked over. And I've seen the promised land."

Libby had listened to that speech and, following King's assassination, came to associate his words with the death of Topper. The two men had become mysteriously linked, fixed like doomed totems in Libby's troubled mind. They had both essayed the mountain, had looked over, and died.

Although invited, Libby could not bring herself to attend King's funeral. She called Coretta instead, and the two women talked for nearly an hour. Later in the year, Libby visited Coretta in Atlanta, helping to dedicate a plaque at her husband's birthplace. The next summer, Coretta and her children spent two weeks with Libby in East Hampton. Libby paid for all their travel expenses, renting a car for Coretta and bicycles for the children. In Coretta's honor, Libby gave one of her sardine squeezes.

For Libby, Martin Luther King had been a symbol of unconquerable strength and courage. Some months before, she had written to him: "There are no words that I have to express to you the gratefulness in my heart that you exist." And now, he too was gone.

62

ON JUNE 5, LIBBY GAVE WHAT WOULD PROVE TO BE HER final concert at the Theresa L. Kaufman Concert Hall at the Ninety-second Street YMHA—a benefit for the World Federation of the United Nations Association. The concert coincided with the assassination of Senator Robert F. Kennedy in Los Angeles. Libby was distraught and considered canceling, but was persuaded to go on, dedicating her program to the slain presidential candidate.

Libby was sixty-four and, for the first time in her career, used a microphone. But she believed she was singing better than ever, admitting, however, that she might be prejudiced or hard-of-hearing. Her material included many songs she had never performed before—Duke Ellington's "The Blues," and Irving Berlin's "Suppertime" and "The Four Marys." She added humor to her repertoire with such songs as "Mosquito in My Kitchen" and "A Draught of Lewis Carroll." The enthusiastic audience showered Libby with continuous applause; and she returned the compliment by curling up on Gerald Cook's piano and singing her old torch songs—"Body and Soul," "Can't We Be Friends?" and "Something to Remember You By." Libby concluded her program with "Moanin' Low," rolling the song out with a deep and vibrant growl. The crowd's cheers turned to chants of joy.

Afterward, Libby was ecstatic. "People who remember me,"

she said, "feel cheated if I don't sing some torch songs. But now I do them differently, without the rinky-tink-tink of the thirties. I have changed the interpretation of them. One has to, as one gets more mature."

Libby spent the summer and early autumn of 1968 in East Hampton. She contributed to the defense of Dr. Benjamin Spock, who had been arrested for demonstrating against the war in Vietnam, and vigorously supported Eugene McCarthy's unsuccessful campaign for the presidency. "Our horrible election is over," she wrote to her friend the British politician Tom Driberg. "Ix! Ugggh! They were all kind of dogs, but I was thinking for the sake of our country and our relationship with the world, that Humphrey was the least bad. However, we still have a Democratic Congress and there will be constant problems. Do you think our country is obsolete? We are quite depressed about it."

Libby continued to think of herself as a fierce, unswerving liberal. Her challenges were always for the obscure, the bizarre, the disparate—her passions for Zen and Quakerism; her pro-black and anti-Vietnam stances; her love for such plays as *Waiting for Godot*, "the best play of all time," she claimed. For most of her life, she had concerned herself with the plight of the poor and with the world's injustices, and became grave and indignant that "so many people fared so badly so much of the time." She was unstintingly generous toward those she loved and the causes she supported, yet worried continually that people loved her for her money alone. Concerning her wealth, Libby liked to say: "If I *can't* take it with me, I *won't* go."

Death preoccupied her increasingly. She complained bitterly of failing health, of depression and a lack of energy. She suffered from low blood pressure, and took daily injections for allergies and anemia. She maintained vast quantities of pills in her bathroom cabinet—a place Alice Byrd called "the drugstore." She began to identify with the plight of her friend Jane Bowles, and, that autumn, wrote the fifty-one-year-old writer a sympathetic letter: "I seem to have some of the same symptoms you have," she said, "a toxic condition from too many drugs. Dr. Resnick took me off most of them, or changed some. He said it would take months for me to get rid of the toxic condition. This may be true of you, too, but here I am, the lay diagnostician, and I don't know anything about anything.

"Janie, I feel terrible I didn't get to see your play this summer in Southampton. I wanted to go but again I didn't have the energy. Can you imagine an energyless Libby? I can't, but here it is smack in front of me."

Libby's weariness enveloped her, and her deepening depressions were becoming more prolonged. Unable to combat them, she voluntarily committed herself to the Four Winds Sanatorium in Katonah, New York, where doctors were conducting experiments with lithium in an attempt to cure, or at least to alleviate, manic-depression. Libby was treated with the new drug for three months. She rested, underwent occupational therapy, and received medical treatment for her lesser maladies. Only Schanker was permitted to visit her, but he came infrequently.

Libby resisted the lithium treatments. Not only did they make her physically ill, but she feared that she would lose her energy altogether. When she returned to Treetops, her behavior manifested itself in periods of frantic, overwrought talk, during which she chattered volubly to Alice Byrd of Topper—how much Alice would have liked the boy, how marvelous, how intelligent, how noble he had been. These periods alternated with protracted bouts of moody silence, during which she did little more than sob.

During the early summer of 1970, she received a letter from Paul Bowles that reduced her to a state of near collapse. Bowles had just returned to Tangier from Málaga in Spain, where Jane was now institutionalized in the Clínica de Los Angeles. "Jane is in a terrible state," he wrote. "I don't think there is any hope that she will ever talk again, or move at all. The doctor seems to have abandoned hope, and says we can only wait. She did recognize me, I'm sure, but it was something far away and fleeting, the recognition. Everyone tells me she does not suffer, either physically or mentally, but *how* can one tell?"

Libby knew that suffering did not have to be visible to exist. Jane suffered, just as she suffered. Unlike Jane, however, Libby could still talk, she could still move about the house; and, in a curious way, she envied her stricken friend. "I, too," she wrote, "long for my body to overtake my mind."

Libby welcomed death, but she wished to know how it was possible to die with equanimity. In October, she and Alec Wilder drove from Treetops to Sarah Lawrence College to attend a lecture given by a venerated teacher of Zen. The roshi was dying but taking it stoically—the theme of his talk that afternoon, and the reason Libby had come to hear him.

The sixty-three-year-old Wilder was almost the only friend Libby continued to see from what she liked to think of as "the old vagabond days." During the drive to Sarah Lawrence, Libby snipped her cigarettes in half and lined them up on the dashboard, smoking them like whole cigarettes in her white-plastic cigarette holder. As they turned into the college grounds, Libby said to Wilder: "There's nothing left, you know. It's all bullshit." She could no longer tolerate what she called "the coming dark age," an age in which there were "no manners, no wit, no elegance." In Libby's view, the world was an alien place with little purpose or meaning. She didn't say it self-pityingly; and when they reached the lecture hall, Libby instructed the chauffeur to turn around and take them home. She didn't need a Buddhist monk to teach her how to die.

On May 23, 1971, Libby turned sixty-seven. She continued to tell everyone she was two years younger (and everyone believed her) and, after all the years of saying so, she had come to believe it herself. Now that she was "sixty-five," Libby insisted on obtaining her Social Security benefits and instructed her lawyer to secure them. She didn't need the money, of course, and she was two years overdue, but the principle was inviolate. On this birthday, Libby informed Aiko, her Japanese cook, not to make a cake; then, when none appeared, she was furious. She spent her birthday sitting by the oval pool drinking Soave Bolla.

For more than twenty years, Libby had opened Treetops to the public for the annual blooming of her million daffodils. That spring, some two hundred fifty people came, including Libby's acquaintances Irina Alexander Reede and Frederic Bradlee. Initially, Libby couldn't face them; she was depressed and despised her new hairdo—marcelled in waves down the sides of her head. But she changed her mind, mingling with her guests in a white cotton embroidered Mexican dress with a divided skirt. She sported dark glasses and wore gold rings on every finger but her thumbs. Bradlee thought she looked like her old self—"a lithe and bronzed Mata Hari."

After strolling through the fields of daffodils, Irina Reede and Frederic Bradlee walked down to the playroom at the bottom of the house. The walls of the room were cluttered with photographs of Libby's old friends—signed photographs in red wooden frames which she had collected over the years—photographs of Tallulah and Monty and Clifton and Phillips and Ralph and Josh and Lucius and Dwight and Martin and Touche and dozens and dozens of others.

They had been in the playroom for only a moment or two when Libby appeared from the direction of the pool. "I should have known I'd find you two down here," she said. And then, indicating the photographs, she thrust her thin tanned arm through the air and, without a trace of emotion, said, "Everybody's *dead, dead, dead.* This place is like a mortuary."

63

A T SIXTY-SEVEN, ALL OF LIBBY'S ASSETS SEEMED TO HER LIKE liabilities. All was age and sorrow. She had worked and spent, she had reaped and acquired. She had fulfilled all her adolescent dreams only to discover that they were not what she had imagined them to be. With few friends, and locked into a loveless marriage, she turned more and more to her staff. They had become her sustenance, the few people for whom she genuinely cared. For some years now, Libby had maintained twelve employees at Treetops: First and foremost, there was Alice Byrd, her personal maid; then Roger McStocker, the superintendent, and his three gardeners; William Hill, the Scottish butler; Mara Dragbratovitch, the Yugoslavian housemaid; Lewis Trigg, the black houseman and chauffeur; Joseph Barash, the Syrian second houseman; Mary Panaszy, the Romanian laundress; Aiko, the Japanese cook; and Rose Minor, Libby's secretary.

Rose had worked for Libby for fifteen years, a period she described as "blissful" but for the odious presence of Louis

Schanker. She had been prepared at first to overlook his craven manner, his bullying behavior, but she refused to ignore his cruel treatment of Libby. Schanker in turn was jealous of Rose's close relationship with his wife. Finally, he forced Rose to resign, and Libby, clutching on to her and crying fitfully, agreed to let her go. After ten years of marriage, Schanker brooked no opposition; he was completely in control.

Libby promptly hired a new secretary, a widow named Marie Stevens. The fifty-year-old Mrs. Stevens was hesitant about accepting the position since she had heard that Libby had a drinking problem but, on meeting her, changed her mind. Mrs. Stevens was expected to type Libby's correspondence, make the household purchases and pay the salaries and bills. At first, the rest of the staff was hostile toward her. They had been fond of Rose and believed she had been fired unjustly. It took Mrs. Stevens several weeks to win them over.

For the first few months of her employment, Mrs. Stevens was unaware that Libby nurtured a preoccupation with death. One evening, however, she mentioned, in passing, that when her time came, she would not wish to be a burden on anyone. Libby asked how she intended to avoid this, and Mrs. Stevens explained that following her husband's terminal illness, she had saved a certain quantity of Demerol, which she would use if life became intolerable. Libby brightened immediately, demanding to know where she concealed her cache. Sensing that Libby's interest was a morbid one, Mrs. Stevens said she wasn't sure, that she probably kept it in her New York apartment. Libby never asked her about it again; but her eerie curiosity had shaken Mrs. Stevens, and she decided to keep a more vigilant eye on her employer.

In recent months, Libby had noticed she was losing her hearing, an adversity her mother had endured. She was emaciated and had great difficulty walking. But these maladies were trifles compared with the more subtle afflictions that troubled Libby's mind: her chronic feelings of frustration and despair; her inability to laugh easily anymore. For Libby, laughter had been the only remedy "to keep," as she said, "the blues at bay."

As her depressions became more severe, Libby began again to seek that person she imagined to be her true self—only to discern a stranger, and worse, a stranger she disliked and feared.

She had come to think of herself as a ghost town, populated by ominous shadows, by errant winds and creaking doors. To survive required hope, or the illusion of hope, but Libby had failed to keep that dream alive. She had lost it somewhere—in one or another of the countless cul-de-sacs into which she had strayed.

Summer descended on the eastern coast of America early that year. By noon at Treetops, on Friday, June 18, the temperature was over ninety degrees. Other than Libby and Louis Schanker, there was no one in the house but the servants—except for William Hill, who was in East Hampton, readying Dune House for Libby's annual summer sojourn.

Libby slept late that morning. She rose after ten, dressed, and came downstairs. She ate no breakfast and went directly to the library, where, moments later, she was joined by Schanker. She felt particularly weary, especially depressed, and almost at once initiated a loud and raucous argument with her husband. Normally, Libby took two Seconals each day; but for weeks she had badgered Schanker for an additional supply. That morning, she demanded twenty more. Schanker, as he had always done, refused and Libby began to cry.

Unable to control herself, she was sobbing silently, tears running down her face. Schanker looked out the window, exasperated. Alice Byrd entered the library and, scowling at Schanker, knelt at Libby's side, squeezed her hand, and assured her that everything would be just fine. But Libby was inconsolable. It broke Alice's heart to see her so weakened, so vulnerable. Reckoning there was little she could do until the tantrum passed, Alice withdrew to the flower room and arranged a bouquet of chrysanthemums.

Schanker had never seen his wife so distraught. He called Dr. Ruth Brickner, Libby's psychiatrist. When he reached her, Libby took the telephone, attempting to explain just how her depressions affected her. "You don't understand," she screamed. "They're *bottomless.*" Dr. Brickner suggested that Libby admit herself to a nursing home. Libby refused.

Shortly afterward, Mrs. Stevens entered the library. Libby was sitting on the sofa alone, her face contorted from crying. She bade Mrs. Stevens good morning and reminded her to call her lawyer. Nine days before, Libby had changed the codicils of her will, inexplicably cutting out many friends and relatives, and she wanted to assure herself that her lawyer had completed everything to her satisfaction.

Mrs. Stevens nodded and handed her the morning mail. She watched as Libby dropped the envelopes, piece by piece, into the wastebasket, saying, *"Drek, drek, drek."* She then opened a small pink envelope—an invitation from Coretta King asking Libby to a recital in Atlanta in which her daughter was singing. Libby brightened and said: "Darling, make out a check for five hundred dollars and write a nice little note wishing her success and happiness."

She began to cry again. Mrs. Stevens took her hand, asking if there was anything she could do. "Nothing, nothing," said Libby. *"Nothing* can help me now." Mrs. Stevens recommended vitamin B therapy, pointing out that Libby was excessively thin. Libby laughed, almost angrily. "Oh, Mrs. Stevens, A.A.D.," she said—a reference to a recent joke the two women shared—A.A.D. standing for "Also A Doctor." But Libby agreed to take the vitamin B. "I'm so miserable, I'll take anything," she said.

Mrs. Stevens went up to her room to fetch the pills, and when she returned, Libby had gone. From the window that overlooked the oval swimming pool, she saw Libby sitting in a chaise longue in the sun. Her bra, her purse and her sunglasses lay on a table beside her.

Some minutes later, Aiko, the cook, asked Mrs. Stevens if Mrs. Reynolds would like to have some lunch. Mrs. Stevens told her that Mrs. Reynolds was outside and that Aiko should ask her. Twenty minutes later, Libby ate lunch by the pool—a bowl of beef broth with tofu and a salad of wilted greens left over from dinner the night before. She had to be helped to the table by Schanker.

At one o'clock, Mrs. Stevens went out to the pool to see if Libby wanted anything, but she had disappeared again. She rushed upstairs to Libby's bedroom; the door was closed, and Mrs. Stevens assumed, as Alice had assumed, that Libby was napping as she sometimes did in the early afternoon. She returned to her office on the ground floor, wrote out the check to Coretta King and typed a note, which Libby would sign when she awakened.

* * *

Earlier that day, Shirley Stowe began the long drive from her home outside Philadelphia to Stamford. Miss Stowe, Michael Kahn's ex-wife, had been invited by Libby to spend the weekend at Treetops. Despite Libby's cheerfulness on the telephone the night before, Miss Stowe knew that she had been enervated by her depressions, and she was concerned.

She drove into Treetops at about four o'clock, and Mrs. Stevens told her that Libby was sleeping. It was a hot steamy afternoon and Miss Stowe decided to swim in the pool. Afterward, she noticed Libby's purse on the poolside table and carried it into the library.

At five-thirty, when Libby had still not emerged from her bedroom, Alice Byrd began to worry. It was unlike Libby to sleep so long. She went up to the bedroom, opened the door, and peered into the darkened room. Libby's bed was empty, unrumpled. Alice rushed downstairs and told Mara, the maid, Mrs. Stevens, and Shirley Stowe that Libby had disappeared. Nothing else was said, but the four women exchanged taut looks of concern and began a methodical search of every room in the large house. Shirley ran to the studio, where Schanker had retreated after lunch, and they scoured the surrounding woods.

It was soon obvious that Libby was not in the house. Alice and Mara checked the greenhouse, which was empty also. On the way back to the main house, they looked into the garage, entering through the side door. It was intolerably hot inside and they saw what appeared to be a huge cloud of steam. The massive oak garage doors had been closed and all the windows were tightly shut; but Libby was not to be found in the garage either. Just before leaving, Mara suggested they look inside the Rolls-Royce. "*Surely*, not the Rolls?" said Alice. But they looked anyway.

Opening the door on the driver's side, they found Libby—wearing only a bikini bottom, stretched out on the front seat, her head resting beneath the steering wheel. The key was in the ignition in the off position. Curiously, Libby was not lying as though she had been sitting behind the steering wheel and had then slumped over; she looked, Alice thought, as though someone had laid her there. She was still breathing. She was warm and limp, and the most extraordinary expression of happiness illuminated her face. Alice and Mara began to scream. They screamed and screamed and were unable to stop.

Hearing them, Mrs. Stevens ran to the garage, glanced at

Libby, then raced up the drive to summon Schanker and Shirley
Stowe. She shouted, but no sound came from her throat. Just
then, Roger McStocker pulled into the drive in his jeep. Mrs.
Stevens told him what had happened, and McStocker yelled for
Schanker and Shirley. Moments later, they raced from the
woods, Schanker dashing into the house to call Dr. William Resnick, Libby's retired physician. Resnick told him to rush Libby to
Stamford Hospital. He would call ahead, he said, and tell the
doctors to expect them.

Alice Byrd fetched a quilt from her room and carried it to
the garage. Then, Schanker and Mara raised Libby from the
Rolls and laid her down on the quilt. Schanker gave her mouth-
to-mouth resuscitation, but Libby did not respond. She neither
groaned nor spoke. Only once did she even open her eyes, looking as though she were trying to remember something.

Libby was lifted into the back of her Buick station wagon and
placed on the floor. Mrs. Stevens lay next to her, giving her
mouth-to-mouth resuscitation. She felt a slight pulse in Libby's
neck; the emaciated body was still warm. McStocker drove
rapidly, taking the shortcut to Stamford Hospital. About halfway
there, Mrs. Stevens realized that the quilt and her hand were
soaked with urine. Libby's sphincter muscles had relaxed.

They arrived at Stamford General Hospital's emergency
room at 6:45 P.M. The doctors were waiting and Libby was carried to an upstairs operating room. Schanker, McStocker, Shirley
Stowe and Marie Stevens huddled together in the station wagon,
neither looking at nor speaking to one another. Ten minutes
later, a doctor appeared at the hospital door and beckoned to
Schanker, and Schanker wearily left the car and walked into the
hospital. He stood in silence for a moment or two, listening to
the doctor, then trudged back to the station wagon. His head was
bowed, his eyes were dry, and he muttered, so softly at first that
it was difficult to hear him: "We've lost her." And then again
more loudly: "We've lost her."

They drove slowly back to Treetops. All the passengers were
miserable, and they snapped at one another unreasonably. The
next morning, Shirley Stowe returned to Philadelphia. Tim and
Tony, whom Schanker had called the night before, arrived, and
they wandered through the house, shocked and desolate. The

days that followed were, as Mrs. Stevens said, "a nightmare." The house seemed filled with a kind of eerie muttering—"If only. If only"—repeated endlessly like a litany. If only Shirley Stowe had come to Treetops earlier. If only Tim and Tony had been there. If only Mrs. Stevens had looked for Libby the first time she missed her. If only Schanker had not retreated to his studio. If only Libby had not been left alone.

But she had been left alone too long, and there remained behind the shroud of mystery that had clung to Libby all her life. June 18 had been a torrid summer's day, yet all the windows in the garage had been shut and the massive garage doors, which Roger McStocker raised every morning and did not close until dusk, had been rolled down. The ninety-five-pound Libby could not have closed the doors herself; a strong healthy woman could not have rolled them down. But someone had done so.

When Libby was found, there were no gasoline fumes in the garage, no exhaust stain on the garage door behind the car. The ignition key was in the off position. It was assumed that at the last minute, Libby had changed her mind and switched off the motor. But where had Libby obtained the keys—keys Schanker normally kept with him? She rarely drove anymore and never went to the garage. Most curious, Louis Schanker had told Joseph, the houseman, not to clean the cars that day. It was an odd request, since Joseph cleaned the cars daily, but he had complied with Schanker's wishes.

Libby had been weak and walking awkwardly that morning. The swimming pool and the garage were at opposite ends of the sprawling house. It was a long walk and the servants would always wonder how she had gotten there. The shortest route to the garage was through the kitchen and the servants' quarters, where Aiko, Mara, Alice and Mrs. Stevens had spent the afternoon. But they had not seen Libby pass nor had anyone heard the car engine. Libby's servants discussed these mysteries for years thereafter without ever making any sense of them.

Some days before, Libby had arranged a dinner party for the next night, June 19. Under the circumstances, it seemed perfectly reasonable to cancel it, but Schanker insisted on going ahead as planned. The guests were Libby's friends Olga and Joseph Hirshhorn, and a couple called Greenwald, whom Libby had met on holiday in Cozumel. It had long rankled Schanker that Hirshhorn, one of America's most prestigious collectors of contemporary paintings and sculpture, had only purchased two of his own works of art. Schanker intended to remedy the matter.

That evening, Schanker declared that no one would inhabit Libby's chair and it remained empty at the head of the table, the guests casting furtive glances of horror in its direction. The Greenwalds, who had not been informed of Libby's death until after they had arrived, were mortified; Joseph Hirshhorn was unable to eat; and the conversation trickled away into brief and then longer silences, punctuated by the hearty sounds of Schanker's appetite. Before dinner ended, the four guests made polite excuses and exited hastily, leaving Schanker to devour his dessert alone.

Libby's death certificate, issued on June 23, stated that her death was due to suicide, pending further study, adding that she had had a history of drinking and depression. The official coroner's report was not made public until July 12. Dr. Elliot Gross said that the cause of death was acute carbon-monoxide poisoning. Libby's blood was filled with 70 percent carbon monoxide, almost twice the amount required to kill her. She also had 0.12 percent alcohol in her blood, making her legally intoxicated.

In her last will, executed nine days before her death, Libby bequeathed Treetops and forty acres of land to the School of Applied and Fine Arts of Boston University. She left some $3,354,000 to her family and associates, including bequests of $1 million apiece to her sons, Tim and Tony, $850,000 to Louis Schanker, and substantial sums to Jane Bowles, Gerald Cook, Marcus Blechman, Alice Byrd, William Hill and the Zen Studies Society, Inc., in New York. For federal tax purposes, Libby's estate was valued at $13.2 million, the bulk of which was donated to the Christopher Reynolds Foundation.

Libby's body was taken to the Boulton Funeral Home in Stamford and cremated. Her ashes were scattered at Treetops in one of her favorite places—a daffodil bed next to an enormous boulder on a path leading up to the tennis court. In her memory, Roger McStocker planted six pure-white Libby Holman daffodils there.

*   *   *

Ned Rorem was at Yaddo, an artists' retreat near Saratoga Springs, New York, for the summer, where he read Libby's obituary in the New York *Times*. On June 22, he made a lengthy entry in his diary:

> Libby Holman has killed herself. Somehow this doesn't come as a surprise. For if Libby was the richest woman in the world (becoming richer as the men in her life died off), also celebrated and humored with special friendships, the specter of violence tracked her from the start. There are a very few people of talent you can thoroughly know within an hour, and who yet continue to nourish you for years. Their capacity comes not so much from their genius as from their generosity. Cocteau was like that. So certainly was John Latouche. Marc Blitzstein somewhat, and Libby too. She was lavish with warmth, and owned the most original of baritone voices, which she gave to us all. I remember dining with her and Marc (1959? 1960?), just the three of us, in a bistro near Marc's one evening, before a lecture by Alan Watts. A few years later Marc would be painfully slain on the island of Martinique and last night in the garage of her Connecticut home Libby died. My intuition was that Libby, like other famous female talents with a penchant for beautiful cripples, in deciding at fifty to reverse the coin and espouse a stolid middle-aged painter, would have found a certain peace through Louis Schanker, as Marie Laure found through Oscar Dominquez. Intuition's discouragingly false.

Tragedy had shadowed Libby from the beginning, had shaped and colored all her dreams, and it was not to end with her death. On April 30, 1973, Jane Bowles, who had lost her sight, her speech and her sanity, died a hopeless schizophrenic at the Clínica del Los Angeles in Málaga. She was fifty-six and was buried by her husband, Paul, in Málaga in an unmarked grave. On February 8, 1976, Louisa Carpenter, while approaching Wilmington Airport in her private plane, crashed, the plane bursting into flames on impact. She was sixty-eight. Although horrified, there were those of Libby's friends who liked to claim that she had been a witch after all, that her hand stretched far beyond the grave.

MANHATTAN: SUMMER 1971

64

O N WEDNESDAY, JUNE 30, A MEMORIAL SERVICE WAS HELD for Libby at the Friends Meeting House at 15 Rutherford Place off East Sixteenth Street in New York. In the back of the room on the center aisle, Roger McStocker and Alice Byrd had arranged an enormous bouquet of chrysanthemums that they had brought down from Treetops. It was a traditional Quaker service with people rising as the spirit moved them to murmur a prayer or to extol the virtues of the deceased.

The little meeting house was crowded. Louis Schanker was there, as were Tim and Tony, David Holman and Michael Kahn, and Libby's younger brother, Alfred Holman, Jr. There were Libby's close associates—her lawyer, Jack Clareman; her pianist, Gerald Cook; and her psychiatrist, Dr. Ruth Brickner. Many of her staff had come—Roger McStocker, Alice Byrd, William Hill and Marie Stevens. Also in attendance were numerous old friends such as Kay Swift, Tamara Geva, George Lloyd, Frank Williams, Peter and Susan Caldwell, Ruth Escherick, Alec Wilder and Mrs. Martin Luther King, Jr. Few of them believed that Libby had actually committed suicide.

Dr. Brickner was the first to speak, berating herself for failing to heed the warnings that Libby had given that final day. She grieved, she said, for the loss of a close friend and considered Libby's death a dereliction of her duties. Alfred Holman bared his soul, attempting to explain why he and his sister had failed to understand one another over the years. Tamara Geva spoke of Libby's irrepressible spirit and energy, a Libby of the thirties that few people thereafter had had the opportunity to know. George Lloyd talked of Libby's magic, her terrifying, seductive charm. She had taught him, he said, the freedoms that come from laughter, and the end of inhibition. Michael Kahn gave a brief soliloquy on Libby's life and troubled times, concluding by saying that no one, not even himself, had recognized that she had been reaching out for help. Coretta King talked of how devoted Libby had been to championing the underdog, the downtrodden and underprivileged. Mrs. King asked one of her daughters to speak and the little girl spoke fondly of "Aunt Libby," hoping she would be happy in heaven.

Alec Wilder stood at the back of the meeting house next to the large spray of chrysanthemums. He disapproved of memorial services. The mourners tended to flatter blatantly or employ the unctuous art of equivocation. In any event, this was not the Libby he remembered—this soft-hearted samaritan, this champion of the underdog. She had been grander and, yes, more wicked than any of these testimonials revealed.

As Coretta King's daughter expressed the hope that Libby be happy in heaven, Wilder groaned and left the room. Walking down Sixteenth Street, he began to laugh, remembering Libby's saying: "Alec, can you imagine spending an *eternity* in heaven? So *dull,* so *commonplace,* like being detained in some quack's waiting room."

That was the Libby Wilder chose to remember: the joyous wit, the naughty voice, the passionate poses, the bright, unconquerable savoir-faire. He would love her for as long as he lived. And then, he remembered something else—a snatch of a poem, a proverb perhaps, that Libby had loved to quote. It was French, he believed, an old saying she had heard in Paris many years before, and was, he felt, as good an epitaph for her as any. It would have made her laugh. Now, turning up Fifth Avenue, Wilder recited it out loud, repeating it over and over again, trying, as best he could, to imitate Libby's throaty baritone. Strangers turned to stare as he intoned:

> I owe much
> I have nothing
> The rest I give to the poor.

ACKNOWLEDGMENTS

It goes without saying, and so it must be said, that a great number of people contributed incalculably to this book. Without their generous assistance, remarkable memories and, in some cases, lengthy annotations of my various drafts, I would not have been able to complete it. I am particularly grateful to Lucinda Ballard (Mrs. Howard Dietz); Paul Bowles, who talked and corresponded volubly; the unstinting generosity of Emily Coleman and Terry Ferrer; Dr. Alexander Cox, who remained silent for nearly fifty years before telling me of his crucial role in the Smith Reynolds affair; Ray Dennis for his hilarious anecdotes; Mrs. Eleanor Dickson for her encyclopedic knowledge of music, nighteries, dances and fashions of the twenties; Alice Byrd Edwards, Libby's noble personal maid and creator of the finest southern-fried chicken in Connecticut; George Lloyd, pantomimist and peanut butter man, whose wit and kindliness spurred me on; Mrs. Gladys Orton, gracious hostess, the belle of Cincinnati; Mary Overton, lioness of the links; Frances Pfeiffer, my mother-in-law, who housed me and fed me and kept me out of the local bars during innumerable research trips to North Carolina; R. H. Shepherd, who meticulously annotated the seven separate drafts of the North Carolina section; Lynn Vinson for providing me with Topper's essays, poetry and short stories; and the late Alec Wilder, whose droll insights into Libby's life were invaluable.

To those named below and those too numerous to list, I offer my heartfelt thanks: Howard Baer, James Baggs, the late Eugenia Bankhead, Ted Benedict, Bill Broadwater, Susan Caldwell, Peter Caldwell

391

and Jane Waters, Dick and Edie Chatham, the late Delancy Cleveland, Tamara Geva, Gigi Gilpin, Peter Glenville, Paul Godkin, the late Carlisle Higgins, William Hill, David Holman, Jack Larson, Mrs. Elizabeth Levy, Bobby Lewis, Dalton McMichael, Edith Meiser, Rose Minor, Terence Netter, Joseph J. O'Donahue IV, Jennings Perry, Tony Reynolds, Ned Rorem, the late Arthur Schwartz, the late Guy Scott, Marie Stevens Shapiro, the late Leonard Sillman, Mrs. Mimi Spear, Ray Stark, Mrs. Vincent Stegeman, Mrs. Sunny Tingle, Dr. Frank Williams and the late Tennessee Williams.

I would also like to thank Ellen S. Dunlap, research librarian of the University of Texas; Susan Sims of the Rochester *Sentinel* in Rochester, Indiana; Linda Ellis of the Special Collections Department at the Carl Blegen Library at the University of Cincinnati; Miles Kreuger of the Institute of the American Musical in Los Angeles; Dr. Howard Gottlieb, director of special collections at the Mugar Memorial Library at Boston University, wherein resides the Libby Holman Collection, and Ned Rorem for allowing me to use excerpts from his published diaries.

Then, too, there were individual contributions for which I am greatly indebted: John Dodds; Arlene Donovan; my researcher Jane Furth; Bert Padell; my illustrious agent, Amanda Urban of ICM; and most important, the shrewd and inestimable assistance of my editor Harvey Ginsberg. I am also thankful for the cunning counsels of such writers as Nik Cohn, Elizabeth Dobell, A. J. Langguth, Dory Previn, Frances Ring and, particularly, A. Scott Berg, who labored over my penultimate draft with the patience of Job, the wisdom of Solomon.

Finally, this book could never have been completed without the unending encouragement, patience and support of my wife, Carolyn. It is dedicated to her (and to our daughter, Shannon) with love and gratitude.

NOTES

Most of my material came from primary sources—that is, from interviews I conducted with almost everyone living who knew her. Aside from that, for early Cincinnati history, I relied on the Cincinnati Historical Society or old issues of the Cincinnati *Enquirer* and the Cincinnati *Post*, and her early interviews, particularly a long account in *Collier's* magazine on November 16, 1929.

All information directly concerning the Reynolds family history was taken from the files of the Winston-Salem Public Library, from the Winston-Salem *Journal* and *Sentinel*, and Smith Reynolds's account of his solo flight from England to Hong Kong from his log—privately published by his sister Nancy in New York in 1932. In the North Carolina section, most of the direct quotes were derived from the complete transcript of the coroner's inquest (309 pages long), given to me by the late Carlisle Higgins, the state solicitor in the case. The assistance of Slick Shepherd was invaluable since he covered the inquest for UP and had grown up in Winston with most of its participants.

The one other principal source on which I relied was the collection of Libby's papers and memorabilia which, prior to her death, she presented to Boston University.

A few supplementary notes:

CHAPTER 2.

(Page 15) According to family legend, the Holzmans were from Alsace-Lorraine in eastern France, their original name being Boishomme. In 1871, when Germany annexed the

393

provinces, they required all intellectuals to Teutonize
their names, Boishomme being altered to Holzman. That
was merely legend, but it was the legend Libby preferred.

CHAPTER 4.

(Page 24)   Rachel detested Libby's singing voice, its peculiarity, and
insisted she take up the violin. For two years, Libby was
forced to endure violin lessons and was always an inept
student. Whenever relatives visited the apartment, Libby
would be called on to perform. As one of those relatives
recalled, it was "a fond if not melodious memory."

One night in 1915, Mischa Elman, the noted Russian
violinist, was persuaded to attend one of Libby's recitals in
the Holzman living room. When Libby concluded her
brief repertoire, Rachel asked the maestro what he recommended she do with Libby's ear. "Washing them twice
a day has its advantages," he said.

(Page 27)   Libby was not raised in the Jewish faith, her parents having converted to the Christian Science Church.

(Page 33)   Castle Farm was a huge hall just beyond Cincinnati's city
limits. Many of the big bands of the period came there to
play. At Castle Farm, Libby and her friends listened and
danced to the music of Paul Whiteman, Ben Bernie, the
Goldkette Band, Coon-Saunders and his Kansas City
Nighthawks, Guy Lombardo, and Ted Lewis, known as
"The High-Hatted Tragedian of Song."

CHAPTER 5.

(Page 34)   Smith's suicide notes were introduced as evidence at the
coroner's inquest by Libby.

CHAPTER 9.

(Page 40)   ". . . to no apparent end": The tale was told of a brilliant
young man who had consumed prodigious quantities of
cognac since Prohibition began. When asked by a sympathetic bartender why he had commenced his spree, the
young man explained that he had started to drink in
order to forget a girl, that he continued to drink because
he could not remember her name. He was trying to remember who he was trying to forget.

CHAPTER 14.

(Page 85)   "Still, he was always there . . .": Libby was arrested for indecent exposure on a beach near Saint-Jean-de-Luz and Smith gallantly paid the fine.

(Page 87)   "Body and Soul" is one of the biggest selling records of all time. In 1974 it was elected to the National Academy of Recording Arts and Sciences Hall of Fame.

CHAPTER 16.

(Page 96)   "As the Depression slipped further and further . . .": By the end of 1932, there would be some 16 million unemployed in America and 21,000 Americans committed suicide that year.

CHAPTER 17.

(Page 109) The vast majority of the quotations in chapters 17 through 22 are taken verbatim from the 309-page transcript of the coroner's inquest set up to investigate "the mysterious death of Smith Reynolds."

(Page 110) "The evening was spent discussing Libby . . .": Carlisle Higgins told me that Smith and Ab had imported two prostitutes from Newport News to the Robert E. Lee Hotel that night, but that fact was never introduced as evidence at the inquest and seems, in fact, little more than innuendo.

CHAPTER 18.

(Page 112) "Smith had promised them an unforgettable evening . . .": There would have been other guests that evening, but it was the Fourth of July weekend and many of Smith's friends had withdrawn to the mountains, to Roaring Gap. Elizabeth 'Blitz' Dillard, who would marry Dick Reynolds six months later, had wanted to come, but her father had packed her off to Rocky Mount to keep her out of trouble. Martha Maslin's family maid had had a miscarriage that afternoon so Martha was compelled to remain at home. Caldwell Roane was called suddenly out of town. Albert "Judge" Wharton, whose father was superintendent of Reynolda House, and who would later become Anne Cannon Reynolds's fourth husband, had intended to come, but he had gotten drunk and woke up the next morning in Greensboro. David Lybrook had also planned to come, but he too had gotten drunk that afternoon, so drunk, in fact, that while flying home, he negotiated his plane beneath every bridge along the Yadkin River. Adela "Pet" Sheppard longed to go; she had attended several of the Reynolda parties in June. But her father had forbidden her to go to Reynolda House again. He disapproved of actresses and did not want his eighteen-year-old daughter consorting with too high-stepping a crowd.

CHAPTER 23.

(Page 149)   The majority of Sheriff Transou Scott's "puzzlements" were given to me by his brother, the late Guy Scott.

(Page 150)   The series in the New York *Daily Mirror* began on August 15 and ran for the rest of that summer.

CHAPTER 24.

(Page 155)   After talking to Slick, Dick Reynolds told reporters: "I knew Libby only slightly. I suppose I knew less about Smith's married life than any other person in the world. His marriage was a surprise to me, since we were very close and had no secrets from each other. There never was any suicide complex with Smith so that angle seems very strange to me."

CHAPTER 29.

(Page 173)   "The history of that night will always remain obscure . . .": The fatal bullet was never found, although Carlisle Higgins claimed to have found it, but he never produced it as evidence. The empty shell casings were never checked to see if they had actually come from the Mauser, and the trajectory of the bullet was inconsistent with Libby's view that Smith had been standing up when he shot himself. Also, it was never conclusively proved whether Smith was right- or left-handed.

(Page 176)   ". . . Ab had another, and what seemed at the time more sensible, idea": This crucial omission in Ab's testimony was given to me by C. G. Hill's widow, Nancy.

(Page 177)   "But upstairs alone in her bedroom . . .": Libby told this story to at least three people, all of whom related it to me.

CHAPTER 31.

(Page 184)   In the first two years after Topper's birth, Libby turned down many chances to return to Broadway, including a request from Vinton Freedley, the Broadway producer, that she join the cast of Cole Porter's *Anything Goes*. The show, ultimately to be called the quintessential musical comedy of the thirties, opened in New York on November 21, 1934, running for 420 performances. It increased the fame of Libby's "replacement," Ethel Merman, who sang such songs as "You're the Top" and "I Get a Kick Out of You."

CHAPTER 33.

(Page 192)   ". . . was temporarily banned on the radio": The lyric began:
You and the night and the music
Fill me with flaming desire
Setting my being completely on fire.

You and the night and the music
Thrill me
But will we
Be one?

(Page 195)   *Reckless* was not the only film to have been based on Libby's life. In 1956, MGM released a film called *Written on the Wind*. Directed by Douglas Sirk, it starred Rock Hudson, Lauren Bacall, Robert Stack and Dorothy Malone, who won an Oscar for best supporting actress that year in the role of the alcoholic nymphomaniac. It was based on the novel of the same title, written in 1945 by Robert Wilder, but the producers, fearing libel perhaps, changed the locale from North Carolina to Texas, from tobacco to oil.

    The novel is an obvious reconstruction of Libby's tragic marriage to Smith Reynolds. When the book was published, Libby wanted to bring a libel suit against the publishers, but her lawyer dissuaded her on the grounds that it would only help to increase the sales of the book. Libby never saw the film.

CHAPTER 36.

(Page 215) Nicholas Ray had been involved with folk singing since before the war, directing a weekly show for Columbia Broadcasting System called *Back Where I Come From,* which included Burl Ives, Earl Robinson, Woody Guthrie, young Pete Seeger, Leadbelly, Josh White and the Golden Gate Quartet.

CHAPTER 38.

(Page 226) Chinky Collins is a pseudonym.

CHAPTER 39.

(Page 232) Nancy Overland is a pseudonym.

CHAPTER 40.

(Page 241) Libby despised Harry Truman. Three years later, in 1948, Libby was listed among the financial angels backing Henry Wallace's third-party candidacy for President. "The Wallace vote," she said, "will be important enough to make the politicians sit up and take notice of the liberal-thinking American's wishes." Harry Truman, of course, won the 1948 presidential campaign, narrowly defeating Thomas Dewey. Wallace won less than 2 percent of the popular vote.

(Page 243) Following her affair with Gary Cooper, Clara Bow is alleged to have said: "Poor Gary. Poor Gary. He's got the biggest cock in Hollywood, but no ass to push it with."

CHAPTER 46.

(Page 276) The quotation is from an affectionate tribute to Alec Wilder by Whitney Balliett in *The New Yorker,* 1981.

CHAPTER 47.

(Page 280) Lynda Williams is a pseudonym.
(Page 283) Luke Readdy is a pseudonym.

CHAPTER **48.**

(Page 293)   "Flight invariably follows failure . . .": George Lloyd paraphrasing a line of Tennessee Williams's.

(Page 294)   "Cold, dead period": "In terms of memory," Tim Reynolds told me, "I can't remember anything of that period.
But I'm sure I must have said *something*."

CHAPTER **52.**

(Page 318)   "She's in between murders . . .": Tallulah told Patsy Kelly:
"I don't mean she actually *killed* all those people. But they
were kind of set up, as though their deaths were meant to
be."

CHAPTER **55.**

(Page 333)   Several of the quips and stories I have attributed to Libby
have also been attributed to other actresses. Their origins
are impossible to ascertain and the tales may even be
apocryphal, mere gossip or hearsay; but I have ascribed
them to Libby because they were ascribed to her by others
and because they were funny.

CHAPTER **59.**

(Page 359)   "Libby wrote McDowall a letter": During the mid-sixties,
Libby maintained a far-flung correspondence with such
people as Frith Banbury, the British theater director; with
Tom Driberg, the British Member of Parliament; with
Jane and Paul Bowles; with Joan Littlewood, the British
director; and with novelist James Jones, who wrote to her
from Paris in 1966: "I too enjoyed very much meeting
and talking with you. But I must say I did get such a
feeling of immense sanity about you yourself that it was a
considerable pleasure. The older I get the less and less
sane people I seem to see." And Libby replied: "I don't
think I know what 'sanity' is. Please let us all stay being
friends. As I said before, I don't understand about sanity,
but I think I have a vague idea about friendship. When I
want it, I want it bad."

(Page 361)   "7. Lipsy Colmar Collection": In 1965, Boston University
asked Libby to donate a collection of her memorabilia to
them and Libby agreed. "Isn't it silly," she wrote. "I have
thrown practically everything away. I have never been a

'keeper,' so to speak. However, they have dug up quite a lot of paraphernalia about me. I don't feel people should be keeping a collection of me anyway. It made me feel dead. So I insisted on going up and doing a concert for them. They had a Libby Holman Week . . . I loved giving the concert but hated having a reception in the midst of all my past. I took off my glasses so the whole thing became a blur and was bearable."

(Page 361) "11. Teller of My Life History to Biographer . . .": During 1965 and 1966, Libby attempted to tell her story (for the purposes of a book) to a young friend named Susan Caldwell, the wife of Peter Caldwell, Topper's best friend at the Putney School. Ironically (an irony not lost on Libby), Mrs. Caldwell was from North Carolina, a member of the Hanes family, and her uncle, Dr. Fred Hanes, was the chief doctor who had worked over the unconscious body of Smith Reynolds at Baptist Hospital. The series of taped interviews was finally aborted. Libby always refused to talk about Smith Reynolds's death and, whenever she mentioned her father, broke down and cried.

CHAPTER 63.

(Page 378) "As her depressions became more severe . . .": From a conversation with Alec Wilder.

(Page 385) "Tragedy had shadowed Libby from the beginning . . .": Libby was a prominent member of the pantheon of doomed American women—Zelda Fitzgerald, Frances Farmer, Judy Garland, Sylvia Plath, Jane Bowles, Carson McCullers, Diane Arbus and Marilyn Monroe. And she knew two of them very well. A few years after Libby died, Harold Clurman and David Diamond were walking in the Rose Garden at Yaddo, the artists' colony near Saratoga Springs, New York, reminiscing about several of the tragic women they had known in common—McCullers, Farmer, Bowles, Monroe and Libby—and Diamond said: "They all had great, expansive, tortured souls, as far as one can sense the 'soul,' and they seemed not only to enjoy their tragedies, but seemed somehow to seek them out."

ADDENDA:

Louis Schanker died on May 8, 1981, at the Lenox Hill Hospital in Manhattan. He was seventy-eight. Up until his death, he lived, for the most part, in Libby's New York brownstone and in Dune House in East Hampton.

Libby's adopted sons, Tim and Tony, live and work in New England.

Libby's three homes are now occupied by others. Dune House was recently purchased by Roone Arledge of ABC Television.

The New York brownstone at 121 East Sixty-first Street is now the headquarters of the Christopher Reynolds Foundation, although Libby's quarters on the top two floors are rented privately.

Treetops was bequeathed to the School of Applied and Fine Arts at Boston University, but because it was not sufficiently endowed, the estate was returned to the foundation and was subsequently purchased by the Champion International Corporation who use it as a retreat for their senior executives. Champion International maintains Treetops as Libby would have wished and the estate is opened to the public every spring for the blooming of Libby's million daffodils.

Since its founding in 1952, the Christopher Reynolds Foundation has made grants and endowments of $3.5 million, nearly a third of which was donated to programs dealing with civil rights. Today, with assets of about $13 million, annual grants are devoted, in the main, to international relations, with emphasis on peace and disarmament programs. Its current focus is on Southeast Asia. Grants have been made for providing humanitarian aid to Vietnam, Laos and Cambodia, and in support of programs designed to bring about reconciliation and normalization of relations between the United States and these countries.

DISCOGRAPHY

The following is believed to be a complete listing of all Libby Holman's commercial phonograph records, arranged in the order of their release. Because records are not always issued in the same order in which they are made, the titles are numbered in the order of their recording session. Occasionally, Miss Holman will not appear on both sides of a disc. Selections on which she does not appear are unnumbered. In was the custom of Brunswick to issue dance-band records on which the artist performed brief vocals. For release in Germany, variant takes were made omitting her vocals; these appropriate take numbers are also listed.

Wherever possible, the following information is included: date and location of recording, release date, song titles, composers, stage or screen productions when applicable, accompanying musicians, matrix numbers, and catalog numbers.

Probably the most fascinating of the artist's recordings are her early Brunswicks, which coincide with the roots of her stage career. The sketchy information about their recording and release dates is due to the reluctance of MCA Records, the current owner, to assist in this research. Much crucial information about these recordings was supplied by Milton Gabler, retired vice-president of the company. I wish to thank also Tina McCarthy (Columbia), Bernadette Moore (RCA Victor), Kathleen E. Brown (Polygram), Bill Borden (Monmouth Evergreen) and Libby Holman's longtime accompanist, Gerald Cook, for their generous assistance in preparing this discography.

—MILES KREUGER

403

recorded 7-27, New York City   released 9-28-27

1. WHO'S THAT KNOCKIN' AT MY DOOR? (Seymour B. Simons, Gus Kahn)
   mx E-24575/6/7   Brunswick 3667-A

2. CAREFREE (Jo Trent, Peter de Rose)
   mx E-24578/9/80/81   Brunswick 3667-B

recorded c. 1-28, New York City   released 1-25-28

3. THERE AIN'T NO SWEET MAN THAT'S WORTH THE SALT OF MY TEARS (Fred Fisher)
   mx E-26219/20   Brunswick 3798-A

4. THE WAY HE LOVES IS JUST TOO BAD (Billy Curtis, Jackie Rose, Andy Robbins)
   mx E-26221/2   Brunswick 3798-B

recorded c. 6-28, New York City   unreleased Brunswick

5. AFTER YOU'VE GONE (Henry Creamer, Turner Layton)
   mx E-27628 a/b   ———

6. I MUST HAVE THAT MAN (Dorothy Fields, Jimmy McHugh) (from *Lew Leslie's Blackbirds of 1928*)
   mx E-27629 a/b   ———

recorded 6-5-29, New York City   unreleased Victor test
piano accompaniment by
Ralph Rainger

7. CAN'T WE BE FRIENDS? (James Warburg aka Paul James, Kay Swift) (from *The Little Show*)
   mx BVE-417-1   ———

8. MOANIN' LOW (Howard Dietz, Ralph Rainger) (from *The Little Show*)
   mx BVE-418-1   ———

recorded c. 7-10-29, New York City   released 7-13-29

10. AM I BLUE? (Grant Clarke, Harry Akst) (from the film *On with the Show*)
    mx E-30296 a/b   Brunswick 4445

11. MOANIN' LOW (from *The Little Show*)
    mx E-30297 a/b   Brunswick 4445

recorded c. 5-25-29, New York City   released 7-16-29

—. AFTER THINKING IT OVER (Benny Davis, Carmen Lombardo) Al Goodman and His Orchestra, vocal chorus
    mx E-30001   Brunswick 4446

recording date unknown

12. MOANIN' LOW (from *The Little Show*)
The Cotton Pickers, vocal chorus Libby Holman
    mx E-30326 (E-30327   Brunswick 4446   no vocal)

recording date unknown   released 7-15-29

13. HE'S A GOOD MAN TO HAVE AROUND (Jack Yellen, Milton Ager) (from the film *Honky Tonk*)
The Cotton Pickers, vocal chorus Libby Holman
    mx E-30328 (E-30329 no   Brunswick 4447   vocal)

—. SHOO SHOO BOOGEY BOO (Leo Robin, Sam Coslow, Richard Whiting) (from the film *Why Bring That Up?*)
The Cotton Pickers, vocal chorus
    mx E-30330 (E-30331 no   Brunswick 4447
    vocal)

recorded c. 6-30-29, New York City   released 7-17-29

—. PRETTY LITTLE MAID OF OLD MADRID (Benny Davis, J. Fred Coots, Arnold Johnson)
Arnold Johnson and His Orchestra, vocal chorus
    mx E-30097   Brunswick 4453

recorded late 6-29, New York City

9. I'M DOING WHAT I'M DOING FOR LOVE (Jack Yellen, Milton Ager) (from the film *Honky Tonk*)
Colonial Club Orchestra, vocal chorus Libby Holman
    mx E-30288 (E-30289 no   Brunswick 4453
    vocal)

recorded 9-29, New York City   released 9-13-29

14. CAN'T WE BE FRIENDS? (from *The Little Show*)
    mx E-30829 a/b   Brunswick 4506

15. I MAY BE WRONG (BUT I THINK YOU'RE WONDERFUL) (Harry Ruskin, Henry Sullivan) (from *Murray Anderson's Almanac*)
    mx-E-30830 a/b   Brunswick 4506

recorded 11-29, New York City   unreleased 12″ Brunswick

18. MOANIN' LOW (from *The Little Show*)
mx XE-31349 a/b ⎯⎯⎯

19. CAN'T WE BE FRIENDS?
(from *The Little Show*)
mx XE-31350 a/b ⎯⎯⎯

recorded 11-29, New York City   released 11-18-29

20. MY MAN IS ON THE MAKE (Lorenz Hart, Richard Rodgers) (from *Heads Up*)
Colonial Club Orchestra, vocal chorus Libby Holman
mx E-31351   Brunswick 4554

—. I CAN DO WONDERS WITH YOU (Lorenz Hart, Richard Rodgers) (from *Heads Up*)
Colonial Club Orchestra, vocal chorus
mx E- ?   Brunswick 4554
Note: Because this song was deleted from the score of *Heads Up* prior to the show's Broadway opening, it was replaced by the following selection as a recoupling. Libby Holman sings on neither recording.

recorded 12-29, New York City

—. WHY DO YOU SUPPOSE? (Lorenz Hart, Richard Rodgers) (from *Heads Up*)
Colonial Club Orchestra, vocal chorus
mx E-31534/5   Brunswick 4554

recorded 10-29, New York City   released 10-10-29

16. HERE AM I (Oscar Hammerstein II, Jerome Kern) (from *Sweet Adeline*)
mx E-31148 a/b   Brunswick 4570

17. WHY WAS I BORN? (Oscar Hammerstein II, Jerome Kern) (from *Sweet Adeline*)
mx E-31149 a/b   Brunswick 4570

recorded 11-29, New York   released 11-18-29
City

22. MORE THAN YOU KNOW (Billy Rose, Edward Eliscu, Vincent Youmans) (from *Great Day*)
    mx E-31527 a/b   Brunswick 4613

21. HAPPY BECAUSE I'M IN LOVE (Billy Rose, Edward Eliscu, Vincent Youmans) (from *Great Day*)
    mx E-31526 a/b   Brunswick 4613

recorded 12-29, New York   released 12-30-29
City

—. YOU'VE GOT THAT THING (Cole Porter) (from *Fifty Million Frenchmen*)
    Colonial Club Orchestra, vocal chorus Dick Robertson
    mx E-31686/7   Brunswick 4666

23. FIND ME A PRIMITIVE MAN (Cole Porter) (from *Fifty Million Frenchmen*)
    Colonial Club Orchestra, vocal chorus Libby Holman
    mx 31690 a/b   Brunswick 4666

recorded c. 1-22-30, New   released c. 2-30
York City

25. WHEN A WOMAN LOVES A MAN (Billy Rose, Ralph Rainger) (from the film *Be Yourself*)
    Roger Wolfe Kahn and His Orchestra, vocal chorus Libby Holman
    mx E-31962/3   Brunswick 4699

24. COOKING BREAKFAST FOR THE ONE I LOVE (Billy Rose, Henry Tobias) (from the film *Be Yourself*)
    Roger Wolfe Kahn and His Orchestra, vocal chorus Libby Holman
    mx E-31960/1   Brunswick 4699

recorded 1-30, New York City   released 1-30-30

27. WHAT IS THIS THING CALLED LOVE? (Cole Porter) (from *Wake Up and Dream*)
    mx E-31974 a/b   Brunswick 4700

26. A SHIP WITHOUT A SAIL (Lorenz Hart, Richard Rodgers) (from *Heads Up*)
    mx E-31973 a/b   Brunswick 4700

unknown recording date   unreleased Brunswick

28. BODY AND SOUL (Edward Eliscu, Robert Sour, Frank Eyton, John W. Green) (from *Three's a Crowd*)
    mx E-34387 a/b   ———

29. SOMETHING TO REMEMBER YOU BY (Howard Dietz, Arthur Schwartz) (from *Three's a Crowd*)
    mx E-34388 a/b   ———
    Note: The above coupling was scheduled for 9-22-30 release but was canceled. Both selections were rerecorded and released 10-30.

recorded 10-30, New York   released 10-13-30
City

30. BODY AND SOUL (from *Three's a Crowd*)
    mx E-34705/6 (E-34707 test   Brunswick 4910
    piano accompaniment)

31. SOMETHING TO REMEMBER YOU BY (from *Three's a Crowd*)
    mx 34388 a/b   Brunswick 4910

recorded 1-31, New York City   released 2-2-31

32. I'M ONE OF GOD'S CHILDREN (WHO HASN'T GOT WINGS) (Oscar Hammerstein II, Harry Ruskin, Louis Alter) (from *Ballyhoo*)
    mx 35972 a/b   Brunswick 6044

33. LOVE FOR SALE (Cole Porter) (from *The New Yorkers*)
    mx 35973 a/b   Brunswick 6044

recorded 12-19-34, New York
City
accompanied by Richard Himber and His Ritz-Carlton Orchestra

34. YOU AND THE NIGHT AND THE MUSIC (Howard Dietz, Arthur Schwartz) (from *Revenge with Music*)
    mx BS-86484 1/2/2A   Victor 24839-A

35. WHEN YOU LOVE ONLY ONE (Howard Dietz, Arthur Schwartz) (from *Revenge with Music*)
    mx BS-86485 1/1A   Victor 24839-B

36. WANDRIN' HEART (Howard Dietz, Arthur Schwartz) (from *Revenge with Music*)
    mx 86486 1/1A/2   unreleased Victor

recorded 3-23-42, New York
City
album: *Blues Till Dawn*, A-316, accompanied by Josh White

37. BABY BABY (Ma Rainey)
    mx 70561   Decca 18304 A

42. FARE THEE WELL (Alston)
    mx 70566   Decca 18304 B

41. GOOD MORNIN' BLUES
    mx 70565   Decca 18305 A

40. WHEN THE SUN GOES DOWN (Leroy Carr)
    mx 70564   Decca 18305 B

39. HOUSE OF THE RISING SUN
    mx 70563   Decca 18306 A

38. 1. HANSOM' WINSOME JOHNNY   2. OLD SMOKY
    mx 70562   Decca 18306 B

recorded c. 10-47, New York
City
accompanied by Johnny Richards Orchestra

43. SOMETHING TO REMEMBER YOU BY (from *Three's a Crowd*)
    mx 1088-1   Mercury 5071

44. BODY AND SOUL (from *Three's a Crowd*)
    mx 1089-1   Mercury 5071

recorded 1953, New York City
10″ LP album: *Libby Holman Sings*, MB 101, ensembles conducted
by Gerald Cook

45. SOMETHING TO REMEMBER YOU BY (from *Three's a Crowd*)
    CAN'T WE BE FRIENDS? (from *The Little Show*)
    BODY AND SOUL (from *Three's a Crowd*)
    MOANIN' LOW (from *The Little Show*)
    mx E3KL-7649-1   MB 101A

46. MORE THAN YOU KNOW (from *Great Day*)
    AM I BLUE? (from the film *On with the Show*)
    LOVE FOR SALE (from *The New Yorkers*)
    THERE AIN'T NO SWEET MAN THAT'S WORTH THE SALT OF MY
    TEARS
    mx E3KL-7650-1   MB 101B

recorded 1954, New York City
12″ LP album: *Libby Holman Sings Blues, Ballads and Sin-Songs,* MB
102, songs arranged and played by Gerald Cook

47. EVIL HEARTED ME
FARE THEE WELL
RIBBON BOW
BABY BABY
THE BLUES (Duke Ellington) (from *Black, Brown and Beige*)
RED RIVER
STRANGE FRUIT (Lewis Allan)
  mx E4-KP-3598   MB 102A

48. CARELESS LOVE
JOHNNY HAS GONE FAR AWAY
NUMBER TWELVE TRAIN
I KNOW WHERE I'M GOING
IN THE EVENING
TAKE IT AWAY FROM HERE (Johnson)
HOUSE OF THE RISING SUN
  mx E4-KP-3599   MB 102B

recorded 1965, New York City
12″ stereo LP album: *The Legendary Libby Holman,* Evergreen MRS
6501, in collaboration with Gerald Cook

49. The Ballads and Blues:
GOOD MORNING, BLUES
IN THE EVENING
RED RIVER
FARE THEE WELL
EVIL HEARTED ME
EASY RIDER
HOUSE OF THE RISING SUN
  mx ?   Evergreen MRS-6501 A

50. The Torch Songs:
BODY AND SOUL (from *Three's a Crowd*)
LOVE FOR SALE (from *The New Yorkers*)
I WANT A MAN (Oscar Hammerstein II, Vincent Youmans) (from
Rainbow)
CAN'T WE BE FRIENDS? (from *The Little Show*)
A SHIP WITHOUT A SAIL (from *Heads Up*)
MOANIN' LOW (from *The Little Show*)
SOMETHING TO REMEMBER YOU BY (from *Three's a Crowd*)
  mx ?   Evergreen MRS-6501 B

recorded 1954, New York City

12″ LP album: *Something to Remember Her By*, Monmouth Evergreen MES/7067, previously unreleased recordings from her 1954 sessions and her final recordings in 1965, issued in 1974 after her death, musical direction and accompaniment by Gerald Cook

51. From 1954:

AM I BLUE? (from the film *On with the Show*)

SUPPERTIME (Irving Berlin) (from *As Thousands Cheer*)

'BUKED AND SCORNED (Gerald Cook)

OH WAILLIE WAILLIE (Gerald Cook)

GO AWAY FROM MY WINDOW (Gerald Cook)

I GAVE MY LOVE A CHERRY (Gerald Cook)

MORE THAN YOU KNOW (from *Great Day*)

THERE AIN'T NO SWEET MAN THAT'S WORTH THE SALT OF MY TEARS

    mx ?   Monmouth Evergreen MES/7067

recorded 1965, New York City

12″ stereo LP album

52. From 1965:

THE BLUES (from *Black, Brown and Beige*)

IN BETWEEN (John Latouche, Duke Ellington) (from *Beggar's Holiday*)

MOSQUITO BLUES (Gerald Cook)

HE'S GONE AWAY (Gerald Cook)

TORNADO BLUES (Gerald Cook)

BAD GIRL (Gerald Cook)

    mx ?   Monmouth Evergreen MES/7067

Libby Holman records and radio air checks appear on the following LP reissues:

Curtain Call Series, Volume 4 10″ Decca DL 7021

Originals Musical Comedy 1909–1935 12″ RCA Victor LPV-560

The Thirties' Girls 12″ Totem 1026

The Original Torch Singers 12″ Take Two TT 207

Vintage Libby Holman 12″ Take Two TT 212

BROADWAY CHRONOLOGY

The Sapphire Ring

Opened at the Selwyn Theatre on April 15, 1925. Written by Lazzlo Lakatos. Presented by George Choos. Adapted by Isabel Leighton. Staged by Lester Lonergan. Cast Included: Milano Tilden, Helen Gahagan, Frank Conroy, Elizabeth Holman, Kenneth MacKenna, Mildred Florence, Marcel Rousseau.

The Garrick Gaieties

Opened at the Garrick Theatre on June 8, 1925. Produced by the Theatre Guild. Directed by Philip Loeb. Music by Richard Rodgers. Lyrics by Lorenz Hart. Settings and Costumes by Carolyn Hancock. Dances by Herbert Fields. Sets by Covarrubias. Conducted by Richard Rodgers. Sketches by Benjamin M. Kaye, Edith Meiser, Arthur Sullivan, Morrie Ryskind, Howard Green, Norman Levy, Sam Jaffe. Stage Manager, Harold Clurman.

Cast Included: Sally Bates, Alvah Bessie, T. Brewster Board, Romney Brent, Dorthea Chard, Harold Clurman, June Cochrane, Harold Conklin, Peggy Conway, Henry Geiger, Hildegarde Halliday, Inez Foster, Edward Hogan, Elizabeth Holman, Sterling Holloway, Frances Hyde, Feliz Jacoves, Paul Jones, House Jameson, Philip Loeb, Stanley Lindahl, William Marsh, Edith Meiser, Sanford Meisner, James Norris, Jack Quigley, Louise Richardson, Rosa Rolando, Starr Jones, Eleanor Shaler, Sylvia Shear, Betty Starbuck, Lee Strasberg, Willard Tobias, Hariette Woodruff.

Pincipal Songs: "Manhattan," "April Fool," "Sentimental Me," "An Old-Fashioned Girl," "On with the Dance."

The Greenwich Village Follies

Opened at the Shubert Theatre on May 10, 1926. Staged by Hassard Short. Revised and Restaged by A. L. Jones and Morris Green. Lyrics and Music by Harold Levey and Owen Murphy, Richard Meyers and Harry Ruby. Lyrics by Leo Robin, Harry Ruskin, Herman J. Mankiewicz, Lew Brown and Sidney Clare. Dances and Ensembles arranged by Larry Ceballos. Settings by Clark Robinson.

Cast Included: Irene Delroy, Teddy Gill, Arnold Gluck, Tom Howard, Joe Lyons, Elsbeth Holman, Philip Conyers, Sam Hearn, Fraun Koski, William V. Powers, Dorothy Hathaway, Maxine Wells, Gladys Glad, Moran and Mack.

Principal Songs: "Follow Me," "Whistle Away Your Blues," "Go South," "The Sincerest Form of Flattery."

Merry-Go-Round

Opened at the Klaw Theatre on August 1, 1927. Presented by Richard Herndon. Book and Lyrics by Morrie Ryskind and Howard Dietz. Ballets and Pantomimes by Walt Kuhn. Music by Henry Souvaine and Jay Gorney. Dances arranged by Raymond Midgley. Staged by Allan Dinehart. Orchestra under the direction of Gene Salzer. Settings by P. Dodd Ackerman Studios.

Cast Included: Joe Kirk, Jack Lenny, Jimmy Ormande, Jack Edwards, Knox Herold, Blanche O'Donahue, Rose Wenzel, Devah Worrell, Vida Manuel, Dorothy Justin, Frances Gershwin, Winnie Kerwin, Patricia Bowman, Margaret Byers, Libby Holman, Leonard Sillman, Philip Loeb, Arthur Lipson, William Liebling, John Picorri, Burt Harger, Blanche Fleming, Mary Stills, Georgia Ingram, Helen Howell, Clifford Walker, James Jolley, Marie Cahill, Tom Burton, Francis Pierlot, Francis Edwards, Maryon Dale, Daniel Higgins, George F. Fitzgerald, Don Barclay, Dorothy Chilton, Doris Vinton.

Principal Songs: "Sentimental Silly," "Gabriel," "What D'Ya Say," "Hogan's Alley."

Rainbow

Opened at the Gallo Theatre on November 21, 1928. Book by Laurence Stallings and Oscar Hammerstein II. Lyrics by Oscar Hammerstein II. Produced by Philip Goodman. Directed by Oscar Hammerstein II. Dances by Busby Berkeley. Music by Vincent Youmans.

Cast Included: Rupert Lucas, Ned McGurn, Harland Dixon, Helen Lynd, Henry Pemberton, Libby Holman, Charles Ruggles, Brian Donlevy, Louise Brown, Allan Prior, Leo Mack, Stewart Edwards, Leo Dugan, Ward Arnold, Randall Fryer, Frank King, Mary Carney, Leo Nash, Charles Ralph, Valla Valentinova, Sadie Black, George Magis, Chester Bree, Edward Nemo, Ralph Walker, Kitty Coleman, May Barnes.

Principal Songs: "I Want A Man," "The One Girl," "I Like You as You Are," "Hay Straw," "The Bride Was Dressed in White."

Ned Wayburn's Gambols

Opened at the Knickerbocker Theatre on January 15, 1929. Produced by Ned Wayburn. Lyrics by Morrie Ryskind. Music by Walter G. Samuels. Additional Melodies by Arthur Schwartz and Lew Kesler.

Cast Included: Libby Holman, Charles Irwin, William Holbrook, Roger Gray, Lew Hearn, Fuzzy Knight, Charles Elbey, Ann Pritchard, Shirley Richards, Olive McClure, Grace Bowman, Virginia Alexander, Helen Koster, John Byam, Priscilla Gurney.

Principal Songs: "Savannah Stomp," "I Bring My Boys Along," "Mothers o' Men," "Montmartre," "No Sweet Man Is Worth the Salt of My Tears."

The Little Show

Opened at the Music Box Theatre on April 30, 1929. Produced by William K. Brady, Jr., and Dwight Deere Wiman in association with Tom Weatherly, Sketches by Howard Dietz, Fred Allen, Newman Levy, Marya Mannes, George S. Kaufman. Songs mostly by Howard Dietz and Arthur Schwartz. Other contributors included Frank Gray, Henry Sullivan, Morris Hamilton, Kay Swift, Earle Crooker, Grace Henry, Paul James, Lew Levinson, Henry Myers, Herman Hupfeld, Charlotte Kent, Henry Ruskin. Directed by Dwight Deere Wiman and Alexander Leftwich. Dances by Danny Dare. Costumes by Ruth Brenner. Sets by Jo Mielziner.

Cast Included: Fred Allen, Libby Holman, Clifton Webb, Bettina Hall, Ernest Scharpe, John McCauley, Romney Brent, Helen Lynd, Peggy Conklin, Portland Hoffa, Joan Carter-Waddell, Harold Moffet, Paul Bissinger, Dorothy Humphreys, Constance Cummings, Adam Carroll and Ralph Rainger (duo-pianists).

Principal Songs: "I Guess I'll Have to Change My Plan," "I've Made a Habit of You," "Hammacher-Schlemmer, I Love You," "Moanin' Low," "Can't We Be Friends?"

Three's a Crowd

Opened at the Selwyn Theatre on October 15, 1930. Produced by Max Gordon. A Revue conceived and compiled by Howard Dietz. Sketches by Howard Dietz, Fred Allen, Laurence Schwab, Corey Ford, Groucho Marx, William B. Miles, Donald Blackwell, Arthur Sheekman and Hazel Flynn. Lyrics by Howard Dietz. Music by Arthur Schwartz. Music and Lyrics also by Alec Wilder and Edward Brandt, Johnny Green, Edward Heyman and Robert Sour, Burton Lane, Phil Charig, Charles Schwab and Richard Myers. Staged and Lighted by Hassard Short. Dances by Albertina Rasch. Settings by Albert R. Johnson. Costumes by Kiviette.

Cast Included: Clifton Webb, Libby Holman, Fred Allen, Wally Coyle, Earl Oxford, Harold Moffett, Tamara Geva, Margaret Lee, Portland Hoffa, Marybeth Conoly, Joan Clement, Amy Revere, The California Collegians (including Fred MacMurray).

Principal Songs: "The Moment I Saw You," "Right at the Start of It," "Someting to Remember You By," "All the King's Horses," "Forget All Your Books," "Yaller," "Body and Soul."

Revenge with Music

Opened at the New Amsterdam Theatre on November 28, 1934. Produced by Arch Selwyn and Harold B. Franklin. Book and Lyrics by Howard Dietz. Music by Arthur Schwartz. Directed by Komisarjevsky, Worthington Miner, Howard Dietz, Marc Connelly. Dances by Michael Mordkin. Settings by Albert R. Johnson. Costumes by Constance Ripley. Music Director: Victor Baravalle.

Cast Included: Libby Holman, Charles Winninger, George Metaxa, Ilka Chase, Rex O'Malley, Joseph Macauley, Ivy Scott, Detmar Poppen, Margaret Lee, George Kirk, Imogene Coca, Natalia Danezi.

Principal Songs: "When You Love Only One," "Never Marry a Dancer," "If There Is Someone Lovelier Than You," "That Fellow Manuelo," "Maria," "Wandrin' Heart," "You and the Night and the Music."

You Never Know

Opened at the Winter Garden on September 21, 1938. Produced by Messrs. Shubert. Book by Rowland Leigh. Based on Siegfried Geyer's play *Candlelight*. Directed by Rowland Leigh and George Abbott. Music and Lyrics by Cole Porter. Music and Lyrics also by Dana Suesse, Robert Katscher and Rowland Leigh, Alex Fogarty and Edwin Gilbert. Dances by Robert Alton.

Cast Included: Clifton Webb, Libby Holman, Lupe Velez, Paul and Grace Hartman, Toby Wing, Rex O'Malley, June Preisser, Roger Stearns, Charles Kemper, Truman Gaige, Gus Schirmir, Ray Dennis.

Principal Songs: "You Never Know," "At Long Last Love," "For No Rhyme or Reason," "From Alpha to Omega," "What Shall I Do?"

Mexican Mural

Opened at the Chanin Auditorium on April 27, 1942. Presented by Robert Lewis. Written by Ramon Naya. Scenery Designed by Herbert Andrews. Lighting by Wil Washcoe. Stage Manager: William Le Massena. Production Staged and Directed by Robert Lewis.

Cast Included: Montgomery Clift, Libby Holman, Wallace House, Priscilla Newton, Robert Lander, Perry Wilson, Kathryn Grill, Eda Reiss, Terry Dicks, Spencer James, Gertrude Gilpin, Norma Chambers, Henrietta Lovelace, Mira Rosovskaya, Kevin McCarthy, Owen Jordan, David Opatashu, Larry Hugo, Morton Amster, Tom Barry, Viola Kates, Kenneth Tobey.

Blues, Ballads, and Sin-Songs

Opened at the Bijou Theatre On October 4, 1954. A One-Woman Show starring Libby Holman. Accompanied by Gerald Cook.

Principal songs: "Good Morning Blues," "Smoky," "Go Away from My Window," "In the Evening," "Barbara Allen," "Rolly Trudum," "Yandre," "Cindy," "Baby, Baby," "Fare Thee Well," "Careless Love," "Riddle Song," "Four Marys," "The Loathly Bride," "Johnny Has Gone," "The Blues," "You Can't Go to Heaven," "Number Twelve Train," "Evil Hearted Me," "House of the Rising Sun."

BIBLIOGRAPHY

Adams, Cindy. *Lee Strasberg.* New York: Doubleday, 1980.

Adams, Samuel Hopkins. *A. Woollcott.* New York: Reynal & Hitchcock, 1945.

Adler, Polly. *A House Is Not a Home.* New York: Popular Library, 1959.

Albertson, Chris. *Bessie.* New York: Stein & Day, 1974.

Allen, Frederick Lewis. *Only Yesterday.* New York: Harper & Brothers, 1931.

Allen, Frederick Lewis. *Since Yesterday.* New York: Harper & Brothers, 1939.

Amory, Cleveland. *Who Killed Society?* New York: Harper & Brothers, 1960.

Anger, Kenneth. *Hollywood Babylon.* San Francisco: Straight Arrow Books, 1975.

Baral, Robert. *Revue: A Nostalgic Reprise of the Great Broadway Period.* New York: Fleet Publishing Corp., 1962.

Beebe, Lucius. *Shoot If You Must.* New York: D. Appleton Century Co., 1943.

Benchley, Nathaniel. *Robert Benchley: A Biography.* New York: McGraw Hill, 1955.

Bishop, Jim. *The Mark Hellinger Story.* New York: Appleton, Century, Crofts, 1952.

Bordman, Gerald. *American Musical Theatre: A Chronicle.* New York: Oxford University Press, 1979.

Bosworth, Patricia. *Montgomery Clift.* New York: Harcourt Brace Javanovich, 1977.

Bowles, Jane. *The Collected Works*. New York: Farrar, Straus & Giroux, 1966.

Bowles, Paul. *The Delicate Prey and Other Stories*. New York: Random House, 1950.

Bowles, Paul. *Without Stopping* (An Autobiography). London: Peter Owen, 1972.

Brown, Eve. *Champagne Cholly*. New York: Dutton, 1947.

Brownlee, Fambrough L. *Winston-Salem: A Pictorial History*. Norfolk, Va.: The Donning Co., 1979.

Churchill, Allen. *The Theatrical Twenties*. New York: McGraw-Hill, 1975.

Clurman, Harold. *The Fervent Years*. New York: Alfred Knopf, 1945.

Coward, Noel. *Present Indicative*. New York: Doubleday, Doran & Co., 1937.

de Acosta, Mercedes. *Here Lies the Heart*. New York: Reynal & Co., 1960.

de Mille, Agnes. *Dance to the Piper*. New York: Grosset & Dunlap, 1952.

Dietz, Howard. *Dancing in the Dark*. New York: Quadrangle, 1974.

Dillon, Millicent. *A Little Original Sin: The Life and Work of Jane Bowles*. Holt, Rinehart & Winston, 1981.

Drutman, Irving. *Good Company*. Boston: Little Brown, 1976.

Eells, George. *The Life That Late He Led: A Biography of Cole Porter*. New York: Putnam & Sons, 1967.

Engel, Lehman. *The American Musical Theater*. New York: A CBS Legacy Collection Book, 1967.

Ewen, David. *Richard Rodgers*. New York: Henry Holt & Company, 1957.

Ewen, David. *The Complete Book of the American Musical Theater*. New York: Henry Holt & Company, 1959.

Farr, Finis. *O'Hara*. Boston: Little Brown, 1973.

Feck, Luke. *Yesterday's Cincinnati*. Miami, Fla.: E. A. Seemann Publishing, 1975.

Fordin, Hugh. *Getting to Know Him: A Biography of Oscar Hammerstein*. New York: Random House, 1977.

Gates, John D. *The Du Pont Family*. New York: Doubleday, 1979.

Geva, Tamara. *Split Seconds: A Remembrance*. New York: Harper & Row, 1972.

Gill, Brendan. *Tallulah*. New York: Holt, Rinehart & Winston, 1972.

Gordon, Max. *Max Gordon Presents*. New York: Bernard Geis Associates, 1963.

Graham, Sheilah. *The Garden of Allah*. New York: Crown, Inc., 1970.

Green, Stanley. *Ring Bells, Sing Songs: Broadway Musicals of the 1930's*. New Rochelle, N.Y.: Arlington House, 1971.

Green, Stanley. *The World of Musical Comedy*. New York: A. S. Barnes & Co., 1974.

Hart, Dorothy. *Thou Swell, Thou Witty*. New York: Harper & Row, 1976.

Haskins, Jim. *The Cotton Club*. New York: Random House, 1977.

Holiday, Billie. *Lady Sings the Blues*. New York: Doubleday, 1956.

Houseman, John. *Front and Center*. New York: Simon & Schuster, 1979.

Israel, Lee. *Miss Tallulah Bankhead*. New York: G. P. Putnam's Sons, 1972.

Jenkins, Alan. *The Twenties*. New York: Universe Books, 1974.

Kahn, E. J., Jr. *The World of Swope*. New York: Simon & Schuster, 1965.

Keats, John. *You Might as Well Live*. New York: Simon & Schuster, 1970.

Kellner, Bruce. *Carl Van Vechten and the Irreverent Decades*. Norman, Okla.: The University of Oklahoma Press, 1963.

Kronenberger, Louis. *No Whippings, No Gold Watches*. Boston: Atlantic, Little Brown, 1970.

La Guardia, Robert. *Monty*. New York: Arbor House, 1977.

Lamparski, Richard. *Whatever Became of. . . ?* New York: Crown, 1967.

Lawrence, Gertrude. *A Star Danced*. New York: Doubleday, 1945.

Lawrenson, Helen. *Stranger at the Party*. New York: Random House, 1974.

Lewis, David Levering. *When Harlem Was in Vogue*. New York: Alfred Knopf, 1981.

Lillie, Beatrice. *Every Other Inch a Lady*. New York: Doubleday, 1972.

Logan, Joshua. *Josh*. New York: Delacorte Press, 1976.

MacShane, Frank. *The Life of John O'Hara*. New York: E. P. Dutton, 1980.

Marx, Samuel, and Jan Clayton. *Rodgers and Hart*. New York: G. P. Putnam's Sons, 1976.

Matthews, T. S. *Name and Address*. London: Anthony Blond, 1961.

Maxwell, Gilbert. *Helen Morgan, Her Life and Legend*. New York: Hawthorn Books, Inc., 1974.

Meredith, Scott. *George Kaufman and His Friends*. New York: Doubleday, 1974.

Meryman, Richard. *Mank*. New York: William Morrow, 1978.

Mordden, Ethan. *Better Foot Forward*. New York: Grossman, 1976.

Mosedale, John. *The Men Who Invented Broadway: Damon Runyon and Walter Winchell*. New York: Richard Marek Publishers, 1981.

Nolan, Frederick. *The Sound of Their Music*. New York: Walter & Co., 1978.

Parks, Melvin. *Musicals of the 1930's*. New York: Museum of the City of New York, 1966.

Pollock, Channing. *Harvest of My Years*. New York: Bobbs Merrill, 1943.

Richman, Harry. *A Hell of a Life*. New York: Duell, Sloan & Pearce, 1966.

Rodgers, Richard. *Musical Stages*. New York: Random House, 1975.

Rorem, Ned. *The Final Diary*. New York: Holt, Rinehart & Winston, 1974.

Rorem, Ned. *The New York Diary*. New York: George Braziller, 1967.

Rosmond, Babette. *Robert Benchley, His Life and Good Times*. New York: Doubleday, 1970.

Schwartz, Charles, *Cole Porter*. New York: Dial Press, 1977.

Sillman, Leonard. *Here Lies Leonard Sillman*. New York: Citadel Press, 1959.

Smith, Cecil. *Musical Comedy in America*. New York: Theatre Arts Books, 1950.

Sobol, Louis. *The Longest Street*. New York, Crown, 1968.

Taylor, Deems. *Some Enchanted Evenings*. New York: Harper & Brothers, 1953.

Tebbel, John. *The Inheritors*. New York: G. P. Putnam's Sons, 1962.

Teichmann, Howard. *Smart Aleck: The Wit, World and Life of Alexander Woollcott*. New York: William Morrow, 1976.

Thompson, C.V.R. *Trousers Must Be Worn*. New York: G. P. Putnam's Sons, 1941.

Thurber, James. *The Years with Ross*. New York: Grosset & Dunlap, 1957.

Townsend, Irving. *John Hammond, On Record*. New York: Ridge Press, 1977.

Walker, Stanley. *The Night Club Era*. New York: Blue Ribbon Books, 1933.

Waters, Ethel. *His Eye Is on the Sparrow*. New York: Doubleday, 1950.

Weiner, Ed. *Let's Go to Press: A Profile of Walter Winchell*. New York: G. P. Putnam's Sons, 1955.

Wilder, Alec. *American Popular Song*. New York: Oxford University Press, 1972.

Wilder, Robert. *Written on the Wind*. G. P. Putnam's Sons, 1945.

Williams, Tennessee. *Memoirs*. New York: Doubleday, 1975.

Wilson, Edmund. *The Twenties*. New York: Farrar, Straus & Giroux, 1975.

Wofford, Harris. *Of Kennedys and Kings*. New York: Farrar, Straus & Giroux, 1980.

Yablonsky, Lewis. *George Raft*. New York: McGraw-Hill, 1974.

Yurka, Blanche. *Bohemian Girl*. Athens, Ohio: Ohio University Press, 1970.

Zerbe, Jerome, and Brendan Gill. *Happy Times*. New York: Harcourt Brace Javanovich, 1973.

INDEX